# Full-Throttle Franchise

# Full-Throttle Franchise

*The Culture, Business and Politics of*
Fast & Furious

Edited by

Joshua Gulam, Fraser Elliott and Sarah Feinstein

BLOOMSBURY ACADEMIC
NEW YORK • LONDON • OXFORD • NEW DELHI • SYDNEY

BLOOMSBURY ACADEMIC
Bloomsbury Publishing Inc
1385 Broadway, New York, NY 10018, USA
50 Bedford Square, London, WC1B 3DP, UK
29 Earlsfort Terrace, Dublin 2, Ireland

BLOOMSBURY, BLOOMSBURY ACADEMIC and the Diana logo
are trademarks of Bloomsbury Publishing Plc

First published in the United States of America 2023
Paperback edition published 2024

Volume Editor's Part of the Work © Joshua Gulam, Fraser Elliott and Sarah Feinstein, 2023, 2024
Each chapter © of Contributors, 2023

Cover design: Eleanor Rose
Cover image: A still from *The Fast and the Furious*, 2001 © MCA/Courtesy
Everett Collection/Alamy

All rights reserved. No part of this publication may be reproduced or transmitted
in any form or by any means, electronic or mechanical, including photocopying,
recording, or any information storage or retrieval system, without prior
permission in writing from the publishers.

Bloomsbury Publishing Inc does not have any control over, or responsibility for,
any third-party websites referred to or in this book. All internet addresses given in this book were
correct at the time of going to press. The author and publisher regret any inconvenience caused if
addresses have changed or sites have ceased to exist,
but can accept no responsibility for any such changes.

Library of Congress Cataloging-in-Publication Data
Names: Gulam, Joshua, editor. | Elliott, Fraser (Lecturer), editor. |
Feinstein, Sarah, active 2001- editor.
Title: Full-throttle franchise : the culture, business and politics of the
Fast & furious / edited by Joshua Gulam, Fraser Elliott, and Sarah Feinstein.
Description: New York : Bloomsbury Academic, 2023. |
Includes bibliographical references and index. |
Summary: "Offers an in-depth critical analysis of the Fast & Furious films,
bringing together a range of scholars to explore not only the style and themes
of the multibillion-dollar franchise, but also its broader cultural impact and
industry legacy"– Provided by publisher.
Identifiers: LCCN 2022028566 (print) | LCCN 2022028567 (ebook) |
ISBN 9781501378904 (hardback) | ISBN 9781501378874 (paperback) |
ISBN 9781501378898 (epub) | ISBN 9781501378881 (pdf) |
ISBN 9781501378867 (ebook other)
Subjects: LCSH: Fast & furious films–History and criticism. | Action and
adventure films–History and criticism. | Motion picture
industry–United States–History–21st century. | Motion
pictures–Social aspects–United States.
Classification: LCC PN1995.9.F398 F85 2023 (print) | LCC PN1995.9.F398
(ebook) | DDC 791.45/75–dc23/eng/20220919
LC record available at https://lccn.loc.gov/2022028566
LC ebook record available at https://lccn.loc.gov/2022028567

| | | |
|---|---|---|
| ISBN: | HB: | 978-1-5013-7890-4 |
| | PB: | 978-1-5013-7887-4 |
| | ePDF: | 978-1-5013-7888-1 |
| | eBook: | 978-1-5013-7889-8 |

Typeset by Integra Software Services Pvt. Ltd.

To find out more about our authors and books visit www.bloomsbury.com
and sign up for our newsletters.

# Contents

| | |
|---|---|
| List of figures | vi |
| List of tables | viii |
| List of contributors | ix |
| Acknowledgements | xii |

1. Researching *Fast & Furious* in the franchise era of Hollywood  *Joshua Gulam, Fraser Elliott and Sarah Feinstein* — 1
2. From Mission Impossible to Mission Insanity: A longitudinal analysis of action sequences in the *Fast & Furious* franchise  *Lennart Soberon* — 37
3. 'For those ten seconds, I'm free': Temporality, affect and spectacle in the *Fast & Furious* franchise  *Naja Later* — 57
4. A critical quantitative analysis of race and representation in the *Fast Saga* films  *Pete Jones and Joshua Gulam* — 73
5. Vin Diesel as franchise auteur: Intersectional authorship and the cuddly hardbody in *Los Bandoleros*  *CarrieLynn D. Reinhard and Christopher J. Olson* — 103
6. Fast, Furious and Free of Sex: Dom, Brian and hetero male affection  *Aaron Hunter* — 121
7. 'What's real is family': Maternal bodies, paternal labour and parenting roles in *Fast & Furious*  *Bianca Batti* — 141
8. 'I never want to lose a fight': Masculinity, machismo and high-octane action in the *Fast & Furious* franchise  *Rebecca Feasey* — 157
9. The on- and off-screen bromances of *Fast & Furious*  *Jackie Raphael and Celia Lam* — 175
10. 'It's so so so so so so important': China's role in shaping the *Fast & Furious* franchise  *Fraser Elliott* — 193
11. Fun for all the family: Adapting *Fast & Furious* as animated children's television  *Sam Summers* — 213
12. 'Zero tolerance for candy asses': World Wrestling Entertainment and *Fast & Furious* as transmedia storytelling  *Robert Watts* — 233

| | |
|---|---|
| Filmography | 251 |
| Index | 258 |

# Figures

| | | |
|---|---|---|
| 1.1 | Abu Dhabi skyscraper jump, *Furious 7* (2015 Universal) | 15 |
| 1.2 | Two-shot of Hobbs and Alameida, *Fast Five* (2011 Universal) | 18 |
| 3.1 | Racing scene, *The Fast and the Furious* (2001 Universal) | 59 |
| 3.2 | Letty holding Dom, *Furious 7* (2015 Universal) | 69 |
| 4.1 | Annenberg Inclusion Initiative – Proportion of characters by ethnic group in top-grossing films (our elaboration from data presented in Smith, Choueiti and Pieper 2020) | 76 |
| 4.2 | UCLA Hollywood Diversity Report – Proportion of characters by ethnic group in top-grossing films (our elaboration from data presented in Hunt and Ramón 2020) | 77 |
| 4.3 | Annenberg Inclusion Initiative – Proportion of characters from non-white ethnic groups in top-grossing films by genre (our elaboration from data presented in Smith, Choueiti and Pieper 2020) | 78 |
| 4.4 | Proportion of speaking characters by ethnic group | 83 |
| 4.5 | Proportion of lines of dialogue spoken by ethnic group | 83 |
| 4.6 | *The Fast and the Furious* (2001 Universal), dialogue network | 88 |
| 4.7 | *2 Fast 2 Furious* (2003 Universal), dialogue network | 88 |
| 4.8 | *The Fast and the Furious: Tokyo Drift* (2006 Universal), dialogue network | 89 |
| 4.9 | *Fast & Furious* (2009 Universal), dialogue network | 90 |
| 4.10 | *Fast Five* (2011 Universal), dialogue network | 91 |
| 4.11 | *Fast & Furious 6* (2013 Universal), dialogue network | 91 |
| 4.12 | *Furious 7* (2015 Universal), dialogue network | 92 |
| 4.13 | *The Fate of the Furious* (2017 Universal), dialogue network | 93 |
| 6.1 | Brian gazes at Dom in their first on-screen meeting, *The Fast and the Furious* (2001 Universal) | 122 |
| 6.2 | Dom briefly glances back at him, *The Fast and the Furious* (2001 Universal) | 122 |
| 6.3 | Brian, Dom and Mia embrace after she informs them of her pregnancy, *Fast Five* (2011 Universal) | 133 |

6.4 Brian gazes at Dom one last time, *Furious 7* (2015 Universal)    134
6.5 Dom returns Brian's gaze with affection, *Furious 7* (2015 Universal)    135
6.6 Brian and Dom part for the last time, *Furious 7* (2015 Universal)    135

# Tables

| | | |
|---|---|---|
| 1.1 | Box office figures for *Fast & Furious* films | 7 |
| 2.1 | Action sequences and run time | 43 |
| 2.2 | Evolution in percentage of action | 45 |
| 2.3 | Type of action events | 47 |

# Contributors

**Bianca Batti** is a Marion L. Brittain Postdoctoral Fellow at the Georgia Institute of Technology, USA. She received her PhD in Literary Studies from Purdue University with a graduate concentration in Women, Gender and Sexuality Studies. Her feminist research and scholarship occur at the intersection of popular culture studies, game studies and science fiction studies. Her work has been published in *The Popular Cultural Studies Journal* and *Kairos: A Journal of Rhetoric, Technology, and Pedagogy*, as well as *Haywire Magazine*, *Not Your Mama's Gamer*, and edited anthologies.

**Dr Fraser Elliott** is a Lecturer of Film, Exhibition and Curation at the University of Edinburgh, UK, where he teaches on a postgraduate course of the same name. His research specializes in the circulation of Chinese-language cinema in international locations, particularly in the UK. In addition to academic work, he was previously on the programming team at HOME, an independent cinema in Manchester, and continues to curate screenings as a member of the Chinese Film Forum UK and collaborate with the Taiwan Film Festival Edinburgh, 2021.

**Dr Rebecca Feasey** is Subject Leader for Media at Bath Spa University, UK, in the School of Art, Film and Media. She has published a range of works on the representation of gender in popular media culture. She has written book-length studies on masculinity and popular television (EUP 2008), motherhood on the small screen (Anthem 2012), maternal audiences (Peter Lang 2016) and infertility and the media (Palgrave 2019).

**Dr Sarah Feinstein** is a Teaching Fellow and the Audience Engagement Participation Programme Leader at the University of Leeds, UK, in the School of Performance and Cultural Industries. She has published in *Liminalities* (2022) and *The Prison Memory Archive: A Case Study in Filmed Memory of Conflict* (2022).

**Dr Joshua Gulam** is a Lecturer in Film & Visual Culture at Liverpool Hope University, UK, with a particular interest in star studies and commercial genre cinema. He has published several chapters and articles looking at the on- and off-screen campaigning of stars such as Angelina Jolie, Ben Affleck and George Clooney, in addition to work on contemporary horror cinema.

**Dr Aaron Hunter** is a Teaching Fellow in the Department of Film at Trinity College Dublin, Ireland. His publications include *Authoring Hal Ashby: The Myth of the New Hollywood Auteur* (2016) and *Polly Platt: Hollywood Production Design and Creative Authorship* (2022). His collection *Women and New Hollywood: Gender, Creative Labor, and 1970s American Cinema*, co-edited with Martha Shearer, will be published in 2023.

**Dr Pete Jones** is an interdisciplinary researcher and postdoctoral fellow at the University of Alberta, Canada. His work combines social research methods and the study of film industry inequalities, with a focus on social network analysis. He received his PhD from the University of Manchester for a thesis exploring the use of character networks for understanding the narrative marginalization of women in popular Hollywood cinema.

**Dr Celia Lam** is Associate Professor of Media and Cultural Studies at the School of International Communications, University of Nottingham Ningbo China. She has published in the area of celebrity culture, bromances, fan fiction and fandoms. Her latest book is *Celebrity Bromances: Constructing, Interpreting and Utilising Persona* (2022) with Jackie Raphael.

**Dr Naja Later** is an academic tutor at Swinburne University of Technology, Australia. They study intersections between pop culture and politics, with a focus on superhero and horror genres. They have published papers in the *Quarterly Review of Film and Video* and *Participations: Journal of Audience & Reception Studies* and chapters with Rutgers University Press, University of Mississippi Press and McFarland.

**Christopher J. Olson** is a PhD candidate at the University of Wisconsin – Milwaukee, USA, with a Media, Cinema and Digital Studies concentration. His books include *Normalizing Mental Illness and Neurodiversity in Entertainment Media: Quieting the Madness* (2021), *The Greatest Cult Television Shows of All Time* (2020), *Convergent Wrestling: Participatory Culture, Transmedia Storytelling, and Intertextuality in the Squared Circle* (2019) and *100 Greatest Cult Films* (2018).

**Dr Jackie Raphael** works at Murdoch University, Perth. She has published several books and papers on celebrity culture, bromance, endorsements, branding, iconic status, persona and social media. Her latest book is *Celebrity Bromances: Constructing, Interpreting and Utilising Persona* (2022) with Celia Lam.

**Dr CarrieLynn D. Reinhard** is a Professor of Communication Arts and Sciences at Dominican University, USA. Her research considers how people make sense of and engage with media products, such as virtual worlds, films and professional wrestling. She is Editor for the *Popular Culture Studies Journal* and the inaugural President for the Professional Wrestling Studies Association.

**Dr Lennart Soberon** is a post-doctoral researcher at the Vrije Universiteit Brussel (VUB) and artistic coordinator of non-profit film theatre KASKcinema (Ghent, Belgium). His prior research project focused on enemy image construction in the American action film. He is currently part of the ERC-funded project 'Reel Borders' that studies the cinematic representation of Europe's border regions. Apart from working on forms of cinematic othering and bordering, he has also published on themes of emotion, masculinity, trauma and spectacle.

**Dr Sam Summers** is an Associate Lecturer in Animation at Middlesex University, UK, in the Visual Arts Department. He is the author of *DreamWorks Animation: Intertextuality and Aesthetics in Shrek and Beyond* (2020) and co-editor of *Toy Story: How Pixar Re-Invented the Animated Feature* (2018), and has written a number of book chapters and articles looking at adaptation, aesthetics and intertextuality in animation history.

**Dr Robert Watts** is a Lecturer in Television and Creative Industries at the University of Manchester, UK. His research centres on TV drama aesthetics, transnational prestige drama and discourses of media industry convergence. He has contributed chapters for *Convergent Wrestling: Participatory Culture, Transmedia Storytelling, and Intertextuality in the Squared Circle* (2019) and *Binge-Watching and Contemporary Television Studies* (2021).

# Acknowledgements

This book grew out of a shared love of *Fast & Furious*, so our gratitude first lies with the creators of the franchise themselves for providing a consistent source of joy over the last two decades and counting. We would of course like to thank the authors who contributed work to this volume, for their scholarship, enthusiasm, compassion and patience while working on a book during a global pandemic. While Covid-19 made the realization of this book less fast than anticipated, the generosity of these contributors ensured the final volume is no less furious ('nice or die').

The early direction of the volume was shaped through the thoughtful feedback of our reviewers and the steering guidance from the team at Bloomsbury of Katie Gallof, Stephanie Grace-Petinos and Erin Duffy. We thank them all for their help. We would also like to thank colleagues and peers who fed into or provided feedback on key elements, especially Noel Brown, Peter Krämer and Eithne Quinn, as well as Sudhagaran Thandapani at Integra for their vital support. Finally, in the vein of Dom and his team, we owe huge thanks to our families, partners and friends for not only bearing with us as we worked on this formal outlet for our fannish enthusiasm, but supporting us so generously too.

It is our hope that *Full-Throttle Franchise* plays a part in accelerating scholarly interest around this franchise as we approach the *Fast Saga*'s (supposed) conclusion …

*Salud, mi familia*

1

# Researching *Fast & Furious* in the franchise era of Hollywood

Joshua Gulam, Fraser Elliott and Sarah Feinstein

On 5 July 2021, *F9* (2021), the ninth feature in the *Fast Saga* and the tenth in the *Fast & Furious* franchise overall, surpassed $500 million at the worldwide box office, becoming the first Hollywood film to reach this milestone since the Covid-19 pandemic began. That *F9* was the first to do so didn't come as a huge surprise. After all, each *Fast & Furious* film since *Fast Five* (2011) has earned over $500 million globally.[1] What's more, *F9* was one of the few Hollywood blockbusters in the summer of 2021 to pursue a theatre-only release. Whereas other big titles such as *Black Widow* (2021), the latest film in the Marvel Cinematic Universe (MCU), were released in cinemas and on streaming platforms simultaneously, Universal's *F9* retained a theatrical window of thirty-one days, meaning that audiences had to visit cinemas if they wished to be among the first to see the film (Mendelson 2021).

Going on to gross $720 million off a production budget of $200 million, *F9* was by no means the franchise's biggest hit, its box office total falling a long way short of the $1.5 billion made by *Furious 7* (2017), a film that cost $10 million less to produce. However, in the context of contemporary theatrical exhibition, where cinemas across the globe were still struggling to adapt to the impacts of Covid-19, the box office performance of *F9* was certainly cause for celebration, providing the clearest sign yet that audiences were still eager to see big-budget franchise movies on the big screen. Writing in *The Hollywood Reporter*, Pamela McClintock (2021) argued that the film's $70 million opening weekend represented 'a major victory for Hollywood and theatres', while *Forbes*' Scott Mendelson (2021) speculated that *F9* might help to kick-start a much-needed theatrical recovery, following one of the most difficult periods in the industry's history. Vin Diesel, the film's biggest star and co-producer, offered an equally bullish account of its record-breaking total in his interviews with the trade press.

Speaking at a charity event, he announced that 'Cinema is back!', before going on to praise Universal Pictures, the studio responsible for distributing the *Fast & Furious* films, for having the foresight to delay *F9* until most movie theatres were ready to open up again (Malkin 2021).

How did *Fast & Furious* become so crucial to Hollywood that its box office performance was being talked about as a barometer of the continuing viability of franchise cinema more generally? What can the journey of this series, from a mid-budget crime thriller about street racing to a multibillion-dollar action-spy franchise, tell us about the contemporary film industry? These questions are two of many we explore across this book which positions the development of *Fast & Furious* alongside broader discussions of the 'franchise era' of Hollywood (Fleury, Hartzheim and Mamber 2019). In his book *The Big Picture*, journalist Ben Fritz (2018: xv) explores the accelerated turn towards franchise filmmaking within post-millennium Hollywood, noting how the explosion of branded content that began in the late-2000s marks 'the most meaningful revolution in the movie business since the studio system ended'. Typified by the activities of media conglomerates like Disney, the contemporary franchise often takes the form of a 'cinematic universe'. In this structure, films are just one element in 'a diversified product range', and their narratives are designed to expand into other media such as TV and games (Maltby 2003: 28). This approach builds on the 'synergistic model' that has long been vital to the industry; but what's different in the current era is the way this model has been honed and extended, helping to restore the type of 'stabilisation of creative form and economic growth that [Hollywood] enjoyed during its golden age' (Lomax 2019). As of April 2022, all but one of the top-30 highest-grossing films at the worldwide box office are part of transmedia franchises, almost all released within the last twenty-five years. The effect of this success on the media landscape has been significant: star vehicles have been reformulated to support the continued development of intellectual property (IP), while the stable production of the type of mid-range films that once found a market on home video has been more or less lost, edged out by the increasing consolidation of media production into a small oligarchy of mega-corporations focused on creating expandable 'storyworlds' (Fleury, Hartzheim and Mamber 2019).

*Fast & Furious* occupies a curious place in this contemporary Hollywood. As of April 2022, it ranks as the eighth highest-grossing film franchise of all time, appearing in the top-10 alongside mega-properties such as *Star Wars* (Disney), *Harry Potter* (Warner Bros.), *James Bond* (MGM) and the MCU (Disney). With a worldwide box office total of $6.6 billion and counting, *Fast & Furious* has earned more in cinema ticket sales than the likes of *X-Men* ($6 billion), *Lord of the Rings* ($5.8 billion), *Transformers* ($4.8 billion) and *Mission: Impossible* ($3.5 billion). Unsurprisingly, then, it is often cited as an exemplar of current trends, with a development history that reflects 'the way in which blockbuster filmmaking has shifted and evolved in the twenty-first century', according to one *BBC* writer (Campbell 2021). Hyperbolic phrases like those from *IndieWire*'s David Erlich (2017) tell us that the 'history of the *Fast and the Furious* franchise is nothing less than the story of Hollywood filmmaking in the twenty-first century.'

These readings are certainly tempting, and *Fast & Furious* has, in many ways, come to resemble an archetype of the contemporary franchise. In addition to the nine feature films in its core series, the *Fast Saga*, the franchise also includes: a spin-off film, *Fast & Furious Presents: Hobbs & Shaw* (2019), with rumours of many more in the works; an animated television series targeted primarily at children, *Fast & Furious: Spy Racers* (2019–21); nine video games, with *Fast & Furious: Crossroads* (2020) being the most recent; a board game, *Fast & Furious: Highway Heist* (2021); a theme park ride at Universal Studios Florida, *Fast & Furious: Supercharged*; and, perhaps most surprisingly, the *Fast & Furious Live* show. The latter of these – an arena show that cost Universal £25 million and only lasted for around six months – gives an indication, however, of how surprising and often ill-conceived these ventures can be. *The Guardian*'s Ryan Gilbey (2018) was one of many to note that the bizarre pairing of a franchise based on high-speed, globe-trotting chases and the confines of a small indoor stage, 'just doesn't work'. Critical responses to most other releases have been similarly negative, from the widely derided video games (Ivan 2022), to the theme park ride dubbed as 'Universal's biggest misstep of the decade' (Gregory 2019).

While seemingly representative of the contemporary franchise through its multiple sequels and spinoffs, vast box office returns and transmedia offshoots, a look under the hood of *Fast & Furious* reveals a vehicle whose continued running is surprising, if not miraculous. The haphazard picture painted by these tie-ins (and, to be honest, the films themselves) suggests a franchise whose journey to box office success has, in fact, been much less straightforward than the other properties listed above. Indeed, unlike many of its closest competitors, *Fast & Furious* did not begin as an adaptation of an ongoing IP; as Diesel himself explains, 'this has never been IP with pre-existing comics and books … it's been built from the ground up' (Lawrence 2021b). The first film in the franchise, *The Fast and The Furious* (2001), was adapted from a 1998 *Vibe* magazine article by Kenneth Li ('Racer X'), which detailed the contemporary, illegal street racing scene in New York. The project was the collaborative brainchild of producer Neal H. Moritz, director Rob Cohen and star Paul Walker. Moritz was drawn to the cinematic potential of the *Vibe* article, noting: 'it was *Point Break*, it was *Donnie Brasco*, with the thematic values of *The Godfather*, which was family, family, family'; and he took the title from a 1954 Roger Corman film, preferring 'The Fast and the Furious' to the then-working title 'Redline' (Lawrence 2021a). Walker assumed the joint lead role in the film as Brian O'Conner, sharing the screen with Diesel's Dom Toretto, in what became an unanticipated success: *The Fast and the Furious* grossed $207 million worldwide, with $145 million of that in domestic receipts.

This initial release, then, did not bring with it an established fanbase, especially as its stars were mostly B-list names at this point; nor did it bring a set of rules for narrative and character possibility, beyond perhaps expectations determined by genre. This is certainly not true for many of the other top-grossing franchises we have referred to thus far: those based on existing moving image properties (*Star Wars*, *Transformers*, *Mission: Impossible*), for example, or that were adapted from popular literature (*Lord of the Rings*, *Harry Potter*, the MCU). When developing these types of transmedia universes, meticulous forward planning is required to ensure legibility across their interconnected spaces. Indeed, Shawna Kidman (2021) identifies this type of forward planning as one of the crucial differences between the franchise era and the blockbuster period that preceded it. Kidman notes that while sequels were a consistent feature of the Hollywood economy in the 1990s and 2000s (and long before), they were generally 'greenlit in response to a previous film's success'. Instead, today's franchises are 'preconceived': they are 'planned from the beginning as stories that … unfurl across not only multiple films but also multiple media' (Ibid: 8). This approach is most clear in the work of Disney-owned franchises such as the MCU, where each new film is released as part of a broader slate ('phase') that includes numerous other sequels and spin-off TV shows (Flanagan, Livingstone and McKenny 2016).

This meticulous planning could not be further from the unexpected success of 2001's *The Fast and the Furious* and the sequels and spinoffs that followed. In truth, the story of the making of *Fast & Furious* – its surprise success, circuitous plotting, ill-informed transmedia ventures and approach to audience responses – uncovers a franchise that succeeded without a plan, stumbling onto a winning formula by a mixture of chance and opportunism. In charting the histories of *Fast & Furious* across this chapter, we note how this unique trajectory has allowed it to be particularly responsive to industry and audience shifts, in ways that have not always been possible for more established, long-running franchises, where there's often a requirement to remain true to 'the canon' or source text (Proctor 2019). We see the effects of this time and again over the course of *Fast & Furious*: from its decision to make sequels starring none of the mainline cast, to resurrect characters who were previously killed off, to largely abandon the domestic audience in favour of pursuing international markets such as China, or to perform a mid-franchise rebrand, transitioning into a series of globe-trotting spy capers from *Fast Five* onward.

It's this haphazard development that we're mapping not only here, but more holistically throughout the book. *Fast & Furious* emerged from a space of possibility that was opened up by an initial lack of expectations and forward planning; and it was steered to its current destination through a collection of individuals that included Diesel, Moritz and Universal's executives, as well as director Justin Lin and screenwriter Chris Morgan. Together, these agents made vital choices, demonstrating a degree of foresight (and luck) in the ways that they reacted to key shifts going on within the industry around them. These choices allowed *Fast & Furious* to reach a position where it now competes with the likes of *Star Wars* and the MCU, at least in box office terms. What emerges across these collected chapters is a story of a franchise that succeeded against the odds, defying its humble origins to ascend the ranks of Hollywood's highest-grossing cinematic properties. If anything, the hectic nature of its development forms a key part of the franchise's appeal. Popular criticism of *Fast & Furious* often remarks that the franchise has an off-the-cuff feel, which distinguishes it from more intricately planned and 'corporatized' properties such as the MCU and *Star Wars* (Campbell 2021). In fact, there's a curious symmetry here between the franchise and the street racers-turned-superspies that it depicts, whereby – much like Dom and his ragtag 'family' – *Fast & Furious* exists as something of an outlier within contemporary Hollywood: an outlaw property that has played by its own rules from the start.

## Sequel struggles: Stumbling onto a winning formula in the first four films

After the success of *The Fast and the Furious*, Universal began to make plans for a sequel which would develop the relationship between Brian and Dom. However, the studio failed to convince Diesel to sign on, with the star leaving to pursue other projects after expressing concerns with the script (Lawrence 2021a). Diesel's exit was the first in a series of cast and crew changes that hampered the production, resulting in a film that's less of a sequel and more of a spinoff. Directed by John Singleton, *2 Fast 2 Furious* (2003) keeps Walker's hero but shifts the street racing action to Miami and introduces an entirely new supporting cast, including Chris 'Ludacris' Bridges and Tyrese Gibson as Tej Parker and Roman Pearce, respectively. So disconnected is the sequel from *The Fast and the Furious* that Universal produced an accompanying short to try to bridge the gap: included on special edition home releases of the first film, *The Turbo Charged Prelude to 2 Fast 2 Furious* (2003) details Brian's journey to Miami following his escape from the police.

Due to its disjointedness, *2 Fast 2 Furious* failed to build on the success of *The Fast and the Furious*, earning just $20 million more at the box office ($236 million in total), despite a production budget two times that of the previous film. These underwhelming returns, coupled with the lukewarm response from critics and fans, prompted Universal to ditch Walker from their future plans (Kaufman 2015). Left with a property they were keen to continue, but one without its original stars, the studio changed tack once again for the third film, which represented a near-total relaunch of the franchise. While *The Fast and the Furious: Tokyo Drift* (2006) retains a strong focus on street racing, its main storyline features no pre-existing characters, and it also abandons the cops-and-criminals dynamic that defined the first two films. Set in and around a Tokyo high school, the film follows Lucas Black's Sean, an American teenager who must adapt to a new way of life (and of driving) when he's sent to live with his father in Japan. Dismissed by critics at the time of release, many of whom bemoaned its lack of connection to the earlier films (Tobias 2006), *Tokyo Drift* marked the franchise's lowest point commercially, grossing $158 million from a production budget of $85 million.

Critics and journalists tend to frame *Tokyo Drift* as a curious failure, a pitstop on the franchise's journey to bigger and better things (Hassenger 2015; Thurm 2015). While there's certainly a degree of truth to this reading, it understates the pivotal role that the film played in the franchise's development. Despite its poor domestic returns, for example, *Tokyo Drift* performed strongly overseas, earning $96 million (61 per cent of its total) in the types of markets that would become increasingly important to *Fast & Furious* as it evolved. Thus, the third instalment set up a pattern whereby each *Fast & Furious* film has grossed significantly more internationally than domestically (see Table 1.1). This growing emphasis on overseas markets reflects broader trends within contemporary Hollywood,

Table 1.1 Box office figures for *Fast & Furious* films (Source: Box Office Mojo).

| Film | Production budget | Domestic opening weekend | Domestic | International (% of worldwide total) | Worldwide |
| --- | --- | --- | --- | --- | --- |
| *The Fast and the Furious* (2001) | $38 million | $40,089,015 | $144,533,925 | $62,750,000 (30.3%) | $207,283,925 |
| *2 Fast 2 Furious* (2003) | $76 million | $50,472,480 | $127,154,901 | $109,195,760 (46.2%) | $236,350,661 |
| *The Fast and the Furious: Tokyo Drift* (2006) | $85 million | $23,973,840 | $62,514,415 | $96,450,195 (60.7%) | $158,964,610 |
| *Fast & Furious* (2009) | $85 million | $70,950,500 | $155,064,265 | $205,302,605 (57%) | $360,366,870 |
| *Fast Five* (2011) | $125 million | $86,198,765 | $209,837,675 | $416,300,000 (66.5%) | $626,137,675 |
| *Fast & Furious 6* (2013) | $160 million | $97,375,245 | $238,679,850 | $550,001,118 (69.7%) | $788,680,968 |
| *Furious 7* (2015) | $190 million | $147,187,040 | $353,007,020 | $1,162,334,379 (76.7%) | $1,515,341,399 |
| *The Fate of the Furious* (2017) | $250 million | $98,786,705 | $226,008,385 | $1,009,996,733 (81.7%) | $1,236,005,118 |
| *Fast & Furious Presents: Hobbs & Shaw* (2019) | $200 million | $60,038,950 | $173,956,935 | $585,100,000 (77.1%) | $759,056,935 |
| *F9: The Fast Saga* (2021) | $200 million | $70,043,165 | $173,005,945 | $553,223,556 (76.2%) | $726,229,501 |
| **Overall total** | **$1.409 billion** | **$745,115,705** | **$1,863,960,151** | **$4,750,675,930 (71.8%)** | **$6,614,439,246** |

where there has been an accelerated turn towards international audiences since the turn of the millennium. While Hollywood has a long and storied history of targeting revenues overseas (Balio 1996; Krämer 2022; Trumpbour 2008), the key differences of this contemporary formulation begin with the fact that Hollywood is now largely reliant on international markets, targeting them in the first instance. Crucially, Hollywood's key markets in the franchise era are emerging ones, within mostly non-European locations such as China, and these 'foreign investors' hold larger stakes – both aesthetic and economic – than they did previously (Fleury, Hartzheim and Mamber 2019; Song 2018). According to Kailash Koushik and Jennifer M. Proffitt (2019: 28), America's blockbuster productions are now 'global events', designed from the ground up to 'attract global audiences and increase global investments'.

*Tokyo Drift* also marked key changes behind the scenes, heralding the arrival of two filmmakers – screenwriter Chris Morgan and director Justin Lin – who would help to oversee the franchise's evolution into a multibillion-dollar property. A relative newcomer to the industry, with just one screenwriting credit prior to 2006, Morgan was hired to write *Tokyo Drift* after Universal issued an open call for screenplays (Lawrence 2019). Morgan recognized that the strengths of the first two films revolved around their strong emphasis on action and family; but he also had the ambition to build a deeper franchise mythology, one which incorporated the types of shocking narrative twists that have lent *Fast & Furious* its distinctive 'soap opera' quality (Ibid). In Morgan, Universal found a screenwriter who was able to mould the franchise's disparate elements into a unified whole, and he would proceed to pen every main saga film until *F9*, as well as the spinoff, *Hobbs & Shaw*.

Lin was recruited to direct *Tokyo Drift* by Neal Moritz and then-Universal Pictures Chair Stacey Snider; and, like Morgan, he would play a key role going forward, helming the next three sequels, before taking a two-film hiatus and returning to the franchise for *F9*. Prior to *Tokyo Drift*, Lin was best known for his solo directorial debut *Better Luck Tomorrow* (2002), a low-budget crime film which received praise for its 'stereotype-shattering' portrayal of East Asian Americans (Ansen 2002). This 'stereotype-shattering' sensibility was something Lin brought to his first big studio film. With *Tokyo Drift*, the director explicitly sought to improve the problematic representational politics of the franchise, having 'disliked the ways in which … non-white characters were portrayed in the original film'; and he did this by making several changes in pre-production, such as cutting some of the more 'stereotypical elements' from Morgan's initial script (Beltrán 2013: 93). As part of this process, Lin also took the opportunity to incorporate elements directly from his earlier work including Han Seoul-Oh, a character who originally appears in *Better Luck Tomorrow*. Played by Sung Kang, Han performs a key function within the narrative of *Tokyo Drift*, teaching Lucas Black's hero how to 'drift'. In keeping with Lin's aim, he emerges as a figure deserving of the audience's respect: a skilled and courageous driver, Han is not only willing to risk himself (and his car) to protect his friends, but he also embodies a type of cool and sophistication that's rarely associated with East Asian characters in Hollywood action cinema.

While Morgan brought renewed vigour to the page, devising the type of elaborately plotted action scenarios that would soon become *Fast & Furious*' modus operandi, Lin was responsible for translating that energy and ambition to the big screen. The director has described *Tokyo Drift* as 'a big $80-million indie', referring to the lack of studio interference at the production stage. In fact, due to a series of changes within Universal Pictures at the time, including Stacey Snider's impending move to DreamWorks, Lin had something of a free hand when shaping the film's style and tone (Saito 2014); and he used that freedom to begin to bring 'more scope' and experimentation to the franchise's action scenes. This scope is evident in the Shibuya chase sequence, which takes the drivers through Tokyo's iconic Shibuya Crossing and functions as both the action centrepiece of the film and its dramatic apex – given that it results in Han's (apparent) death.[2] The range of camera movements represents a shift from the flat aesthetic of *2 Fast 2 Furious*, culminating in a shot that performs a 360° motion around the bend as the cars zoom past. In order to capture this moment, Lin's stunt coordinators constructed a camera rig out of a high-speed shifter kart. Capable of reaching speeds of 80 mph, this rig allowed Lin to film the cars from close proximity and at ground level, bringing greater emphasis to the drifting motion that was the film's key selling point (Lin 2006). This visual sensibility, partnered with Morgan's penmanship, laid the groundwork for the types of outrageous action we see within the franchise today.

What Lin and Morgan both recognized was the value of bringing back Diesel. When he first met with Universal about writing *Tokyo Drift*, Morgan pitched a version of the film where Dom travels to Japan to solve a friend's murder; and both he and Lin remained keen to pair the likes of Han with characters from the original film (Lawrence 2019). Thus, together with Universal executive Jeffrey Kirschenbaum, Lin met with Diesel in the months prior to production, where they discussed future possibilities for Dom and the franchise (Saito 2014).

Off the back of these conversations, the actor agreed to make an appearance in the film. Diesel took no pay for *Tokyo Drift*, waiving his salary in exchange for greater creative control over any subsequent sequels, as well as the rights to the Riddick character – a deal that allowed him to co-produce and star in the 2013 film *Riddick* (Mendelson 2015a).

Diesel's appearance in *Tokyo Drift* is brief. In a 90-second sequence at the film's close, Dom reminisces with Sean about the recently deceased Han, before challenging the teenager to a race. However brief this moment is, its significance in the *Fast & Furious* production lore is paramount. With Diesel's return, the centrality of Dom had been re-established, giving Universal an avenue through which they could pursue a more conventional sequel arrangement. In the initial screenings, Dom's cameo proved a huge success with fans. It was the first moment of unanimous consensus across the various stakeholders in its production that there was a franchise worth developing in a less scattered way than it had been prior. Adam Fogelson, then-Chair of Universal Pictures, recalls the cameo fondly: 'That last scene when audiences saw him was explosive. All of us sitting in that test screening in Chatsworth realised the franchise wasn't over. We said, "Let's get started"' (Finke 2011a).

In that moment, Universal had stumbled upon a version of the end-credits stinger, anticipating some of the trends that Disney and Marvel would perfect into the 2010s, with the 'post-credits sequence' functioning as a key audience development tool in the MCU (Flanagan, Livingstone and McKenny 2016: 184). While Dom's arrival actually precedes the credits, it works in much the same fashion, adding a post-resolution tease which sets up the possibility of further sequels and spinoffs. In this sense, it's a realization of the type of 'incompleteness' that Chuck Tryon identifies as pivotal to cinema in the age of media convergence, wherein narrative elements are deliberately left dangling in order 'to foster the vast expansion of the story world of major Hollywood franchises, and by extension their marketability' (Tryon 2009: 19; Jenkins 2006). This 'incompleteness' would subsequently help *Fast & Furious* open up into a more expansive, multi-film narrative – what later became known as 'The *Fast Saga*' (Hedash 2020). In the initial instance, though, it consolidated the series and returned it to its roots, by reintegrating the starting roster of characters.

*Fast & Furious* (2009, hereinafter *Fast Four*) was the sequel that Universal had originally wanted to make with *2 Fast 2 Furious*. Crafted by *Tokyo Drift*'s creative collaborators of Lin and Morgan, *Fast Four* was developed as a franchise reboot – as indicated by its rather confusing 'Fast & Furious' title – and finely tuned to follow in the footsteps of *The Fast and the Furious*. It reunites Dom with Brian as buddy protagonists and brings back the supporting cast of Letty (Michelle Rodriguez) and Mia (Jordana Brewster) from the first film. The action scenes take on the visual flair that Lin developed in *Tokyo Drift* while consciously referring to set pieces from the original film, with the gang using the same technique to hijack oil trucks as they did for haulage trucks previously. Likewise, the global sensibility that Lin and Morgan brought to the franchise is maintained, with the heroes moving between the Dominican Republic, Panama, Mexico and the United States over the course of the film.

Most crucially, though, amid all of these important changes, was that *Fast Four* resurrected Han (from the dead) to incorporate him into the 'family' proper. On first viewing, it's a surprise to see Han with Dom and his team in *Fast Four*'s opening heist, given his death at the climax of *Tokyo Drift*. We hear later in the film that he plans to move to Tokyo in the future to avoid arrest, meaning that *Fast Four* takes place before the fateful events of *Tokyo Drift*. In truth, this was not a smooth manoeuvre but a clumsy fudge, which Morgan and Lin have laughed about getting away with: 'And nobody asked!' (Ryan 2017). This rejig had significant repercussions, as Morgan gleefully reminds us: 'the timeline is, you know, it's one-two-four-five-six-three-seven, right?' (Ibid). In resurrecting Han, *Fast & Furious* initiated the strange chronology that has gone on to become a part of the franchise's distinctive appeal.

For a franchise finally able to produce a clean sequel to the first film, this seems an oddly convoluted creative decision to bring to the table, but it captures the off-the-cuff feel which is vital to the series. The timeline shift was created entirely out of the desire to accommodate Han, who was not only beloved by Lin and Morgan but also by the vocal *Fast & Furious* fan base. Dubbed the 'greatest *Fast & Furious* character' by *Buzzfeed,* Han is understood to personify the franchise's progressive representational politics (Willmore 2015). In test screenings for *Tokyo Drift*, Han earned a 100 per cent approval rating, the highest for any character in Universal's history (Saito 2014). This transitional moment established a pattern of resurrecting (sometimes quite literally) fan favourites and characters from earlier films. Indeed, it laid the foundations for a deeper *Fast & Furious* mythology that Universal would seek to unify in its most meaningful form in *Fast & Furious 6* (2013), a film which attempts to tie together all the loose threads from the previous instalments into a unified 'family' roster.

Since *Fast Four*'s sweeping adjustment, Han has remained central to the franchise, appearing in all but two of the subsequent main saga films (we discuss his absence from the seventh and eighth entries below). Moreover, the combination of unusual plot choices and necromancy that brought Han into the family is now key to the *Fast & Furious* brand. These characteristics had their foundations laid in those pivotal moments of *Fast Four* and in the authors of the franchise seeking to mould the films into a unified, sequential series. Such character arcs might not seem as remarkable if the studio had stuck with the tangentially-related sequels approach used in the first three releases, when Universal were unable to secure Diesel's continued involvement. Thus, the seeds for the franchise's later development were sown in the transition between *Tokyo Drift* and *Fast Four*: between Dom's return and the timeline accommodation of Han on screen, and the collaboration of Diesel, Lin and Morgan off screen.

While *Fast Four* was unpopular with critics, it represented a significant upturn in the franchise's commercial fortunes, especially after the disappointing returns of *Tokyo Drift*: the film grossed $360 million worldwide, $205 million of its total coming from locations outside North America. However, if it wasn't for the obstacles surrounding *2 Fast 2 Furious* and *Tokyo Drift*, Universal and the core creative team of Lin, Morgan and Diesel would not have landed on the formula that proved so successful in *Fast Four*. In fact, as Mendelson (2015a) notes, it was precisely 'the "failure" to make a proper sequel for the first eight years', that led the franchise to initiate the 'kind of expanded universe that Hollywood now craves'. By surrendering to what was easy in the moment, the producers of *Fast & Furious* might have sacrificed logical coherence, but in doing so they opened up a strange chronology and a much deeper roster of characters on which to build. And build on it they did, honing the formula into a fine craft in the subsequent sequels and spinoffs. But not before one more pivot: this time at the level of style and genre, with *Fast Five* ushering in new types of spectacular action.

## A franchise re-branded: Incorporating new styles of action after *Fast Four*

For the first four films, *Fast & Furious* stuck closely to its genre roots: these were crime pictures set in and around the street racing world, where the stakes rarely extended beyond the lives of the protagonists themselves; and, while each film contained spectacular chases, the action sequences were generally 'grounded in some sense of … physical reality', meaning the cars and their drivers did things that cars and their drivers 'can actually do' (Suderman 2017). Starting with *Fast Five*, however, the franchise began to shift gears, moving away from a focus on street racing and towards more expansive and high-stakes forms of action. Set in Rio de Janeiro, the fifth film contains just one street race, a four-way contest which functions primarily as a comic interlude. Instead, the spectacular action in *Fast Five* stems from the central heist plot – Dom and his team's plan to steal $100 million from Brazilian drug kingpin, Herman Reyes (Joaquin de Almeida). Although other races are set up and referenced in the film, these take place off screen to allow time for more elaborate and lengthy set pieces such as the climactic robbery, a twelve-minute sequence that features over 200 vehicles and culminates with Dom and Brian using two Dodge Vipers to drag a 9000-lb. bank vault through the streets of Rio. *Fast & Furious 6* continues the pattern established in *Fast Five*. Here, the solitary street race involves Dom and Letty and is more concerned with rekindling their romance than providing thrilling action, while the thirteen-minute finale sees the team tether their vehicles to a cargo plane in order to prevent it from taking off.

The primary motivation for this transition away from street racing was commercial, as the studio behind the franchise sought to broaden its appeal. Speaking with *Deadline* in April 2011, one week after the release of the fifth film, then-Universal Pictures Chair Adam Fogelson (Finke 2011a) explained:

> The question putting *Fast Five* and [*Fast & Furious 6*] together for us was: Can we take it out of being a pure car culture movie and into being a true action franchise in the spirit of those great heist films made 10 or 15 years ago? … if these movies were still about street racing, there was probably a ceiling on how many people would buy tickets. We wanted to see if we could raise it … and make car driving ability just a part of the movie.

After *Fast Four*, then, the franchise sought to up the ante with each new instalment. So, while the cars remained front and centre in the fifth and sixth films, they were tied to more and more elaborate action scenarios and plots, as *Fast & Furious* incorporated elements from not just the heist movie but also the spy thriller subgenre. *Fast & Furious 6* introduced the franchise's first supervillain, for instance, pitting Dom and his team against Luke Evans's Owen Shaw – a former SAS agent who is building a superweapon, 'Nightshade', that can disable the world's power grid. At the close of the film, Dom and his team not only stop Owen Shaw from activating Nightshade, thereby saving the world;

they also successfully reintegrate Letty into the group, helping her to recover from the amnesia that she is shown to have suffered as a result of her apparent death in *Fast Four*.

Between the fifth and sixth films, therefore, *Fast & Furious* underwent a significant evolution, transplanting its street racer heroes into the arenas of international espionage and counterterrorism, while also building a complicated overarching narrative through the frequent use of plot twists – such as the revelation, included in a mid-credits sequence at the end of *Fast & Furious 6*, that Owen Shaw's brother, Deckard (Jason Statham), was responsible for Han's death in *Tokyo Drift*. These plot twists continued the work that began in the third and fourth films, fleshing out character backstories as a way to reward audience investment and produce a deeper mythology. Indeed, *Fast Five* and *Fast & Furious 6* also marked the first consistent use of post-credits scenes within the franchise. Although the original film contains a brief post-credits scene, which shows Dom escaping to Mexico, these only became a recurring feature after *Fast Four*, when the producers began to engage much more systematically with the types of world-building best associated with transmedia mega-properties like the MCU (Flanagan, Livingstone and McKenny 2016).

This evolution paid off commercially. While *Fast Five* and *Fast & Furious 6* cost more to make than the earlier entries, with production budgets over three times that of the first film, they also earned far more at the box office, grossing $626 million and $789 million, respectively. What's more, these two films consolidated the franchise's global appeal, as the shift to over-the-top action and family-based melodrama proved especially popular outside North America. Building on the international success of the third and fourth films, for example, *Fast Five* set records for Universal's biggest opening weekend in multiple overseas markets, including Mexico, Brazil and Russia, and was the seventh highest-grossing film of 2011 worldwide (Finke 2011b; Stewart 2011). Likewise, $550 million (70 per cent) of *Fast & Furious 6*'s total came internationally, with the film placing number one in each of the fifty-nine markets outside of North America where it opened (McClintock 2013). Particularly significant in this regard was the $66 million that *Fast & Furious 6* grossed in Mainland China, a territory that emerged as one of the franchise's major markets in the period after *Fast Four* (see Table 1.1).

Unsurprisingly, Universal continued this bigger is better strategy with the next two sequels, *Furious 7* and *The Fate of the Furious* (2017, hereinafter *Fast Eight*), which cost $190 million and $250 million to produce and grossed

$1.5 billion and $1.2 billion, respectively. The cars in these films, even more so than in the fifth and sixth entries, are 'completely and unapologetically unbound from any real-world understanding of how cars actually work' (Suderman 2017); and the action sequences as a whole make use of a far wider range of vehicles and settings. In *Furious 7*, the first act concludes with a set piece in which the team parachute their cars out of a plane and onto the Caucasus Mountains in Azerbaijan, while a later sequence sees Dom use a supercar to jump between two of Abu Dhabi's tallest skyscrapers (Figure 1.1). *Fast Eight* sought to raise the stakes even higher with the introduction of antagonist Cipher (Charlize Theron), a cyberterrorist who functions as a sort of master villain across the franchise's later films. Early in *Fast Eight*, Cipher is revealed as the architect behind the terrorist plots in the sixth and seventh films; and, here, she forces Dom to betray the team by kidnapping his son, Marcos. Set against the icy backdrop of the Arctic, the film's climactic set piece features a nuclear submarine that's remote-piloted by Theron's villain, one which Dom eventually destroys by redirecting a heat-seeking missile back towards it.

With their growing roster of supervillains and strong emphasis on high-tech weaponry, these later instalments are much closer in style to action-adventure spy franchises such as *James Bond* and *Mission: Impossible*, than the B-movie car and crime pictures from which *Fast & Furious* originally derived. This shift at the level of genre is also reflected in the design of the franchise's cars, which have become more combat-focused in films five through to nine. Writing for *BBC Culture*, Kambole Campbell (2021) observes the sharp contrast between the vehicles in the earlier and later films, noting that while the first three pictures 'set out to convey the allure of street racing' – through the use of bright colours and

**Figure 1.1** Abu Dhabi skyscraper jump, *Furious 7* (2015 Universal).

dialogue detailing 'the technical specificity' of the engine parts – the cars from the sixth film onward are 'stripped back, and sometimes even military-looking, in their appearance'. Certain features have remained consistent throughout the franchise, including the dependence on NOS. However, starting with *Fast & Furious 6*, there was a focus on more than just speed, as the franchise moved away from its original, underpinning philosophy of the '10-second car'. Instead, the vehicles in these later sequels are superpowered, kitted out with a growing arsenal of military-grade weapons and gadgets, such as the electromagnets that allow the team to attract and repel other cars in *F9*.

Lisa Purse (2011: 79) points to a 'credibility continuum' in the action film. She notes that within action cinema, 'the relationship of the hero's feats to real-world laws of physics and physiology' differs from film to film, placing anywhere along a continuum 'between highly naturalistic and radically non-naturalistic'. This is evident in *Fast & Furious*, a franchise which becomes progressively less naturalistic as it develops. Indeed, at the same time *Fast & Furious* pivoted towards the spy film, it also began to absorb elements of the nascent superhero movie trend. The first instalment in the MCU, *Iron Man* (2008), was released just three years prior to *Fast Five*, its success leading to an explosion of superhero content that has seen the subgenre dominate the box office in subsequent years (Flanagan, Livingstone and McKenny 2016).[3] The MCU's influence can be seen in the later *Fast & Furious* films, where it's not only the cars that possess superpowers but also the protagonists themselves. A growing proportion of the action after *Fast Four* takes place outside the cars, as fistfights inside abandoned warehouses (*Fast & Furious 6*) or foot chases across rooftops (*Fast Five*). This shift provided more opportunities to incorporate hand-to-hand combat within the franchise, as the team were shown punching and grappling in a manner that far exceeded anything in the earlier films. The gravitation towards spectacular bodily action was partly a result of casting choices, namely, the decision to bring in skilled physical performers such as Dwayne Johnson and Jason Statham. However, these superhuman abilities also extended to the original cast. In *F9*, for example, Dom fights an entire platoon of mercenaries alone, before using his bare hands to tear down a steel bridge.

For a franchise that began in such modest fashion, incorporating this style of action hasn't always been straightforward. Indeed, reviews of the later instalments – even where they express a positive opinion overall – tend to mock the 'ludicrous' idea that the US government would recruit a gang of street racers to prevent terrorist plots (Grierson 2021). One way that *Fast & Furious* has sought to offset these criticisms is by engaging in a metacommentary on its own absurdity. An example of this is found in *Fast & Furious* 6, when Roman stops to voice his disbelief following the team's first chastening encounter with Owen Shaw: 'This is crazy … So, now we've got cars flying through the air? On some 007-type shit? *This is not what we do!*' The reference to 007 here serves a comic purpose, making light of just how far the franchise and its protagonists have come. This type of knowing humour is central to the brand. On the one hand, it encourages audiences to reflect (like Roman) on what they have just witnessed, to better appreciate the epic scale of *Fast & Furious*' action sequences. On the other, it lends the franchise a sense of playfulness, whereby the films seem to revel in their reputation as 'ludicrous' and over the top. As actor John Cena explains, '*Fast* isn't afraid to occasionally wink [back] at the audience to say, "Thanks for allowing us to do this"' (Lawrence 2021b), a feature that further underlines its offbeat and cultish tone (Mack 2019).

## Stardom and performance in *Fast & Furious*

It wasn't just the action that got bigger as the franchise developed; the stars got bigger, too. In *Fast Five*, Dwayne Johnson boarded the cast as Luke Hobbs, a US federal agent who is sent to Rio de Janeiro to arrest Dom and Brian but ends up joining forces with them in the final act. Standing at 6 foot 5 inches tall and weighing 260 lbs., Johnson was a perfect fit for the rebranded *Fast & Furious*, his huge frame embodying the franchise's commitment to more and more spectacular action. Julie Lobalzo Wright (2019: 204–8) argues that Johnson's stardom centres on his 'seemingly impossible' physique, noting how 'even in comparison with other muscle-men, Johnson is enormous'. This is clearly apparent in *Fast Five*, where early scenes underscore his sheer size and power. When Hobbs first appears in Rio, for example, arriving aboard a military cargo plane, he is framed in a two-shot with a much smaller man – the local police chief, João Alameida (Joseph Melendez; Figure 1.2). In the background of the shot, a convoy of armoured cars emerge from the plane, prompting Alameida to ask, 'Is all of this really necessary?' Alameida is referring here to the vast arsenal of high-tech weapons and vehicles Hobbs has brought with him to Rio, and that he will use in his efforts to apprehend the two fugitives. However, as the film cuts to a medium close-up of Hobbs, where his muscular shoulders and square jaw dominate the frame, it's clear that the question applies just as much to the star

**Figure 1.2** Two-shot of Hobbs and Alameida, *Fast Five* (2011 Universal).

himself. Indeed, in the way it offers up Hobbs's body as a source of spectacle – by pairing him with Alameida and drawing a link between his ripped physique and the armoured cars – *Fast Five* suggests that Johnson is precisely what's necessary for the franchise to evolve.

Beyond his physical attributes, Johnson also brought wide name recognition to *Fast & Furious*, in large part due to his earlier career as a World Wrestling Entertainment (WWE) star. Prior to *Fast Five*, Johnson had already begun to translate his success as a professional wrestler into theatrical returns, with starring roles in action-adventure blockbusters such as *The Scorpion King* (2002), alongside well-received supporting turns in *Be Cool* (2005) and *The Other Guys* (2010), two crime-comedies which play on his arrogant WWE persona, 'The Rock'. However, it was *Fast & Furious* that elevated Johnson into the Hollywood A-list, with its combination of spectacular action and macho banter providing an ideal vehicle for him to showcase the athleticism and verbal dexterity that were crucial to his popularity in the ring.

Johnson's introduction to the franchise proved to be a hit. Grossing $626 million worldwide, *Fast Five* more than doubled the box office of the previous film, with over $400 million of that total coming from international markets. Moreover, unlike the much-maligned *Fast Four*, the fifth film received generally positive reviews (Eichler 2011), while numerous critics also singled out Johnson for praise. Writing in *Variety*, Robert Koehler (2011) noted how Johnson brought 'a welcome injection of tough-guy vigour' to the franchise, identifying his muscular performance as a 'perfect counter to the easy bond' between the rest of the cast. By assuming the role of Hobbs, then, Johnson established himself as a major box office draw, someone whose larger-than-life persona appealed to a wide range of audiences both at home and abroad. Indeed, it was in the period immediately after *Fast Five* – when Johnson appeared in a string of lucrative sequels including *Fast & Furious 6*, *Journey 2: The Mysterious Island* (2012), and *G.I. Joe: Retaliation* (2013) – that he earned the nickname 'franchise Viagra', a reference to his capacity to reinvigorate cinematic properties by joining them mid-stream (Mendelson 2015b).

Following the success of the fifth film, *Fast & Furious* continued to recruit big-name talent as a way to broaden its appeal. In *Fast & Furious 6*, British actor Jason Statham made his first appearance as Deckard Shaw, a rogue MI6 agent and brother of Owen Shaw. Statham's character would go on to play a major role in the next two sequels: after a mid-credits cameo in the sixth film, Shaw serves as the primary antagonist of *Furious 7*, before teaming up with Dom and the others in *Fast Eight*. Shaw follows a very similar trajectory to Hobbs in this regard, transitioning from adversary to ally in the space of just two films; and his redemption – after appearing to kill Han – once again illustrates the kind of 'unusual, unexpected choices' for which *Fast & Furious* has become known (Mack 2019: 66).

By the time he joined the franchise in 2013, Statham was already a major action star, having appeared in popular films such as *Crank* (2006) and *The Expendables* (2010). Although these early Statham films earned less than his subsequent work on *Fast & Furious*, each was a success in its own right, leading to one or more sequels in which the actor also starred. In casting Statham, therefore, *Fast & Furious* was gaining an international star with a proven track record in the action genre as well as his own loyal fan base, something that contributed significantly to the box office performance of the seventh and eighth films. *Fast Eight*, for example, was specifically marketed as another opportunity to see Statham square off against Johnson, following the positive response to their fight at the start of *Furious 7* (Heritage 2016). In this instance, the trailers not only teased the friction (and spectacular brawls) generated by Shaw's unlikely addition to the team, but also the odd-couple chemistry between Johnson and Statham, which would form the basis of their own 2019 spinoff, *Hobbs & Shaw*.

With the introduction of Johnson and Statham, and other prominent actors such as Charlize Theron, the cast of *Fast & Furious* 'moved from B-list forgettable to formidable' (Thurm 2015). Crucially, this growing emphasis on stardom appears to run up against broader Hollywood trends. Fritz (2018) suggests that 'the dawn of the franchise era' has coincided with a downturn in star power, noting how the involvement of A-list talent no longer provides the same guarantee of box office success that it did in the early 2000s and before. Fritz's argument echoes wider observations about the emergence of a character-centric economy in post-millennium Hollywood. According to scholars Fleury, Hartzheim and Mamber (2019: 10), for example, 'characters, rather than stars, now dominate the box office', a shift that has led the major studios to redirect much of the money they once spent on star vehicles into developing pre-existing properties and brands. Summarizing these changes, Fritz (2018: 84–5) writes: 'Today, no person has the box-office track record that [Tom] Cruise once did, and it's hard to imagine that anyone will again. But Marvel Studios does. Harry Potter does. Fast & Furious does.'

The accounts of these scholars and journalists are persuasive in showing that for most of Hollywood's mega-franchises, iconic characters are important, but the actors playing them are not. However, far less persuasive is Fritz's idea that *Fast & Furious* fits neatly within this paradigm. Indeed, while other franchises such as *Spider-Man* and *Batman* have enjoyed success when recasting their central characters, it's hard to imagine the same strategy working for *Fast & Furious* – because Dom, Letty, Hobbs and Shaw are so intimately tied to the star images of Diesel, Rodriguez, Johnson and Statham, respectively. Again, this speaks to the unusual nature of the franchise: the fact that *Fast & Furious* wasn't adapted from a long-established IP, and that the vast majority of its revenue still derives overwhelmingly from box office receipts and home video sales. In contrast to the likes of Spider-Man and Batman, then, these *Fast & Furious* characters have a limited presence beyond the actors who currently play them on the big screen, despite recent efforts to expand the franchise into theme park rides and TV shows. Framed against the backdrop of the franchise era, *Fast & Furious* emerges as something of an anachronism, recalling earlier decades of Hollywood filmmaking in its strong emphasis on stardom, including the way in which it became more star-driven during a period when Hollywood was transitioning to a character-centric model.

For all the high-profile additions to the later films, it's an original cast member, Diesel, who still looms largest within the franchise. Indeed, it's not possible to explore the importance of stardom to *Fast & Furious* without looking closely at Diesel's contributions on-screen and off. According to reports, Diesel was pivotal in shaping the style of the films from the outset (Lawrence 2021a), and he sought to exert further control over the franchise when he made a full return for the fourth film. The star did this by combining his acting with a behind-the-scenes role. Via One Race, the company he established in 1995, Diesel has co-produced each of the *Fast Saga* films since *Fast Four*; and it's a role in which he is said to consult on everything from story structure and the soundtrack, to casting and costume choices (Lin 2009). As such, the actor-producer is often credited with overseeing the franchise's evolution into a multibillion-dollar property (Lawrence 2021b), an idea which he himself has cultivated by claiming the title of 'saga visionary' in interviews (Acuna 2019).

Authorship in a collaborative medium such as film is notoriously difficult to ascertain. This is particularly true in the case of big-budget franchise pictures which are financed by multimedia conglomerates for the purpose of realizing profits in several divisions of the company. In these instances, authorship becomes even more dispersed, spread out across a vast number of individuals working on many different media platforms (Johnson 2012; Kidman 2021). Given the complex nature of authorship in franchise cinema, we certainly don't want to suggest that Diesel is the primary force behind *Fast & Furious*: that argument would ignore the crucial work undertaken not only by the likes of Lin, Morgan and Diesel's fellow cast members, but also by below-the-line crew such as the stunt drivers and coordinators.[4] However, it's clear from the examples above that the actor wields a degree of influence over a major franchise which is largely unrivalled in post-millennium Hollywood (or, at least, Diesel performs such influence through the leverage of his star persona). Indeed, in an era where star power has declined significantly, Diesel is distinctive for the way in which he has helped to steer *Fast & Furious* for such a sustained period of time.

The star has managed to achieve this level of influence through his savvy use of social media. Like Johnson, Diesel is among the most-followed Hollywood actors on Facebook and Instagram, and he regularly uses these platforms to communicate directly with the franchise's fans, a group he addresses as his '*Fast* family'. During pre-production on the tenth film, for example, the actor posted an update to his 80 million Instagram followers, reminding them: 'you all have been a part of this journey. You all have been a part of this family … I hope to make you proud' (Diesel 2022). Across these posts, Diesel emerges as the franchise's custodian, rather than its author: someone who works for the fans, drawing on their feedback and suggestions to deliver what's best for 'the family'. In this sense, he offers an example of what Suzanne Scott (2012: 44) terms the 'fanboy auteur', a mode of authorship where the filmmaker presents themselves as 'simultaneously one of "us" and one of "them"'. Diesel's social media posts are one element within a wider corporate strategy to generate strong audience investment in the franchise. This is something we turn to in the next section, when we consider the ways in which *Fast & Furious* has positioned itself as a fan-driven franchise.

## 'Join the *Fast* Family': *Fast & Furious* as a fan-driven franchise

In March 2020, *F9* was among the first Hollywood blockbusters to be postponed because of Covid-19, its release date moving from May 2020 to spring the next year. When announcing the delay, Universal Pictures issued a lengthy press release addressed to the franchise's fans via their Facebook page:

> To our family of Fast fans everywhere, We feel all the love and the anticipation you have for the next chapter in our saga. That's why it's especially tough to let you know that we have to move the release date of the film. It's become clear that it won't be possible for all our fans around the world to see the film this May. We are moving the global release date to April 2021, with North America opening on April 2. While we know there is disappointment in having to wait a little longer, this move is made with the safety of everyone as our foremost consideration. Moving will allow our global family to experience our new chapter together. We'll see you next spring. Much love, Your Fast Family. (The Fast Saga 2020)

Circulated on social media, what stands out most from this statement is its repeated use of the phrase 'family' and its assurance that fans of the franchise will understand and accept the delay as a gesture of solidarity with their 'global family' members. Indicative of the international reach of the franchise, these repeated references to ideas of a global family have been central to *Fast & Furious*' success at cultivating a large, loyal fan base for its films.

Throughout this introduction we have alluded to the use of 'family' as an umbrella term within the films used for the group of Dom and his accomplices. This term functions well as a semantic manoeuvre that allows each film to smooth over the shady morality of its protagonists' actions and accommodate characters (living, dead or resurrected) who flip-flop across lines of 'good' and 'evil' with abandon. However, moving beyond its prominence within the films themselves, we can see through strategies like this Facebook post how 'family' also serves a larger purpose in terms of audience development: it is a concept used to cultivate a large and loyal fan base, engendering modes of appreciation for *Fast & Furious* that mark the franchise as somewhat distinct from its closest competitors. These modes are multifaceted – at once sincere and ironic, intimate but distanced – and they work to maintain a relationship with audiences in which fans are granted agency in dictating the direction of the characters and their world.

As the March 2020 Facebook post reminds us, this family is a broad church which takes in viewers from a variety of ethnic, class and geographic groups. Excluding the first two releases, each film in the franchise has made more money outside of North America, with both *Furious 7* and *Fast Eight* breaking box office records for international releases in China and elsewhere (Frater 2017). Within the limited *Fast & Furious* scholarship that currently exists, Mary Beltrán (2005, 2013) has explored the relationship between the franchise's audiences and the demographically diverse cast which make up the on-screen family. For Beltrán (2005: 50), *Fast & Furious* is the pinnacle of the 'multiculti' film which embodies through its casting – and Diesel as a star – contemporary concerns in the United States towards race relations: 'with respect to the nation's burgeoning cultural creolization and multiethnic population'. The statistics back up Beltrán's assessment: the theatrical audience for *F9* in the US was made up of 37 per cent Latino, 35 per cent Caucasian, 16 per cent Black, 8 per cent Asian and 4 per cent 'Native American/Other' audiences (McClintock 2021). This signifies the wide-ranging, multi-demographic appeal that has been central to *Fast & Furious* since its inception, and which is articulated through the framework of 'family', with all of its attendant ideas of unconditional love and support. There is an ethics of inclusivity on display throughout *Fast & Furious*, from its rewriting of the initial *Vibe* magazine article adaptation to include better representation of the Latinx community of Los Angeles, to Lin's corrective work on *Tokyo Drift* and its portrayal of East Asian (and Asian American) characters. This approach has helped the franchise navigate, and to some extent pre-empt, the specific character of the turn to global audiences which Hollywood has undertaken in the last decade.

It helps that, within the diegetic world of *Fast & Furious*, 'family' is a wholly positive concept: it signifies a moral code that favours notions of loyalty, respect and camaraderie over those of legality, respectability and competition. As such, it is a welcoming concept that Universal (and Diesel in particular) have managed to successfully leverage in the promotion and marketing of the films. We see this in Diesel's mediation between audiences and Universal through his role of the 'fanboy auteur', discussed above, but also through more formal material shared by the studio itself: when one goes to the official website for the franchise to join its mailing list, for example, they are invited to 'Join the *Fast* Family' rather than simply 'sign up'. Indeed, when asked how *F9* overcame the obstacle of a twelve-month delay caused by a global pandemic, Universal's President of Domestic Distribution Jim Orr claimed that it was because 'fans consider themselves to be family' (McClintock 2021). It appears, as with many of us during the Covid-19 pandemic, reuniting with family was worth the risks of transmission.

A vital part of this sense of familiarity believed to be felt by audiences of *Fast & Furious* is the sense of ownership it engenders; and fans have good reason to believe their proximity to the franchise is genuine and not just empty marketing platitudes from a Hollywood studio. This is a franchise which has, on more than one occasion, responded directly to fan suggestions in surprising ways, at the often alarming cost of narrative coherence and believability. We see this most clearly in the franchise's treatment of Sung Kang's character, Han, whose circuitous inclusion in the *Fast Saga* shows how reactively the series has worked to accommodate fan suggestion or, in this case, outrage (Acuna 2021). Han, in particular, shows that this is a unique approach through which *Fast & Furious* interacts with its audiences. We have, earlier in this introduction, traced Han's narrative arc (at the time of writing): from his appearance and 'death' in *Tokyo Drift*, through a timeline rejig to support his appearances between the fourth and sixth films, to his resurrection in *F9*. We noted that this was related to Han's rare popularity with audiences, shown by his 100 per cent approval rating at test screenings for *Tokyo Drift*. But this popularity only translated into on-screen changes thanks to Universal's negotiation with a large, vocal group of fans who felt betrayed by the decision to have Han's (then-suspected) murderer, Deckard Shaw, join the core 'family' at the end of *Fast Eight*.

Following the release of *Fast Eight*, a social media movement sprang up demanding 'Justice for Han', claiming that Shaw's rushed redemption pointed to a new 'hypocrisy' in the *Fast Saga* and a sign that the franchise was losing touch with the emotional core that many were invested in (Dumaraog 2021). The movement called for retribution for Shaw, rather than redemption, which they would see as *Fast & Furious* returning to its roots: pulling back from the spurious unravelling of its core themes that occurred as the franchise grew in scale, scope and popularity. Ever keen to accommodate fan requests – especially when they line up with desires of Lin and the creative team – Han was resurrected, again, for *F9*. In this film, we learn that Han did *not* die in Tokyo, actually, but rather, his 'death' was orchestrated by government agent Mr Nobody (Kurt Russell) as a means of getting him out of the spotlight to undertake a secret mission. As we write this, Han is alive and well on the precipice of *Fast X* and the exhaustingly complex, haphazard and unpredictable plot lines of *Fast & Furious* are common knowledge.

In addition to the #JusticeForHan social media campaign, Lin has said that when he returned to the franchise to direct *F9* after a six-year hiatus, he spoke to numerous audiences who were confused by Han's suspected death at the hands of Shaw. They were particularly upset at the fact that Universal made the decision without Lin's involvement or approval during his absence (Acuna 2021). For Lin, these vocal fans were directly to thank for Han's return to the films, suggesting that if the character's death 'was handled in a way that didn't result in outrage from the fans', then 'it would have been "appropriate" to leave Han dead' (Ibid). The return of Han – in both instances – was driven by this inclination to work with the requests and desires of the franchise's most vocal fans. While his is the most notorious, Han's character arc is not the only one to be shaped this way: Letty was similarly resurrected after her 'death' in *Fast Four*, thanks to fans who lobbied for the change on Diesel's Facebook page (Nobel 2019); and Diesel has claimed that *both* Johnson and Statham were brought into the franchise after he asked fans which actors they'd most like to see join the 'family' (Robinson 2016).

These latter examples again point towards Diesel's important role as broker between the *Fast* fandom and its creatives. While Diesel believes this is just how filmmaking works in the twenty-first century – 'I always say Clark Gable would have made a sequel to *Gone with the Wind* if he had a Facebook page' (Nobel 2019) – the truth is that this is quite specific to *Fast & Furious*. Though there may have been creative decisions made at Disney for, say, the direction of *The Rise of Skywalker* (2019) following a negative fan reaction to *The Last Jedi* (2017), few other franchises appear to have responded so directly and collaboratively to fan suggestions as *Fast & Furious*, or with such seismic consequences for their narrative coherence (see Santos and Wilkinson 2019). In this way, *Fast & Furious* cultivates a different kind of shared authorship which is generally perceived as collaborative – instead of combative – with its most invested fans. Like the seemingly slapdash nature of the franchise's development, these interactions with audiences and fans (and critics within them) are vital. They take Scott's (2012) considerations of the 'fanboy auteur' to the extreme, cementing the perception within its broad and heterogeneous fan base that *Fast & Furious* is more 'authentic' (less managed), organic and endearingly chaotic than other franchises.

This carves out a useful niche for *Fast & Furious* in the contemporary franchise era. While successful and hegemonic (enjoying near-total dominance over the marketplace), the explosion of branded franchise content in post-milennium Hollywood also has the potential to engender cynicism within the movie-going public – a so-called 'franchise fatigue' (Proctor 2019: 321). Being able to claim some kind of 'authenticity' in this space is a valuable, distinguishing asset. As Shawna Kidman (2021: 9) explores, a 'sense of integrity in the texts' is exactly what audiences seek out when IP expand through sequels and spinoffs and spread out across multiple media. This sense of integrity is something that *Fast & Furious* cultivates by positioning itself as a fan-driven and cultish property, one which plays by its own rules (just like Dom and his 'family' do in the films). For Kidman (2021: 10), other studios have tried to navigate this space through the development of 'corporate auteurism', where notions of authorship have elevated beyond individual directors and toward executives, producers and brands like the MCU itself. Universal, however, are doing the opposite, working to undercut the visible role of corporate structures through these marketing strategies which, instead, direct attention to the human messiness of the *Fast Saga* 'family'. To this end, Michael Moses, Universal's Co-President for Marketing, encourages the stars to share photos directly from the film sets which would normally be shrouded in secrecy. The aim here is to 'remove the studio filter as much as possible' because he views it to make for more 'authentic and organic interaction with fans' (Barnes 2013).

Framed in this fashion, 'family' becomes a focal point around which both producer and viewer energies appear to coalesce harmoniously. This returns us again to what's different about *Fast & Furious* in the current space. 'Organic' and 'authentic' are not necessarily words we would associate with the well-oiled and exhaustively-planned world of the contemporary franchise, where Disney's ten-year road maps and the MCU's meticulously prepared 'phases' are commonplace. Yet, through its consistent use of family within the films and extratextually, *Fast & Furious* has crafted such an identity, distinguishing itself in the crowded marketplace of contemporary franchises. Bringing a critical eye to this employment of 'family' by the authorial voices of *Fast & Furious* functions as a kind of code breaker. It provides a way into understanding the franchise and its idiosyncrasies in all their complexity, something that the contributors to this book explore.

## About this book

*Full-Throttle Franchise* is the first book to offer an in-depth analysis of *Fast & Furious*, bringing together a range of scholars to explore the key elements we have set up in this introductory chapter, in addition to many more. Despite its commercial success and wide cultural reach, surprisingly little has been written about *Fast & Furious* from an academic perspective. Mary Beltrán (2005, 2013) has produced the most significant body of work in this regard, publishing two insightful studies of the early films' racial politics – both of which form a key reference point for the chapters that follow. What other scholarship there is can be found in the form of short journal articles, such as Peter Turner's (2019) valuable analysis of the social media posts made by the franchise's actors, or book chapters that refer to *Fast & Furious* as part of broader studies of product placement (Schulze 2022), and the careers of particular stars (Mack 2019; Thomas 2019).[5] It is our hope that *Full-Throttle Franchise* will contribute to this small but important body of literature.

*Full-Throttle Franchise* contains twelve chapters, each of which examines core aspects of *Fast & Furious*, from the style of the films' action sequences and how they communicate on an ideological level, to the franchise's transmedia offshoots and its links to other prominent entertainment brands. The broader purpose of the book is to introduce readers to a range of perspectives on the franchise and its impact, with a particular focus on how *Fast & Furious* is both representative of wider cultural and industrial forces and curiously out of step with them, too. It was never going to be possible for one book to cover every element of the franchise's strange journey. However, in the chapters assembled here, we hope to have taken a first step towards opening up a wider critical dialogue about what makes *Fast & Furious* so unusual within the franchise era, as well as some of the key reasons behind its enduring popularity.

The first two chapters in the collection explore aesthetic issues (or 'Fast-thetics'), especially as they relate the franchise's trademark action sequences. Firstly, Lennart Soberon (Chapter 2) combines quantitative and qualitative methods to offer a longitudinal analysis of action sequences in the first nine *Fast & Furious* films, showing some of the key ways in which these sequences have evolved over the course of the franchise's twenty-year history. In Chapter 3, Naja Later explores the technique of temporal deferral in the films' street racing scenes. Drawing on Tom Gunning's 'cinema of attractions', Later extends their analysis to consider how – through the use of digital effects to render the deceased actor Paul Walker in *Furious 7* – the franchise expands and plays with conventional ideas of time, both aesthetically and narratively.

The next five chapters turn towards broad issues of representation and ideology, paying particular attention to the way in which the films intersect with dominant ideas of race, gender and sexuality. In Chapter 4, Pete Jones and Joshua Gulam explore the franchise's reputation as a model of blockbuster diversity, whereby the films have been praised for utilizing actors and directors from many different racial and ethnic groups. Here, Jones and Gulam develop a 'critical quantitative approach' to analysing race in popular Hollywood cinema, one which allows them to not only measure the *Fast Saga*'s level of diversity against that of other contemporary blockbusters, but to unpack the franchise's deeper racial politics as it appears in the texts. CarrieLynn D. Reinhard and Christopher J. Olson (Chapter 5) also look at race in their chapter on Vin Diesel as 'an intersectional auteur'. Focusing on his short film *Los Bandoleros* (2009), produced as a lead-in to *Fast Four*, they argue that Diesel offers up a new perspective on male action heroism through his performance as Dom, which combines traditional ideas of masculinity with a strong emphasis on familial bonding and cooperative action.

Building on Reinhard and Olson, the following three chapters take a deep dive into notions of gender within *Fast & Furious*, by both detailing and critiquing its hyper-masculine logic and themes. Aaron Hunter (Chapter 6) starts us off with a detailed discussion of the central bromance between Dom and Brian. Here, Hunter notes that, despite their close friendship, the pair very rarely touch or embrace; and he considers what this means in terms of the franchise's ambivalent ideas around male affection and sexuality. In Chapter 7, Bianca Batti focuses on the franchise's themes of family, considering how the films re-centre heteronormative familial frameworks through the paternalistic figure of Dom. As part of this discussion, Batti also offers a valuable insight into some of the franchise's key female characters, noting the way in which the potentially transgressive elements of Mia, Elena and Letty are undermined by their transition into various forms of motherhood. Rebecca Feasey (Chapter 8) rounds off this mini-section with a detailed examination of the hierarchy of masculinity that exists within the films. Here, Feasey considers the tensions generated by performing male heroism within the ensemble action film, focusing on the revelation that stars such as Diesel, Johnson and Statham have 'no loss' clauses in their contracts which prevent their characters from losing fights.

The remaining chapters move beyond the big screen to examine the franchise's extratextual dimensions and transmedia offshoots. In Chapter 9, Jackie Raphael and Celia Lam examine the way that the on-screen bromance between Brian and Dom is continued off screen in the promotional and publicity work of Diesel. Drawing on various frameworks from celebrity studies, they examine the way in which Diesel legitimates his bromance with Walker via social media and interviews, with a particular focus on how this process has continued after Walker's death. Fraser Elliott, in Chapter 10, looks at the franchise's success internationally, focusing on its box office performance within Mainland China. Framing his analysis in terms of the growing importance of the Chinese market for Hollywood more generally, Elliott notes how, from the fifth film onward, *Fast & Furious* has been specifically geared towards maximizing its profits in Mainland China.

This theme of industry and adaptation continues with the next two chapters. In Chapter 11, Sam Summers examines one of the films' transmedia offshoots – the DreamWorks Animation TV show, *Fast & Furious: Spy Racers*. Framing his analysis against a much longer history of film-to-TV animated adaptations, Summers considers the various ways in which *Spy Racers* adapts the films' core styles and themes 'in order to satisfy, and take advantage of, the unique conditions of television, animation, and children's media'. Finally, in Chapter 12, Robert Watts addresses the commonalities and convergences that the franchise shares with WWE, noting the multiple times in which WWE stars have crossed over into the world of *Fast & Furious*. Crucial here is Dwayne Johnson as Hobbs. Through close analysis of films such as *Hobbs & Shaw*, Watts argues that Johnson's performances in the franchise draw heavily on his earlier career as a professional wrestler, to the point where he directly reproduces 'signature wrestling moves and taunts' within the action sequences. Taken together, these twelve chapters will help to fill an important gap in scholarship on contemporary Hollywood cinema, whereby one of the biggest movie franchises of the last twenty years has been largely ignored.

# Notes

1   Throughout this book, box office is listed in US dollars, and, unless otherwise stated, all figures are sourced from Box Office Mojo (n.d.).
2   Prohibited from filming in central Tokyo, Lin and his team recreated Shibuya Crossing in a car park in Burbank, CA (Lin 2006).

3   The recent growth of the superhero movie can also be viewed as part of a larger trend where, from the late-1970s onwards, most of Hollywood's biggest hits have been sci-fi and/or fantasy pictures with a 'special emphasis on … global threats and devastation' (Krämer 2022: 571).
4   Stunt coordinators and drivers such as Terry Leonard and Rhys Millen were pivotal to the action sequences in *Tokyo Drift*, for instance, helping to realize the trademark drifting sequences through both their driving expertise and their development of specialist camera rigs (Lin 2006).
5   At the time of writing, though, several other pieces of work are in progress that take *Fast & Furious* as a point of focus, including book chapters on the representation of the US-Mexico border in *Fast Four* (Llamas-Rodriguez, forthcoming) and a journal special issue on the *Fast Saga* (Boyd, forthcoming).

# References

Acuna, K. (2019), 'How Vin Diesel Helped Save the *Fast and Furious* Franchise from Going Straight to Video', *Insider*, 2 August. Available online: https://www.insider.com/fast-and-furious-almost-went-straight-to-video-2017-4 (accessed 9 May 2022).

Acuna, K. (2021), '*F9* Director Justin Lin Says Han "Probably" Would've Stayed Dead if a Scene at the End of the Last Film Didn't Cause Fan Outrage', *Insider*, 22 September. Available online: https://news.yahoo.com/fast-9-director-justin-lin-020914357.html (accessed 9 May 2022).

Ansen, D. (2002), 'Fest Bets', *Newsweek*, 16 January. Available online: https://www.newsweek.com/fest-bets-143751 (accessed 21 March 2022).

Balio, T. (1996), 'Adjusting to the New Global Economy: Hollywood in the 1990s', in A. Moran (ed), *Film Policy: International, National, and Regional*, 23–38, London: Routledge.

Barnes, B. (2013), '*Fast & Furious* Stresses the Social Side of Fandom', *The New York Times*, 17 February. Available online: https://www.nytimes.com/2013/02/18/business/fast-furious-6-focuses-on-its-online-following-for-promotion.html?smid=fb-share&_r=1& (accessed 10 May 2022).

*Be Cool* (2005), [Film] Dir. F. Gary Gray, USA: MGM Distribution Company.

Beltrán, M. C. (2005), 'The New Hollywood Racelessness: Only the Fast, Furious, (and multiracial) Will Survive', *Cinema Journal*, 44 (2): 50–67.

Beltrán, M. (2013), 'Fast and Bilingual: "Fast & Furious" and the Latinization of Racelessness', *Cinema Journal*, 53 (1): 75–96.

*Better Luck Tomorrow* (2002), [Film] Dir. Justin Lin, USA: MTV Films.

*Black Widow* (2021), [Film] Dir. Cate Shortland, USA: Walt Disney Studios.

Box Office Mojo (n.d.), 'Franchise: *The Fast and the Furious*'. Available online: https://www.boxofficemojo.com/franchise/fr3628568325/ (accessed 14 May 2022).

Boyd, M. (forthcoming), 'Special Issue: The Art of Drag (Racing) – Reading *The Fast and the Furious*', *Contemporaries Post45*.

Campbell, K. (2021), '*F9*: How the *Fast & Furious* Films Define the 21st Century', *BBC Culture*, 25 June. Available online: https://www.bbc.com/culture/article/20210624-f9-and-how-the-fast-furious-films-define-the-21st-century (accessed 22 March 2022).

*Crank* (2006), [Film] Dir. Mark Neveldine and Brian Taylor, USA: Lakeshore Entertainment.

Diesel, V. (2022), [Instagram] 'Good morning planet …', 21 March. Available online: https://www.instagram.com/p/CbXyR5hFKtZ/ (accessed 10 May 2022).

Dumaraog, A. (2021), 'Justice for Han Highlights the *Fast Saga*'s Hypocrisy', *Screen Rant*, 3 July. Available online: https://screenrant.com/f9-justice-han-fast-furious-dom-jesse-johnny-problem/ (accessed 9 May 2022).

Eichler, A. (2011), 'Critics Give You Permission to Enjoy *Fast Five*', *The Atlantic*, 29 April. Available online: https://www.theatlantic.com/culture/archive/2011/04/critics-give-you-permission-enjoy-fast-five/350174/ (accessed 9 May 2022).

Erlich, D. (2017), 'All 8 *Fast and Furious* Movies, Ranked from Worst to Best', *IndieWire*, 10 April. Available online: https://www.indiewire.com/2017/04/the-fast-and-furious-movies-ranked-worst-to-best-fate-of-the-furious-vin-diesel-1201803720/ (accessed 10 May 2022).

*The Expendables* (2010), [Film] Dir. Sylvester Stallone, USA: Lionsgate.

*Fast & Furious: Crossroads* (2020), PlayStation4 [Game], Tokyo: Bandai Namco Entertainment.

The Fast Saga (2020), [Facebook] 'To Our Family of *Fast* Fans Everywhere', 12 March. Available online: https://www.facebook.com/TheFastSaga/posts/10157556744242631 (accessed 9 May 2022).

Finke, N. (2011a), '*Fast Five* Will Transition Franchise from Street Racing to Future Full of Heist Action', *Deadline*, 25 April. Available online: https://deadline.com/2011/04/fast-five-will-transition-franchise-from-street-racing-to-heist-action-125552/ (accessed 10 May 2022).

Finke, N. (2011b), 'Mighty *Thor* Hammers $242M Global Cume; *Fast Five* $324M; *Jumping Broom* $13.7M; *Something Borrowed* $13.1M', *Deadline*, 8 May. Available online: https://deadline.com/2011/05/thor-divines-3-25-million-in-midnight-b-o-129162/ (accessed 9 May 2022).

Flanagan, M., A. Livingstone and M. McKenny (2016), *The Marvel Studios Phenomenon: Inside a Transmedia Universe*, New York: Bloomsbury.

Fleury, J., B. H. Hartzheim and S. Mamber (2019), *The Franchise Era: Managing Media in the Digital Economy*, Edinburgh: Edinburgh University Press.

Frater, P. (2017), '*Fate of the Furious* Speeds to Record-breaking $65 million Opening Day in China', *Variety*, 14 April. Available online: https://variety.com/2017/film/news/fate-of-the-furious-china-openieg-records-1202030781/ (accessed 9 May 2022).

Fritz, B. (2018), *The Big Picture: The Fight for the Future of Movies*, New York: Houghton Mifflin Harcourt.

*G.I. Joe: Retaliation* (2013), [Film] Dir. Jon Chu, USA: Paramount Pictures.

Gilbey, R. (2018), 'Fast & Furious Live Review – A Stinker in Both Senses', *The Guardian*, 19 January. Available online: https://www.theguardian.com/film/2018/jan/19/not-fast-and-curious-car-chase-movie-just-doesnt-work-on-stage (accessed 9 May 2022).

Gregory, J. (2019), '"Worst Ride Ever": Universal's *Fast & Furious* Seen as Major Misstep a Year Later', *Theme Park Tribune*, 13 May. Available online: https://www.themeparktribune.com/worst-ride-ever-universals-fast-furious-seen-as-major-misstep-a-year-later/ (accessed 9 May 2022).

Grierson, T. (2021), '*F9*: Review', *Screen Daily*, 18 May. Available online: https://www.screendaily.com/reviews/f9-review/5159709.article (accessed 10 May 2022).

Hassenger, J. (2015), 'We Ride the *Fast and Furious* Series from B-Movie Start to A-List Finish', *AV Club*, 23 April. Available online: https://www.avclub.com/we-ride-the-fast-and-furious-series-from-b-movie-start-1798278878 (accessed 3 May 2022).

Hedash, K. (2020), 'Why *Fast & Furious* Franchise Is Now Called the *Fast Saga*', *Screen Rant*, 28 January. Available online: https://screenrant.com/fast-furious-saga-movies-franchise-name-meaning-change-explained/ (accessed 25 June 2021).

Heritage, S. (2016), '*Fast & Furious 8* Trailer Review: A Reassuring, Obscene Platter of Murder', *The Guardian*, 12 December. Available online: https://www.theguardian.com/film/2016/dec/12/fast-furious-8-trailer-review (accessed 2 March 2022).

*Iron Man* (2008), [Film] Dir. Jon Favreau, USA: Marvel Studios.

Ivan, T. (2022), '*Fast & Furious Crossroads* Is Being Pulled from Sale Less Than 2 Years After Its Release', *VGC*, 29 March. Available online: https://www.videogameschronicle.com/news/fast-furious-crossroads-is-being-pulled-from-sale-less-than-2-years-after-its-release/ (accessed 10 May 2022).

Jenkins, H. (2006), *Convergence Culture: Where Old and New Media Collide*, New York: NYU Press.

Johnson, D. (2012), 'Cinematic Destiny: Marvel Studios and the Trade Stories of Industrial Convergence', *Cinema Journal*, 52 (1): 1–24.

*Journey 2: The Mysterious Island* (2012), [Film] Dir. Brad Peyton, USA: Warner Bros. Pictures.

Kaufman, A. (2015), 'How Paul Walker Nearly Quit the *Furious* Franchise', *LA Times*, 6 April. Available online: https://www.latimes.com/entertainment/movies/moviesnow/la-et-mn-paul-walker-furious-death-20150406-story.html (accessed 10 May 2022).

Kidman, S. (2021), 'The Disneyfication of Authorship: Above-the-Line Creative Labour in the Franchise Era', *Journal of Film and Video*, 73 (3): 3–22.

Koehler, R. (2011), '*Fast Five*', *Variety*, 21 April. Available online: https://web.archive.org/web/20110426022937/http://www.variety.com/review/VE1117945052?refcatid=31 (accessed 9 May 2022).

Koushik, K. and J. M. Proffitt (2019), 'Global Capital, Global Labour, and Global Dominance: The Case of *xXx: Return of Xander Cage*', *International Journal of Media & Cultural Politics*, 15 (1): 27–47.

Krämer, P. (2022), 'The Walt Disney Company, Family Entertainment, and Hollywood's Global Hits', in N. Brown (ed), *The Oxford Handbook of Children's Film*, 569–90, Oxford: Oxford University Press.

*The Last Jedi* (2017), [Film] Dir. Rian Johnson, USA: Walt Disney Studios.

Lawrence, D. (2019), 'From Stolen DVD Players to Black Superman, *Fast & Furious* Writer Shares Secrets of the Franchise', *Entertainment Weekly*, 1 August. Available online: https://ew.com/movies/2019/08/01/chris-morgan-fast-furious-look-back-hobbs-shaw/ (accessed 9 May 2022).

Lawrence, D. (2021a), '"F—, Let's Go do it": An Oral History of *The Fast and the Furious*', *Entertainment Weekly*, 3 May. Available online: https://ew.com/movies/the-fast-and-the-furious-oral-history/ (accessed 9 May 2022).

Lawrence, D. (2021b), '2 Brothers 2 Furious: How Vin Diesel and John Cena are Redefining Fast Family in *F9*', *Entertainment Weekly*, 15 June. Available online: https://ew.com/movies/f9-vin-diesel-john-cena-digital-cover/ (accessed 9 May 2022).

Li, K. (2015), 'From The VIBE Vault: "Racer X" (The "Fast & Furious" Inspiration)', *Vibe*, 26 March. Available online: https://www.vibe.com/features/editorial/racer-x-rafael-estevez-kenneth-li-fast-and-furious-inspiration-may-1998-336369/ (accessed 22 May 2022).

Lin, J. (2006), [DVD] 'Feature Commentary with Director Justin Lin', *The Fast and the Furious: Tokyo Drift*, USA: Universal Pictures, Region 2.

Lin, J. (2009), [DVD] 'Feature Commentary with Director Justin Lin', *Fast & Furious*, USA: Universal Pictures, Region 2.

Llamas-Rodriguez, J. (forthcoming), *Border Tunnels: Media and the Infrastructures of the U.S.-Mexico Divide*, Minneapolis: University of Minnesota Press.

Lomax, T. (2019), 'The franchise era: Blockbuster Hollywood in the 2010s… and beyond', *Senses of Cinema*, (92). Available online: https://www.sensesofcinema.com/2019/cinema-in-the-2010s/the-franchise-era-blockbuster-hollywood-in-the-2010sand-beyond/.

Mack, J. (2019), '"It's that Peasant Mentality": The Cult Persona of Jason Statham, Hollywood Outsider', in S. Gerrard and R. Shail (eds), *Crank It Up. Jason Statham: Star!*, 56–70, Manchester: Manchester University Press.

Malkin, M. (2021), 'F9 Stars Vin Diesel, Charlize Theron React to Record-breaking Box Office Debut: "Cinema Is Back!"', *Variety*, 27 June. Available online: https://variety.com/2021/film/news/f9-vin-diesel-charlize-theron-donna-langley-universal-1235006174/ (accessible 29 April 2022).

Maltby, R. (2003), *Hollywood Cinema*, Oxford: Blackwell.

McClintock, P. (2013), 'Box Office Report: *Fast 6* No. 1 with $300 Million Globally; *Hangover III* Sputters', *Hollywood Reporter*, 27 May. Available online: https://www.hollywoodreporter.com/movies/movie-news/box-office-report-fast-6-558856/ (accessed 29 June 2021).

McClintock, P. (2021), 'Box Office: How *F9* Sped to Record $70M U.S. Opening', *Hollywood Reporter*, 28 June. Available online: https://www.hollywoodreporter.com/movies/movie-news/f9-huge-opening-box-office-1234974643/ (accessed 29 June 2021).

Mendelson, S. (2015a), 'How *Fast and The Furious* Won by Losing', *Forbes*, 17 March. Available online: https://www.forbes.com/sites/scottmendelson/2015/03/17/the-fast-and-furious-series-had-to-lose-before-it-could-win/?sh=29f9e2bd4280 (accessed 29 June 2021).

Mendelson, S. (2015b), 'The Rock Isn't Just Franchise Viagra, He Is Red Bull for Cinematic Universes', *Forbes*, 2 June. Available online: https://www.forbes.com/sites/scottmendelson/2015/06/02/the-rock-isnt-just-franchise-viagra-he-is-red-bull-for-cinematic-universes/?sh=3495a0311b31 (accessed 29 June 2021).

Mendelson, S. (2021), '*F9* Races Past Two Huge Box Office Milestones', *Forbes*, 20 July. Available online: https://www.forbes.com/sites/scottmendelson/2021/07/20/f9-races-past-two-huge-box-office-milestones/?sh=6e7def1813b3 (accessed 21 July 2021).

Newman, K. (2008), '*Fast & Furious* Review', *Empire*, 8 September. Available online: https://www.empireonline.com/movies/reviews/fast-furious-2-review/ (accessed 29 June 2021).

Nobel, A. (2019), 'How Vin Diesel's Facebook Fans Brought Letty Back from the Dead', *Heavy*, 5 March. Available online: https://heavy.com/entertainment/2013/02/fast-furious-letty-back-vin-diesel-facebook/ (accessed 21 September 2021).

*The Other Guys* (2010), [Film] Dir. Adam McKay, USA: Columbia Pictures.

Proctor, W. (2019), 'A New Hate? The War for Disney's *Star Wars*', in W. Proctor and R. McCulloch (eds), *Disney's Star Wars: Forces of Production, Promotion, and Reception*, 301–22, Iowa, IA: Iowa University Press.

Purse, L. (2011), *Contemporary Action Cinema*, Edinburgh: Edinburgh University Press.

*Riddick* (2013), [Film] Dir. David Twohy, USA: Universal Pictures.

*The Rise of Skywalker* (2019), [Film] Dir. J. J. Abrams, USA: Walt Disney Studios.

Robinson, J. (2016), 'The Three Huge Fan Suggestions That Forever Changed the *Fast and Furious* Franchise', *Vanity Fair*, 23 August. Available online: https://www.vanityfair.com/hollywood/2016/08/fast-furious-tommy-lee-jones-the-rock (accessed 29 June 2021).

Ryan, M. (2017), '*The Fast and The Furious: Tokyo Drift* Was Originally Written to Star Vin Diesel', *Uproxx*, 11 April. Available online: https://uproxx.com/movies/the-fast-and-the-furious-tokyo-drift/ (accessed 23 December 2021).

Saito, S. (2014), 'Justin Lin on *Tokyo Drift* and the Four Hours That Saved the *Fast & Furious* Franchise', *The Moveable Feast*, 6 July. Available online: https://moveablefest.com/justin-lin-tokyo-drift/ (accessed 24 February 2021).

Santos, A. A. and A. Wilkinson (2019), '*Star Wars: The Rise of Skywalker* Was Designed to be the Opposite of *The Last Jedi*', *Vox*, 27 December. Available online: https://www.vox.com/culture/2019/12/27/21034725/star-wars-the-rise-of-skywalker-last-jedi-j-j-abrams-rian-johnson (accessed 6 January 2022).

Schulze, J. (2022), '"I'm More of a Corona Man, Myself": The Narrative and Semiotic Function of a Corona in the *Fast and Furious* Franchise', in S. Lefait and S. Villers (eds), *The Faces and Stakes of Brand Insertion*, 143–57, Wilmington, DE: Vernon Press.

*The Scorpion King* (2002), [Film] Dir. Chuck Russell, USA: WWF Entertainment.

Scott, S. (2012), 'Who's Steering the Mothership? The Role of the Fanboy Auteur in Transmedia Storytelling', in A. Delwiche and J. J. Henderson (eds), *The Participatory Cultures Handbook*, 43–52, London: Routledge.

Song, X. (2018), 'Hollywood Movies and China: Analysis of Hollywood Globalization and Relationship Management in China's Cinema Market', *Global Media and China*, 3 (3): 177–94.

Stewart, A. (2011), '*Fast Five* Drives to No. 1 Overseas', *Variety*, 14 May. Available online: https://variety.com/2011/film/box-office/fast-five-drives-to-no-1-overseas-1118037011/ (accessed 21 February 2021).

Suderman, P. (2017), 'Hollywood's New Blockbuster Model, as Explained by *Fast & Furious* Action Scenes', *Vox*, 12 April. Available online: https://www.vox.com/culture/2017/4/12/15211086/fast-and-furious-action-scenes (accessed 14 May 2022).

Thomas, S. (2019), 'A Balancing Act(or): Jason Statham and the Ensemble Film', in S. Gerrard and R. Shail (eds), *Crank It Up. Jason Statham: Star!*, 71–85, Manchester: Manchester University Press.

Thurm, E. (2015), 'How *Fast & Furious* Took Over the World', *Rolling Stone*, 6 April. Available online: https://www.rollingstone.com/movies/movie-news/how-fast-furious-took-over-the-world-236649/ (accessed 12 September 2021).

Tobias, S. (2006), '*The Fast And The Furious: Tokyo Drift*', *AV Club*, 15 June. Available online: https://www.avclub.com/the-fast-and-the-furious-tokyo-drift-1798201826 (accessed 25 March 2022).

Trumpbour, J. (2008), 'Hollywood and the World: Export or Die', in P. McDonald and J. Wasko (eds), *The Contemporary Hollywood Film Industry*, 209–19, Oxford: Blackwell.

Tryon, C. (2009), *Reinventing Cinema: Movies in the Age of Media Convergence*, New Brunswick: Rutgers University Press.

Turner, P. (2019), 'Fast Marketing, Furious Interactions: An Interstellar Community on Instagram', *Celebrity Studies*, 10 (4): 469–78.

Willmore, A. (2015), 'Han Seoul-Oh Is the Greatest *Fast and Furious* Character', *Buzzfeed*, 8 April. Available online: https://www.buzzfeed.com/alisonwillmore/why-han-seoul-oh-is-the-greatest-fast-and-furious-character (accessed 29 April 2022).

Wright, J. L. (2019), 'Animation and the Star Body', *Film-Philosophy*, 23 (2): 194–211.

2

# From Mission Impossible to Mission Insanity: A longitudinal analysis of action sequences in the *Fast & Furious* franchise

Lennart Soberon

'Ask any racer. Any real racer. It don't matter if you win by an inch or a mile. Winning's winning', states street racer Dom Torretto (Vin Diesel) in *The Fast and the Furious* (2001). Within the merciless world of street racing, it's all about staying ahead of the competition. It takes skill, quick thinking and originality to keep up in the race. Big-budget action filmmaking is similar in many ways: with so many different properties competing in a cutthroat marketplace, just one wrong turn or unsuccessful instalment can cause a franchise to stall. Like its high-octane heroes, *Fast & Furious* has proved to be a 'winner'. With ten films to date and over $6 billion in worldwide ticket sales (Box Office Mojo 2021), *Fast & Furious* ranks as one of contemporary Hollywood's most successful and enduring movie franchises. This chapter will investigate the way in which *Fast & Furious* has maintained its success for a period of more than twenty years. How did it manage to stay ahead of the curve at a time when a vast number of Hollywood franchises were competing to provide audiences with ever more spectacular thrills? There's no singular answer to this question; however, I approach it by focusing on one of the action genre's most essential components: the action sequences themselves.

The display of spectacular action is the *raison d'etre* of the action film. Writing at the turn of the millennium, Geoff King (2000) noted that action sequences are both the driving force of the genre and a way for individual action films to distinguish themselves from their competitors. In the years since, the action blockbuster film has arguably become Hollywood's standard unit of output (Kendrick 2019). Fully conscious that action is how they differentiate themselves in an already saturated market, action filmmakers have started to choreograph ever more ambitious and complex set pieces to provide audiences with something they've not yet seen before. Due to its longevity, *Fast & Furious* offers an excellent case study for examining the changing nature of the action sequence in millennial Hollywood cinema. The following study conducts a longitudinal analysis of action sequences in the first nine *Fast & Furious* films, one which not only measures how the formal and narrative properties of these sequences have developed over time, but also seeks to understand any such developments in terms of broader genre shifts within the franchise. In his review of *The Fast and the Furious*, Roger Ebert (2003) pointed to its 'pirate spirit', whereby the film 'wants to raid its betters and carry off the loot'. Ebert's words ring true for the franchise as a whole: as explored in the introduction to this book, subsequent *Fast & Furious* films have sought to revitalize the franchise's initial street racing formula by incorporating elements of other genres, such as the heist film and spy thriller. These genre shifts offer convenient benchmarks from which this analysis can depart. By departing from the role of genre in the franchise, we can track how the introduction of heist film and spy thriller elements has affected the structure and function of action sequences within and across each of the *Fast & Furious* films.

In contrast to studies that look at the aesthetics of race and chase action scenes, the focus of this analysis is on the narrative dimensions of such action sequences (cf. Barker 2009; Musser 1994). Indeed, I employ a multangular approach that investigates both the importance of action to the overall narrative and how individual action sequences function as micro-narratives. This is done through a combination of qualitative and quantitative types of textual analysis. Firstly, the chapter records and presents data on the duration, sum, type and other properties of the action sequences within the first nine *Fast & Furious* films. This metric data is then combined with a more in-depth close reading of how the franchise's action sequences have changed function throughout the years. Although quantitative approaches are still a rare breed in the field of film studies, the form of the action film makes it especially suited to a metric-oriented approach. After all, the action sequence is easily recognizable on an aesthetic level, meaning it can be demarcated from other narrative units in a film (Purse 2011). As the chapter demonstrates, the combination of quantitative and qualitative methods is particularly useful for exploring questions of film form and narrative. In this case, analysing both the hard numbers and the intricate working of action sequences in relation to narrative, provides a better understanding of what lies under the hood of one of contemporary Hollywood's most lucrative franchises.

## The *Fast* and the functional: How does action work?

This chapter builds on my previous research on contemporary Hollywood action cinema (Soberon 2021). In this comparative analysis between action sequences of the 1980s and the 2010s, I elaborated on how the contemporary action sequence is defined by a relatively high degree of narrative complexity. In contrast to action cinema's formative years, where action sequences were traditionally limited to one type of action-related event (fistfights, shootouts, chases and so on), millennial action sequences string together a series of action events to form complex narratives of their own. Using narrative techniques of plotting to intensify the amount of suspense and spectacle, the contemporary action sequence features several narrative strands which run through the action and are interwoven via parallel editing. These principles help to highlight the fact that filmmakers do not just present action; instead, they carefully craft multiple spectacular events for the viewer into a tightly wound package. The average action film in post-millennium Hollywood contains five specific action sequences that attempt to dose the viewer with just the right amount of excitement to keep them engaged without the spectacle becoming tiring to watch. In this chapter, I will further elaborate on this premise using *Fast & Furious* both in comparison and contrast to current standards of action sequence organization and plotting. More specifically, three strategies will be identified of how filmmakers heighten the amount of action while keeping their audiences narratively engaged: acceleration, intensification and diversification.

While action sequences are often considered as moments of excess spectacle that are systematically detached from, or even antithetical to, narrative development, authors such as David Bordwell (2006) argue that the relationship between spectacle and narrative is much more symbiotic than often assumed (cf. Dixon 1998; Gurevitch 2009; Stauven 2006). Action sequences are capable of moving the plot forward, providing character exposition, or even developing a film's themes. Moreover, as Anderson (1998) argues, action sequences not only help to advance the larger narrative of the film, they are also small stories in their own right. Every action sequence has a clear beginning, middle and end, and is neatly bookended to create a further degree of narrative coherence. As explored in my earlier research (Soberon 2021), the micro-narrative of the action sequence often consists of action events that are organized through principles of cause and effect. As such, these action events simultaneously provide building blocks that narrativize the spectacle that action films seek to deliver.

Approaching action sequences as isolated yet interconnected micro-narratives helps us to better understand how and why they function in relation to a film's wider narrative and the action sequences that are a part of it. In essence, all action films operate around the idea of taking action, setting up a structure in which obstacles are introduced and conquered. Indeed, Purse (2011) considers the action film in general as being about the thrill of mastery: heroes are by genre-ordained rule required to venture into chaotic situations and struggle through action sequences in order to master a situation and ultimately regain control. However, since action films – and, by extension, action sequences – endeavour to provide maximum excitement, the narrative will provide new and increasingly difficult challenges for its heroes to face. One way these films are capable of stringing together action events within one action sequence is by introducing complicating scenarios within the action. This is what Bordwell (2006: 37) refers to when discussing 'complicating actions'. Complicating scenarios are plot turns that alter the status quo of the narrative, introducing a problem which the protagonist then needs to resolve. Action films can be said to rely on these complicating scenarios to create new problems and challenges that need to be overcome, thereby supplying the film with an increasingly more spectacular stream of action until the narrative comes to a close.

This desire to offer consistent and continuous action, whilst simultaneously heightening the stakes in terms of spectacle, lies at the heart of my analysis. Action sequences are especially vulnerable to signs of inflation. In order to keep the viewer engaged, filmmakers have to consistently top the sequence that came before. In order to do so, filmmakers either invest in the acceleration, diversification or intensification of action. In the context of acceleration, filmmakers simply provide more action in a film's given running time. Diversification involves featuring different types of action events that are mixed and matched throughout one or several action sequences. Intensification, on the other hand, is a figurative shifting of gears of the action sequence in which sequences attempt to provide increasingly intense viewer experiences. These three principles take both intra-textual (the competition between different action sequences) and inter-textual (between different action films) form, and they meet in the action sequence's need to make its action distinctive from whatever spectacular feats might have preceded it.

Acceleration, intensification and diversification are essential concepts for considering how the action sequences of *Fast & Furious* have developed and transformed over time. If action films are caught up in their own mechanics of seemingly ever-increasing intensity, how does this phenomenon manifest in a franchise with ten instalments spread over twenty years? In the remaining sections, I set about trying to answer these questions by providing both quantitative and qualitative analysis of the franchise's many action sequences.

## Methodology

Since the interrelation between action and narrative is far from one-sided, the development of action sequences needs to be studied in a multangular manner that fully accommodates their complexity. Therefore, I approach action in two different dimensions: action in narrative (the amount and type of action spread over the narrative) and narrative in action (the narrative qualities of action scenes themselves). To undertake this analysis, the first nine *Fast & Furious* films underwent quantitative analysis that coded the number of action sequences (Table 2.1), as well as the duration of these sequences and the contents of their action events (Table 2.3). Framing these data against the findings of my earlier 2021 study, I was able to explore action in *Fast & Furious* by closely observing how the action escalates over time. Additionally, all nine films were subjected to a close reading that studied the way in which these action sequences both operate as distinct narrative units and stand in relation to one another. This allows me to better understand how these action sequences intensify in narrative complexity, as well as how they diversify in terms of the types of action events depicted.

Firstly, as its name already hints, action sequences can primarily be understood as sequences of action-packed events, such as explosions, acrobatics and fistfights. It's important to note that the introduction of action can come in all kinds of shapes and sizes. Bordwell (2006: 211) makes a distinction between short action beats (or 'whammos') and longer lasting series of action events that together form an *action sequence*. An action beat generally lasts under three minutes and has little influence on the wider narrative of the film, while action sequences have no apparent limit in time and offer a concentration of action events that alter the shape of the narrative. Action beats and action sequences are also different in the amount of action events they can feature. While the first is usually centred on one type of spectacular action (either a chase or a shootout), the second functions by stringing together several of these events into a diverse composition of destructive action. A single explosion therefore does not constitute an action sequence. Secondly, action sequences can be identified by a set of formal characteristics that are activated once the action sequence commences and stop when the action sequence is finished. A quicker editing pace, bombastic movement, more dramatic camera angles and other formal properties help to constitute an 'impact aesthetic' that is meant to accentuate dynamic movement and spectacular awe (King 2000: 95). This shifting of registers is further emphasized by some sort of auditory kick-off such as a moment of silence interrupted by an explosion, a gunshot or an alarm siren. *Fast & Furious,* for example, has its own distinct kick-offs in the form of a set of starting flags or a foot hitting the pedal within the context of race sequences. Alongside its contents, the formal characteristics of action sequences make it possible to conveniently capture and measure action sequences.

## Action in narrative

Starting from the numbers, it becomes apparent that *Fast & Furious* does have some notable differences with the standards set for contemporary Hollywood action cinema. The average millennial action film consists out of 20:26 minutes of action of its average 108 minutes runtime (Soberon 2021). This means that roughly 19 per cent of the contemporary action film consists of action. As stated above, this action is spread over five action sequences, making the average runtime of an action sequence close to four minutes. In comparison with this sample, *Fast & Furious* is considerably more action-packed (Table 2.1). With 35:32 minutes action time of its 122 minutes running time, *Fast & Furious* films consist averagely of 10 per cent more action (29 per cent) than is typical for contemporary Hollywood action cinema. Interestingly enough, *Fast & Furious* does contain, on average, only five action sequences, relying on both longer action runtimes and a higher number of action beats.

In terms of action placement and timing, *Fast & Furious* also distinguishes itself. The average Hollywood action film uses two sequences for the first act, two for the second act and one final (longer) one to close the movie (Soberon 2021). In contrast, *Fast & Furious* films tend to operate on a 1-3-1 or 1-2-2 model, exchanging one of the action sequences typically found in the first act for either three in the middle or two in the final act. Aside from the opening action vignettes, which have become a trademark of the films, it takes a relatively long time for *Fast & Furious* to (re)introduce action to the plot. It's ironic that while having the reputation of being one of contemporary Hollywood's

Table 2.1 Action sequences and run time.

| Title | Year | Runtime | Action sequences | Beats | Action time | Percentage |
|---|---|---|---|---|---|---|
| The Fast and the Furious | 2001 | 107 min | 3 | 5 | 26 min 10 sec | 24% |
| 2 Fast 2 Furious | 2003 | 108 min | 4 | 2 | 32 min 10 sec | 30% |
| Tokyo Drift | 2006 | 104 min | 4 | 2 | 21 min 28 sec | 21% |
| Fast & Furious 4 | 2009 | 107 min | 5 | 1 | 28 min 56 sec | 27% |
| Fast Five | 2011 | 132 min | 4 | 2 | 30 min 06 sec | 23% |
| Fast & Furious 6 | 2013 | 131 min | 5 | 3 | 38 min 42 sec | 30% |
| Furious 7 | 2015 | 137 min | 5 | 2 | 54 min 50 sec | 40% |
| The Fate | 2017 | 136 min | 5 | 0 | 51 min 42 sec | 38% |
| Hobbs & Shaw | 2019 | 137 min | 5 | 2 | 37 min 42 sec | 27% |
| **Average** | | 122 min | 4 | 2 | 35 min 32 sec | 29% |

busiest and loudest action franchises, *Fast & Furious* actually takes its time to get into the action. One possible explanation for this is that with its thematic focus on family bonds, the franchise has a keen interest in foregrounding the interpersonal dynamics between the various characters that comprise the core ensemble. The relationship between Dom and Letty, for example, goes through major changes over the course of the franchise, and the filmmakers spend relatively large amounts of screen time detailing its development. With time, *Fast & Furious* became so comfortable with its commitment to character engagement that it began to postpone the (re)introduction of action sequences even more, introducing them unusually late for films in the action genre. In *Fast & Furious 6* (2013), the first action sequence doesn't appear until the twenty-two-minute mark. What we are offered prior to this is all narrative set-up and character development as Dom has to deal with the re-emergence of Letty, who he believed to be dead.

This is all because the film prioritizes the viewer's emotional investment with the story and characters over immediate action thrills. The decision to let the viewer catch up with the various characters and to introduce them to a relatively large degree of exposition in regard to other action films is a classic *Fast & Furious* trait, which can be tied to what Mary Beltrán (2013) understands as the franchise's thematic focus on familial bonds. In contrast to other, more individual-oriented action franchises such as *James Bond* or *John Wick*, *Fast & Furious* opts to utilize its opening sequences to draw the viewer back into the interpersonal relationships and dynamics of the films. Naturally, that doesn't mean these opening acts are devoid of action altogether. *Fast & Furious* simply displaces its first-act action sequences to action beats that function as a type of teaser for the amazing feats to come.

When comparing the individual films, it becomes apparent that the amount of action is relatively unstable across the franchise. *The Fast and the Furious: Tokyo Drift* (2006), the third film in the franchise and its low point in terms of action, is almost doubled in action runtime by the action high point, *Furious 7* (2015). One might assume that the discrepancy between *Tokyo Drift* and *Furious 7* stems largely from their respective positions in the franchise, as per the widely held idea that *Fast & Furious* has become bigger and more spectacular over time. However, instead of exponentially increasing with each new instalment, action time in *Fast & Furious* tends to swing back and forth in a pendulum-like manner. Indeed, while *2 Fast 2 Furious* (2003) did respond to the success of its predecessor with an increase in action, this amount of action is not surpassed for the next four instalments. This is because, as Bordwell (2006) states, filmmakers carefully dose their action sequences, so the viewer doesn't get too overwhelmed or bored by them. Genre is another particularly important variable in this respect. The first and second films in the franchise are composed primarily as crime thrillers, with each narrative centring on the protagonist's infiltration of a criminal gang. Although a suitable arena for many action events in their own right, the conventions of the crime thriller placed certain limitations on the type of action sequences the filmmakers could feature. Because *2 Fast 2 Furious* simply offers more of the same, the concept of what a *Fast & Furious* film could be in terms of action sequences seemed to have already reached its peak potential.

However, once *Fast & Furious* started tinkering with its genre DNA, the action and how this is divided throughout the narrative began to change. *Toyo Drift*, for example, signals the first departure from the crime thriller mould that characterized the first two films. Besides featuring a different lead character and a different location (Japan), the film stands out from other *Fast & Furious* instalments because of its genre properties. While retaining a broad focus on organized crime, the film fits much more in line with the generic structure of a sports film, where the hero's narrative of becoming is often given more importance than the action itself (Babington 2014). It also introduces a new type of racing spectacle to the franchise – the act of oversteering through a corner, referred to as 'drifting'. In *Tokyo Drift*, then, drift racing serves as a type of gimmick, a novel addition that supports and provides a frame for the film's action sequences. Nearly all the action sequences and beats here fall into three categories: introductions to drifting, training sequences where the protagonist learns how to drift, and tournaments/races where drifting is required. Apart from racing and chasing, close to no other action events are featured in the film (see Table 2.2). Such discrepancies with the rest of the franchise are not surprising since *Tokyo Drift* is something between a spinoff and a sequel to *2 Fast 2 Furious*. As such, the film occupies a curious space in the franchise's history: at this point, the filmmakers were still experimenting with the direction in which to take the franchise, before they eventually offered a reboot in the shape of *Fast & Furious* (2009; hereinafter *Fast Four*) and its pivot towards action in the international crime thriller mould. Moreover, because new characters are introduced in *Tokyo Drift* and their motivations need to be established, these alternate timelines tend to invest more intensely in character exposition. This phenomenon seems to repeat with the franchise's other spinoff, *Hobbs & Shaw*, which equally signifies a drop of action time in favour of character exposition and interaction.

**Table 2.2** Evolution in percentage of action.

Further evidence of the importance of genre to action identity can be found in the direction the franchise took after *Fast Four*. With the franchise's fourth instalment, there's a much stronger emphasis on the world of organized crime, meaning that some of the previous focus on street racing culture is lost or marginalized. This trend was continued with Justin Lin's *Fast Five* (2011) and *Fast & Furious 6*, both of which tinkered with the formula to incorporate elements of the heist film. From *Fast Five* on, street racing features much less prominently in the franchise, only appearing in brief, isolated sequences that pay lip service to the franchise's roots. In exchange, viewers got a shift from racing to chasing, together with a higher proportion of heist sequences, shootouts and fistfights. Subsequently, James Wan's *Furious 7* (2015) and F. Gary Gray's *The Fate of the Furious* (2017; hereinafter *Fast Eight*) pushed the action-envelope even further by introducing the franchise to the world of geopolitical espionage: here, the crew from the original street racing films (Dom, Brian and their family) are recruited to work for the US government, represented by the enigmatic Mr. Nobody (Kurt Russell). This development led to *Fast & Furious* adopting many different genre tropes and conventions from spy franchises such as *Mission: Impossible* and *James Bond*, including the injection of geopolitical intrigue, high-tech gadgets and an even more international approach to action.

Tables 2.1 and 2.2 both show how these shifts at the level of genre coincide with a significant increase in action (plus 10 per cent). Taking further cues from *Mission: Impossible*, the action sequences started to become ever more elaborate in terms of setting and plotting after *Fast Five*. From this point on, the action sequences generally last longer, partially because the filmmakers started to diversify the types of action that were foregrounded in the films. Table 2.3 shows how action events such as shootouts, fistfights and stuntplay became the centre of the franchise's action sequences. Other, more familiar action events such as car chases even got an upgrade in terms of scale. *Fast & Furious 6*, for example, presents cat-and-mouse sequences similar to the earlier films, but now the cars of the villains have all been upgraded with military-grade technology. As if *James Bond*'s Q took an interest in car tuning, the vehicles in the film start to resemble highly-mobile tanks that provide the franchise with new opportunities for action – something we'll revisit below. Interestingly, though, *Hobbs & Shaw* represents another possible shift in the franchise's identity. While the franchise appeared to have made its final transformation by incorporating elements of the spy film, the data for *Hobbs & Shaw* hints at a further shift in the direction of the

**Table 2.3** Type of action events.

| Title | Action event/proportion in film | | | | | | |
|---|---|---|---|---|---|---|---|
| | Car race | Car chase | Varia chase | Foot chase | Shootout | Fist fight | Stunts |
| The Fast and the Furious | 0.63% | 0.50% | 0.13% | 0.13% | 0.13% | 0.38% | 0.25% |
| 2 Fast 2 Furious | 0.33% | 0.67% | 0.17% | 0.00% | 0.17% | 0.25% | 0.00% |
| Tokyo Drift | 0.83% | 0.17% | 0.00% | 0.17% | 0.17% | 0.17% | 0.00% |
| Fast & Furious | 0.17% | 0.67% | 0.00% | 0.17% | 0.00% | 0.33% | 0.17% |
| Fast Five | 0.17% | 0.50% | 0.33% | 0.33% | 0.50% | 0.50% | 0.33% |
| Fast & Furious 6 | 0.13% | 0.50% | 0.13% | 0.13% | 0.13% | 0.50% | 0.25% |
| Furious 7 | 0.14% | 0.57% | 0.14% | 0.14% | 0.86% | 0.71% | 0.43% |
| The Fate | 0.20% | 0.60% | 0.40% | 0.20% | 0.40% | 0.20% | 0.40% |
| Hobbs & Shaw | 0.00% | 0.43% | 0.43% | 0.29% | 0.43% | 1.00% | 0.57% |
| **Average** | 0.29% | 0.51% | 0.19% | 0.17% | 0.46% | 0.45% | 0.27% |

buddy cop comedy and, in some respects, the superhero genre. While keeping one foot firmly in the terrain of *Mission: Impossible*, the action amount in this film dips compared with previous instalments, in order to allow for the development of the dynamic between its titular odd couple.

Another interesting trend is that the franchise seems to develop a more self-conscious attitude towards its trademark action sequences, most notably scenes of street racing. While the plot does draw its characters into street racing situations from *Fast Five* on, the franchise sometimes refrains from actually showing the action. In both *Fast Five* and *Furious 7*, for example, there are specific scenes in which someone needs to acquire a fast car for the purpose of pulling off a mission/heist. The set-up of these scenes is nearly identical to those in previous instalments. However, whereas earlier films in the franchise proceeded to a sequence of spectacular street racing, *Fast Five* cuts away right before the action to the moment after the street race. In this manner, the film deliberately withholds the street racing action – that was once the franchise's hallmark – from its audience. This phenomenon could be read as a sign of action sequence anxiety. Like any long-running franchise, *Fast & Furious* needs to constantly update and renew its own design. Thus, it's possible the producers of these later films calculated that audiences would get tired of seeing the same type of action sequence over and over again. At the same time, though, street racing remains a crucial part of the *Fast & Furious* universe, something that many audiences expect to see acknowledged within the film's narrative. This might help to explain why the producers chose to minimize the time spent on these street racing sequences, gesturing to but also downplaying them in favour of emphasizing other, less familiar forms of action.

Ironically, some types of action in the action sequence can thus become expendable. This is further confirmed in *Furious 7*'s opening sequence. In the film's pre-credit scene, villain Deckard Shaw (Jason Statham) – a former SAS agent who is now on America's most wanted list – is seen at the hospital bed of his brother Owen (Luke Evans). After exiting the hospital, the camera follows him to show the destruction he caused in order to get to his brother. Dead security officers are littered all over the hospital floor and the building seems to be on the verge of collapsing. While in other instalments this scenario would be the basis of an extensive action vignette, *Furious 7* confidently shifts the attention to the post-action part of an action sequence that took place off-camera. The promotional discourse around the franchise's latest instalments seems to adhere to the hypothesis that anxieties stemming from tensions between repetition and innovation are influencing the filmmaking process. Indeed, recent interviews with the cast and crew emphasize how each new film 'pushes the boundary' and 'sets the bar higher', whilst also seeking to reassure fans that the franchise remains grounded in its original spirit and values (see Goh 2021).

As the amount of action time shows, the duration and position of action sequences is something that *Fast & Furious* filmmakers plan with great care. *Fast & Furious'* developments in terms of action duration showcase that action franchises don't simply evolve by providing their audiences with more action. While the pivot towards the spy genre coincided with an increase in action, *Fast & Furious* did not simply rely on extending action runtime to intensify its viewing experience. Indeed, the acceleration of action does not appear to be a strategy on which *Fast & Furious* consistently relies. On the contrary, the franchise seems to deliberately omit certain action events in order to create a more engaging wider narrative. Therefore, in addition to looking at action in narrative, it benefits the analysis to examine how the action sequences themselves seem to change over time.

## Narrative in action

Comparing action across the nine films shows that in order to innovate and intensify its action, *Fast & Furious* greatly elaborated the narrative complexity of its action sequences over time. It should firstly be noted that throughout the franchise the action sequences are narratively tight. *Fast & Furious* tends to include a staggering number of tonal shifts, lengthy dialogue, subplots and other strategies that ensure a high degree of narrative development. This falls somewhat in line with the wider development in Hollywood action cinema of action becoming more narratively complicated (Soberon 2021). In *Fast & Furious*, however, this trend can be tied to the role cars play in these action sequences. After all, the car is also a type of setting: it's both a means of transportation and an interior space in which characters can have conversations. In this sense, *Fast & Furious* uses its cars for both spectacular action and narrative exposition. The car as a setting provides filmmakers opportunity to include clear dialogue between two or more individuals in the midst of a spectacular chase sequence. Because the characters share an enclosed space, they are in constant interaction and have more opportunity to exchange conversation while the action unfolds. In *Tokyo Drift,* for example, spectacular car races and chase sequences allow for plot exposition, character development and even narrative turning points. In this film, action is what often drives people closer and fosters intimate bonds. The first date between lead character Sean (Lucas Black) and his love interest, Neela (Nathalie Kelley), even takes the form of a car racing action beat. This offers potential for both high-octane thrills and romantic development. Indeed, the strong emphasis on cars and racing (especially in the early films) means that the action sequences of *Fast & Furious* have a very clear narrative focus/purpose. Whether its introducing new destinations or plot points, or simply putting two or more characters in close proximity, the franchise's car rides always seem to move the story forward on some level.

Although action sequences might not increase in terms of runtime, they do get more and more ambitious in terms of scale and narrative plotting across the franchise. In addition to the focus on cars, the filmmakers rely on two strategies to heighten the spectacular stakes of their action sequences: intensification and diversification. Firstly, when looking at the principle of action intensification, it's clear that the franchise distinguishes itself from other contemporary Hollywood action films by utilizing a larger proportion of chapters within its action sequences. Apart from nearly always featuring a set-up type prologue to its action, *Fast & Furious* constructs its action into a micro-narrative by installing different variables, such as breaks, twists and combinations of action events. This principle of action intensification relies on several aspects. Firstly, breaks help to provide breathing space in an action sequence, which in turn helps to extend the duration of these sequences. In *The Fast and the Furious*, after Dom is being chased by the police, he finds a space to dump his car and shake off the heat. From this point on, the action scene has seemingly ended as Dom casually walks through the streets. However, when a police patrol drives by and notices Dom, the action reignites again in the form of a foot chase. This break helps to add a level of narrative complexity to a straightforward action sequence by splitting it into two distinct chapters (before and after the action break) and layering it with an additional moment of suspense. As such, the action sequence can be doubled in duration whilst ensuring that the viewer remains engaged. These types of breaks are common in the franchise and serve a range of different narrative functions. In *Furious 7*, for example, the film's central heist is paused briefly to provide a humorous intermezzo: here, the audience is shown a brief shot of a family enjoying dinner in a luxury Abu Dhabi apartment while – unbeknownst to them – cars hurtle past their window. *Fast Eight* even makes room for a mid-action flashback scene during the final action sequence in which past events are retold from Dom's point of view, thus providing yet another layer to the complex nesting dolls these action sequences have become.

Secondly, diversification shows that *Fast & Furious* attempts to appeal to the audience by incorporating a wide range of action events within its action sequences. *Fast & Furious* ensures this type of narrative complexity by mixing and matching different types of action beats. This strategy of diversification is similar to the way in which a car chase continues as a foot chase in the first film, and it reminds us once again of how the filmmakers seek to pursue ever more intricate combinations of action events as the franchise develops. Indeed, this process of diversification largely relies on the incorporation of other genres, with the shift towards the spy genre after *Fast Five* offering the franchise a new set of toys and threats for its heroes to interact with. In *Furious 7*, a car chase is combined with an explosive drone strike, whilst being intercut with a fistfight and a shootout, before culminating in a stunt sequence where Dom attempts to escape a collapsing parking lot. *Fast Eight* goes to such extreme lengths to improve on the spectacle of its predecessor that it relies on an arctic submarine and remote-controlled avalanche of cars in its action sequences. At this point, the car chase no longer warrants an action sequence of its own and is demoted to one of many action beats that are strung together into more complicated action sequences. As the franchise progresses, it's clear that *Fast & Furious* is involved in a type of bidding war with itself. In attempting to one-up its previous instalment, every new addition to the franchise attempts to raise the bar even higher in terms of the type of action an action sequence consists of. While *Fast & Furious* internal competition takes on many forms, it manifests most clearly in rises in both the number and the types of action events per action sequence. *Fast & Furious* can therefore be considered to constantly intensify and diversify in order to exhilarate.

Similarly, each *Fast & Furious* film's action sequences build and variate on those of their predecessors, appealing to what the audience has seen before while adding further elements and complications. These complications function both intra- and intertextually. In *2 Fast 2 Furious*, for example, the second major action sequence mirrors the first: here, the action once again takes the form of a spectacular highway chase; however, this time the heroes are pursued by not just criminals but also the police, thereby escalating the earlier scene's vehicular combat. On a broader, intertextual level, each *Fast & Furious* film communicates with its past instalments to simultaneously evoke and surpass iconic previous action sequences. Indeed, the motorized heist sequences – a key part of the franchise since its beginning – keep returning in new and intensified ways. While the complications in the first film were only minor, such as Vince's (Matt Schulze) watch getting caught on the wing mirror, its sequels find challenges in the heist that are more and more outlandish. *Furious 7* is a strong example in this regard. Here, the main heist sequence is set in the Caucasus Mountains in Azerbaijan and raises both the number of action events and complicating scenarios. The sequence starts off with an airdrop of muscle cars before evolving into a high-speed ambush of an armed convoy. After some familiar car stunts, the first complicating scenario pops up in the shape of a manned turret gun in one of the enemy's trucks. The heroes adapt by aligning their cars, so a second complication is added in the shape of side-turrets. From that point, the sequence switches from driving to both fist and gun fighting in order to save a hostage, before this stability turns out to be short-lived and Deckard Shaw shows up to intervene. This complicating action subsequently triggers a downhill drag race between Deckard and Dom, which is then complicated by the truck driver being knocked unconscious.

The pattern that emerges from *Fast Five* on is that complicating scenarios and action events interact with one another. When the action risks becoming monotonous, complicating scenarios help to introduce new action events which are needed to solve the situation. Therefore, the logic of complication is seemingly what makes the action sequence tick. Complicating scenarios help with both the diversification of action and the intensification of narrative engagement in the sequences, because they supply the hero with a consistent stream of new challenges. Like Sisyphus on steroids, the action hero uses their powers to roll a boulder up the mountain, only to lose grip of it again once a complicating scenario is initiated.

A final way in which *Fast & Furious* intensifies the narrative complexity of its action sequences lies with the number of narrative strands per action sequence. A narrative strand can best be described as a focalization of one or several characters' experiences of events. In the first instalments of the franchise, one action sequence usually consists out of three or four viewpoints of the same events. However, the later instalments again take this narrative strategy to new extremes. *Fast Five*'s second-act train heist displays how the franchise combines narrative strands, complication events and the diversification of action to produce one enthralling entity. While this sequence starts from one narrative strand of the team approaching the train, the strands start multiplying once the complicating scenario of the team's betrayal kicks in and everyone splits up. This creates a distinction between Dom's point of view (on the train) and that of Brian (atop the heist buggy). From this point on, the two characters are each at the centre of their own distinctive set of action events. While still part of the same action sequence, the action goes back and forth between both narrative strands through parallel editing, until a point where both strands intersect and begin to influence each other. Brian's fistfight in the heist buggy eventually leads to him crashing the buggy into the moving train, which then serves as a complicating scenario to Dom's fight. This crash subsequently leads to an explosion that triggers an action event in which Brian now has to avoid flames released by the blast.

As this example shows, splitting up and tying together narrative strands centred on individual characters becomes one of the main ways that these films make their action sequences more intense. With every instalment the number of strands increases, as well as the complicating scenarios that they help to set up. *Fast Eight* even boasts as many as eight different narrative strands in its final-act action sequence. Lasting around 29 minutes, this action sequence is the longest of the entire franchise. Moreover, it features almost every type of action event that the franchise has heretofore shown, moving from land to sea to air over the course of its duration. The reason why this action can be stretched to such lengths has everything to do with the amount of narrative complexity this sequence is embedded with.

## Conclusion

Action cinema is its own perpetuum mobile. As Jones (2019: 100) states, 'whatever their subject matter, whenever their year of production, and whatever their budget, action films operate in a register of movement and dynamism.' This is as true for an action franchise as it is for an individual action film. If the opaque nature of the genre is characterized by anything, it's by a relentless drive to continue forward, pushing the spectacular action and the heroes' ordeals to ever greater extremes in the process. *Fast & Furious* is probably more susceptible to this logic than any other franchise. Its long-lasting success and consistent output have led to a constant need to intensify and diversify in order to revitalize its brand. This chapter adopted a longitudinal analysis to further understand how this process of enhancement affects the franchise's approach towards action. By way of a quantitative and qualitative approach to nine *Fast & Furious* films, the franchise's employment of action sequences could be studied from the angle of action in the narrative on the one hand, and narrative in action on the other. Although an instinctive guess would assume that the *Fast & Furious* accelerates its treatment of action by increasing the amount of action in its films, the quantitative study showed that there's no consistent rise of action across the franchise.

However, what did influence the amount of action across these films was *Fast & Furious*' interaction of with new genre forms. It's this same genre hybridity that largely defines the type of action events which are present throughout its respective instalments and offers new opportunities for the intensification and diversification of action. Rather than simply amp up action duration, *Fast & Furious* chooses to surpass its own instalments by making its action sequences consistently more narratively complex and varied in scope. If action sequences are micro-narratives, the recent *Fast & Furious* films present them as diverse, incident-rich and multi-layered plots. Through extensive use of complicating scenarios, narrative strands and action diversification, *Fast & Furious* has continued to raise the bar of what makes an engaging action sequence. Thus, while the criticism that action film plots are increasingly getting thinner can be arguably confirmed, this analysis also shows that this observation might be entirely beside the point. Action sequences have overtaken and surpassed the importance of the wider narrative, providing spectacular thrills at the same time as functioning as engaging and intertextually-connected narratives in their own right. With the tenth film already released (*F9* [2021]), and an eleventh currently in production, the immediate future of the franchise looks assured. Indeed, now that *Fast & Furious* has set off into space, one can study its departure into the sci-fi terrain and wonder what lies beyond the stars for Dom and his family. But one thing remains certain: in terms of action, *Fast & Furious* will always find new frontiers to cross.

# References

Anderson, A. (1998), 'Kinesthesia in Martial Arts Films: Action in Motion', *Jump Cut*, 42 (1): 1–11.
Babington, B. (2014), *The Sports Film*, New York: Columbia University Press.
Barker, J. (2009), *The Tactile Eye: Touch and the Cinematic Experience*, Berkeley: University of California Press.
Beltrán, M. (2013), 'Fast and Bilingual: *Fast & Furious* and the Latinization of Racelessness', *Cinema Journal*, 53 (1): 75–96.
Bordwell, D. (2006), *The Way Hollywood Tells It: Story and Style in Modern Movies*, Berkeley: University of California Press.
Box Office Mojo (2021), 'Franchise: *The Fast and the Furious*'. Available online: https://www.boxofficemojo.com/franchise/fr3628568325/?ref_=bo_frs_table_14 (accessed 23 April 2022).
Dixon, W. (1998), *The Transparency of Spectacle: Meditations on the Moving Image*, Albany: SUNY Press.
Ebert, R. (2003), *Roger Ebert's Movie Yearbook 2003*, Kansas City: Andrews McMeel Publishing.
Goh, M. (2021), '*Fast & Furious* Director Justin Lin: *F9* Is the Most Challenging Movie by Far', *Yahoo! Style*, 23 April. Available online: https://sg.style.yahoo.com/director-justin-lin-f9-most-challenging-fast-furious-movie-051944356.html (accessed 23 April 2022).

Gurevitch, L. (2009), 'Problematic Dichotomies: Narrative and Spectacle in Advertising and Media Scholarship', *Popular Narrative Media*, 2 (2): 143–58.

Jones, N. (2019), 'The Perpetual Motion Aesthetic of Action Cinema', in J. Kendrick (ed), *A Companion to the Action Film*, 97–117, Hoboken: Wiley Blackwell.

Kendrick, J. (2019), *A Companion to the Action Film*, Hoboken: Wiley Blackwell.

King, G. (2000), *Spectacular Narratives: Contemporary Hollywood and Frontier Mythology*, London: I.B. Tauris.

Musser, C. (1994), 'Rethinking Early Cinema: Cinema of Attractions and Narrativity', *Yale Journal of Criticism*, 7: 203–32.

Purse, L. (2011), *Contemporary Action Cinema*, Edinburgh: Edinburgh University Press.

Soberon, L. (2021), 'The Ultimate Ride: A Comparative Narrative Analysis of Action Sequences in 1980s and Contemporary Hollywood Action Cinema', *The Journal of Film and Video*, 72 (1): 18–32.

Stauven, W. (2006), *The Cinema of Attractions Re-Loaded*, Amsterdam: Amsterdam University Press.

# 3

## 'For those ten seconds, I'm free': Temporality, affect and spectacle in the *Fast & Furious* franchise

Naja Later

Reflecting on *The Fast and the Furious*, director Rob Cohen (2009) described the difficulty of constructing a 100-minute picture around the spectacle of quarter-mile races, which – if filmed in real time – would take up just ten seconds. Instead, Cohen learned to rely on digital visual effects, such as animating the mechanical processes of the car's ignition, and complex character shots to exaggerate and delay the conclusion of the race without sacrificing an authentic experience of speed. These aesthetic choices allowed for both spectacular and narratively significant action sequences: sequences that felt like real thing but, for the purposes of telling a feature-length story about the thrill of racing, could be extended to last for two minutes or more.

Despite numerous changes to the franchise's directorial personnel over the last twenty years, this technique of temporal deferral and spectacle has remained a key feature of *Fast & Furious* and was particularly important to the marketing and storytelling of *Furious 7* (2015), following the untimely death of actor Paul Walker: Walker, who played police officer-turned-street racer Brian O'Conner, died midway through production of the seventh film. With limited footage of Walker's final performance, director James Wan was forced to shoot multiple key scenes with stand-ins and visual effects substantiating the role. In the marketing, visual effects company Weta Digital were lauded for their mastery in digitally re-animating the recently deceased star. Crucially, this strategy replicated aspects of the visual effects process used for the quarter-mile races, in this case expanding on and exaggerating the limited footage of Walker. Here, Walker's final moment is spectacularly deferred until his character's arc reaches emotionally satisfying closure.

This relationship between temporality, affect and spectacle plays out on narrative and meta-narrative levels: it shapes the storyworld, its stars and its success. The ability for action cinema to sustain and suspend the highly affective moment of spectacle can be likened to Tom Gunning's (1993) discussion of the 'cinema of attractions'. Gunning's theory characterizes attractions as a perpetual present, a 'now' that thrills the audience through temporal defiance. Reading the franchise's narrative and aesthetic approaches to temporality through the cinema of attractions, this chapter argues that Walker's death is one of many spectacular deferrals, inviting the audience to linger in an illusory 'now' between life and death.

## The 'cinema of attractions'

Writing about early film history, Gunning (1993: 11) defines 'attractions' as spectacular films or sequences which favour novel temporality over narrative causality. Gunning articulates his theory of narrative temporality through the concept of a perpetual and recurring 'now' or discontinuous instants, rather than the cause-and-effect temporality of '*now* and *then*'. Shifting away from narrative analysis as a primary framework for understanding cinema, Gunning reframes spectacular temporality as thrilling moments unbound from the constrictions of causality. When applied to ostensibly classical Hollywood narratives like *Fast & Furious,* the cinema of attractions helps us analyse the significance of extravagant visual-effects sequences.

The magical 'now' of the *Fast & Furious* franchise, as Dom Toretto (Vin Diesel) articulates it in the first film, happens a quarter mile at a time. Dom is the seasoned outlaw who draws Brian, an undercover police officer, into both the world of underground street racing and his extended family/crew. Describing his love of racing to Brian in *The Fast and the Furious*, Dom states: 'For those ten seconds or less, I'm free.' The films are structured around a series of adrenaline-pumping car chases and races, presented as surreal, supernaturally drawn-out spectacles that last significantly longer than ten seconds. While of course we remain intimately aware that time and sequentially are crucial – the hero's car *must* cross the finish line *before* a rival's car – the ambiguity and anxiety surround *when* the finish line will appear. In those prolonged moments, Dom and the audience are free from causality.

Gunning identifies a distinctive set of aesthetic qualities in attractions. Attractions feature conspicuous spectacle and self-reflexive virtuosity. The showmanship is designed to provoke a thrilling affective response:

... a fascination with visual experiences which seem to fold back on the very pleasure of looking (colours, forms of motions ... ); an interest in novelty (ranging from actual current events to physical freaks and oddities); an often sexualized fascination with socially taboo subject matter dealing with the body (female nudity or revealing clothing, decay and death); a peculiarly modern obsession with violent and aggressive sensations (such as speed or the threat of injury). (Gunning 1993: 5–6)

These attributes are found in the highly-stylized races of the *Fast & Furious* franchise: the abstract blur of colours and movement, the novelty of cutting-edge technology as the camera travels through the cars, the voyeuristic shots of gyrating women bystanders and, of course, speed with the threat of injury. When Dom claims that those ten seconds are 'free', we could interpret them as free from time itself. Gunning (1993: 10) states: 'Rather than a developing configuration of narrative, the attraction offers a jolt of pure presence, soliciting surprise, astonishment, or pure curiosity instead of following the enigmas on which narrative depends.' In Brian's first race, we are eager to see him prove himself as the newcomer among the street racers, and to see whether his new rival Dom's reputation is earned. The pivotal affect is the thrill of the moment: Brian loses to Dom, but he basks in the triumph of having 'almost had' Dom. In that moment, the affect of racing is more important than the consequences of losing.

It is tempting to position attractions and narrative cinemas as antonymous, though Gunning (1993) argues that attractions find their way into classical

**Figure 3.1** Racing scene, *The Fast and the Furious* (2001 Universal).

narrative cinema. For a story driven by speed, *Fast & Furious* often slows down its fastest moments to ludicrously drawn-out sequences, forestalling narrative progression to favour the thrill of the chase. The spectacle presents a moment blissfully free of consequence: while the plot's timely conclusion is forestalled by the racing sequences, the spectacle ironically upholds the franchise's overarching theme of the protagonists escaping the consequences of their reckless driving.

Similarly, the high-speed thrill of slow-motion sequences might seem counter-intuitive, but Vivian Sobchack (2006) argues the opposite. Sobchack uses Gunning's work to contextualize how action cinema has 'what appears to be (but is not) a dialectical opposition between slowness and speed, forestalment and action'. Sobchack's valuable analysis focuses slow motion as a spectacular attraction, emphasizing its affective qualities. The slow motion of action scenes 'make their constitutive and elemental micro-rhythms viscerally visible'. Sobchack's essay uses 'cut to the quick' as a metaphor, where the visceral 'quick' is both time and a physical sore spot. She writes: 'Thus, cut to the quick, we are compelled to recognize that we are, at once, too temporally fast and too slow, too spatially large and too small, to apprehend the movements of movement – not merely our own but also, and more significantly, those of *physis*: the elemental micro- and macro-movements of the natural world.' Slow motion is just one device used to forestall and prolong the racing sequences, but functionally, every racing scene in *Fast & Furious* is *slow* in the sense that it takes a ludicrous amount of the film's runtime for high-speed cars to cross short distances. The invitation to linger in these moments, and their coding through the dialogue as 'free', offers a way of contextualizing the attraction of cinema itself. It is a glimpse at what Sobchack calls 'beyond' and yet 'beneath' all human 'perception and endeavour' (Sobchack 2006: 337–345).

Attractions disrupt temporality by deferring narrative advancement in favour of affect: a life-changing race that would take ten diegetic seconds to resolve is stretched into two minutes, functionally stalling the plot. On a larger scale, causality is still intrinsic to the storytelling, but the chronology becomes enigmatic: the films may be superficially straightforward, but the re-emergence and resurrection of former cast members produces a surprisingly complicated non-linear narrative. Following the stop-start, out-of-order story rewards an attentive audience who can take a flexible approach to temporality. In the races, effect does not follow cause in a timely manner, and in the overarching continuity, entire films can be squeezed between cause and effect. One effect – Han Seoul-Oh dying in Tokyo during the third film, *The Fast and the Furious: Tokyo Drift* (2006) – precedes its cause by three films. Only at the conclusion of the sixth film does Han (played by Sung Kang) depart for Japan, leaving the audience with their haunting meta-knowledge of his imminent death in Tokyo. The films are not discontinuous, though an audience might be forgiven for simply accepting Han somehow survived – despite the fact that the details of his survival are not confirmed until *F9* (2021). The conceit of the temporally uncanny, slow-but-fast spectacle allows for similar narrative diversions, forestalling the death of both major characters and a major star in the franchise. How Han's particular twist is achieved – and how *Furious 7* reconciles the loss of a lead character – relies on the franchise's perpetual and delighted deferral of the narrative through spectacle.

## Promoting *Furious 7* after Walker's death

Paul Walker was killed in a high-speed car crash in 2013, halfway through shooting *Furious 7* (Duke 2013). Production was delayed for a year as the studio decided how to proceed. Ultimately, it was announced that the film would resume shooting, with the role of Brian O'Conner to be completed with a combination of existing footage, stand-ins and visual effects from globally renowned Weta Digital (Stampler 2014). Brian would be written out of the franchise, his arc brought to a satisfying end with rewrites and reshoots. Despite earlier films following the arc of Brian's rejection of conventional life in favour of his outlaw family, *Furious 7* ends with Brian succumbing to the call of domesticity. This allows the character to withdraw gracefully from the foreground where the action takes place.

By staging Brian's departure as an in-universe retirement, the film avoids the plausible but ghoulish possibility of killing the character off despite – and *because* of – the fact that many previous franchise characters have died in similar circumstances to Walker. While Brian chooses to quit the racing life, and implicitly continues his relationships with the characters off screen during subsequent films, it is impossible to avoid the fourth wall of the audience's meta knowledge, and the film does not attempt to. The performances and mise-en-scène of *Furious 7* frame Brian's departure as permanent and heart-breaking, to a degree that might actually be jarring if an audience were unaware of the film's production history. In the closing scenes, two of Brian's close friends drink on a beach and discuss him leaving the crew, with the tone and finality of a funerary wake. Dom and Brian race together down a highway, and while their roads diverge, the narrative explanation of Brian's permanent retirement from driving would seem at odds with his commitment to the crew. However, the studio safely bets on the audience's awareness of Walker's final performance, carefully shaping the narrative through entryway paratexts – material Jonathan Gray (2009: 16) describes as 'providing an initial context and reading strategy for the text'. Drew Ayers (2019: 180) analyses how Universal 'rhetorically situated the completion of the film as honouring Walker's legacy', where Walker died as Brian lived. This breach of the fourth wall is befitting of Gunning's attractions, and the spectacle of Walker's face becomes an attraction in itself: 'Attractions pose a very different relation to the spectator [when compared with that of the classic voyeur]. The attraction does not hide behind the pretence of an unacknowledged spectator' (Gunning 1993: 5). We know going in that Walker's performance is only partially embodied, and, indeed, we are invited to marvel at it.

The success of this promotional narrative, and the emotional integrity of the film itself, depends on three key factors: Weta's digital visual effects, Walker's stand-ins and the ethereal styling of Brian's face. Indeed, the promotion for *Furious 7* placed strong emphasis on Weta's mastery, by reminding audiences of their previous work on *The Lord of the Rings: The Fellowship of the Ring* (2001; see Giardina 2015). Alongside their general technical expertise, the *Lord of the Rings* association emphasizes Weta's particular wizardry as magical storytellers, rather than Frankensteinian necromancers. If, by contrast, Universal had collaborated with Industrial Light and Magic (ILM), the studio would be reckoning with a brand identity of risky experimentation and eerie effects. An oft-compared example is ILM's reanimation of Peter Cushing in *Rogue One* (2016), which was a twitching, corpse-like affair that ultimately suited the villainous character and envelope-pushing effects of *Star Wars,* but would have been inappropriate for Walker (Walsh 2016).

The second consideration was the primary stand-ins Weta worked from: Universal hired Walker's brothers, Caleb and Cody (Giardina 2015). The striking family resemblance helped Universal sell the idea that the performance was still *a* Walker, if not *the* Walker, thereby also feeding into the franchise's themes of family. The audience's paratextual awareness of the Walkers' performances accounts for potential inconsistencies of Brian's appearance within the film. Of course, this does not account for uncredited stand-ins, such as the stunt performers who have shared the role of Brian O'Conner since the franchise began: stunt performers do less to affirm the authenticity of Walker's real-life passion for street racing, or echo themes of family. The most spectacular sequence from the trailer, where Brian leaps from a bus as it falls off a cliff, would always have been performed by a stunt professional, but the thrill elicited from viewing comes from the anxiety of seeing someone who is *almost* Paul Walker *almost* die.

Finally, there are the specific aesthetic choices made when reanimating Walker. In most of his scenes he appears to glow, soft edges obscuring the technical seams of his amalgamated performance. While it is apparent there was limited footage of Walker, obvious effort is made to obscure *how* limited this footage was. All Walker's scenes have a consistently ethereal visual quality, and so it is uncertain exactly when he was present, and when he was not. With his signature blond hair and blue eyes, Walker always possessed angelic looks. In *Furious 7*, he is often surrounded by a halo of source-less light, adding a beatific quality to his ambiguously posthumous scenes. This particular design choice recalls Vin Diesel's public grief of Walker, where Diesel described Walker in angelic terms. Ayers (2019: 180) quotes an interview where he describes 'the legacy that was Paul, the legacy of that angel', while in Lisbeth Klastrup's (2018: 6) analysis of Diesel's Facebook page – where fans prolifically share their grief for Walker – there are frequent references to Walker as an angel. The wizardry of Weta, the authenticity of Walker's brothers, and the angelic characterization of Walker by Diesel and fans, combine here to create a particularly sentimental affect in the spectacle of reanimation.

Still, there is an undeniable and unavoidable ghoulishness to what Ellis-Petersen called 'digital necromancy', a term coined in a think-piece released a week after *Furious 7*. Kasey Clawson Hudak (2014) cites examples that call such performances '"hauntological", "a Frankensteinian experiment" and "necrofilmia"', demonstrating the fantastical and surreal associations we have with reanimated performances. However, Hudak argues that all media is phantasmagorical to a degree, and our mythology of celebrities has always been caught up in anxieties of time and death. Hudak's (2014: 385) analysis of dead celebrities ('delebs') characterizes them as 'phantasms', noting that 'viewers are not so much confused about the status of the phantasm as living or dead, embodied or disembodied, but rather are apprehensive about how they feel'. In Walker's case, there is some genuine ambiguity and obscurity around which specific shots portray his embodied performance, and the degree to which all acting is altered in post-production, as Stephen Prince (2012: 101) compellingly argues. Hudak (2014: 385) emphasizes that 'celebrities are always and already phantasms that owe their continued existence to the very media that binds them.'

Cinema is always a snapshot of lost moments, and actors' performances are always an incomplete, discontinuous compilation of editing and post-production. Hudak's (2014: 385) transhistorical analysis describes the uncanny affect of early photography and sound technologies, suddenly able to portray voices and faces of their absent subjects, speculating whether all media-recorded performances are, to some degree, phantasmagorical: 'media permits the flow of time to be inscribed into voices, images, and ethereal bodies that can be played back at will (resurrected?).' Prince (2012: 101) similarly argues that ambiguity is inherent in cinematic performance: 'A viewer's impression of wholeness – the actor as a unified being in front of the camera – and of psychological and emotional continuity – the actor-as-character unfolding in narrative time and space – is a manufactured impression that often fails to correlate with what was.' When an actor's death is highly publicized, the 'manufactured impression' is unavoidable, so the entryway paratexts emphasize the mastery of manufacturing, drawing attention to the attraction *as* attraction. Angela Ndalianis (2000: 259) describes how the wizardry of digital visual effects invites 'simultaneous acceptance of the fantastic illusion as both technological achievement and a realistic, alternative reality; thus the effects technology is both exposed and disguised.' The logic of attractions presents a self-reflexive invitation to marvel at the ambiguity and artifice of Walker's performance.

Acknowledging the careful cultivation of media texts surrounding a celebrity's image, Hudak (2014: 289) argues that 'the passage of time poses a threat to living celebrities and their fame', because the celebrity's star persona is subject to change with future performances. However, '[c]elebrities that passed away when their image as a cultural icon was still intact remain that way possibly forever', and this embeds their image with a timeless quality (Ibid: 390). Walker's death in a car accident was entirely congruent with the characterization of Brian O'Conner, and an indirect consequence of the role: his passion for fast cars was sparked by his involvement in the franchise, cementing a permanent iconic status inextricable from the values of the *Fast & Furious* franchise (Jurnecka 2020). Between Walker's well-publicized passion for racing, his death at a pivotal point in the *Fast Saga* and the careful styling of his phantasmagorical performance as angelic, Universal was ideally positioned to tastefully argue that the show must go on.

## The longest ten seconds in history

As noted, the *Fast & Furious* franchise has always presented attractions through their ability to stall time. In *Furious 7*, the time being stalled is the time before useable footage of Walker runs out. Wan spectacularly prolongs the end (of Walker's performance) by masterfully teasing out the limited time (embodied performance footage) remaining. In many ways, the franchise has been developing this theme of spectacular forestalling since its beginning. The central conflict of every *Fast & Furious* narrative is speed. We crave the thrill of the chase, hoping the characters will swiftly pass the finish line or stop the bad guys. But the pleasure lies in the anticipation, in the thrill of the race itself. In every film, but especially in *Furious 7*, we don't want it to be over. This powerful affect is described by Thomas Elsaesser (2005) in his theory of cinephilia. He breaks the theory down into two stages, or 'takes': take one, a love of cinema that embraces the ephemerality of celluloid is 'the love that never lies'. This manifests in *Furious 7* as euphoria at the fleeting possibility of embodied authenticity in Walker's scenes. Elsaesser's take two describes the 'love that never dies', typical of the digital age where a film can be watched in perpetuity, the spectacle always available to revisit: an apt metaphor for a film that digitally defies death. Reflecting on take one and take two of cinephilia, Elsaesser (2005: 39–41) describes how take one 'was an anxious love, because it was love in deferral and denial'. While Elsaesser's analysis focuses on the experience of attending the cinema in the 1960s–1980s (and digital reanimation is a distinctly take-two aesthetic) the same affect of deferral and denial underpins the storytelling of the entire *Fast & Furious* franchise. For those two hours, we are free.

This problem of deferral means every race must *feel* fast while actually being drastically prolonged to capitalize on its narrative tension. The anxious dissonance has been a problem since the first instalment. In the director's commentary, Rob Cohen (2009) frames the approach to the first racing scene entirely through the techniques of spectacle:

> I took ten seconds and expanded it to two minutes. [Sound designer Bruce Stambler and I] began to dig into how to do speed in a new way, ... in a way that we go in the cars, through the cars, around the cars, from car to car. I realised ... the only way to get speed was to not treat racing as it lived in the real world, but treat it like it's a science fiction film ... At any rate, most of the cars you're seeing, like [Walker's car] they don't exist. These cars are created in

the computer, and we put the actors in them. [The VFX department] all worked together on this sequence to create each of these moments with me to take you aboard the street race. And let you know what it felt like to go 140 to 180 miles an hour.

Cohen attributes the spectacle to the masterful visual effects companies and their ability to expand the limited window of a ten-second race into a full action sequence. When Dom claims those ten seconds are free, they are free from even *being* ten seconds: the sequence offers a lingering glimpse at a world without the inevitable progress of time. In essence, this is the same strategy applied to Walker seven films later. It is the spectacle of dazzling effects which makes the temporal rupture possible, and indeed a hallmark of cinema history. While there may be scepticism of the franchise crossing into science fiction with the supervillains of *Fast & Furious Presents: Hobbs & Shaw* (2019), the franchise has always possessed supernatural affectations – not to mention plot twists that border on time travel (Hood 2019).

The motif of deferral, and the anxious pleasure of anticipation lengthened by that deferral, is also used to address in-universe character death. Han Lue was introduced in *The Fast and the Furious: Tokyo Drift* as a mentor to protagonist Sean Boswell (played by Lucas Black). Han's death in the second act of the film seems to present a conclusive end for the character, though a surprise appearance from Dom alludes to some shared off-screen history that predates *Tokyo Drift*. Then the fourth instalment, *Fast & Furious* (2009: hereinafter *Fast Four*), begins with an unusual surprise: Han is alive and well. Did he somehow survive the explosion? No, a throwaway line reveals: Han has *not yet* been to Tokyo, but he plans to go soon. The audience is left to presume that *Fast Four* must actually be the third film, chronologically, and *Tokyo Drift* must be the fourth. Next, Han reappears in *Fast Five* (2011) the film teasing out into its final scenes whether Han is planning to finally go to Tokyo and meet his death. 'We'll get there, eventually,' he assures us, leaving the audience guessing that the fifth instalment is in fact the chronological fourth, and the sixth will be the fifth, so the third may in fact end up being the sixth – which was confirmed to be so when the *Fast & Furious 6* (2013) mid-credits stinger recapped Han's death. This turned out to be a flash-forward to the first act of *Furious 7*, finally bringing the timeline back into alignment.

This narrative game, cramming three films' worth of chronology between the third and fourth instalments, prolongs the pleasure of spending more time with the character, mingled with the anxiety of knowing *how* things will end – the suspense comes from *when*. The time loop does not close perfectly: Han's apparent death is retconned as a foiled assassination, not an accident. The actors have visibly aged: the re-enactment of Dom meeting a teenage Sean in *Furious 7*, and the noticeable ageing of Sean and his crew in the brief in-universe years before their reappearance in *F9* requires some suspension of disbelief. The cutting-edge technologies and street fashions featured prominently in every film are amusingly anachronistic if we entertain the idea that *Tokyo Drift* takes place in 2015. These amusing tensions between past, present and future support the franchise's increasing use of non-linear storytelling to develop new back stories and relationships, seen in *F9* with the introduction of Dom's brother Jake (John Cena). Through a complex string of flashbacks, we learn that Dom and Mia's (Jordana Brewster) confrontation with the lost Toretto has taken decades to reach its climax, while the character was only introduced to audiences in the 2020 trailer.

As Cohen (2009) states in his analysis of the first race, the aim is 'not to treat racing as if it lived in the real world, but to treat it like it's a science fiction films … and to be free'. This particular affective experience, delighting at the cleverness of the storytelling without nitpicking its superficial anachronisms, is an established conceit that accounts for the occasionally eerie glow of Brian in *Furious 7*. Indeed, the plot of *Furious 7* depends on our ability to stitch together disparate timelines: the re-staging of Kang and Black's *Tokyo Drift* scenes create an ironic cohesion of visual oddities, relying on the audience's ability to reorder the narrative chronology across four films as the events unfold out of order.

A faithful audience is primed to anxiously anticipate the end, while thrilled by its uncannily exaggerated deferral. While Sung Kang is alive and can deliver embodied performances for films shot after Han's fictional death, there are affective parallels between Han and Brian that depend on our meta-knowledge of the films. Han's allusions to Tokyo carry the same ominous weight as Brian's longing for domesticity in *Furious 7*. The series invites us to cling to those remaining moments we will share before their inevitable departure, exaggerating and aestheticizing that impossible time the same way it does with the races that form the backbone of the franchise. We know the characters' arcs *must* end (or not, with Han's reappearance in *F9*), but our anxiety lingers on *when* it will end. Gunning (1993: 10–11) finds a similar experience in Georges Méliès films:

> The sudden flash (or equally sudden curtailing) of an erotic spectacle, the burst into motion of a terroristic locomotive, or the rhythm of appearance, transformation, and sudden disappearance that rules a magic film all invoke a spectator whose delight comes from the unpredictability of the instant, a

succession of excitements and frustrations whose order cannot be predicted by narrative logic and whose pleasures are never sure of being prolonged. Each instant offers the possibility of radical alteration and termination.

It is the pleasure of *not yet* compounded by the anticipation of *soon*, and it has been a core tenet of the franchise since Brian's first race.

## Time in *Furious 7*

Time is a malleable force in *Furious 7,* to be played with and warped at will. Establishing shots of the exotic global locations the heroes zip between pulse and jitter to the pounding trap beats of the soundtrack. Caught somewhere between the stylistic influences of a hand-crank and a buffering web video, the rhythm of the film is beholden to its aesthetic contrivances rather than naturalistic continuity. The cacophonous strobing shots of disjointed bodies recall *Furious 7* director James Wan's first hit, *Saw* (2004), though the sensory overload is now staged for pleasure, rather than disgust. The spectacle takes precedence over realism, and like the traps of *Saw* the races of *Furious 7* present a vaudevillian revue of death-defying attractions interspersed with a high-stakes plot and an unpredictable twist revealed through flashbacks.

The twist comes as a revelation that Letty (played by Michelle Rodriguez) has regained her lost memories, following her apparent death in the fourth film and surprise return in the sixth. Although romance in the franchise has always played second fiddle to the love of found family, *Furious 7* rushes to assure the audience that Letty and Dom had a fairy-tale love story: we just didn't see it. Letty's relationship with Dom was never particularly effusive, as demonstrated by the necessity of retconned flashbacks purpose-shot for the film. As Dom appears to be dying, Letty confesses that her memories have returned. In a flurry of brightly coloured smash cuts and soft-focus scenes, we realize that Letty and Dom must have married sometime around the events of *Los Bandoleros* (2009), the prequel to *Fast Four*. Dom's trademark cross necklace sealed their marriage.

The film clearly displaces the audience's grief for Walker onto a heterosexual relationship we never truly saw: Brian stands to one side, frowning in frustration as Letty holds Dom. The moment cannot help but recall the finale of *Fast Four*, where Dom cradled Brian in the aftermath of the final chase, and Brian carried Dom's necklace when he rescued Dom from prison. It is Dom and Brian's relationship that had driven the franchise thus far, and their homoerotic chemistry fuelled

**Figure 3.2** Letty holding Dom, *Furious 7* (2015 Universal).

the tension in many of the spectacular racing sequences. It is unclear whether Wan lacked the footage to show Brian grieving Dom, or whether this would have brought the romantic subtext too near to the surface: either way, Brian stands to one side, shaking his head in denial as Letty articulates grief over Dom that could easily apply to the audience's grief – and Diesel's – for Walker. The film never goes so far as to disambiguate Dom and Brian's closeness, offering an alternative: Dom has a romantic life that has been taking place off-screen, ostensibly with Letty. This scene promises to the audience that relationships – whether between Dom and Letty or Dom and Brian – are stronger and deeper than can be shown in the film, and memories can be conjured from pure imagination in the face of death. And so, we are reassured that Brian's life will continue even if we do not see it, that he will be loved. Letty makes those promises to Dom on Brian's behalf. 'I'm not ready to leave this place yet,' she tearfully pleads with Dom: 'This moment is still ours.'

The film itself is 'this moment', minutes spun into hours that spectacularly forestall the end. The audience are forgiven if, like Letty, we are not ready to leave. 'This place' and 'this moment' collapse time and space, and although the focus is superficially on Dom and Letty's relationship, this articulation of time fits neatly into Halberstam's queer temporality. Reflecting on how the AIDS crisis shaped theories of queer time, Halberstam (2005: 2) argues: 'The constantly diminishing future creates a new emphasis on the here, the present, the now, and while the threat of no future hovers overhead like a storm cloud, the urgency of being also expands the potential of the moment, and as [poet

Mark] Doty explores, squeezes new possibilities out of the time at hand.' The squeezing of new possibilities for scenes from the diminishing footage of Walker defers the threatening storm cloud of his death. So the film expands the potential of the moment, the urgent 'now' that Gunning describes in the cinema of attractions. Expanding beyond the temporal disruption of racing, entire film becomes a spectacular: from the establishing shots to the face of its star, the film invites 'a jolt of pure presence' (Gunning 1993: 10).

The moment is timeless and fleeting: it cannot be one without being the other. Comparing Walker's reanimation to similar action stars, Ayers (2019: 179) argues that 'the immortality offered in *Furious 7* is more timeless in nature, visualizing a kind of perpetual present that could be recreated *ad infinitum*'. Ayers' argument hinges on the digitization of Walker's image, a spectacular immortality offered by the virtuosity of cinema. This immortality echoes Sobchack's (2006: 349) argument that the slow motion spectacle 'serves as both the uncanny affirmation and *memento mori* of modernity. Interrogating the differential speed of modernity's earliest and latest phases, the essential revelations of slow motion are radical – potentially sublime and dangerous in their capacity to wound.'

The spectacle offers potential to disrupt linearity and the limits of perception, defying death by bringing us to its edge. Elsaesser (2005: 35) describes a similar experience in describing the illusionism of American cinema: 'one takes pleasure in being a witness to magic, to seeing with one's own eyes and ears what the mind knows to be impossible, or to experience the uncanny force of cinema as a parallel universe, peopled by a hundred years of un-dead presences, of ghosts more real than ourselves.' This has always been the promise made by the *Fast & Furious* franchise, and the reason it is able to deliver a timeless moment in *Furious 7*. Time is not time; death is not death; illusions are not illusions; and ten seconds are not ten seconds. After the denouement and each of the actors – ostensibly in-character – eulogize Brian, the film takes one more moment to reassure us that Dom and Brian will always have time for one more race.

## Conclusion

The *Fast & Furious* franchise has always offered deferral through spectacle. In reanimating Walker, the studio uses the same techniques that once stretched and expanded the conclusion of the races to defer the death of a lead actor. The films characteristically defy a steady chronological progression in favour of the thrilling affect of spectacle in defiance of death. Narratively, Han's surprise returns and Letty's lost memories create a plausible precedent for Brian's arc closing. Aesthetically, the stylized effects-driven races codify the non-naturalistic forestalling of the end. The racing spectacle invites audiences to linger in the instant, to marvel at how skilful and dazzling this prolonging of the inevitable can be. Gunning (1993: 11) calls the cinema of attractions: 'an alternative temporality based ... on an intense interaction between an astonished spectator and the cinematic smack of the instant, the flicker of presence and absence.' The protracted present of the *Fast & Furious* films always threatens to flicker into absence, and the cinema of attractions does not attempt to deceive or conceal this truth: instead, it offers a chance at freedom, fleeting but prolonged by the magic of the movies. This is the promise of all cinema: that we can have just a little more time, even if it's only an illusion.

## References

Ayers, D. (2019), 'The Composite Body: Action Stars and Embodiment in the Digital Age', in J. Kendrick (ed), *A Companion to the Action Film*, 165–86, Hoboken, NJ: John Wiley & Sons.

Cohen, R. (2009), 'Director's Commentary' [Blu Ray] *The Fast and the Furious*, USA: Universal Studios.

Duke, A. (2013), '*Fast & Furious* Star Paul Walker Killed in Car Crash', *CNN*, 30 October. Available online: https://edition.cnn.com/2013/11/30/showbiz/actor-paul-walker-dies (accessed 30 August 2021).

Ellis-Petersen, H. (2015), 'Bruce Lee, Audrey Hepburn and the Ethics of Digital Necromancy', *The Guardian*, 11 April. Available online: https://www.theguardian.com/culture/2015/apr/10/bruce-lee-audrey-hepburn-ethics-digital-necromancy (accessed 30 August 2021).

Elsaesser, T. (2005), 'Cinephilia or the Uses of Disenchantment', in M. de Valck and M. Hagener (eds), *Cinephilia: Movies, Love and Memory*, 27–42, Amsterdam: Amsterdam University Press.

Giardina, C. (2015), 'How *Furious 7* Brought the Late Paul Walker Back to Life', *Hollywood Reporter*, 11 December. Available online: https://www.hollywoodreporter.com/behind-screen/how-furious-7-brought-late-845763 (accessed 30 August 2021).

Gray, J. (2009), *Show Sold Separately: Promos, Spoilers, and Other Media Paratexts*, New York: New York University Press.

Gunning, T. (1993), '"Now You See It, Now You Don't": The Temporality of the Cinema of Attractions', *The Velvet Light Trap*, 32: 3–12.

Halberstam, J. (2005), *In a Queer Time and Place: Transgender Bodies, Subcultural Lives*, New York: New York University Press.

Hood, C. (2019), 'Idris Elba's Powers Can Explain *Fast & Furious* Most Over-the-Top Action Scenes', *Screen Rant*, 3 February. Available Online: https://screenrant.com/idris-elba-fast-furious-powers-explain-action-scenes/ (accessed 30 August 2021).

Hudak, K. C. (2014), 'A "Phantasmic Experience: Narrative Connection of Dead Celebrities in Advertisements', *Culture, Theory and Critique*, 55 (3): 383–400.

Jurnecka, R. (2020), 'Inside Paul Walker's Treasure Trove of Collector Cars', *Automobile*, 1 January. Available online: https://www.automobilemag.com/news/paul-walker-collection-drive-photos/ (accessed 30 August 2021).

Klastrup, L. (2018), 'Death and Communal Mass-Mourning: Vin Diesel and the Remembrance of Paul Walker', *Social Media + Society*, 4 (1): 1–11.

*The Lord of the Rings: The Fellowship of the Ring* (2001), [Film] Dir. Peter Jackson, USA: Warner Bros.

Ndalianis, A. (2000), 'Special Effects, Morphing Magic, and the 1990s Cinema of Attractions', in V. Sobchack (ed), *Meta-morphing: Visual Transformation and the Culture of Quick Change*, 251–65, Minneapolis: University of Minnesota Press.

Prince, S. (2012), *Digital Visual Effects in Cinema: The Seduction of Reality*, New Brunswick: Rutgers University Press.

*Rogue One* (2016), [Film] Dir. Garreth Edwards, USA: Walt Disney Studio Motion Pictures.

*Saw* (2004), [Film] Dir. James Wan, USA: Lionsgate Films.

Sobchack, V. (2006), '"Cutting to the Quick": Techne, Physis, and Poiesis and the Attractions of Slow Motion', in W. Strauven (ed), *The Cinema of Attractions Reloaded*, 337–52, Amsterdam: Amsterdam University Press.

Stampler, L. (2014), 'Here's What Will Happen to Paul Walker's Character in *Fast and Furious 7*', *Time*, 6 January. Available online: https://entertainment.time.com/2014/01/06/heres-what-will-happen-to-paul-walkers-character-in-fast-and-furious-7/ (accessed 30 August 2021).

Walsh, J. (2016), '*Rogue One*: the CGI Resurrection of Peter Cushing Is Thrilling – but Is It Right?', *The Guardian*, 16 December. Available online: https://www.theguardian.com/film/filmblog/2016/dec/16/rogue-one-star-wars-cgi-resurrection-peter-cushing (accessed 30 August 2021).

4

# A critical quantitative analysis of race and representation in the *Fast Saga* films

Pete Jones and Joshua Gulam

The *Fast & Furious* franchise offers a fascinating nexus for exploring racial representation in contemporary Hollywood cinema. Produced by Universal Pictures, the nine films in the *Fast Saga* have consistently featured a central team of protagonists drawn from a range of racial and ethnic groups, and eight of these films have also been directed by people of colour. In both regards, *Fast & Furious* is anomalous in a landscape of blockbuster cinema marked by a clear and persistent white dominance at all levels: figures for cast and crew diversity from 2011 to 2019 – a key period in the *Fast Saga*'s development – show that, at its most inclusive, white actors occupied two out of every three roles in top-grossing Hollywood cinema, while people of colour accounted for just 15 per cent of directors (Hunt and Ramón 2020).

From the perspective of on- and off-screen representation, then, *Fast & Furious* appears to stand out as a model of Hollywood blockbuster diversity, as much of the recent press reception of the franchise suggests. For example, *USA Today*'s review of *Furious 7* (2015) proclaimed that 'the franchise's ethnically diverse cast ... is a wonderful example for Hollywood of how most films should look' (Puig 2015); and *Variety*'s review of the same film remarked on the difficulty of identifying 'another mainstream Hollywood blockbuster, past or present, with this level of ethnic ... diversity on display' (Foundas 2015). Similarly, *L.A. Times* critic Justin Chang (2017), in an otherwise scathing review of *The Fate of the Furious* (2017), applauded the franchise for its long-standing commitment to inclusive casting, noting that: 'Years before #OscarsSoWhite became the depressing industry catchphrase, the *Fast & Furious* movies were the glorious standard-bearer for multiplex multiculturalism.'

Compared with the enthusiastic press coverage, the academic literature on *Fast & Furious* tends to be far more sceptical about its supposed racial progressivism.

In her discussion of *The Fast and the Furious* (2001), Mary Beltrán (2005) notes how the film's 'multiculti' aesthetic belies a problematic racial hierarchy that privileges lighter-skinned characters such as Paul Walker's Brian O'Conner and Vin Diesel's Dom Toretto. For Beltrán (2005: 59–62), the casting of multiracial actor Diesel is especially significant: it lends the franchise a 'bronzer whiteness', which provides the appearance of meaningful racial difference but is also deeply invested in 'notions of white superiority'. Likewise, Lisa Purse (2011: 125–8) cautions against overstating the 'progressive agenda' of *Fast & Furious*, noting how these types of multicultural action films 'too often simply reconfirm white dominance'. These arguments sit within a much wider, well-established critique of post-civil rights representational politics that has been dubbed 'post-racial' or 'colour-blind' – terms that capture a celebration of progress which serves to deny continuing forms of white material and discursive domination (Gray 2013; Quinn 2020; Saha 2018). This critique complicates and sheds doubt on the praise that *Fast & Furious* has received for showcasing 'characters of all races' (Blay 2016).

This chapter explores the fault line that exists between these two competing accounts. In doing so, it contributes not only to scholarship about the racial politics of *Fast & Furious*, but also wider debates around the implications of quantitative data for assessing representational inequality in Hollywood cinema (Cobb 2018). Celebration of the franchise's on- and off-screen diversity – noteworthy and novel though it is – fails to register some of the more contradictory and regressive racial themes identified by Beltrán and Purse, scholars whose work is consistent with a broader cultural-theory critique of the post-racial entertainment industries (Saha 2018). One of our central aims therefore is to consider whether these scholarly arguments still ring true, in light of both the franchise's significant commercial growth over the last decade and the representational hype that currently surrounds it.

The secondary interventions of our chapter are methodological. Here, we use *Fast & Furious* to engage with a broader discussion about how best to approach the auditing and evaluation of on-screen representation. On their own, basic empirical measures of racial prevalence are insufficient, and can too easily mask the neoliberal and post-racial displays of multiculturalism that are found in texts like the *Fast Saga* films (Gray 2016; Warner 2017). However, questioning the politics of crude prevalence models shouldn't lead us to jettison empirical and quantitative methods altogether. Instead, drawing on insights from critical race scholars, we can push these methods in different directions and develop a hybrid 'critical quantitative' approach. By combining a prevalence-based content analysis with other measures of on-screen representation, this approach enables us to delve more deeply into the films, uncovering the types of embedded textual dynamics and hierarchies that aren't always picked up by a focus on visibility alone. We also consider the questions that this throws up about racial classification for auditing purposes. Quantitative approaches, often rooted in the measurement techniques of the social sciences, provide scope for more than just a dualistic Black/white logic, allowing us to gather representational data on the wide range of racial/ethnic groups that appear in the *Fast Saga*. At the same time, though, this highlights the complexity and arbitrariness of racial categorization in the first place, a fact that is brought into acute relief by the franchise's 'ethnically ambiguous' protagonists (Beltrán 2005: 50).

To address these issues, the chapter employs a range of quantitative and qualitative methods. First, we review existing Hollywood diversity data to assess their strengths and limitations, and to establish some empirical benchmarks against which to evaluate the *Fast Saga* films. We then conduct a content analysis of the proportion of speaking roles among characters from different racial/ethnic groups to explore how the franchise 'performs' relative to dominant industry patterns. In addition to the proportion of speaking roles, our approach measures the distribution of dialogue in a character network analysis, something that allows us to further examine the relationships between and across characters (Jones 2020). Close analysis of this dialogue data, when paired with critical race studies insights and textual readings of specific films, reveals a complex picture of on-screen representation in *Fast & Furious*. Thus, by taking a critical approach to quantitative analysis of representation, our findings are able to usefully engage with previous arguments and illustrate how the films of the *Fast Saga* – despite surpassing the industry average for non-white visibility – reproduce a post-racial logic that confirms but also complicates the franchise's reputation as a model of blockbuster diversity.

## Establishing an empirical picture of the representational landscape

As more attention has been paid to representational inequalities in the film and entertainment industries, so too has there been an increase in attempts at auditing on- and off-screen representation quantitatively. Several annual studies offer systematic content analyses of top-grossing films, providing data that can be used to establish empirical benchmarks for the diversity of Hollywood productions both in front of and behind the camera. Here, we review the findings of two studies published in 2020: the UCLA Hollywood Diversity Report (Hunt and Ramón 2020; hereinafter, HDR) and the Annenberg Inclusion Initiative's survey of inequality in popular films (Smith, Choueiti and Pieper 2020; hereinafter, Annenberg). Both studies provide quantitative breakdowns of the highest-grossing films each year, though each takes a slightly different approach to sample selection and analysis.[1] Together, these complementary studies help to map countable representational trends in mainstream Hollywood cinema during the period from 2007 to 2019, trends which provide a useful backdrop for our own analysis of the *Fast Saga* films.

The Annenberg data (Figure 4.1) show that the yearly proportion of speaking characters who are white declined over the course of the thirteen-year sample. This proportion remained relatively stable from 2007 to 2015, averaging 75.2 per cent over this period, but fell more sharply in the subsequent four years, averaging 67.7 per cent from 2016 to 2019. All other groups increased proportionally in conjunction with this; however, the gains were most notably concentrated among Black and multiracial actors. A similar trend is visible in the HDR data

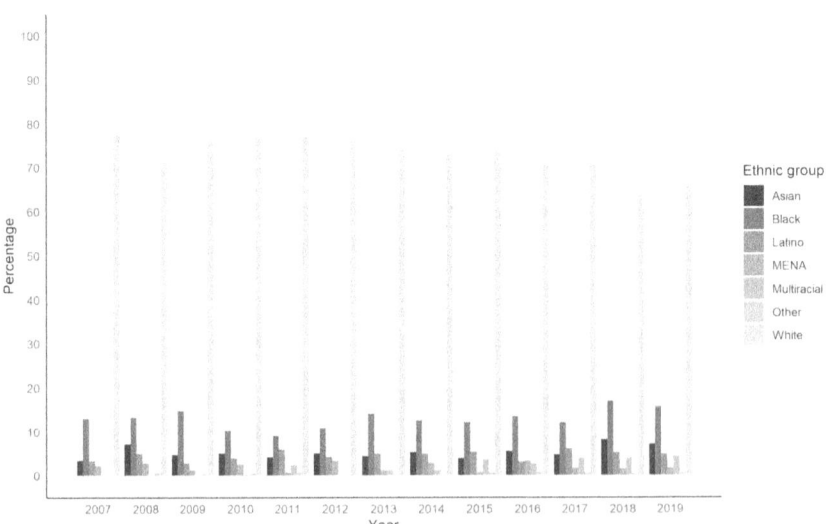

**Figure 4.1** Annenberg Inclusion Initiative – Proportion of characters by ethnic group in top-grossing films (our elaboration from data presented in Smith, Choueiti and Pieper 2020).

(Figure 4.2), which present cast shares broken down by ethnic group over a shorter period, 2016–19. Nevertheless, the pattern was similar, with white actors accounting for 78.1 per cent of all actors in 2016 and 67.3 per cent in 2019.

Together, these studies suggest that levels of non-white visibility increased substantially between 2007 and 2019, with viewers more likely each year to see people of colour in popular Hollywood films. However, it's not clear from these numbers what kind of roles these characters played in the narrative, or the extent to which their inclusion was reductive or tokenistic. HDR aims to get a little closer to identifying depth of representation by also analysing proportionality among 'film leads' over time. The study finds that white actors' share of film leads fell from 89.5 per cent in 2011 to 72.4 per cent in 2019, which was a shift from a ratio of 9 white leads per non-white lead to under 3-to-1. Again, this shift is more pronounced in later years: the average for 2011–16 was 86.2 per cent, whereas the proportion fell more steeply after this period to 75.3 per cent for 2017–19. These figures are not broken down further by ethnic group, meaning that they offer a rather broad means for assessing representational progress. Overall, though, the fact that white dominance among film leads is considerably higher than across the total cast suggests that little was done in this period to address the longstanding white-centrism of popular Hollywood films.

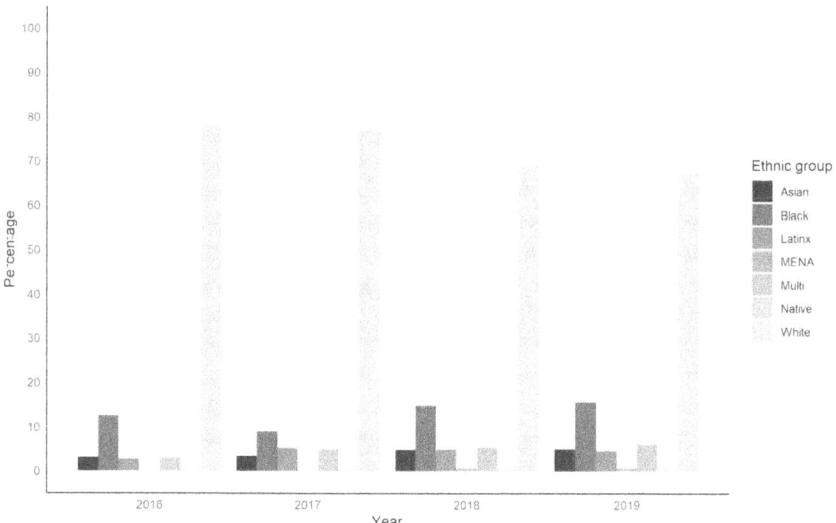

**Figure 4.2** UCLA Hollywood Diversity Report – Proportion of characters by ethnic group in top-grossing films (our elaboration from data presented in Hunt and Ramón 2020).

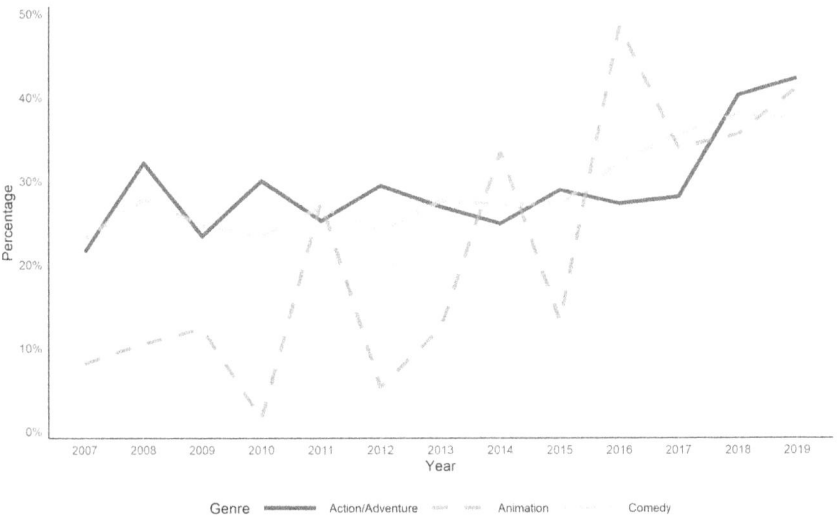

**Figure 4.3** Annenberg Inclusion Initiative – Proportion of characters from non-white ethnic groups in top-grossing films by genre (our elaboration from data presented in Smith, Choueiti and Pieper 2020).

There are limited data for assessing how these trends might interact with the genre of a film, which is an important factor in determining the expectations for an action-oriented franchise like *Fast & Furious*. However, Annenberg does offer the proportion of non-white speaking characters in their sample each year in three genres – Action/Adventure, Animation and Comedy. Figure 4.3 illustrates that the level of non-white representation in the Action/Adventure genre remained largely static from 2007 to 2019, though there is evidence of a jump in the later years. Significantly, this jump occurs in the two years *after* the 2017 release of *The Fate of the Furious* (hereinafter, *Fast Eight*), the most recent film in our analysis. Thus, the benchmark of 20–30 per cent non-white visibility provides a valid backdrop for this study, allowing us to measure the *Fast Saga* films against other Hollywood action blockbusters released in the period from 2007 to 2017.

## Diversity data, headcounts and the limits of visibility

The data in these reports are crucial in piecing together an understanding of the extent of under-representation in quantitative terms. The empirical picture established here would not have been possible a decade ago. What's more, the annual publication of such data helps keep the question of Hollywood labour force inequities in the public and industry discourse. In this section, however, we wish to reflect on some of the limitations of relying only on prevalence data such as these in light of key critiques of visibility-driven approaches to representation. Our aim here is not to dismiss the value of prevalence data or the conversations that surround them, especially as those conversations constitute an important and growing effort among critics, audiences and the industry, to reflect upon Hollywood's ongoing racial disparities. Instead, we want to acknowledge that a more critical approach to quantification can advance our understanding of what it means for a franchise like *Fast & Furious* to be labelled 'diverse'.

Current conversations about racial representation in Hollywood tend to centre around questions of numerical visibility, embracing a particular kind of quantification which aims to measure 'diversity' and 'inclusion' in terms of headcounts of people from various demographic groups. Recent scholarship on screen sector inequalities has paid increasing attention to the discourse surrounding 'diversity' and diversity policy, including analysing the important role of 'diversity data' within this arena (Cobb 2019; Nwonka 2020). This scholarship calls for a more critical engagement with the data that's used to audit representational inequalities and the way it structures how 'diversity' is understood and addressed (Newsinger and Eikhof 2019).

Issues of and demands for representation have become increasingly central to the commentary and debate on pop culture texts in recent years – something that we see very clearly in the press reception of the *Fast Saga* films (Blay 2016; Chang 2017). Often, these conversations make reference to the phrase 'representation matters', which has come to symbolize the current moment of increased awareness of ongoing and historical deficits in the visibility of certain groups in the media. Here, calls for a wider diversity of representations stem from an understanding that seeing someone who looks like you in popular media can have powerful and affirming effects. For example, an implicit (and sometimes explicit) assumption of much of the discussion surrounding Hollywood representation is that demographic visibility levels should be in line with the general US population – that is, Hollywood films should 'look like' the wider country in racial/ethnic terms (Gray 2016).

Critical media scholars have expressed scepticism regarding a 'cultural politics of diversity [which] seeks recognition and visibility as the end itself' (Gray 2013: 772). For example, Herman Gray (2013, 2016) and Sarah Banet-Weiser (2007) have both raised concerns over how the focus on representation-as-visibility has enabled the neoliberal entertainment industries to simultaneously increase the levels of visible presence of people of colour in the media while limiting the terms of diversity talk to individualistic definitions of race as a marketable visual identity category. These perspectives caution that representation-as-visibility is insufficient for addressing the entrenched racism within representational systems, as it discursively constructs diversity in such a depoliticized way that 'racial neoliberalism willingly concedes, even celebrates difference' (Gray 2013: 780). Indeed, they ask us to think about how strategies such as quantitative diversity standards allow productions to 'adopt practices which in turn permit the achievement of *certain forms of diversity* within a film's production whilst racial inequality and underrepresentation remain undiminished' (Nwonka 2020, emphasis added).

Kristen Warner (2017) develops a similar critique in her work on popular film and television. She explores how the proliferation and dominance of a visibility-based perspective helps to produce 'plastic representation': 'a combination of synthetic elements put together and shaped to look like meaningful imagery, but which can only approximate depth and substance'. For Warner, this 'plasticity' is the inevitable consequence of reducing demands for diversity to 'quantifiable difference alone'. Indeed, one of the limitations of benchmarks based on racial prevalence models is that they can be satisfied through tokenism, whereby the addition of a handful of non-white characters may significantly impact the data even if their narrative contribution is minimal. Warner's account serves as another reminder that quantitative approaches must go beyond racial head counting, employing measures which are better able to uncover deeper textual dynamics and more of the complexity of a character's portrayal.

What these critiques ultimately highlight is that having the tools to quantify and audit differences in demographic visibility is important and necessary, but it is not in itself a safeguard against the deeply entrenched racism and hierarchies which operate within popular cinema (Newsinger and Eikhof 2019). As such, we must be wary of those discourses which imply that proportionality, or stratified visibility, is the end goal of representational struggles, carefully considering the link between how we think about 'diversity' and how we ultimately audit it. These considerations are central to our analysis of *Fast & Furious*. Given the tendency for current 'diversity talk' to emphasize visibility at the expense of dimensionality, it's not enough to merely analyse levels of non-white representation in the *Fast Saga* films – we must explore the *types* of representation, too. In other words, if these films stand out in the contemporary blockbuster landscape, do they only do so in 'plastic' terms? Or is there a more substantial representational politics underpinning their multicultural aesthetic, one which transcends the post-racial, pro-white logics identified in the scholarly critique?

## Methods and data

To determine whether *Fast & Furious* surpasses the empirical benchmarks established above, we conducted a content analysis of the first eight *Fast Saga* films. Here, we created a codebook with a number of demographic variables to record for each named speaking character in the films, allowing us to compare the representational landscape of *Fast & Furious* against the trends identified in the Annenberg and HDR data.[2] For each character, we recorded the following information: *gender* (Male/Female/Non-binary); *race/ethnicity* (following HDR, we used the categories Black, White, Latinx, Asian/Asian American, Middle Eastern/North African, Native, Multi and Other/Unknown); and *age* (of the actor on the date of the film's release). For the purpose of this analysis, we focus only on the results related to the race/ethnicity variable.

However, while this headcount data provides valuable insights into demographic visibility, it is limited in its capacity to reveal deeper patterns of narrative involvement. Raphael Leung and Bartolomeo Meletti (2021) explore these limitations as part of their development of a '3Ps' framework for measuring on-screen representation, where they distinguish between three 'different aspects of diversity': 'Presence' (i.e., whether someone appears on screen), 'Prominence' (i.e., the amount of 'screen time' a character has and how foregrounded they are within the narrative) and 'Portrayal' (i.e., the nature of a character's depiction, including what 'narratives and stereotypes' it may reproduce or subvert). Reviewing dominant trends in auditing representation, Leung and Meletti note that much of the current data focuses on the former aspect, 'presence', with far less attention paid to 'prominence' and 'portrayal'. This intervention is crucial because it helps to identify some of the gaps in existing quantitative approaches, and how we can begin to address them by utilizing more than just prevalence-based metrics.

Drawing on the '3Ps' framework, we expanded our content analysis for the purpose of capturing some richer information about characters' narrative activity over the course of each film. Thus, in addition to the named speaking characters, we also recorded each line of dialogue in the films, including the sender, receiver(s) and sequence of the character interactions, as per the method outlined by Jones (2020: 22). This meant that we added two further character-level variables to the demographic variables listed above: *number of lines spoken* and *number of times spoken to* (for each film). In total, this produced data on 4,827 lines of dialogue between 107 distinct characters over the course of the eight films.

These character interactions can also be aggregated into 'dialogue networks' which allow us to do more than count the mere fact of a character's *presence* (or visibility) in a film; we can also measure how much that character contributed vocally and track who they spoke to during the film (Jones 2020). The value of looking at dialogue is that it provides a stronger measure of the depth and centrality of characters from different demographic groups, meaning we can evaluate their narrative *prominence* as part of our investigation into the *Fast Saga*'s racial politics. Importantly, as we will explore later in the chapter, prominent characters can still be depicted in stereotypical and regressive ways, and so we complement these data with textual reading to better capture the *portrayal* of characters in the films. When combined, these methods constitute the type of critical quantitative approach that is able to extend our discussion of *Fast & Furious* beyond a basic account of the franchise's visible diversity.

## Visibility and vocality in the *Fast Saga*

Several findings from these data help us to understand how the *Fast Saga* compares with wider industry benchmarks. Figures 4.4 and 4.5 show the proportions of characters and lines spoken in each film respectively, broken down by race/ethnicity. These data reveal that white characters account for fewer than 50 per cent of named speaking characters in all eight films, a significantly lower prevalence level than is typical in mainstream Hollywood cinema. This fact, coupled with the broad range of different racial/ethnic classifications among its speaking characters, suggests that *Fast & Furious* is ahead of the pack when it comes to the kind of visible diversity that's routinely privileged in critical discussions around on-screen representation. What's more, the large number of non-white characters in these films render them somewhat exceptional within a landscape of Hollywood Action/Adventure blockbusters that continues to exhibit a clear and persistent white dominance in front of the camera: as noted,

Race and Representation in the Fast Saga    83

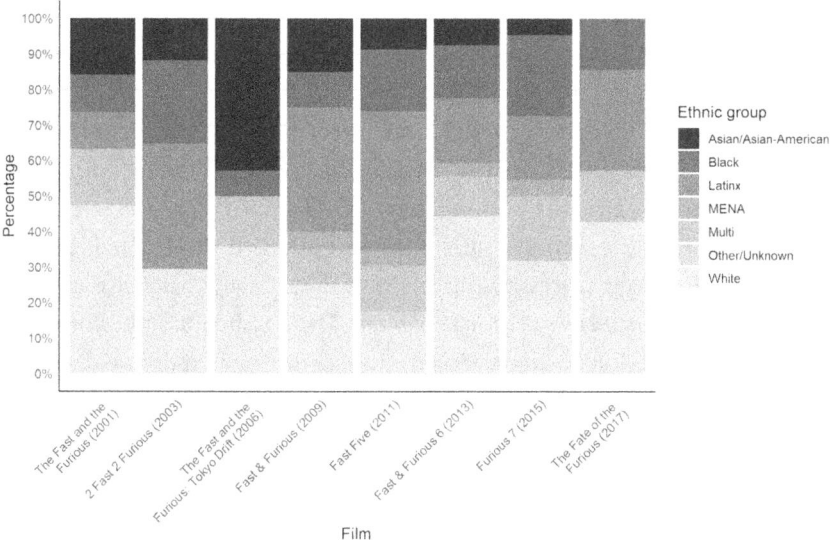

**Figure 4.4** Proportion of speaking characters by ethnic group.

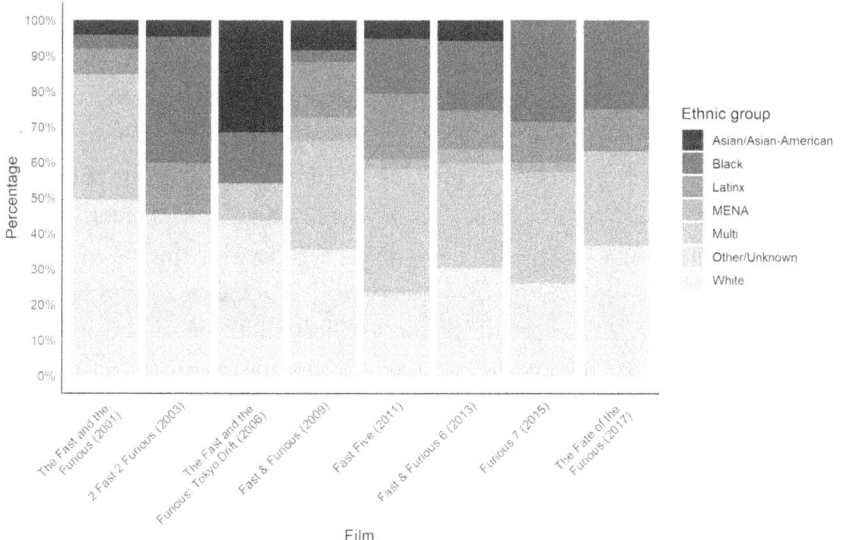

**Figure 4.5** Proportion of lines of dialogue spoken by ethnic group.

the genre as a whole averaged between 20 and 30 per cent non-white visibility from 2007 to 2017; in that same period, the *Fast Saga* films consistently operated above 50 per cent.

From the initial content analysis, it's easy to see why *Fast & Furious* has been lauded for its diversity, with the data showing that the eight films far outpace the visibility-based benchmarks for mainstream Hollywood cinema by featuring a 'majority minority' cast throughout. Interestingly, though, the data in Figure 4.4 also point to a slight regression in this regard, especially when we examine them from the perspective of white visibility. The number of white characters as a proportion of all named speaking characters decreases substantially across the first five films and reaches its lowest point with *Fast Five* (2011), where the ratio of white to non-white characters stands at around 1-to-7. After that low point, however, this figure increases, so that films 6–8 contain a notably higher proportion of white speaking characters than *Fast Five*: the ratio of white to non-white characters here is more than 1-to-2. This shows that the visibility of white characters within the franchise actually increased in the period between films 5 and 8, a shift we consider below.

Looking at the distribution of lines spoken in the eight films (Figure 4.5) helps to uncover further interesting patterns, which offer an insight into the prominence, rather than just the presence, of specific racial/ethnic groups. Overall, the trend is similar to that identified in the initial content analysis: white characters never speak a majority of the lines, and the proportion falls consistently through the first five films before ticking up again in films 6–8. However, this uptick is much less pronounced when considered from the perspective of vocal activity, with non-white characters continuing to deliver over 60 per cent of the lines in these films despite the increased prevalence of white characters. What the data in Figure 4.5 illustrate therefore is that *Fast & Furious* does not just *look* diverse; it *sounds* diverse, too. Here, we can see how the *Fast Saga* consistently centres non-white voices, with non-white characters from various racial/ethnic groups speaking a majority of the lines in each of the eight films. These findings are significant because they point to one of the ways in which the franchise moves beyond representation-as-visibility, investing its non-white characters with a level of 'vocal empowerment' that's not always evident in popular films labelled as 'diverse' (Jones 2020; O'Meara 2016).

However, the data in Figure 4.5 also highlight important disparities. Although *Fast & Furious* can be said to privilege *non-white voices* overall, there are considerable discrepancies between the vocal activity of the different groups within this category. For example, the dialogue data illustrates that while there is a generally high level of visible representation for Latinx characters, much higher than the industry average, the number of lines spoken by these characters is relatively few and declines slightly over the course of films 4–8. This suggests that even though Latinx characters contribute strongly to the multicultural look of the franchise, few are given roles which drive the narrative action. Conversely, Black characters demonstrate a level of vocal activity that is commensurate with and at times exceeds their visibility. By comparing the data in Figures 4.4 and 4.5, therefore, it's apparent that the relationship between these visibility and vocality metrics varies by group, and that Latinx characters in particular experience a representational deficit when it comes to their number of spoken lines.

Of the non-white groups, multiracial characters are by far the most vocally active. Their share of the dialogue across the *Fast Saga* is vast, second only to that of the white characters: in all but two of the films, multiracial characters deliver between 26–36 per cent of the lines, even though they make up a relatively small proportion of the speaking characters. Within this group, it's Vin Diesel's Dom, the legendary street racer, who is the most consistently prominent figure. Appearing in all but one of the films, Dom is the *Fast Saga*'s protagonist, the alpha male the other characters look to and follow. Indeed, the drop in multiracial dialogue that occurs with films 2 and 3 is directly related to his absence, a result of actor Diesel's brief hiatus to pursue other projects.

This high level of vocal activity corresponds with previous scholarship about the privileged position of multiracial characters in the franchise. In her analysis of the first film, Beltrán (2005) situates it within a cycle of post-millennium Hollywood action movies that root their narratives in multicultural urban environments and regularly feature multiracial actors as protagonists. For Beltrán (2005: 59), these 'multiculti action films' embody contradictory racial impulses. On one level, they articulate a 'utopic multiculturalism', wherein the actions of non-white heroes help to promote the idea that 'speed rules, rather than the colour of one's skin'. At the same time, though, films like *The Fast and the Furious* serve to uphold 'notions of natural white superiority' by foregrounding white and light-skinned multiracial characters at the expense of 'darker ethnic bodies' within the diegesis. Central here is Dom's 'ethnic ambiguity' (Ibid: 59–63). Played by Diesel, a mixed-race actor whose heritage has been the subject of intense speculation, Dom is unplaceable: 'a racial blank slate onto which any identity can be applied' (Carter 2008: 210). Indeed, Beltrán (2005: 54–63) argues that Diesel's hero exemplifies a type of 'racelessness' that is prized within the multiculti action film, one which allows him to traverse 'cultural borders' with a degree of ease that's rarely afforded to darker-skinned characters. This combination of mobility and 'cultural competence' places Dom at the top of the 'new, culturally pluralistic society' depicted in these films; and, for Beltrán, it instils him with a 'symbolic whiteness' (Ibid).

Beltrán's arguments offer a useful counterbalance to the representational hype that surrounds *Fast & Furious*, highlighting key tensions in the way the franchise combines visible difference with raceless protagonism. Such tensions are crucial here because they complicate any attempt to categorize characters for the purposes of quantifying racial/ethnic diversity. The Hollywood Diversity Report (HDR), one of the most influential audits of representation in the US film industry, divides characters into the following groups – Asian, Black, Latinx, MENA, Multi, Native and white (Hunt and Ramón 2020). To enable direct comparison, we adopted similar groups in our own content analysis. As part of this process, Dom and his sister, Mia (Jordana Brewster), were included in the Multi category, alongside Dwayne Johnson's Luke Hobbs. However, the type of 'racelessness' that Beltrán discusses – and which is so clearly exemplified by someone like Dom – proves particularly difficult to capture within these groupings.

The Torettos – siblings whose surname hints at Italian heritage but whose depiction evokes a broad range of ethnic identities – illustrate the difficulties of categorizing characters according to race/ethnicity. For example, several aspects of Dom and Mia's characterization could lead them to be included within the Latinx group. Raised in the majority-Latinx neighbourhood of Echo Park, L.A., the pair demonstrates strong links to and affinities for Latin American culture, with the later films confirming that they not only speak fluent Spanish but also have Cuban relatives (Beltrán 2013). At the same time, Dom and Mia manifest their mixedness in very different ways, owing largely to the public personas of the actors who play them. Although Diesel and Brewster are both light-skinned multiracial actors, the former is much more clearly identified as such in the press, where he's described as an 'ethnic mutt' with a mix of African American, Italian and other unknown ancestry (Gleiberman 2017; see Carter 2008). The kind of diversity data generated by the demographic-based auditing strategy of representation-as-visibility is not always suited to capturing such nuances and needs to be complemented with a more critical approach to analysing race. Indeed, by assigning Dom and Mia to the Multi group, without also delving deeply into their on-screen portrayal, we risk losing some of the complexity of the *Fast Saga* and its emphasis on racelessness.

This difficulty is compounded by the casting of white actor John Cena as Jakob Toretto, Dom and Mia's estranged brother, in *F9* (2021). Played by Cena, Jakob's introduction consolidates the idea that Dom (and Mia) inhabits a 'bronzer whiteness'—something that is indirectly acknowledged in the film when one of the characters points to Jakob as evidence of an unexpected 'Nordic strain' within the Toretto 'bloodline'. These character additions and plot twists show how racial identity in the *Fast Saga* is fluid and elusive, with several protagonists embodying a particularly acute form of 'ethnic indeterminacy' (Purse 2011: 124). This makes *Fast & Furious* a fascinating but challenging case study for exploring questions of racial/ethnic diversity in Hollywood. In the next section, we look more intricately at who speaks in the *Fast Saga* and what this reveals about the films' racial politics.

## Character interactions in the *Fast Saga*

Visualizing the character interaction data as dialogue networks provides a further insight into the relationships between characters from different racial/ethnic groups and how these change over the franchise's history. In these network diagrams (Figures 4.6–4.13), the arrows between character nodes show the direction of the dialogue, with darker arrows indicating more interaction over the course of the film than lighter ones. Nodes are sized proportionally to the total number of lines spoken by that character in the film, and only characters who speak more than one line are included. Overall, these dialogue networks offer a more in-depth account of the racial dynamics, allowing us to distinguish between individual characters and make comparisons based on their relative centrality to the narrative (Jones 2020).

These diagrams illustrate that the first, second, and fourth films share the same interracial buddy structure (Figures 4.6, 4.7 and 4.9, respectively). In each of these films, white cop Brian (Paul Walker) is paired with a non-white male ally. In films 1 and 4, this role is occupied by Dom, the multiracial mechanic who initiates Brian into the world of illegal street racing. In the second film, Black actor Tyrese Gibson steps into the void left by Diesel's hiatus, playing a childhood friend of Brian, Roman Pearce. The narratives are also similar with Brian going undercover in all three films to solve a crime. Over the course of his investigations, Brian encounters two highly racialized sites of power: the predominantly white world of the police/authorities, and a criminal underworld populated primarily by people of colour.

88    Full-Throttle Franchise

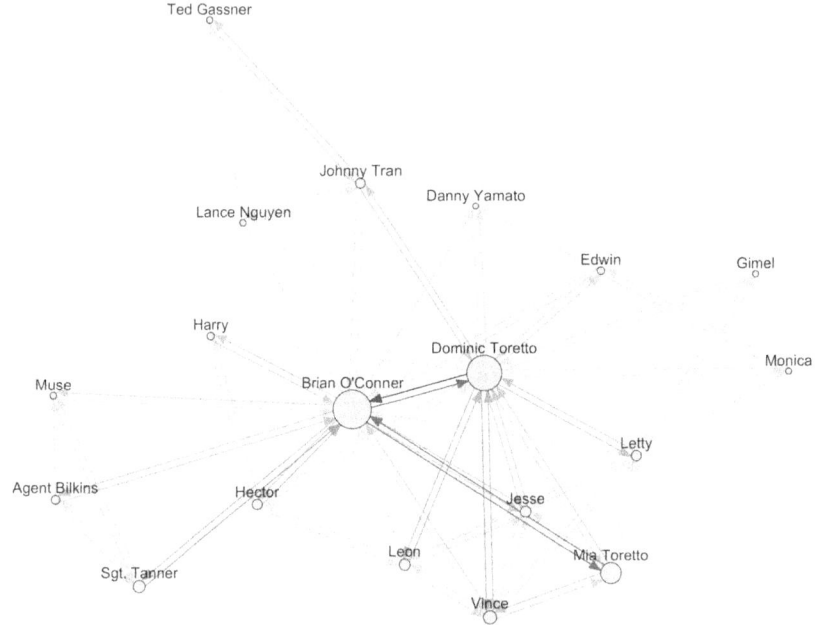

**Figure 4.6** *The Fast and the Furious* (2001 Universal), dialogue network.

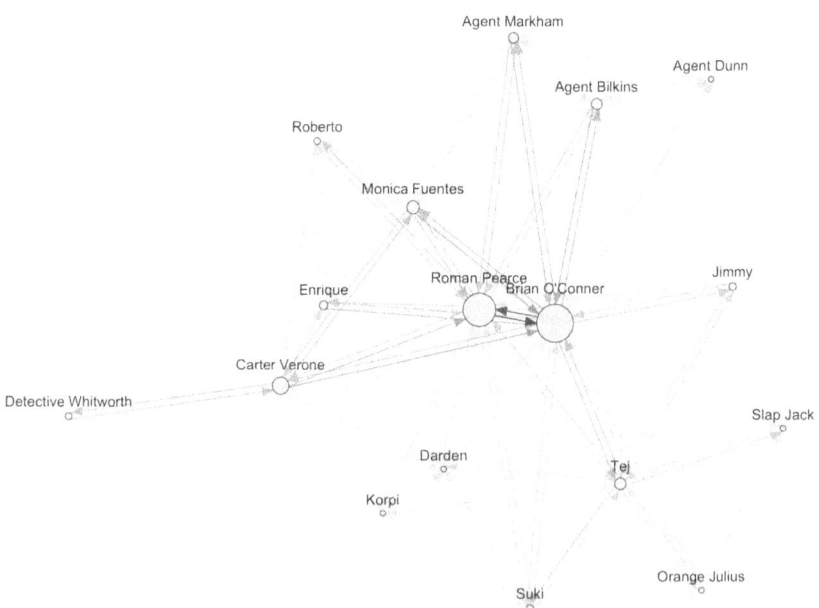

**Figure 4.7** *2 Fast 2 Furious* (2003 Universal), dialogue network.

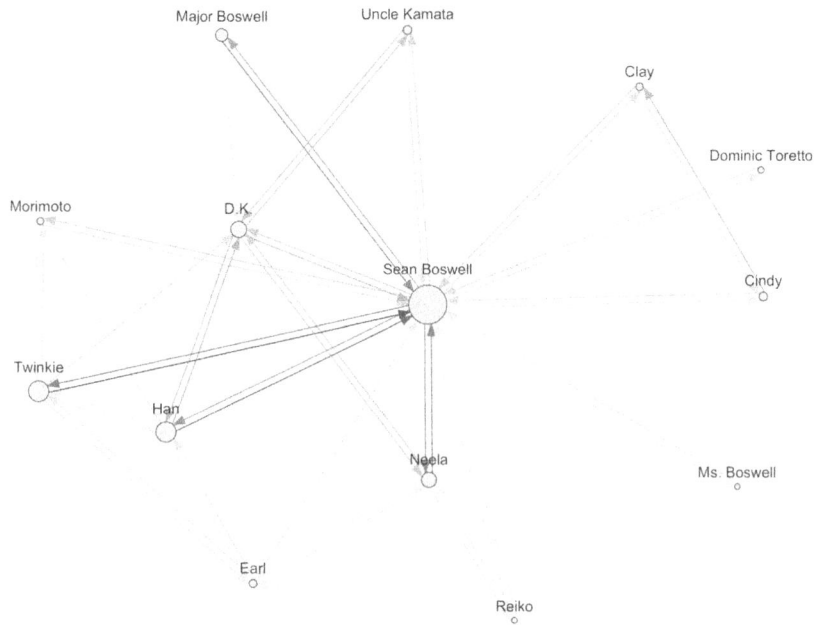

**Figure 4.8** *The Fast and the Furious: Tokyo Drift* (2006 Universal), dialogue network.

Looking closely at the diagrams, the networks for films 1, 2 and 4 confirm an underlying emphasis on white protagonism and mastery. Indeed, Brian's centrality is evident here not just in the size and positioning of his nodes, but also the arrows emanating out from them, which branch off in multiple directions. These ties show how he moves seamlessly between his life as a cop and the criminal underworld that becomes his new home, engaging in the type of 'border crossing' which, according to Beltrán (2005: 50), is a prized skill in the multiculti action film. Except for Roman, someone we discuss below, it's the white and light-skinned multiracial male characters (i.e., Brian and Dom) who are most prominent and active within these three films.

In the third film, *Tokyo Drift* (2006), a different narrative character structure is used (Figure 4.8). Here, the fact that the film takes place in and around a Tokyo high school serves to move it away from the interracial buddy structure and a focus on tensions with the police/authorities. Instead, *Tokyo Drift* presents a more contained narrative, one in which white teenager Sean (Lucas Black) – a recent emigrant from suburban America – struggles to find his place within cosmopolitan Tokyo. However, while Sean is very clearly the sole protagonist

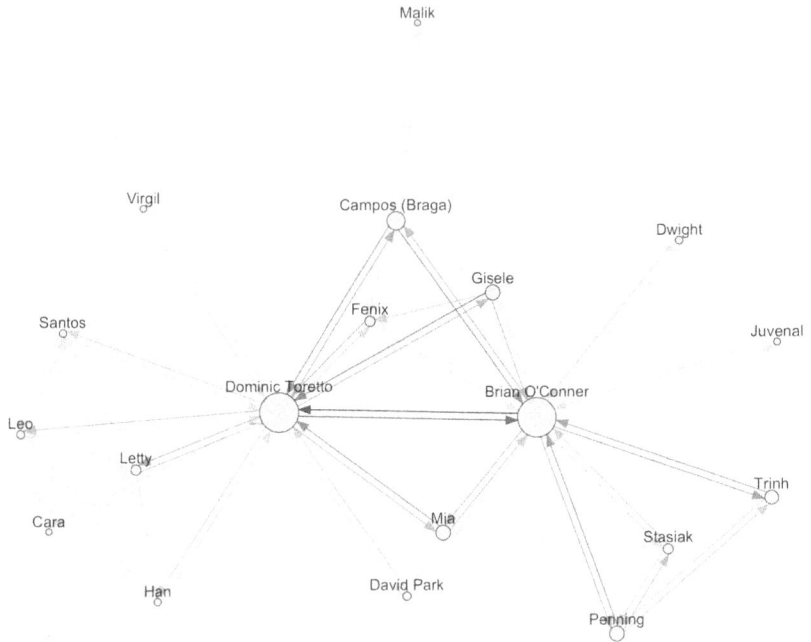

**Figure 4.9** *Fast & Furious* (2009 Universal), dialogue network.

(as indicated by the size of his node), non-white characters still have prominent speaking roles, including Sung Kang's Han, a Korean American criminal who works for the Yakuza, and Twinkie, the Black high school student played by Bow Wow.

In the network diagrams for films 5–8, we see another pattern emerge (Figures 4.10–4.13). The narrative character structure becomes more homogenized across these films as the franchise hits on and consolidates its signature '*Fast family*' formula. This formula is marked by a tight ensemble structure, whereby secondary characters from the first four films are reunited with Brian and Dom to form the central cast (the 'family'). Significantly, none of these characters – Han, Roman, Tej (Chris 'Ludacris' Bridges), Leo (Tego Calderón), Santos (Don Omar) and Gisele (Gal Gadot) – are white, creating a genuinely racially diverse ensemble at the core of the franchise. Here, individuals from Black, Latinx, MENA and Asian/Asian American backgrounds are given prominent speaking roles, as indicated by the size of their respective nodes and their location within the main hub of activity in the centre of the networks.

Race and Representation in the Fast Saga 91

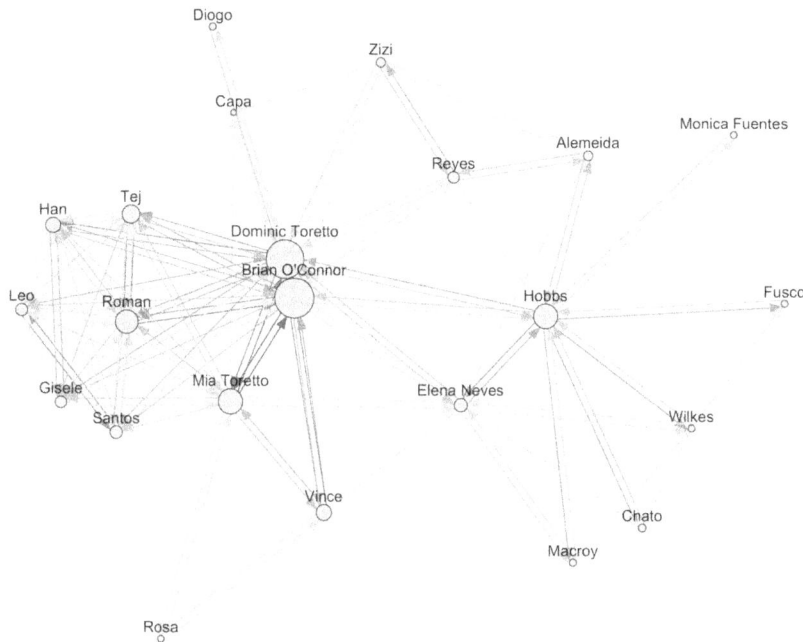

**Figure 4.10** *Fast Five* (2011 Universal), dialogue network.

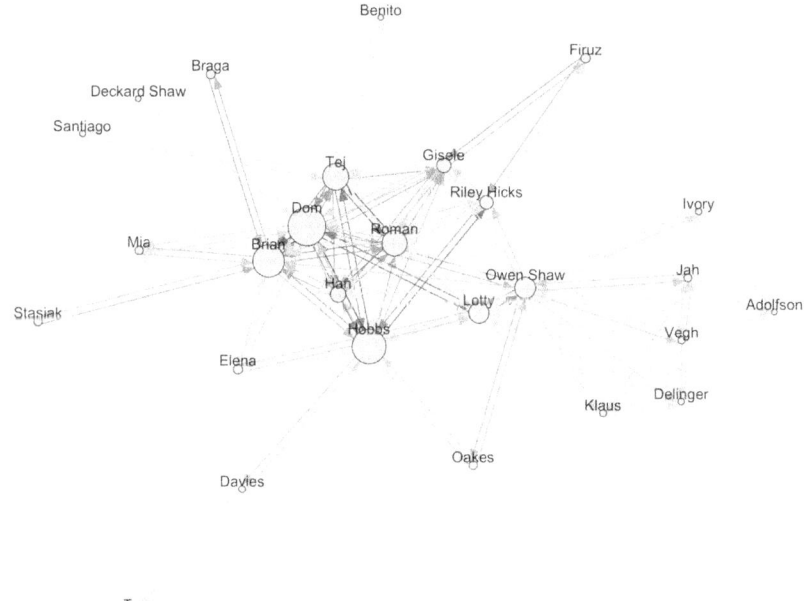

**Figure 4.11** *Fast & Furious 6* (2013 Universal), dialogue network.

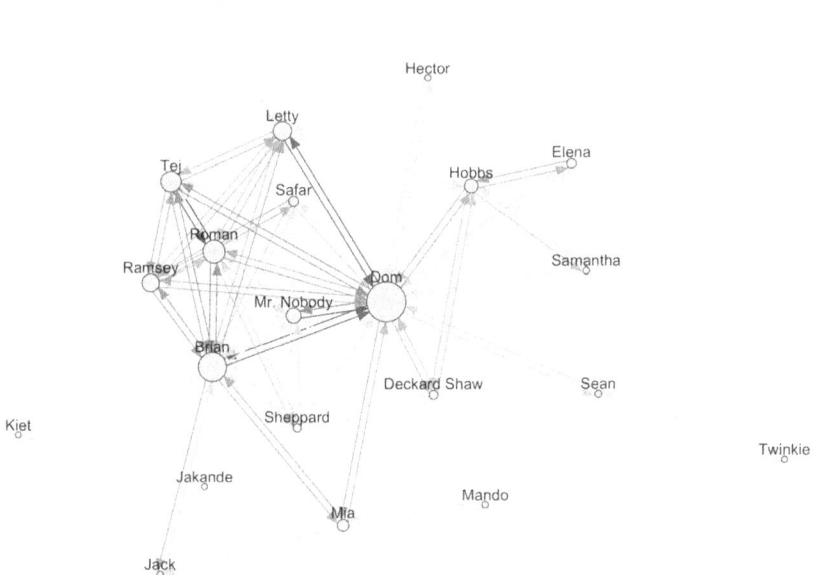

**Figure 4.12** *Furious 7* (2015 Universal), dialogue network.

This is also the point at which multiracial action star Dwayne Johnson joins the cast as Hobbs, a US federal agent who first appears as an antagonist in *Fast Five*, before teaming up with Dom and the others in films 6–8. In *Fast Five*, Hobbs's interactions concentrate on Dom and Brian, as well as his own team of agents – a team that contains a majority of non-white characters, differentiating it from the predominantly white hubs of institutional power in the earlier films. Starting with *Fast & Furious 6* (2013), however, Hobbs assumes a central role, interacting more and more extensively with the core ensemble as he becomes one of the most prominent figures in the franchise (culminating in his co-starring role in the 2019 spinoff, *Fast & Furious Presents: Hobbs & Shaw*). The introduction and development of Johnson's character is significant because it bolsters the multiracial protagonism that has been a consistent feature of *Fast & Furious* since the first film; and that Beltrán (2005) pinpoints as crucial to the franchise's emphasis on racelessness. In the final section, we consider these findings in more detail and what they can (and cannot) tell us about racial representation in the *Fast Saga*.

Race and Representation in the Fast Saga    93

**Figure 4.13** *The Fate of the Furious* (2017 Universal), dialogue network.

## Discussion: *Fast & Furious* Presents …?

The network diagrams offer an interesting account of on-screen representation across the eight films. Combined with the content analysis, they help to show the broad range of non-white groups that are included among the protagonists and secondary characters. Yet, the data in the previous sections also raise important questions about how different racial/ethnic groups are portrayed and the extent to which their presence within the films equates to something more than representation-as-visibility. Thus, for the remainder of the chapter, we complement our earlier findings with a closer look at textual and extratextual themes and patterns, drawing out some of the contradictions and discrepancies within the franchise's ostensible diversity.

As noted, one of the most interesting patterns is how white visibility actually increases in the later films. Several developments suggest that since *Fast Five*, the franchise has adopted a more racially conservative approach to casting, tending to recruit big-name white actors as a way to augment its core ensemble. In *Fast & Furious 6*, the white Shaw family is introduced through Luke Evans's villain Owen Shaw, a former British SAS soldier who plans to disable the world's power. Although Owen Shaw is defeated over the course of the film, his brother, Deckard (Jason Statham), becomes a key figure within the franchise, operating as the primary antagonist of *Furious 7*, before joining the family in *Fast Eight*. Like Hobbs, then, Deckard transitions from villain to hero, a turnaround that's explored further in *Hobbs & Shaw*. *Fast Eight* also marks the first appearance of Deckard and Owen's mother, Magdalene (Helen Mirren), while their sister, Hattie (Vanessa Kirby), plays a prominent role in the spinoff film. In addition to the Shaws, several other white recurring characters enter the franchise after *Fast Five*, including Kurt Russell's Mr Nobody and Charlize Theron's Cipher. The only non-white recurring character introduced in films 6–8 is Ramsey, a hacker-turned-spy played by Nathalie Emmanuel. Collectively, these casting moves (re-)establish a strong white presence at the centre of the franchise, one that has persisted despite the elision of the Brian character following Paul Walker's death between films 6 and 7.

The dialogue data show that this growing emphasis on whiteness has not necessarily displaced the franchise's commitment to narratives built around a racially diverse ensemble. Nevertheless, the timing of this increase merits attention. That so many white recurring characters were added in the period between films 5 and 8 is significant because this is when *Fast & Furious* established its status as one of Hollywood's biggest cinematic properties. *Fast Five* was the first film in the franchise to top $500 million at the worldwide box office, earning $620 million off a production budget of $125 million; and films 6–8 built on this commercial success with ticket sales of $780 million, $1.5 billion and $1.2 billion, respectively. In comparison, films 1–4 earned considerably less at the box office, grossing an average of $240 million per film, and cost far less to make: the first film was produced for a sixth of the budget of *Fast Eight*, for example. This is to say that *Fast & Furious* took a much more circuitous route to the blockbuster A-list than its closest competitors. Indeed, it was not until *Fast Five*, following the return of several original cast members and Johnson's addition, that *Fast & Furious* instigated the family/ensemble structure which has become so pivotal to its brand.

This rapid growth may help to explain two things: firstly, how *Fast & Furious* came to find itself so far ahead of wider representational trends within mainstream Hollywood cinema; and, secondly, why its proportion of non-white characters has reverted closer to the mean in recent years. Starting as a mid-budget film series about street racing, *Fast & Furious* evolved under very different conditions from those other properties which have defined the overdetermined 'franchise era' (Fritz 2018: xv). In contrast to the likes of the Marvel Cinematic Universe, for example, the *Fast Saga* was visibly and vocally diverse from the outset: here, the comparatively low production budgets of the early films helped to facilitate the casting of little-known, non-white actors in prominent roles, as the producers sought to target an increasingly diverse segment of the domestic youth audience (Beltrán 2005). However, since breaking into the top tier of Hollywood franchises, *Fast & Furious* appears to have partly moved away from this strategy, applying the handbrake to its more racially progressive casting choices now that the films' production budgets regularly exceed $200 million. Framed against Hollywood's broader racial conservatism, recent developments within the *Fast Saga* could be indicative of the continued entrenchment of the long-held industry belief that films centring non-white characters are commercially 'risky', despite evidence suggesting that audiences are just as keen to see these films as those which feature white protagonists (Hunt and Ramón 2020).

Turning to the films themselves, it's worth examining the portrayal of Latinx characters, especially in light of the content analysis data. Findings in the previous section show that the vocal activity of these characters does not match their visibility; and textual analysis confirms that while Latinx people and culture are afforded strong presence within the *Fast Saga*, they rarely play a central narrative role. Latin American culture emerges as an increasingly visible presence in films 4–8, where it's foregrounded through the frequent use of elements including reggaetón music, subtitled Spanish and Portuguese, and settings such as Rio de Janeiro. Developing her critique of *Fast & Furious* in relation to the fourth film, Beltrán (2013: 77–85) argues that these recurring elements fail to displace its underlying white centrism. Indeed, she observes how Latinx signifiers are regularly attached to Dom within the films, in a way that further underscores his racial 'fluidity'. According to Beltrán (2013: 85), then, this type of 'progressive visibility' amounts to little more than a 'Latinization of racelessness', whereby Latin American culture functions 'primarily as spectacle' and Latinx characters 'are circumscribed to roles supporting the more traditional American heroes'.

This pattern of Latinx representation – of high visibility but low narrative centrality – is clearly apparent in the pre-title sequence of *Fast Eight*, which shows Dom honeymooning with Letty (Michelle Rodriguez) in Havana, Cuba. The film opens with a montage of tracking shots through the city and surrounding areas, set to a reggaetón beat. Here, a series of (stereotypical) images – sun-kissed beaches, brightly coloured classic cars and bikini-clad women dancing in cobbled streets – combine to establish an exoticized portrait of Cuba and its people. From this initial montage, the sequence cuts to a conversation between Dom and a local mechanic. Speaking Spanish, Dom intones on the ingenuity of the 'Cuban spirit', urging the mechanic, 'Don't ever lose that'. However, while appearing to champion Cuba's distinctive culture, these scenes clearly privilege the resourcefulness of Americans Dom and Letty over that of their Cuban counterparts. Shortly after that conversation, Diesel's hero beats Raldo (Celestine Cornielle), the fastest driver on the island, in a street race: despite driving the inferior car, Dom finds a way to pip his opponent to the finish line, proving (once again) that what matters most, 'is *who's* behind the wheel'. The sequence ends with Dom and Letty surrounded by cheering locals, before cutting to a final aerial shot of Havana.

Sequences like these lend a Latin American dimension to *Fast & Furious*, even though, as the dialogue networks illustrate, the narratives do not cede much centre-ground to Latinx characters. In this sense, the franchise is indicative of the ambivalent status of Latinx audiences within contemporary Hollywood. As explored by Beltrán (2013), the demographics for Hollywood cinema have changed considerably since the 1990s, with Latinx viewers constituting a growing share both domestically and internationally. These changes have proved particularly key to the commercial success of *Fast & Furious*: 46 per cent of *Fast & Furious's* (2009) opening-weekend audience in the United States were Latinx, while *Fast Eight* recorded Universal's highest-ever opening weekends in multiple Latin American markets including Brazil, Mexico and Argentina (Beltrán 2013; D'Alessandro 2017). Critical media scholars highlight the progressive potential of this turn towards a more diverse and global audience, while also pointing to tensions in the racially conservative strategies pursued by Hollywood. For example, Diana Leon-Boys and Angharad Valdivia (2020: 219–28) argue that studios like Disney favour 'strategic ambiguity' when representing Latinx characters in order to avoid 'alienating their normative white audiences'. Leon-Boys and Valdivia observe how this creates a 'flattened Latinidad', whereby certain tropes and themes are deployed, but in such a way that they are simultaneously 'subsumed or represented as … inconsequential'. Within *Fast & Furious*, this plays out in the way the films embed Latin American signifiers at the surface level, without compromising a deeper narrative commitment to their 'bronzed' American heroes (Beltrán 2005: 60–2). Here, Beltrán's account of 'Latinized racelessness' helps to explain why these films have been so adept at navigating Hollywood's changing demographics: it provides a version of Latinidad that's both specific and ambiguous, and therefore capable of appealing to a wide range of audiences (Beltrán 2013: 89).

In contrast to those in the Latinx group, Black characters speak a relatively high proportion of dialogue across the *Fast Saga*, with their vocal activity often exceeding their visibility. They also become more prominent between films 4–8, so that Black characters are among the most vocally active in *Furious 7* and *Fast Eight*. Within this group, Tej (Chris 'Ludacris' Bridges) and Roman (Tyrese Gibson) are the most consistently prominent figures; and Gibson's character, in particular, warrants analysis as one of the darker-skinned members of the family. To conclude this discussion, therefore, it's useful to look at the portrayal of Roman in the films and where he fits within the racial hierarchy identified by Beltrán and Purse.

Roman is introduced in *2 Fast 2 Furious* as the wisecracking friend of Paul Walker's white hero: an ex-con, he helps Brian apprehend a Miami drug kingpin in exchange for a clean criminal record. Like Dom in the first film, then, Roman occupies the role of non-white ally within the sequel's interracial buddy structure. Yet, there are crucial differences in the way that they each join Brian at the centre of the narrative. Although both characters feature prominently, it's the lighter-skinned Dom who is shown to possess superior skill when it comes to the 'cultural border crossings' that are required of the multiculti action hero (Beltrán 2005: 50). In contrast, Roman's lack of mastery is frequently played up for laughs, with *2 Fast 2 Furious* juxtaposing his hot-headedness against Brian's composure and adaptability.

Roman next appears in *Fast Five* and becomes a prominent member of the ensemble thereafter. The network diagrams show that Gibson's character is among the most vocally active in *Fast Eight*, his number of lines surpassed by only Dom and Hobbs (Figure 4.13). Despite his large share of the dialogue, Roman continues to play a supporting role in these films, functioning mainly as a source of comedy. Across films 5–8, he provides a running commentary on, or punchline to, many of the action sequences, usually expressing consternation at what's required of himself and the team. Here, Roman's panic features as a recurring gag, and it's contrasted with the quiet courage of the other characters. In these instances, a high level of vocal activity does not necessarily equate to narrative agency and empowerment. The opposite may in fact be true: Roman's frequent expressions of fear and disbelief undermine his position within a highly gendered and racialized hierarchy of power, one which rewards the cool-headed machismo of the white and multiracial male protagonists.

Moreover, when Roman does perform a pivotal role in the action, it's often in a way that further emphasizes his racial difference. An example of this is the central heist in *Furious 7*, where the team must infiltrate a penthouse party in Abu Dhabi. At the start of the scene, Roman provides the distraction that allows Dom and Brian to make off with a vital piece of equipment: commandeering the DJ's microphone, he draws the attention of the guards by singing and catcalling female partygoers. Unlike the raceless protagonists, who move seamlessly within this new environment, Roman stands out – his designated role within the heist is to cause a scene and stir up trouble. These actions are consistent with Roman's portrayal across the *Fast Saga*, capturing how he is both a comic aside to the action and sexualized in ways that tap into regressive stereotypes of Black masculinity. The development of Gibson's character illustrates that more is not always better when it comes to on-screen representation. In fact, where regressive portrayals already exist – as with Roman's role as the hot-headed Black sidekick in *2 Fast 2 Furious* – increasing the level of prominence may only serve to amplify the potentially harmful impact of these stereotypes (Collins 2011). This is an important caveat of our dialogue-based approach and illustrates why it is valuable to complement presence-based analysis with both prominence *and* portrayal: prominence tells us how involved characters are in the action, but we also need to look at their portrayal to understand the value of this involvement.

## Conclusion

As the 'multiculturalism' and 'diversity' of *Fast & Furious* become more widely recognized as part of its brand identity, there's a need to engage critically and empirically with the complex nature of racial representation in the franchise. Our findings show that the *Fast Saga* films consistently outperform the empirical benchmarks for non-white visibility in mainstream Hollywood cinema, suggesting much of the representational enthusiasm around *Fast & Furious* is warranted (Blay 2016). Thus, when viewed in terms of the headcount data, *Fast & Furious* emerges as something of a Hollywood trailblazer: a long-running and popular series that embraced diversity from the outset, rather than incorporating it after the fact as so many other big-budget franchises have been seen to do. Indeed, the way the *Fast Saga* films use a 'majority minority' cast throughout, while also consistently centring non-white characters and voices within their narratives, stands out as genuinely exceptional in a blockbuster landscape that still skews overwhelmingly white.

However, our exploration in this chapter highlights two reasons to be cautious, both of which serve as a reminder of why it is important to resist totalizing evaluations of how films 'perform' representationally. Firstly, recent instalments appear to have moved away from the racially progressive casting choices that marked the early years of the franchise, investing more heavily in the introduction and recurrence of central white characters. Therefore, at the very moment when *Fast & Furious* began to consolidate its reputation as a model of diversity, the *Fast Saga* seems to have regressed towards the mean of the broader Hollywood landscape.

Secondly, visibility and vocality in the franchise are broadly compatible with an underlying narrative dynamic which privileges those who are least racially salient. Here, we see that the *Fast Saga* generally centres white and light-skinned multiracial characters, with original protagonists Brian and Dom speaking the largest proportion of dialogue across the eight films. Indeed, ambiguously coded multiracial characters are particularly prominent in *Fast & Furious*. Best exemplified by Diesel's hero, they possess a striking degree of vocal empowerment and narrative centrality, confirming Beltrán's (2013: 77) earlier assessment that the franchise 'embrace[s] an ethos of postracial multiculturalism'. Within this dynamic, those from other non-white groups are typically restricted to supporting roles. Latinx characters experience high visibility but low vocal activity, for example, a discrepancy indicative of the type of 'plastic representation' Warner (2017) cautions against. Black characters, on the other hand, are more prominent within the narratives; however, their portrayal sometimes reproduces problematic stereotypes and may ultimately serve to reinforce the mastery of lighter-skinned heroes like Brian and Dom.

Press reception of the franchise tends to overlook these disparities, championing *Fast & Furious* as 'the glorious standard-bearer for multiplex multiculturalism' (Chang 2017). As noted, this account is not without substance: starting with the first film, each entry in the *Fast Saga* has exceeded the industry average for non-white visibility, a level of consistency that's unmatched among other contemporary Hollywood franchises. Yet, it's important that we analyse these figures from a more critical perspective, one that remains alert to the industry's continued investment in 'nourish[ing] racial hierarchies without calling attention to itself' (Purse 2011: 128, quoting Gabbard 2004). Indeed, the *Fast Saga*'s combination of visible gains with a post-racial representational politics illustrates some of the blind spots and failings within the kind of 'diversity talk' that currently dominates. Yes, *Fast & Furious* is 'diverse' in the prevailing sense of representation-as-visibility, but it also presents some more troublesome patterns that illustrate why a focus on visibility alone is insufficient. At the same time, the films' emphasis on 'racelessness' – by way of their 'ethnically ambiguous' protagonists – highlights the challenges of placing characters into racial/ethnic categories for the purposes of quantification (Beltrán 2005: 50). We must therefore remain vigilant about both the value and the limits of quantification for auditing on-screen representational trends, especially where existing methods fail to register the racial hierarchies and contradictory dynamics that lie beneath the surface of texts like the *Fast Saga* films. Critical approaches to quantitative analysis of representation, as we have demonstrated in this chapter, will be invaluable in capturing this complexity.

## Notes

1  The Hollywood Diversity Report (HDR) selects the top 200 films released each year as ranked by global box office, minus foreign language films. The Annenberg Inclusion Initiative's report analyses the top 100 fictional films ranked by US box office. HDR looks at both lead actors (defined as 'the protagonists around whom a film's narrative revolves') and total cast diversity, and its substantive focus is on questions of proportional representation in the film and television industry as well as the relationship between diversity and the bottom line. Annenberg differs in that its unit of analysis is the speaking character and its substantive focus is more on traditional content analysis questions relating to the prevalence of certain types of characters and the frequency with which they are represented through stereotypes.
2  The codebook and data are available at: https://github.com/pj398/furious-chapter.

## References

Banet-Weiser, S. (2007), 'What's Your Flava? Race and Postfeminism in Media Culture', in T. Tasker and D. Negra (eds), *Interrogating Postfeminism: Gender and the Politics of Popular Culture*, 201–26, Durham, NC: Duke University Press.
Beltrán, M. (2005), 'The New Hollywood Racelessness: Only the Fast, Furious, (and Multiracial) Will Survive', *Cinema Journal*, 44 (2): 50–67.

Beltrán, M. (2013), 'Fast and Bilingual: *Fast & Furious* and the Latinization of Racelessness', *Cinema Journal*, 53 (1): 75–96.

Blay, Z. (2016), '15 Years Ago, *The Fast and The Furious* Proved "Diversity" Works', *HuffPost*, 22 June. Available online: https://www.huffpost.com/entry/15-years-ago-the-fast-and-the-furious-proved-diversity-works_n_57683a21e4b0fbbc8beb3a87 (accessed 23 December 2021).

Carter, G. T. (2008), 'From Blaxploitation to Mixploitation: Mixed-Race, Male Leads and Changing Black Identities', in M. Beltrán and C. Fojas (eds), *Mixed Race Hollywood*, 203–20, New York: NYU Press.

Chang, J. (2017), 'Review: *The Fate of the Furious* is Mostly Spinning Its Wheels', *Los Angeles Times*, 13 April. Available online: https://www.latimes.com/entertainment/movies/la-et-mn-fate-of-the-furious-review-20170413-story.html (accessed 23 December 2021).

Cobb, S. (2019), 'What about the Men? Gender Inequality Data and the Rhetoric of Inclusion in the US and UK Film Industries', *Journal of British Cinema and Television*, 17 (1): 112–35.

Collins, R. L. (2011), 'Content Analysis of Gender Roles in Media: Where Are We Now and Where Should We Go?', *Sex Roles*, 64 (3–4): 290–8.

D'Alessandro, A. (2017), '*Fate of the Furious* Sets Massive $532M Global Opening Record', *Deadline*, 17 April. Available online: https://deadline.com/2017/04/the-fate-of-the-furious-weekend-box-office-opening-vin-diesel-dwayne-johnson-1202069983/ (accessed 23 December 2021).

Foundas, S. (2015), 'SXSW Film Review: *Furious 7*', *Variety*, 17 March. Available online: https://variety.com/2015/film/reviews/sxsw-film-review-furious-7-1201453751/ (accessed 23 December 2021).

Fritz, B. (2018), *The Big Picture: The Fight for the Future of Movies*, New York: Houghton Mifflin Harcourt.

Gabbard, K. (2004), *Black Magic: White Hollywood and African American Culture*, New Brunswick: Rutgers University Press.

Gleiberman, O. (2017), 'How Vin Diesel Became the Frog Prince of Movie Stars', *Variety*, 15 April. Available online: https://variety.com/2017/film/columns/vin-diesel-frog-prince-of-movie-stars-1202031349/ (accessed 23 December 2021).

Gray, H. (2013), 'Subject(Ed) to Recognition', *American Quarterly*, 65 (4): 771–98.

Gray, H. (2016), 'Precarious Diversity: Representation and Demography', in M. Curtin and K. Sanson (eds), *Precarious Creativity: Global Media, Local Labor*, 241–53, Oakland: University of California Press.

Hunt, D. and A. Ramón (2020), 'Hollywood Diversity Report 2020: A Tale of Two Hollywoods', *Hollywood Diversity Report*. Available online: https://socialsciences.ucla.edu/wp-content/uploads/2020/02/UCLA-Hollywood-Diversity-Report-2020-Film-2-6-2020.pdf (accessed 23 December 2021).

Jones, P. (2020), 'Diana in the World of Men: A Character Network Approach to Analysing Gendered Vocal Representation in *Wonder Woman*', *Feminist Media Studies*, 20 (1): 18–34.

Leon-Boys, D. and A. N. Valdivia (2021), 'The Location of US Latinidad: *Stuck in the Middle*, Disney, and the in-between Ethnicity', *Journal of Children and Media*, 15 (2): 218–32.

Leung, R. and M. Meletti (2021), 'Part Two: A Framework for Measuring On-Screen Representation', *Creative Industries Policy & Evidence Centre*. Available online: https://pec.ac.uk/research-reports/part-two-a-framework-for-measuring-on-screen-representation (accessed 22 April 2022).

Newsinger, J. and D. R. Eikhof (2019), 'Explicit and Implicit Diversity Policy in the UK Film and Television Industries', *Journal of British Cinema and Television*, 17 (1): 47–69.

Nwonka, C. J. (2021), 'Diversity and Data: An Ontology of Race and Ethnicity in the British Film Institute's Diversity Standards', *Media, Culture & Society*, 43 (3): 460–479.

O'Meara, J. (2016), 'What "The Bechdel Test" Doesn't Tell Us: Examining Women's Verbal and Vocal (Dis)empowerment in Cinema', *Feminist Media Studies*, 16 (6): 1120–3.

Puig, C. (2015), '*Furious 7* Makes Cars Fly, Pulses Race', *USA Today*, 1 April. Available online: https://www.usatoday.com/story/life/movies/2015/04/01/furious-7-review/70732130/ (accessed 23 December 2021).

Purse, L. (2011), *Contemporary Action Cinema*, Edinburgh: Edinburgh University Press.

Quinn, E. (2020), *A Piece of the Action: Race and Labor in Post-Civil Rights Hollywood*, New York, NY: Columbia University Press.

Saha, A. (2018), *Race and the Cultural Industries*, Cambridge: Polity Press.

Smith, S. L., M. Choueiti and K. Pieper (2020), 'Inequality in 1,300 Popular Films: Examining Portrayals of Gender, Race/ Ethnicity, LGBTQ & Disability from 2007 to 2019', *Annenberg Inclusion Initiative*. Available online: https://assets.uscannenberg.org/docs/aii-inequality_1300_popular_films_09-08-2020.pdf (accessed 23 December 2021).

Warner, K. J. (2017), 'In the Time of Plastic Representation', *Film Quarterly*, 71 (2). Available online: https://filmquarterly.org/2017/12/04/in-the-time-of-plastic-representation/ (accessed 23 December 2021).

5

# Vin Diesel as franchise auteur: Intersectional authorship and the cuddly hardbody in *Los Bandoleros*

CarrieLynn D. Reinhard and Christopher J. Olson

Throughout the *Fast & Furious* franchise, lynchpin figure Dominic 'Dom' Toretto repeatedly uses the importance of family to justify his criminal behaviour. Framing his actions this way allows the franchise to position Dom, his friends and his family as honourable people who nevertheless engage in morally and legally questionable behaviour. This framing proved so effective that producers scrapped the original idea of presenting the series as an anthology focused on street racing narratives, and instead centred it on Dom and his 'family' starting with the fourth movie, *Fast & Furious* (2009; hereinafter *Fast Four*). By focusing on Dom, the franchise provides insight into how the sociocultural construct of masculinity is highly intersectional. As portrayed by Vin Diesel, who has also served as a producer on the franchise since the fourth film, Dom's masculinity is informed by his Christian beliefs, his heterosexuality, his ambiguous racial/ethnic heritage and his political ideology. Dom's tough-yet-sensitive masculinity is thereby tempered by his religious and liberal creed. This chapter examines the 2009 short film *Los Bandoleros*, which was directed and co-written (with T. J. Mancini) by Vin Diesel and thus foregrounds his unique perspective on twenty-first-century masculinity. Focusing on this short film allows us to utilize an 'actor as auteur' or 'star as auteur' approach in reading and analysing Diesel as Toretto.

Film critics writing for the French film journal *Cahiers du Cinéma* originally developed auteur theory as a reading strategy to analyse the filmography of a (usually American) director to understand how specific stylistic choices in cinematography, editing, screenwriting and other cinematic techniques help establish an authorial voice (Sarris 2004). Since then, auteur theory has been used to argue for other artistic contributions to films. A subset of auteurism aligns with celebrity studies to analyse how actors can impact the films in which they appear. Richard Dyer's (1998) work on stars helped develop different types of auteurship, including 'stars as author' to recognize the influence of a movie star on production. The 'actor as auteur' approach has been used to analyse works by directors who appear or star in their own films, including Alfred Hitchcock, Bruce Lee and Spike Lee (Hantke 2016; Palis 2018; Pellerin 2019). It has also been employed by mainstream film critics to argue that celebrities such as Arnold Schwarzenegger influence the films in which they appear (Singer 2015). Diesel exemplifies this latter idea, as his star persona, which involves a cuddlier form of hard-bodied masculinity as originally conceptualized by Susan Jeffords (1994a, 1994b), remains consistent across such violent action-oriented franchises as *Fast & Furious*, *xXx*, *Riddick* and *Bloodshot*.

Given its star-driven nature, the *Fast & Furious* franchise stands apart from other contemporary franchises (e.g., *Harry Potter*, *Star Wars*, the Marvel Cinematic Universe). Indeed, the *Fast & Furious* films recall earlier star-driven action blockbusters such as those featuring international hard-bodied superstars like Schwarzenegger and Sylvester Stallone. Given Diesel's pivotal role in the development of the franchise from the fourth film onwards, it is therefore useful to examine the *Fast & Furious* films in general and *Los Bandoleros* specifically through a star-as-auteur lens, positioning Diesel himself as the series' primary auteur. Indeed, critics have noted that his 'behind-the-scenes shepherding of the franchise has led it down paths most fans never have thought it would go originally' (Ryan 2017). Following Paul Walker's death while shooting the seventh film, Diesel 'carried the franchise' and helped it 'keep moving forward' (Hedash 2020). This chapter argues that, as portrayed by Diesel, Dom's identity reflects a twenty-first-century masculinity that remains stoic and hard-edged, emphasizing actions over words, but adds homosocial and familial bonding and cooperative action as necessary ingredients for material success and true happiness. In other words, Diesel's Dom represents what we term a 'cuddly hardbody' that deviates from more traditional conceptions of hard-bodied American hegemonic masculinity seen in American action films such as *Commando* (1985) or *Rambo III* (1988).

## Diesel as auteur-star

Diesel started acting when, as seven-year-old Mark Vincent, he trespassed in Manhattan's Theater for the New City and an artistic director convinced him to 'try acting instead of acting up' (People 2002). Before landing the starring role in the *Fast & Furious* franchise, Diesel remained relatively unknown, appearing only in his own indie films and in small roles in studio pictures (Zakarin 2015). From the beginning, however, he sought to exert control over the films in which he appeared. After failing to secure acting gigs in New York's theatre and film scene or during his initial attempts to make it in Hollywood, Diesel wrote, directed and starred in *Multi-Facial* (1995), a semi-autobiographical short film that drew on his own experiences as a mixed-race actor (Diesel 2016). The film concerns Diesel's 'problems getting cast because of his ethnic looks' (People 2002). Diesel stars as Mike, a young actor trying to make it in the New York film industry. *Multi-Facial* follows Mike as he attends a series of auditions throughout a single day, each of which he fails to land due to his ambiguous ethnicity. Casting directors dismiss him as too light-skinned, unable to speak Spanish, or not enough of a 'Wesley [Snipes] type'. In the final audition, Mike delivers an impassioned monologue about what led him to want to act. Afterwards, the casting directors express admiration for Mike's performance but admit that they are looking for someone with dreadlocks, which disqualifies Mike since he sports a buzzcut. Following the audition, Mike sits at a diner and listens as a young blonde actress decries not getting cast. She then orders a cup of coffee, asking for it to be 'regular' (i.e., 'not too light or too dark'), causing Mike to smirk in recognition.

Shot in three days for a total of $3,000, *Multi-Facial* employs the rough video and audio quality characteristic of 1990s' Indie cinema. It contains static camera shots, long takes, a shaky handheld camera in sequences shot outside and dialogue heavy with street slang, all of which align with a more realistic approach to filmmaking and thus reaffirm the narrative's autobiographical nature. Even the rap song featured on the soundtrack, 'Middleman', written and performed by Diesel, reflects the actor's own experiences of being multiracial based on how others see him. The song accompanies a montage consisting of close-ups of Mike smiling and contorting his face in frustration, which serves to create a more intimate relationship with the performer and subject matter. This intimacy is reinforced during the film's climax, as Diesel performs his monologue directly to the camera which slowly zooms in on him while he speaks; here, his passion for the craft comes through.

*Multi-Facial* earned critical praise and eventually screened at the Cannes film festival, where Steven Spielberg saw it and decided to cast Diesel in *Saving Private Ryan* (1998) (People 2002). Diesel's decision to produce this film aligns him with Stallone, another muscular actor who launched his own career with *Rocky* (1976), which features a script written by Stallone. According to Diesel, 'It took me 20 years to understand that if I was going to make my dreams a reality, I had to take the reins. I had to learn something about being productive and being … self-sufficient … I had to be productive at all costs and I had to make product' (Adler 2004). Diesel saw *Multi-Facial* as 'an artistic expression' of his own casting struggles that resulted from his racially ambiguous appearance (Ibid). As critic Jason Sondhi (2011) notes, Diesel 'desires to be taken seriously' for his craft and not just his 'impressive musculature' developed during his years as a bouncer. Critic Nick Rogers (2020) similarly argues that the film demonstrates Diesel's sincerity and honesty in considering issues of race and Hollywood, which would go on to shape his career.

Per Tom Hanks, the top-billed star of *Saving Private Ryan*, Diesel's passion was apparent on set: 'He's Vin, hellbent to change the industry in his own image … His single-headed pursuit of what he wanted was there' (Wloszczyna 2002). In fact, appearing in the Oscar-winning film failed to temper Diesel's ambitions and desire for creative control over his career, and in 1995 he launched his own production company, One Race. Under this banner, Diesel served as producer on films he headlined such as *A Man Apart* (2000) and *The Chronicles of Riddick* (2004). Diesel followed *Saving Private Ryan* with a breakout role as the roguish antihero Richard B. Riddick in the cult science fiction film *Pitch Black* (2000), which led to a co-starring role (opposite Paul Walker) in *The Fast and the Furious* (2001). Upon receiving the *Fast Four* script, Diesel met with the production team to improve it (Variety 2015).

Over time, this yearning for creative control led to Diesel assuming a more direct role in producing both the *Fast & Furious* sequels and several of his other Hollywood films. Diesel served as producer or executive producer on *xXx* (2002) and its second sequel *xXx: The Return of Xander Cage* (2017), *The Chronicles of Riddick* and its follow-up *Riddick* (2013), the Valiant Comics adaptation *Bloodshot* (2020), and six of the *Fast & Furious* films. In addition, Diesel served as an executive producer on the tie-in video games *The Chronicles of Riddick: Escape from Butcher Bay* (2004) and *The Chronicles of Riddick: Assault on Dark*

*Athena* (2009), as well as the animated Netflix/DreamWorks Animation series *Fast & Furious: Spy Racers* (2019–21), where he reprises his role of Dom, who now serves as a mentor to his young cousin, Tony. Thus, in addition to exerting creative control over the films in which he appears, he also contributes to the expanded transmedia universes spawned from them.

Additionally, Diesel demonstrates the somewhat common activity of an actor dabbling in directing. As Bert Cardullo (2000: 175) observes, 'most actors have turned to directing in part to protect and enhance their own lustre as performers. As such, their filmmaking styles tend to reflect the persona each projects on screen as an actor.' Yet Diesel stands apart from other actors-turned-directors primarily due to the level of control he exerts over the *Fast & Furious* series; it is rare for an actor or director to steer the creative direction of a multibillion-dollar Hollywood franchise. Diesel therefore represents both a celebrity actor and an actor-director-producer in his relationship to the *Fast & Furious* franchise. Though he received second billing in the original film, remained absent from the second and only appeared in a brief cameo during the ending of the third, Diesel's character became central to the franchise starting with the fourth film.

To understand the various masculinities on display in the *Fast & Furious* franchise we must view it through the framework of Diesel's creative control, as it began with *Multi-Facial*. Since his emergence, Dom is more than just a hard-bodied action hero or an outsider intent on saving the world; his pursuits largely focus on protecting his family through criminal acts. After all, he served as the antagonist in the first film, and only became the antihero over time. This positioning of Dom as antihero appears to reflect Diesel's creative influence on the franchise, as Diesel describes himself as 'being drawn to anti-heroes' (Waldron 2001: 54). Indeed, when considering Dom's masculinity, both the intersectionality of his identity and the hybridity of his masculine persona become clear. Through his acting and directing, most notably in *Los Bandoleros* (2009), Diesel creates and portrays Dom as a family-oriented tough guy of faith who balances hard and soft masculinities.

## *Los Bandoleros* and the recentring of Toretto

While Diesel exerted creative control over the *Fast & Furious* films from the beginning, his return to the franchise led to more producer responsibilities. At that time, 'the studio told Diesel that it had plans to use his [*Tokyo Drift*] appearance as a way to relaunch the Dominic story line,' leading to the fourth film being greenlit (Carroll 2009). In addition to his responsibilities as producer, Diesel also returned to the activity that launched his career by stepping behind the camera to direct *Los Bandoleros*. This short film explains Dom's absence between the first and fourth films, thereby bridging these two entries in the franchise (Perry 2020). Set in the Dominican Republic, *Los Bandoleros* follows Dom's efforts to free street racer Tego Leo (Tego Calderon) from prison and hijack a gasoline shipment. Teaming with associates Han Lue aka Han Seoul-Oh (Sung Kang), Rico Santos (Don Omar) and Cara Mirtha (Mirtha Michelle), Dom successfully frees Leo before rekindling his romance with his old flame Letty Ortiz (Michelle Rodriguez), who tracked him down following the events of the first film.

Thematically, the short focuses on Dom's extended family connections and relationship with Letty (Highfill 2013). Interestingly, it also contains messages about social justice, as Dom seeks to hijack a gasoline tanker and give the fuel to poor citizens who need it, thus positioning the crime as 'a Robin Hood-esque caper' while further solidifying Dom as an honourable thief (Hornshaw 2017). The short film also provides backstory for Dom's connection with the characters of Han, Tego Leo and Santos, bringing all these characters together into a single shared universe (Ibid). However, the film also demonstrates inconsistencies in Dom's character, as it reveals that his love for Letty causes him to leave her. Therefore, the film reinforces the idea that by trying to keep Letty safe, Dom inadvertently caused her death (though subsequent films reveal that she survived the explosion that appeared to kill her) (Lalonde 2018). Yet, as demonstrated in this chapter, these inconsistencies in fact reveal a balancing act between a hegemonic hardbody masculinity and a softer cuddly masculinity by demonstrating how Diesel's Dom embodies contradictory characterizations.

## Balancing hard and soft masculinities

Unlike the other films in the franchise, *Los Bandoleros* eschews the big-budget action spectacle of the feature films for something more realist, personal and directly informed by Diesel's early work on *Multi-Facial* and *Strays* (1997). In addition, the short is particularly interesting as it only features the crime of breaking Leo out of jail. The actual gasoline robbery occurs in a different film entirely, *Fast Four*. As such, *Los Bandoleros* is less about Dom being a hardbody action hero or even a criminal, and more about him being an altruistic anti-hero, a family man and a lover. The film first introduces Dom while he, of course, repairs a car. However, this short film marks the first time he speaks Spanish, demonstrating a fluency due to being biracial. Thus, *Los Bandoleros* immediately reminds audiences of Dom's two defining characteristics: cars and family. The latter trait is reinforced through the multicultural meal Dom shares with Santos' family, now part of Dom's own extended family. This meal is a centrepiece to Dom's characterization and brings to light two more important features: the importance of family and Christianity, as a young boy at the table is chided for not following 'Dom's rules' of offering thanks to God before eating. This boy also calls Dom 'godfather', while Santos later calls him 'The Godfather'. The subtitles specifically indicate each utterance as such, suggesting the two different meanings of 'godfather' related to Catholicism and the mafia.

In her analysis of the Hollywood action heroes of the 1980s, Jeffords (1994a) defined the concept of hard-bodied masculinity. According to Jeffords, in the years following the Vietnam War and Jimmy Carter's presidency, Americans wanted new manly icons and got them in the form of steely, musclebound action heroes such as John Matrix (*Commando*) and Alex Murphy (*Robocop* 1987). Drew Ayers (2008: 42) picks up on this thread when defining the parameters of the 'hardbody genre', arguing that such films and characters drew on several key characteristics: 'a central male hero as the lone protagonist charged with "saving the day"' and whose body was 'fetishized for its hard and sculpted muscularity and/or its athletic skill and physical prowess'. Additionally, such films 'fetishize the weapons, vehicles, and other objects used by the heroes in their quests' (Ibid). Yet the 1980s hard-bodied action hero gave way to the softer New Man action hero of the 1990s; critical observations show that the action films of the 1990s increasingly involved more drama and romance, as action heroes suddenly had families to care for and were thus concerned about family values and fatherhood (Ayers 2008; Jeffords 1994b). Nevertheless, the long-standing popularity of this rather consistent portrayal suggests that the hardbody soon emerged as a type of hegemonic masculinity in the United States, whereby muscularity signifies power (Morrison and Halton 2009).

In many ways, Dom conforms to the ideal of the hard-bodied action hero throughout the *Fast & Furious* franchise. Diesel's Dom is a stoic individual who rarely discusses his past: his main characteristics are that he loves the 'street' and his extended family, but he is also a criminal who has perpetrated numerous acts of assault, robbery, hijacking and, of course, reckless driving (Cheeda 2020). At the same time, Dom deviates from the traditional stoic hard-bodied hero due to his propensity to speak candidly about his emotions. Modern conceptions of stoicism often suggest a combination of physical toughness and emotional frigidity. Yet, while Dom embodies the idea of physical toughness, he frequently uses his few words to speak openly about his past and the importance of family. Indeed, one of Dom's defining characteristics is his almost comically sincere display of emotion, as evidenced by his monologue about his father and his climactic arguments with Brian in the franchise's first film. In contrast to other action heroes such as Rambo or John McLane (*Die Hard* 1988), Dom seems not to have any trouble or concerns about expressing his emotions.

Dom further aligns with the hard-bodied action hero due to Diesel's powerful physique, which makes Dom 'look like one of the strongest people on Earth' (Lalonde 2018). Central to his physicality are his biceps; Dom typically wears a vest or a sleeveless tee shirt, which means that these muscles are almost always on display. *Los Bandoleros* is no exception, as Dom first appears onscreen wearing a sleeveless mechanic shirt and later a black vest. In addition, starting with *Fast Five* (2011), Dom even engages in unrealistic pain endurance as 'he never reacts to any pain that is inflicted on him' (Lalonde 2018). In some ways, his hardbody operates more as a deterrent, whereby his 'strength makes him very menacing to his enemies and makes him someone you shouldn't cross' (Ibid). Dom easily fits in with other hard-bodied action heroes who let their actions speak louder than their words – or, in Dom's case, his car's revving engine speaks as loud, if not louder than his icy glares. While his stoicism likely relates to his need to be calm and level-headed as leader of his crew, he also has a temper and lashes out very quickly in the heat of the moment. Dom is most stoic behind the wheel, living life a quarter mile at a time, but when someone threatens his extended family, he sees red and charges in, full throttle, displaying an emotional undercurrent informing his actions.

Dom also represents a type of criminal masculinity commonly seen in mafia films. Crucially, unlike the other films in the franchise, which emphasize outrageous spectacle and thrilling action, *Los Bandoleros* plays out like a low-budget gangster film, more akin to *The Godfather* (1972) and *City of God* (2002) than contemporary action-adventure blockbusters. Such genre hybridity could explain why Dom's hardbody deviates from previous depictions as it exists in an ensemble and revolves around caring for loved ones. Dom runs his crew similarly to a godfather or mafia boss, drawing on codes seen in mafia films. These codes involve a strict moral approach of loyalty, honour and respect that includes an 'absolute allegiance to family and friendship, individual honour, vision, and social duty' (Fields 2004: 616). Adhering to such codes allows mafia films to create a fantasy of criminals and their underworld, whereby they may exist outside of the law while following their own rules (Ibid). The importance of *la familigia nostra*, 'our family', and the justification of any criminal action as occurring for the family is a common theme in the *Fast & Furious* films featuring Dom. When not committing crimes – sanctioned or otherwise – Dom relaxes and parties with his crew, which operates as an extended family. He presides over communal meals, such as with Santos' family, as the paternal figure at the head of the table leading the rest of the group in giving thanks through prayer. The films provide this background on Dom to explain his crime similarly to other gangsters: doing it for the family.

The short film reinforces this importance of family to Dom as the final act of *Los Bandoleros* veers away from crime to focus on sex and romance, yet in doing so it contradicts the stereotypical criminal or hard-bodied action hero. While the hardbody rarely focuses on romance, or at least sex, carnal prowess is a common hypermasculine trope of heterosexual masculinity, especially in Latino cultures involving machismo (Jeffords 1994a; Lieberman 2009). After finalizing the deal, Dom dances seductively with an unnamed woman before retiring to a couch to sit with his arms around two other women, kissing each on the cheek, as someone approaches. The shot lingers on him to register his surprise upon seeing Letty, who says she easily tracked him down by following 'the odour of skanks'. Rather than act embarrassed or defensive, Dom simply smiles and kisses Letty on the mouth, to which she offers no resistance or further admonition. The film then cuts to Dom driving while holding Letty's hand. At one point, she moves to straddle him in the driver's seat, and Dom demonstrates his automotive mastery by continuing to drive, muscles bulging as he controls the car while also holding her. The short concludes with a montage sequence featuring the following images: Dom and Letty visiting a sun-drenched beach where he gives her a piggyback ride to a secluded cave where they kiss passionately; Dom and Letty canoeing on the water; and Dom holding Letty up in the water and kissing her. These images repeatedly show that Dom is the man in control of both the car and his woman. Yet, interestingly, just before the end, Dom also grants Letty some control, allowing her to tip over the canoe and then steer it as he relaxes. Rather than the hypermasculine machismo of the man dominating the woman, the short ends on an incident that suggests he truly cares for her and trusts her to care for him.

In a way, *Los Bandoleros* softens Dom by demonstrating his feelings for Letty, which complicates his masculinity. In this sequence, *Los Bandoleros* presents Dom and Letty's relationship in a positive light as chaste and pure. Letty occupies the role of the 'good' woman whose arrival leads Dom out of the hedonistic bachelor life into which he descended upon arriving in the Dominican Republic. More importantly, perhaps, Letty emerges within this scene as Dom's equal, in that she manages to shake him out of his bad habits and vices. As such, *Los Bandoleros* appears to repudiate Dom's party lifestyle, which is presented as less worthy than the life that he shares with Letty. Overall, the film suggests that Dom is happier at home working on his cars and spending time with his family and loved ones than he is indulging in casual sex. These shots reinforce the softening of Dom, as he relinquishes the vehicle (albeit a canoe rather than a car) to Letty. Indeed, *Los Bandoleros* shows Letty and Dom on more equal footing than the feature films, where Dom remains unequivocally in charge. Bringing more attention to romance and even gender equality reflects Diesel's own approach to love: 'I love women more than anything … I have four more years, then family' (Wloszczyna 2002). While he was 'notoriously guarded when it comes to his romantic relationships' (Wenn 2022), he is reportedly a 'huge family man' and became a father for the first time at age forty, celebrating the achievement by cutting his newborn child's umbilical cord (Marquina 2015). His family operates centrally in his life, and he has apparently positioned Dom to reflect this aspect of his own personality.

Overall, the emphasis on faithfulness and romance in this sequence appears to reinforce the Christian themes found in the *Fast & Furious* franchise. Throughout the franchise, importance is placed on religious faith. Dom identifies as Christian, to the point that he requires saying grace before every meal. Dom's Christian beliefs appear central to his idea of himself as a family man. Diesel has described Dom as a 'strong caretaker' who preaches 'the importance of putting family first and the world after that. His religious background contributes to his belief that people need to have faith in family and God' (Cheeda 2020). Indeed, this religious faith appears to explain his criminal ways: like the mafia's family values, Dom's paternal approach embraces self-sacrifice as a means of protecting those he loves (Lalonde 2018). While religion is not central to the *Fast & Furious* films, Diesel's Dom helps the franchise develop this sacred subtext to present 'religious storytelling without necessarily appearing "religious"' (Kozlovic 2008a: 56). Both *Los Bandoleros* specifically and Dom more broadly demonstrate Christian, religious elements. For example, starting with *Los Bandoleros* and carrying over into *Fast Four*, Dom's cross necklace plays a much more central role in the narrative. From the fourth film on, the necklace signifies Dom and Letty's relationship as it comes to symbolize the pure, almost devout nature of their love, thereby emphasizing their religiosity.

Through this religious framework, the film positions Dom's actions as a form of racial and economic justice and reveals that his willingness to sacrifice his freedom and life for others represents the ultimate form of masculinity to which a man can aspire. In his role as patriarch, Dom constructs a racially diverse crew as a family because they all hold 'a shared set of deeper values' that allows them to function as 'a group of people who know and love one another' (Stevens 2011). They are bound together in fraternity because they share the same social and cultural values about right and wrong, law and crime. As outsiders, legally and ethnically, they view Dom as 'a gruff but affectionate father to his loyal pack of renegades, providing them with barbecue, protection, and a rough moral code to live by' (Ibid). This extended family concept applies to the Dominicans he lives among in *Los Bandoleros* – not just Santos' family but all the people in the barrios where Dom resides.

Diesel reinforces this narrative throughout the short. *Los Bandoleros* routinely relies on documentary-style shots of 'real' people on the barrio's streets playing music, talking, eating and just generally living their lives. The film presents such stylistic tendencies via a shaky handheld camera, natural lighting and real locations, not unlike the approach Diesel first used in *Multi-Facial*. This neorealist approach is intercut with Leo in jail discussing the vicious cycle of rich white Dominicans locking up darker poor Dominicans and keeping them in their place by encouraging them to engage in infighting through gang warfare. Diesel's editing demonstrates the lived conditions of the poor Dominicans with whom he identifies while providing social commentary on the injustices they face. This overt messaging is unique in the *Fast & Furious* franchise, but it aligns with *Multi-Facial* by referencing the systemic and implicit racism that prevents people of colour from succeeding.

Ultimately, this mixture of hardbody, mafioso and Christianity explains the crime Dom and his crew are prepping in *Los Bandoleros* and perhaps offers insights into the *Fast & Furious* movies to follow. In *Los Bandoleros*, a politician wants the crew to steal an oil tanker to bring fuel to the impoverished Dominicans. While talking to the politician, Dom remains cool and calm throughout, despite smiling and joking with Leo only moments prior. Diesel places himself-as-Dom in shadow, separated from those around him and the noise of the club. During much of the conversation Dom's motivation for taking the gig remains unclear, but his monologue following the conversation reveals his altruism: 'at the end of the day, people are gonna get what they need. You can't move forward without fuel and no one wants to get left behind.' To reinforce the Christian nature of Dom's sacrifice, the politician then explains that he wants the fuel to reach the people. Dom's actions reflect a religious, Christian-inflected notion of justice that is less political than it is moral. Moreover, he does not engage in such action from afar, as an outsider, because he refers to the people as 'mi gente' ('my people'). Dom is the 'Anointed One' not because he has a muscular physique, but because he is willing to sacrifice himself for others. Dom's masculinity, then, centres around being physically, mentally and emotionally strong as needed, yet never forgetting that he needs his relationships with his loved ones to truly succeed in life.

This religious faith, then, helps explain the contradictory or ambiguous nature of Dom's masculinity. Hegemonic secular masculinity is often seen as 'much "harder" than religious masculinity; it is presented as tough, violent, emotionally distant, and fixated on heterosexual conquest' (McDowell 2017: 224). To recruit secular men, some Christian hardcore punks 'express a hybrid construction of manhood that is both aggressive and loving' while also emphasizing 'brotherhood' and 'homosocial unity' to normalize 'the idea that men need to express solidarity with other men' (Ibid: 232). Dom reflects this Christian hardcore punk masculinity, especially regarding his conception of family as based on relationships rather than genetics. His masculinity revolves around a focus on family, the notion of the righteous criminal and a racial and ethnic inflection whereby his faith taps into and contributes to his coding as vaguely Latino (Beltrán 2013). The character's religiosity – a border-crossing Catholicism that values family and is at once Latin American and global – functions as the glue that holds many of these interconnecting elements together. Brotherhood is central to his view of his crew and life and helps explain why he is simultaneously aggressive and emotionally distant yet trusting and loving. *Los Bandoleros* serves as the beginning of a more concerted effort to soften Dom across the franchise more broadly, which relies heavily on this new emphasis on piety and religion.

## Dom as cuddly hardbody

Critics have described Vin Diesel as the 'missing link' between 1980s action heroes and 2000s New Men given his muscular build and his theatre training, allowing him to showcase both physicality and vulnerability (Wloszczyna 2002).

As such, they have dubbed him an 'everylug' for the twenty-first century, recalling 'the young Sylvester Stallone, at once fearsome alpha male and loveable lug' (Stevens 2011). Through his various creative expressions, Diesel draws on his experiences and perspectives to ensure that throughout the *Fast & Furious* franchise the Dom character breaks stereotypes and appears complicated: a multiracial family man with a machismo approach to heteronormativity and physicality who also draws on his faith to reinforce his core values.

The breaking with stereotypes could be due to Diesel's own biracial identity. Diesel's parents were Italian American and African American, and the franchise never truly clarifies Dom's own lineage (Dominican Today 2009). This racial and ethnic ambiguity appears to reflect Diesel's own multiracial identity as seen in *Multi-Facial* and how he repeatedly self-identified as multicultural and multiracial. After *Saving Private Ryan*, Diesel came to see his racial ambiguity as a blessing as it allows him access to roles for different types of races and ethnicities (Waldron 2001). From the beginning, the *Fast & Furious* franchise intentionally featured a diverse cast, helping it appeal to a global audience while following in a cinematic tradition for heist films (Gutiérrez 2015). The franchise, then, creates an 'underlying ethos … of an urban, multicultural, and presumably post-racial world' (Beltrán 2013: 76), which reflects Diesel's own outlook, as seen in the name of his production company, One Race, promoting the idea of humanity as one people (Dominican Today 2009). As critics have noted, due to his own experiences, 'Diesel ensures that the ethnic swirl of the faces in his billion-dollar blockbusters feel like no big deal' (Rogers 2020). Specifically for *Los Bandoleros*, Diesel said he identifies with the multicultural nature of the Dominican Republic and that he grew up with Dominicans in Manhattan, which helped him connect with the subject matter (Dominican Today 2009).[1] Critics, and even his own co-stars, noted that this ambiguity allows Diesel to represent an 'amalgamation of all races' and become an 'everyman' (Dagbovie 2007: 225). As with the labelling of 'everylug', Diesel, and by extension Dom, can thus be read as a 'floating signifier' that allows him to be whatever others want him to be (Ibid: 226). This 'floating signifier' designation, however, does not account for Diesel's auteur status or agency, as he appears to have a specific identity he has constructed with Dom.

Instead, Diesel's construction of Dom suggests a willingness to embrace contradictions. *The Fast and the Furious* portrays Dom as an action hero who balances his hard-bodied masculinity with a softer more emotional masculinity. *Los Bandoleros* furthers this characterization as Dom seeks to defend his extended barrio family from the injustices around them. Yet, rather than act as a 'lone wolf' as Schwarzenegger or Stallone may have done decades ago, Dom embraces his role as the patriarch of a criminal crew that functions more as a family, thus aligning him more with a mafia godfather. Dom embodies the concepts of the 'Man-of-Action', a rugged individual who nevertheless works for a more collective goal and communal good (Holt and Thompson 2004), and the 'lone wolf family man', who seeks to defend his family, however defined, from victimization and oppression (Boyle 2019). Dom exemplifies these concepts due to his efforts to balance his stoicism, powerful muscularity and emotional attachment to his friends and family. Thus, Diesel's Dom conforms to a type of action hero that is simultaneously hard and soft, stoic yet romantic, criminal yet pious, lone wolf yet family man.

At the same time, Dom reflects a Christian approach to masculinity, specifically a Black Christian approach that seeks to challenge and undo masculine stereotypes. This reading, in fact, sees parallels with how Cecile B. DeMille brought his masculinity and religiosity into his films, especially his Biblical epics (Kozlovic 2008b). Through Dom, Diesel appears to be creating a similar presentation of masculinity: a selfless, strong man willing to sacrifice for his extended family to ensure justice thrives in the world. Starting with *Los Bandoleros* and leading into *Fast Four*, Dom goes from being just another gangster antihero to becoming a Messiah-type who guides his multiracial family through a series of righteous quests. Seemingly disparate characterizations co-exist, blurring the boundaries of stereotypes to perhaps reflect the complicated intersectional nature of real people.

## Conclusion

In *Multi-Facial*, Diesel reveals contradictions in the entertainment industry that does not know what it wants and stymies Diesel's (and other people of colour) potential. With his characterization of Dom, Diesel embodies these contradictions as Dom's strength, not his weakness: Dom's ambiguity and multifaceted identity help him succeed. Thus, Dom represents a potentially new hegemonic masculinity: the twenty-first-century ideal man, according to Vin Diesel, is not a stoic loner but a fighter for his family and his faith. The hard-bodied action hero has become the cuddly hardbody: a breadwinning rebel willing to risk life and limb to improve the world while refusing to ignore those he loves for his own prosperity. He is a man of powerful physique and great strength willing to support his family above all else. Dom and his crew would likely be less successful without the character's balanced masculinity, and Diesel's portrayal of this masculinity perhaps adds to the franchise's massive global popularity.

## Note

1   To further solidify his fraternity with Dominicans, Diesel signed an agreement in March of 2021 to build a film studio for his company, One Race Films, in the northern part of the country (Dominican Today 2021).

## References

Adler, S. (2004), 'Vin Diesel of *The Chronicles of Riddick* (Universal) Interview', *UnderGround Online*, 16 June. Available online: https://web.archive.org/web/20040616071451/http://www.ugo.com/channels/filmtv/features/thechroniclesofriddick/vindiesel.asp (accessed 23 April 2022).

Ayers, D. (2008), 'Bodies, Bullets, and Bad Guys: Elements of the Hardbody Film', *Film Criticism*, 32 (3): 41–67.

Beltrán, M. (2013), 'Fast and Bilingual: *Fast & Furious* and the Latinization of Racelessness', *Cinema Journal*, 53 (1): 75–96.

*Bloodshot* (2020), [Film] Dir. David S. F. Wilson, USA: Columbia Pictures.

Boyle, B. (2019), 'Lone Wolf Family Man: Individualism, Collectivism and Masculinities in *American Sniper*(s) and *Lone Survivor*(s)', *European Journal of American Culture*, 38 (2): 117–33.

Cardullo, B. (2000), 'Actor Become-Auteur: The Neorealist Films of Vittorio De Sica', *The Massachusetts Review*, 41 (2): 173–92.

Carroll, L. (2009), 'Vin Diesel Explains His Return to the *Fast & Furious* Universe', *MTV News*, 31 March. Available online: http://www.mtv.com/news/1608216/vin-diesel-explains-his-return-to-the-fast-furious-universe (accessed 23 April 2022).

Cheeda, S. (2020), '*Fast & Furious*: 10 Questions about Dominic Toretto Answered', *Screen Rant*, 1 September. Available online: https://screenrant.com/fast-furious-dominic-toretto-questions-answers (accessed 23 April 2022).

*The Chronicles of Riddick* (2004), [Film] Dir. David Twohy, USA: Universal Pictures.

*The Chronicles of Riddick: Assault on Dark Athena* (2009), PlayStation 3 [Game] Belvue, Washington: Tigon Studios.

*The Chronicles of Riddick: Escape from Butcher Bay* (2004), Xbox [Game], Paris: Vivendi Games.
*City of God* (2002), [Film] Dir. Fernando Meirelles and Kátia Lund, USA: Miramax Films.
*Commando* (1985), [Film] Dir. L. Mark Lester, USA: 20th Century Studios.
Dagbovie, S. (2007), 'Star-light, Star-bright, Star Damn Near White: Mixed-race Superstars', *The Journal of Popular Culture*, 40 (2): 217–37.
*Die Hard* (1988), [Film] Dir. John McTieman, USA: 20th Century Studios.
Diesel, V. (2016), [Instagram] 'As you all know …', 7 December. Available online: https://www.instagram.com/p/BNs-L_XjKyf (accessed 23 April 2022).
Dominican Today (2009), 'Vin Diesel "Adores" Dominicans, Presents *Los Bandoleros*', *Dominican Today*, 30 July. Available online https://web.archive.org/web/20141207155144/http:/www.dominicantoday.com/dr/this-and-that/2009/7/30/32762/Vin-Diesel-adores-Dominicans-presents-Los-Bandoleros (accessed 23 April 2022).
Dominican Today (2021), 'Vin Diesel's Neighbors in the Dominican Republic Are Fed Up with the Actor's Security Guards', *Dominican Today*, 12 April. Available online: https://dominicantoday.com/dr/people/2021/04/12/vin-diesels-neighbors-in-the-dominican-republic-are-fed-up-with-the-actors-security-guards (accessed 23 April 2022).
Dyer, R. (1998), *Stars*, London: Palgrave Macmillan.
Fields, I. (2004), 'Family Values and Feudal Codes: The Social Politics of America's Twenty-First Century Gangster', *The Journal of Popular Culture*, 37 (4): 611–33.
*The Godfather* (1972), [Film] Dir. Francis Ford Coppola, USA: Paramount Pictures Studios.
Gutiérrez, P. (2015), 'Safety in Numbers: The Staggering Success of the 'Ensemble Action Movie', *Screen Education*, 9: 38–45.
Hantke, S. (2016), 'Hitchcock at War: *Shadow or a Doubt*, Wartime Propaganda, and the Director as Star', *Journal of Popular Film and Television*, 44 (3): 159–68.
Hedash, K. (2020), 'Why *Fast & Furious* Franchise Is Now Called the Fast Saga', *Screen Rant*, 28 January. Available online: https://screenrant.com/fast-furious-saga-movies-franchise-name-meaning-change-explained (accessed 23 April 2022).
Highfill, S. (2013), '*Los Bandoleros*: The *Fast and Furious* Film You Haven't Seen', *Entertainment Weekly*, 3 June. Available online: https://ew.com/article/2013/06/03/los-bandoleros-the-fast-and-furious-film (accessed 23 April 2022).
Holt, D. and C. Thompson (2004), 'Man-of-Action Heroes: The Pursuit of Heroic Masculinity in Everyday Consumption', *Journal of Consumer Research*, 31 (2): 425–40.
Hornshaw, P. (2017), '*Los Bandoleros* Is the Vin Diesel-directed *Fast and Furious* Movie You've Probably Never Seen,' *The Wrap*, 13 April. Available online: https://www.thewrap.com/los-bandoleros-vin-diesel-fast-furious (accessed 23 April 2022).

Jeffords, S. (1994a), *Hard Bodies: Hollywood Masculinity in the Reagan Era*, New Brunswick: Rutgers University Press.

Jeffords, S. (1994b), 'Can Masculinity Be Terminated?' in S. Cohan and I. R. Hark (eds), *Screening the Male: Exploring Masculinities in Hollywood Cinema*, 245–64, London: Routledge.

Kozlovic, A. (2008a), 'Christian Education and the Popular Cinema: The Creative Fusion of Film, Faith, and Fun', *MJTM*, 9: 50–71.

Kozlovic, A. (2008b), 'Cecil B. DeMille: Hollywood Macho Man and the Theme of Masculinity within His Biblical (and Other) Cinema', *Journal of Men, Masculinities and Spirituality*, 2 (2): 116–38.

Lalonde, C. (2018), '*Fast and Furious*: 20 Things That Make No Sense about Dom Toretto', *Screen Rant*, 12 November. Available online: https://screenrant.com/fast-furious-dom-toretto-biggest-plot-holes-no-sense (accessed 23 April 2022).

Lieberman, E. (2009), 'Mask and Masculinity: Culture, Modernity, and Gender Identity in the Mexican Lucha Libre Films of El Santo', *Studies in Hispanic Cinemas*, 6 (1): 3–17.

*A Man Apart* (2000), [Film] Dir. F. Gary Gary, USA: New Line Cinema.

Marquina, S. (2015), 'Vin Diesel, Girlfriend Paloma Jimenez Welcome Third Child', *US Weekly*, 16 March. Available online https://www.usmagazine.com/celebrity-news/news/vin-diesel-girlfriend-paloma-jimenez-welcome-third-child-2015163 (accessed 23 April 2022).

McDowell, A. (2017), 'Aggressive and Loving Men: Gender Hegemony in Christian Hardcore Punk', *Gender & Society*, 31 (2): 223–44.

Morrison, T. and M. Halton (2009), 'Buff, Tough, and Rough: Representations of Muscularity in Action Motion Pictures', *The Journal of Men's Studies*, 17 (1): 57–74.

*Multi-Facial* (1995), [Film] Dir. Vin Diesel, USA: One Race Productions.

Palis, E. (2018), 'The Economics and Politics of Auteurism: Spike Lee and *Do the Right Thing*', *Cinema Journal*, 57 (2): 1–21.

People (2002), 'Vin Diesel: From Nightclub Bouncer to Action Hero', *CNN*, 12 August. Available online: http://edition.cnn.com/2002/SHOWBIZ/Movies/08/12/people.cel.diesel/index.html (accessed 23 April 2022).

Pellerin, E. (2019), 'Bruce Lee as Director and the Star as Author', *Global Media and China*, 4 (3): 339–47.

Perry, N. (2020), 'How to Watch the *Fast and Furious* Movies in Order', *Digital Trends*, 6 April. Available online: https://www.digitaltrends.com/movies/how-to-watch-fast-and-furious-movies-in-order (accessed 23 April 2022).

*Pitch Black* (2000), [Film] Dir. David Twohy, USA: Universal Pictures.

*Rambo III* (1988), [Film] Dir. Peter MacDonald, USA: TriStar Pictures.

*Riddick* (2013), [Film] Dir. David Twohy, USA: Universal Pictures.

*Robocop* (1987), [Film] Dir. Paul Verhoeven, USA: Metro-Goldwyn-Mayer.

*Rocky* (1976), [Film] Dir. John Avildsen, USA: United Artists.

Rogers, N. (2020), 'All We Do Is Vin: Top It Off with Diesel', *Midwest Film Journal*, 30 March. Available online: https://midwestfilmjournal.com/2020/03/30/all-we-do-is-vin-top-it-off-with-diesel (accessed 23 April 2022).

Ryan, M. (2017), '*The Fast and the Furious: Tokyo Drift* Was Originally Written to Star Vin Diesel', *UpRoxx*, 11 April. Available online: https://uproxx.com/movies/the-fast-and-the-furious-tokyo-drift (accessed 23 April 2022).

Sarris, A. (2004), 'Notes on the Auteur Theory in 1962', in L. Braudy and M. Cohen (eds), *Film Theory and Criticism*, 561–4, Oxford: Oxford University Press.

*Saving Private Ryan* (1998), [Film] Dir. Steven Spielberg, USA: Paramount Pictures Studios.

Singer, M. (2015), 'Arnold Schwarzenegger Is a Serious Auteur and It's Time Everyone Acknowledged It', *ScreenCrush*, 30 June. Available online: https://screencrush.com/arnold-schwarzenegger-is-an-auteur (accessed 23 April 2022).

Sondhi, J. (2011), '*Multi-Facial*: Drama about Identity in Live-action', *Short of the Week*, 29 April. Available online: https://www.shortoftheweek.com/2011/04/29/vin-diesel-in-multi-facial (accessed 23 April 2022).

Stevens, D. (2011), '*Fast Five*: A Tenderhearted Family Drama Starring Vin Diesel', *Slate*, 29 April. Available online: https://slate.com/culture/2011/04/fast-five-reviewed-a-tenderhearted-family-drama-starring-vin-diesel.html (accessed 23 April 2022).

*Strays* (1997), [Film] Dir. Vin Diesel, USA: First Look Studios.

Variety (2015), [YouTube] 'Vin Diesel: 7 Things You Don't Know about Me', *Variety*, 24 March. Available online: https://www.youtube.com/watch?v=v8oxRdBRd3I (accessed 23 April 2022).

Waldron, C. (2001), 'Vin Diesel Shifts Acting Career into High Gear in *The Fast and the Furious*', *Jet*, 9 July, 53–4. Available online: https://books.google.com/books?id=q7UDAAAAMBAJ&q=Vin+Diesel#v=snippet&q=Vin%20Diesel&f=false (accessed 23 April 2022).

Wenn (2022), 'Vin Diesel Slams Gay Rumors', *Hollywood.com*, 24 March. Available online: https://www.hollywood.com/celebrities/vin-diesel-slams-gay-rumors-57155451/ (accessed 23 April 2022).

Wloszczyna, S. (2002), 'Vin Diesel, in High Gear', *USA Today*, 6 August. Available online: https://usatoday30.usatoday.com/life/2002-08-06-vin-diesel_x.htm (accessed 23 April 2022).

*xXx* (2002), [Film] Dir. Rob Cohen, USA: Sony Pictures Releasing.

*xXx: The Return of Xander Cage* (2017), [Film] Dir. D. J. Caruso, USA: Paramount Pictures Studios.

Zakarin, J. (2015), 'Meet the Writer Who Made *The Fast and the Furious* Possible', *Yahoo! Entertainment*, 26 March. Available online: https://www.yahoo.com/entertainment/fast-and-furious-original-article-writer-114662681722.html (accessed 23 April 2022).

6

# Fast, Furious and Free of Sex: Dom, Brian and hetero male affection

Aaron Hunter

A young man approaches an LA sandwich counter. He orders a tuna sandwich. The viewer does not yet know it, but this man, Brian (Paul Walker), is a cop investigating the owners – waitress Mia Toretto (Jordana Brewster) and her brother Dominic, or Dom, Toretto (Vin Diesel), who sits in a back room reading. Dom might be involved in some recent high-speed robberies, and Brian is working undercover at a local garage, hoping to penetrate the illegal street racing culture where Dom is king, thereby getting closer to the suspect. At the counter, Brian flirts with Mia – he has been here before, she knows his order, and they have developed a friendly rapport. But he only has eyes for Dom. He stares at him, his eyes lingering over the well-known street racer and potential criminal. As Dom moves about behind the counter, Brian's gaze follows him. They make eye contact (Figures 6.1 and 6.2), but Dom, oblivious to Brian or the role they will come to play in each other's lives, looks away and returns to his business. Thus begins the saga of Brian and Dom, their relationship the beating heart of the *Fast & Furious* film franchise.

The franchise zoomed into life with *The Fast and the Furious* (2001), a modestly budgeted summer actioner designed as a *Point Break* (1991) with street racing. Featuring a young cast of little-known actors, the film's $200 million box office haul surprised nearly everybody involved and led to the inevitable talk of sequels (Mitchell 2013). After a bumpy couple of entries that offered new characters and storylines, the series underwent a soft reboot with the fourth entry, *Fast & Furious* (2009, hereinafter *Fast Four*), and hit international pay dirt with *Fast Five* (2011). In total, there have been nine films as part of the main 'saga'; there have also been a spin-off film, two short films and an animated series, with at least one more in the series proper and two more spinoffs – including one focusing on the series' female characters – due in the next few years.[1] Despite often lacklustre

**Figure 6.1** Brian gazes at Dom in their first on-screen meeting, *The Fast and the Furious* (2001 Universal).

**Figure 6.2** Dom briefly glances back at him, *The Fast and the Furious* (2001 Universal).

critical reviews, the franchise has proved incredibly popular with international audiences, garnering over $6 billion dollars worldwide and making it one of the highest-grossing film franchises of all time. This has no doubt been aided by its diverse cast, international settings and by a depiction of women that features a deft blend of multi-dimensional main characters with the more scantily clad extras typical of macho action films. Stylistically and narratively, from its humble origins as a medium-budget depiction of cops and bad-guys-with-good-hearts in a neighbourhood turf battle, the franchise has exploded into a massively budgeted story of once-scrappy street punks who now repeatedly save the world in increasingly dangerous missions against increasingly villainous foes. With a now all-star cast, the franchise has morphed into a millennial throwback to

1980s-era action films, which more frequently depicted men as rugged and women as hot, and where no explosion was too explosive.

However, one element noticeably missing from this iteration of action franchise is the sex. There are no sex scenes in the *Fast & Furious* franchise. To be clear, sex is often implied (occasionally resulting in pregnancy), with suggestive foreplay and elliptical sexual encounters. There is also much talk and joking about sex, and the films are rife with gratuitous sexualizing, particularly of women's bodies, which are frequently depicted only from the neck down. But the films include no actual, on-screen sex scenes. In contrast, they do include scenes of intense, if restrained, emotional bonding where the male leads confide in each other about their memories, hopes and fears, scenes that often bridge the second and third acts – moments of quiet before the intensity of each film's climax.

In this chapter, I address how the films feint towards but do not commit to depicting platonic, hetero, male affection. The lack of sex and the male heart-to-heart conversations combine to develop several functions in the series. Firstly, they aid the franchise in positioning itself as an epic tale of traditional, heteronormative 'family' values. At the same time, though, ripples of male affection course throughout the series' dominant relationships, and in subtle ways undermine those traditional values. This is furthered by the way that even the most important male-female relationships are depicted as secondary to the male-male relationships, or as requiring the presence of both males to be legitimate – metaphorical threesomes. Much has been written, particularly in popular media, about homoeroticism in the series, the physical nature of the male relationships and the metaphorical fetishizing of phallic objects like cars, guns and bottles of Corona.[2] It is not my aim to preclude such readings – the films are laden with tropes easily recognizable as representations of male-for-male desire and ripe for numerous plausible readings. Rather, I would like to complement homoerotic interpretations by interrogating how the films depict a longing for platonic male affection and emotional love – apparent in both style and narrative – that the films cannot repress but refuse to commit to.

## Platonic male affection

While romance and the hint of heteronormative sex permeate the *Fast & Furious* franchise, the films' male-male relationships are the series' beating heart. For five of the films, the central relation is between Dom and Brian, but other important examples include Brian and Roman (Tyrese Gibson) in *2 Fast 2 Furious* (2003), Sean (Lucas Black) and Han (Sung Kang) in *The Fast and the Furious: Tokyo Drift* (2006), and Luke Hobbs (Dwayne Johnson) and Deckard Shaw (Jason Statham) in *The Fate of the Furious* (2017, hereinafter *Fast Eight*) and the series spinoff, *Fast & Furious Presents: Hobbs & Shaw* (2019). This chapter focuses mainly on the central relationship between Dom and Brian, but each of these male-male bonding pairs is coded with elements of male affection, often mediated by ambivalent attitudes towards race and ethnicity, as none of the pairings feature two white men. However, the power dynamics and privileges afforded to the men of colour in the films often change based on the number of other men of colour, as well as the presence and number of women in the films who are coded as romantically or sexually available.[3] Because of this ambivalence, before considering how the *Fast & Furious* franchise replicates, but also modifies, previous iterations of male affection in action films, it is worth briefly discussing depictions of race, ethnicity and gender in the films.

The *Fast & Furious* films negotiate a minefield of racial, sexual and domestic tensions and cross-purposes. Mary Beltrán (2005, 2013) has written extensively about how the films reflect and cater to changing demographics in the United States, describing the first film as 'an optimistic vision of race relations' (Beltrán 2005: 59) and has discussed how the series questions 'the place and status of whiteness in an increasingly multicultural US and global culture' (Beltrán 2013: 85). She argues that the films offer a contrast to 'traditional, xenophobic whiteness' by depicting protagonists – regardless of skin colour or tone – who are 'open to cultural learning and flexibility' (Ibid). The films are refreshing in the way they generally avoid white saviour narratives: Brian, the primary white protagonist in six of the films, rarely 'wins' the movie unless in partnership with, in most cases, Dom, an American with Cuban ancestry.[4]

In addition to the franchise's racial and ethnic diversity, many people associated with *Fast & Furious* have expressed pride in and admiration for the films' depiction of women. Cast and crew alike talk about how much input female actors are given into developing their characters and how open the crew are to their suggestions. For example, Michelle Rodriguez (who plays Letty) has described how the fight between her character Letty and Gina Carano's Riley in *Fast & Furious 6* (2013) was originally scripted as a typical cat fight, with face scratching and hair pulling, but how Rodriguez and Carano thought it would work better as a more brutal street brawl that contrasted the two characters' different fighting styles, which is how director Justin Lin ended up shooting it

(*Hand to Hand Fury* 2017). For the most part, across the spectrum of driving, fighting and shooting firearms, the women are as accomplished as the men. When it comes to relationships and sex, the films grant them autonomy and they are rarely shamed or disparaged for being sexually active, which, sadly, remains something of an achievement in twenty-first-century Hollywood. For example, after Brian and Mia's first date, it is Mia who asks Brian if he 'wants to go for a drive', then takes the wheel and drives at high speed, which leads to their first night together. Like Mia, Letty engages in acts of high-speed bravado, as well as fisticuffs and mission planning, and Gisele (Gal Gadot) is just as formidable in a gun fight as her partner Han.

At the same time, however, while the films' gender politics display a patina of inclusive sisterhood and their overall sense of diversity is admirable, the franchise still displays elements of traditional patriarchal hierarchies. These are often based on privileges related to skin colour and tone, and also on heteronormative assumptions about traditional family structures. For example, when it comes to sexual relationships, the black men of the franchise rarely take part, nor do they engage in the male-male bonding so crucial to the films' emotional landscape. The one exception being Roman's intense friendship with Brian in *2 Fast 2 Furious*. Likewise, women in the films are allowed their autonomy only to a certain extent. Thus, in her early appearances, Mia fights and drives like the men, but once she becomes pregnant and then a mother, she is relegated to the narrative margins of *Fast & Furious 6* and *Furious 7* (2015), and her onscreen time is drastically cut. In fact, while Michelle Rodriguez has praised some elements of the production, she has been publicly critical of the franchise's tendency towards a 'macho vibe' that centres the male characters (Mumford 2017).

If depictions of race, ethnicity and gender in the films can be described as ambivalent or even confused, the same can be said of their central male relationships. That ambivalence can be particularly difficult to interpret because film scholarship, along with most other forms of cultural criticism, has inadequate means to evaluate platonic male affection. These films depict their men as solidly, if not aggressively, heterosexual, and the male-male relationships are heavily bro-coded, with the men expressing affection via such standard masculinist tropes as sharing beers, talking trash, racing cars and resorting to fisticuffs. In recent decades, a standard approach to such tropes has been to read them as homoerotic, and the *Fast & Furious* films have been subject to numerous such readings within online film discourse. Jen Yamato (2017) describes 'Diesel and Walker's torrid, homoerotic-bromantic chemistry', built on 'flexed biceps and popped hoods'. Robbie Collin (2015) describes fight scenes in the fifth and sixth films thus: 'Diesel and Johnson mount one another in a ludicrous tussle' and 'Michelle Rodriguez and Gina Carano … clash on the London Underground in a brawl that's basically frottage'. Jeffrey Bloomer (2019) describes how 'Brian gives Dom the keys to a car, which, in *The Fast and the Furious*, is basically a sex act anyway'. In a film world where male emotional expression is generally limited to aggression or humour, seemingly simple acts like passing somebody a beer bottle, gifting them a set of keys or punching them in the face are easy to interpret as expressions of homoerotic affection.

Discerning homoeroticism or an ambivalent homoerotic gaze in action films is not a recent development, of course. Describing the homoerotic gaze in 1980s action films, Patrick Schuckmann (1998: 675) writes: '[T]hat the action genre's display of its heroes' eroticized bodies is mainly addressed to a male, straight audience establishes homoeroticism as a constantly present but highly ambivalent undercurrent. Homoeroticism is both consistently evoked and disavowed by the genre's specific plot devices and visual scenarios.' Yvonne Tasker (1993:154) describes the films more succinctly: 'homoeroticism is central to the male action movie, and while gay desire may be unspoken within dialogue, it is very much present within the frame.' Both scholars identify a specific strain of barely submerged homoeroticism in the action buddy subgenre, with Schuckmann (1998: 675) writing: 'homoeroticism is strongly evoked by the coupling of male partners as buddies, and, at the same time, disavowed by homophobic jokes and remarks.' Tasker (1993: 121) observes that the insistent homophobia in buddy films 'threatens to draw attention to the very fact of homosexual desire that it seeks to deny.'

Furthermore, it is not only the hard-body 1980s actioners of Schwarzeneger and Stallone that have been subject to readings of homoeroticism. For example, numerous scholarly and pop cultural readings of *Top Gun* (1986) have recognized that film's homoerotic gaze.[5] Likewise, as action films underwent a variety of changes in the 1990s, developing a more knowing, irony-laden approach to their subject matter, they maintained a fixation on the possibility of sublimated male desire – often with a knowing wink. This is perhaps most apparent – or at least has been the subject of the most discussion – in the film *Point Break* (1991), which is often considered a spiritual precursor to *The Fast and the Furious*. Christina Lane (1998: 74) describes how 'The homoerotic overtones in Johnny and Bohdi's relationship, which usually occur implicitly in the action and buddy genres, are addressed rather overtly in the film ... Point Break feeds on the sexualized pleasure of the male bonding.' Clifton Evers (2010), on the other hand, finds something more akin to the buddy film's homophobia in the way Point Break replicates surfing's 'policing of male-to-male social bonding'. Thus, while different from the blatant homophobia that some scholars recognized in the muscle-bound buddy films of the 1980s, films like Top Gun and Point Break feature a complicated mix of homoeroticism, homophobia and misogyny in the way they demarcate and then safeguard male-only spaces.

Arriving at the dawn of the new century, the Fast & Furious films generally eschew the blatant homophobia of earlier iterations of the action genre, similar to how they lean away from a strict centring of the white male protagonist of their forebears. However, as the plethora of popular film criticism attests, they remain just as ripe for homoerotic readings. To better understand how Fast & Furious codes a sublimated yearning for platonic male affection, examining the rise of the bromance may prove as fruitful as a discussion of past action films. The bromance, a genre that has experienced a concomitant rise with the Fast Saga, foregrounds the efforts of men to avoid, confront and then accept their affection for other men more explicitly than most action films of any era. A subgenre of comedy, bromances may take action films as a point of comic entry (for example, the Will Ferrell/Mark Wahlberg vehicle The Other Guys [2010]). However, they more often than not replicate the narrative beats and comedic emblems of the screwball or romantic comedy: including variations on the meet-cute, the early obstacles to coupledom, the shaky relationship that crumbles at the end of act two and the final cementing of an emotionally mature and bonded relationship.[6] These films differ in significant ways from action films – their men tend to be less fixated on traditionally performative aspects of masculinity like fighting skills, mechanical and weapon prowess, or bulging muscles and shirtlessness (Will Ferrell goes topless for comedy, not sex appeal). Differences aside, however, in the 2000s and 2010s, bromance films have established themselves as a primary locus in recalibrating how male affection is mediated on screen. Since the Fast & Furious films, like their buddy picture precursors, share with the bromance a dual protagonist nature that grapples with the difficulty of expressing platonic male affection, it is worth considering how readings of heteronormativity and homoeroticism in the bromance might inform a reading of Fast & Furious.

David Hansen-Miller and Rosalind Gill (2011) place the bromance film in a postfeminist context in which depictions of stereotypical heterosexual male attributes are highly knowing and ironized.[7] As such, the films can remain as libidinous as earlier masculinist films in part because they are 'refreshingly honest' about it (Ibid: 41). However, Hansen-Miller and Gill see the bromance, much like the buddy pics that came before them, as 'striking' in their 'dependence on dynamics of intense heterosexual male bonding, paired with explicit homophobic humour'. They argue that 'this connection between homosociality and homophobia is not incidental or innocent but constitutes a structuring feature of the films' (Ibid: 41–5). This structure overlaps with the infused rom-com elements of the films – in developing their bromantic relationships, the dual protagonists construct a homosocial space in which they can perform acts of idealized masculinity that serve as proxy expressions of affection for each other. However, before anything resembling real physical affection occurs, the 'adult' world intercedes and one or both pairs accept or recommit to separate heterosexual relationships. A difference that Hansen-Miller and Gill see between these contemporary films and older buddy films is how they resolve with a sense of ambivalence or even melancholy – the buddies often seem to be settling for rather than actively choosing the films' heteronormative dénouements.

An analysis that reformulates readings like Hansen-Miller and Gill's in intriguing ways comes from R. Colin Tait (2016), who interrogates *Step Brothers* (2008) as an example of bisexual hybridity in which 'the love story between Dale and Brennan is implicit in the level of form and narrative'. Tait acknowledges that *Step Brothers* differs from other bromances in its sometimes paradoxical incorporation or rejection of screwball comedy and rom-com attributes in a way that 'eludes' the 'frameworks' of other bromances (as articulated above). At the same time, however, Tait recognizes that those differences are a result of the film being part of a trend, the 'genre's mutation from the heteronormative ideal to a much more fluid and open trope' about male relationships. He argues that this is a result of the film's polysemous nature, which yields 'multiple interpretations and [provides] a number of entry points for audience identification' (Tait 2016: 61–6). This resembles, if not exactly, the sexual ambivalence that Hansen-Miller and Gill recognize. Because the films are exploring male affectionate relationships through their formal and stylistic strategies, their polysemous nature allows for an inference of sexual relationship or love, while their unwillingness to commit fully to such a relationship renders them ambivalent, or even impotent, in that regard. For the fact remains, as Tait points out, that while *Step Brothers* 'has the potential to present alternative forms of love, sexuality, and brotherhood', the film 'does not present the on-screen depiction of male sexual consummation' (Tait 2016: 61–5), so any such reading of the film must arise from its polysemous nature. Tait's reading, even if applied to a specific film within a different genre, is useful for probing the *Fast Saga's* similarly polysemous presentation of sex and male affection.[8]

A further useful approach to the ambivalence of male affection and sexuality in the bromance comes from Heather Brook (2015), who explores the 'crevices' in the 'representation of monolithically heteronormative masculinity' that continue to widen as the bromance genre advances. Unlike the above, however, Brook seeks to complement readings of the films grounded in homoeroticism by positioning their depictions of male affection within a framework of heterodoxical masculinity. For Brook, masculinity and heterosexuality are too various and intersect in too many ways for heterosexuality to be 'dichotomized with homosexuality', where the danger of doing so is the perpetuation of 'heteronormative privilege'. Brook argues that a reading of the films grounded in a heterodoxical masculinity and heterosexuality can supplement queer readings by enquiring 'from a majority position into the ways that gendered power relations and sexual orientations work together, or fail to work together, as axes of domination and resistance' (Brook 2015: 250–253).

Brook (2015) argues that bromances rarely offer compelling examples of heterodoxical masculinity. Her approach represents a valid and compelling way to think about the *Fast & Furious* films for at least two reasons. First, unlike the bromance films that have been the subject of recent scholarly inquiry into the queering of male affection, *Fast & Furious* does not ground its male relationships in homosociality. The films are insistent that women be present, active and forceful agents. It is true that to participate, these women must exhibit tendencies and behaviours typically coded (at least within Hollywood) as 'male' – they must be able to fix cars, race cars, shoot guns and punch somebody in the face. They also, however, reassert more feminine codes whenever they so desire in how they dress, interact with male villains or engage in romantic relationships with their male partners.[9]

These women's presence and variety of character and desires negate the homosocial milieu of many bromance and buddy films, but it also allows them to mediate between male characters – Mia with Brian and Dom, Elena (Elsa Pataky) with Dom and Hobbs, Neela (Nathalie Kelley) with Sean and Han, and Hattie (Vanessa Kirby) with Hobbs and Shaw. In a sense, they act as conduits via which the men can get to know one another, or as totems about which the men can express their feelings for each other – for example, many of Brian and Dom's most heartfelt conversations have Mia as an ostensible subject. In *The Fast and the Furious*, after Dom finds out that Brian and Mia are going on their first date, he first warns Brian not to break her heart and then immediately takes Brian to see his father's car, where he tells him about his father's death and makes his famous 'quarter-mile-at-a-time' speech. Thus, expressing his concern for Mia allows Dom to confide in Brian in other ways.

Secondly, Brook's (2015) heterodoxical analysis allows us to re-read the franchise's masculinity in a more nuanced fashion, one which accounts for not just its insistent, surface-level heterosexuality, but also its deeper sadness at the men's inability to articulate or formulate new expressions of male affection. This sadness recalls the melancholy that Hansen-Miller and Gill identify in the reinscribed heterosexuality of bromance resolutions. Indeed, turning to the *Fast Saga*, and the way in which its films often replace sex with instances of emotional bonding, let us now delve more deeply into the central relationship between Brian and Dom. Specifically, we can draw on the aforementioned scholarship to re-evaluate the limited heterodoxical masculinity that their relationship appears to embody, paying attention to both the franchise's polysemous efforts to express a new approach to male affection and the melancholy that results from its failure to do so convincingly.

## Brian and Dom's feels

From Brian and Dom's first encounter, there is an implication that their actions – gestures, expressions – and the formal way the films frame and present those actions will convey as much about their intentions and feelings as their dialogue. As with the stylistic elements of the bromance, much of the emotion in Dom and Brian's relationship – and the way Mia often mediates it – comes not from what the characters say or do, but how they say and do it, and how it is presented formally on screen.

An example of this interplay comes at the house party scene in *The Fast and the Furious*. When the police descend upon a street race, Brian saves Dom from potential arrest, thereby earning Dom's trust, which has been his goal thus far. As a reward, Dom invites Brian to a party at his house. The two men arrive in an exterior shot of the house and street. There is then a cut, not to the party downstairs, but to Mia alone in her bedroom, watching through the window. When she realizes Brian is coming in, she panics and begins to adjust her clothes and make-up. Thus, through his early relationship with Mia, Brian was able to get close to Dom, and now that he has earned Dom's trust, he's able to get closer to Mia. Cutting to the party downstairs, Dom is angry at his crew for not having saved him from arrest, and much male jousting takes place. But then Mia comes downstairs and presents herself to Brian, almost as a kind of reward. Finally, as Dom goes upstairs with Letty for 'a massage', he stops and tells Brian, referring to an earlier incident, 'you still owe me a ten-second car.' In close-up, Brian gazes at Dom, replicating the close-ups of his gaze from their first scene together. Brian and Dom's affection for each other has clearly grown throughout this sequence, but so too has Mia's proxy role.

As Brian becomes more enmeshed with the gang, he develops authentic emotional feelings for Mia, which leads to a romantic and sexual relationship. The film's formal nature continues to fasten this relationship to Brian's pursuit of Dom – both narratively as a cop and emotionally as an object of affection. As mentioned above, when Dom finds out Brian and Mia are going on a date, he takes Brian aside and they have the first of the franchise's many male-bonding, heart-to-heart talks. Dom reveals himself emotionally to Brian: he talks about his love for his father, he describes why he was sent to prison and he imparts his 'quarter-mile-at-a-time' philosophy to him. After this heartfelt sequence, there is an immediate cut to Brian and Mia's first date, where Brian tells her pointedly he has no interest in Dom, only her. By now, the film's narrative has demonstrated this statement's lack of veracity, but so too has its formal nature in its choice of shots and edits, which continue as Brian and Mia leave the restaurant. Mia takes the wheel and her driving thrills Brian: a shot inside the car shows him looking at her with admiration – similar to the way he has looked at Dom throughout. This cuts to an exterior shot of their car speeding through the night. There is an immediate cut to the cars of Dom and his crew also speeding through the night, as they take part in another high-speed heist, which is then followed by a cut to Brian and Mia in bed.

Thus, as Brian's emotional attachment to Mia grows, so too does his affection for Dom. So much so that by the first film's end, he sacrifices everything, including his relationship with Mia, to save Dom from being arrested. In the film's climax, Brian must reveal that he is a police officer to save one of Dom's crew. While he radios for a medic, he and Dom make extended eye contact as Mia watches on, and Dom expresses clear heartbreak before fleeing with Mia and the rest of his crew. In the film's denouement, the two meet again, they even race, before Brian intentionally lets Dom escape police capture. This decision will reverberate throughout most of the ensuing saga. One could argue that this action spurs the entirety of the franchise; Brian betrays Dom by being a cop but then lets him go because he loves him. They both run away from L.A. and each other, Brian to Miami and Dom to Mexico. Their fates do not re-entwine until *Fast Four*, when it is again via the connection with women that they come together. Each is independently investigating the (supposed) death of Letty, while at the same time Brian attempts to rekindle his relationship with Mia.

As the franchise progresses, Brian and Dom must rediscover their trust for one another, which they eventually do, often by way of heartfelt conversations. These often come in the form of clandestine meetings or late-night confessionals. Removing themselves from the rest of the team – Brian even leaves Mia alone in bed – the two men talk on their own. They discuss their childhoods, their fathers, their ethical codes and philosophies. They talk about trust. In doing so, they replicate the actions of a couple in the developing stages of a relationship. While the films eschew on-screen depictions of sex, they never forgo an opportunity to depict these conversations, which always deepen the emotional connection of the two men involved. In fact, these conversations often occur in place of or in close proximity to an expected sex scene. However, just as sex scenes often function as on-screen indicators of a relationship's progression, for the men of *Fast & Furious*, these conversations serve to consummate or re-commit to male affection.

The series continues to find novel ways to develop Dom and Brian's emotional attachment, while also withholding the possibility that they might commit to it on their own, without other mediating factors. A key sequence from *Fast Five* illustrates how the films achieve this via a deft blend of narrative and formal functions. Early in the film, the audience becomes aware that Mia is pregnant, but she refrains from telling anybody. During an intense chase scene – the film's antagonists and FBI agent Hobbs simultaneously pursue the gang – Mia, Brian and Dom are on foot in the *favelas* of Rio. At a brief pause in the action, Mia announces her pregnancy to Brian and Dom together. Shot selection and editing in the sequence work to tie three couples – brother and sister, lovers and best friends – together into a group of three. The three are bickering about splitting up, and Mia, alone on screen, punctuates the quarrel with her announcement. There is a cut to a close-up of Brian, followed by a close-up of Dom, then to Mia talking about the importance of family. After some cuts between her and Dom, there is a medium shot of Brian joyfully walking to her and they kiss. Then a medium shot frames Dom alone in the foreground against Brian and Mia embracing in the background. Mia turns to Dom, says his name and after some more close-ups, there is return to the medium shot of Dom standing apart from the couple. He promises Mia they will always 'stick together' and walks towards them, closing the gap. In a tight close-up, all three of them hug, with Brian patting Dom's head and glancing at him with love in his eyes (Figure 6.3). This is one of the few times in the franchise when the two men embrace, and it is fitting that it is a three-way hug with Mia, a surrogate for both men: as Dom's sister, she affords Brian a familial relationship with Dom; as Brian's lover, she encourages Dom's feelings for Brian to transcend friendship.[10] Her baby is both of theirs – in fact, after her announcement, it is Dom who declares, 'the family just got bigger'.

After Mia's announcement, there is a short sequence with Hobbs and his team, then a cut back to the trio, and to the film's major male heart-to-heart, relatively early compared to most of the entries. This is the first time we see them after Mia's announcement, but rather than a celebratory or passionate moment between Brian and Mia, Brian leaves Mia in bed to discuss his fears of fatherhood with Dom. The scene's content is not particularly revelatory – Dom again offers great praise of his own father, Brian worries he'll follow in his own dead-beat father's footsteps, and Dom reassures him not to worry. The scene is important, though, in its reinforcement of Dom and Brian's as the central emotional relationship in the film. Furthermore, it is during this scene when Dom and Brian hatch their plan to put a team together – a team devised of characters the two have known independently in past films. This team will continue in various iterations for the rest of the franchise, dramatically altering the content and tenor of the films from *Fast Five* onward. In a sense, then, while Mia is lying in bed alone, pregnant, Dom and Brian are 'birthing' the family at the heart of the rest of the series.

Through the next two films, with all plot twists and raised stakes, Dom and Brian continue to grow closer. It would have been fascinating to see how the creators planned to develop the relationship through the final stretch of films,

**Figure 6.3** Brian, Dom and Mia embrace after she informs them of her pregnancy, *Fast Five* (2011 Universal).

but extra-filmic events intervened. In November 2013, during production on *Furious 7*, Paul Walker died in a car crash. Production ceased for five months until the decision was made to complete the film in Walker's honour. Brian's arc was rewritten, Walker's brothers acted as stand-ins for several scenes, and the Weta Workshop created digital compositions of Walker's face that were superimposed on the bodies of his brothers and his stunt double. In the film, Mia, pregnant with their second child, is mostly sidelined, while Brian and Dom take part in some of their most outrageous adventures. The film ends with the remnants of Brian and Dom's team on the beach, watching Brian and Mia play with their son at the water's edge. To fans of the series who had followed the news and events around Walker's death, the film's ending enacts a moment of extended trans-diegesis, where Dom and Brian are not just on-screen characters, but also serve as stand-ins for their performers, Vin Diesel and Paul Walker. Dom/Diesel walks away from the beach. He leaves Brian/Walker in the sunshine, with his 'family'. Driving away, in voiceover Dom waxes about his friendship and brotherhood with Brian, accompanied by clips from previous films. Trans-diegetically, this also represents Diesel talking about Walker.[11] Then, as if to cement the affection of their relationship, but also its melancholy, Brian pulls up next to Dom at a stop sign: 'Hey', he says, 'you thought you could leave without saying goodbye?' (Figures 6.4 and 6.5). The scene replicates several earlier in the franchise when Dom and Brian prepare to race each other. Brian's gaze across the space between them also replicates the first look audiences saw him give Dom early in *The Fast and the Furious*, only this time, Dom returns his gaze. And then the two race off. An aerial shot follows the two cars along a winding mountain road until they approach a fork – Brian goes left, while Dom drives right (Figure 6.6).

**Figure 6.4** Brian gazes at Dom one last time, *Furious 7* (2015 Universal).

**Figure 6.5** Dom returns Brian's gaze with affection, *Furious 7* (2015 Universal).

**Figure 6.6** Brian and Dom part for the last time, *Furious 7* (2015 Universal).

The franchise does not kill Brian. However, that fork in the road represents Brian's metaphorical death in the series. Just as he first gazes at Dom while ostensibly flirting with Mia, he chooses to 'die', not in the loving embrace of his family on the beach, but in a revved-up car racing alongside Dom. Diverging at that fork also becomes an apt metaphor for the two's inability to acquire physical closeness – their inability or unwillingness to touch. As much affection as they have developed, they have been unable to establish any sort of new, heterodoxical representation of masculine affection on screen. That failure is melancholic, but maybe more, it's heart-breaking. The films invest much in developing the deep bonds of Dom and Brian's relationship, but their relationship ends with no embrace of each other or of the affection that binds them.

## Conclusion

The presence of homoeroticism throughout Hollywood cinema history has been well documented and discussed. In the 1970s and 1980s, texts by critics and scholars such as Parker Tyler, Richard Dyer and Vito Russo began to articulate a taxonomy of onscreen queerness in Hollywood, including an understanding of the various codes, tropes and metaphors by which a perceptive viewer could recognize veiled homoeroticism in films presumably about straight men and women. These methodologies were advanced by scholars in the 1980s and 1990s whose perceptive readings of muscled masculinity in action films developed a framework for understanding homoeroticism's presence in those most macho of movies – a framework that has persisted and grown with continued engagement and elaboration by scholars over the past two decades. However, as Brook (2015) contends, reading the male affection on display in such films within a heterosexual context can supplement homoerotic readings by expanding and adding nuance to an understanding of masculinity that is too often dichotomized as either homo – or hetero-, either sexual or platonic.

The *Fast & Furious* franchise presents a text ripe for understanding male relationships along what might be better understood as a homo-/hetero-, sexual/platonic axis of affection. In this chapter, I have attempted to articulate both the presence of hetero male affection in the films and their reticence about committing openly to that affection onscreen. Perhaps ironically, the platonic affection displayed by the male leads in *Fast & Furious* is as veiled, or more so, than the homoerotic gestures that populate so many action films. At the same time, the films' depiction of women taking part in activities previously coded as male – planning, racing and fighting – reduces the presence of homosocial spaces on-screen, complicating (although certainly not erasing) the homoerotic readings that were so applicable to 1980s and 1990s, male-centred action films. On the other hand, but also unlike their forebears, the *Fast & Furious* films eschew gratuitous, or even demure, sex scenes. There are moments of heightened sexual foreplay in the films, but overall they seem unconcerned with depicting sex on screen, even as the films are peopled with attractive Hollywood bodies in various states of undress. And while they do not completely eschew the rituals of male dominance typical of the genre, they prioritize scenes of emotional male bonding. These scenes are enhanced by intimations of female mediation or even surrogacy for male emotional attachment, by actors' performance choices, and by formal decisions about framing and editing. However, the potential for these emotional relationships to flourish remains limited by the films' unwillingness to let the performers touch one another with affection or express their feelings directly, thus the construction of a different kind of veiled male relationship. For while the films' depictions of male sexuality are complex and often contradictory, and the primary male relationship at their heart is one of respect, admiration, affection and love, it is a love that in the end remains unwilling to transcend the strict precepts of heteronormative masculinity.

## Notes

1. The ninth film, *F9*, was released internationally in May 2021, and in the United States in June 2021, not soon enough to be considered for this chapter.
2. See for example: Bloomer (2019), Collin (2015) and Yamato (2017).
3. There is much to be said about how the films reward white or light-skinned men with sexual partners, while withholding sexual relationships from Black men.
4. The films rarely allude to the Torettos' ethnicity or ancestry, but in an April 2016 Instagram post, Vin Diesel describes Cuba as 'where the Torettos started' (Diesel 2016).
5. Other readings recognize a more decidedly misogynistic element to *Top Gun*'s privileging of male-only spaces. See Modleski (2007).
6. For more on the bromance as rom-com, see Tait (2016).
7. Writing before the term 'bromance' was fully cemented, David Hansen-Miller and Rosalind Gill (2011) use the term 'lad flicks'. However, they analyse many of the same films that appear in scholarly work on the bromance.
8. Tait's (2016) reading of the film, and of the evolution of the bromance more generally, is much more intricate and nuanced than I have time to explicate here, including a wide-ranging discussion of Hollywood history's depiction of male love and affection and scholarly accounts of it.
9. The only female characters who might be 'punished' for their sexuality are Eva Mendes's Monica in *2 Fast 2 Furious*, whose sexual relationship with a villain while undercover is the subject of Roman's scorn, and Elena who suffers an inglorious, misogynist 'fridging' in *Fast Eight*.
10. By my count, Brian and Dom touch each other fourteen times in the saga, sometimes aggressively. Five of these instances can be considered affectionate hugs or embraces.
11. Diesel and Walker developed a tight bond off-screen, with Diesel acting as godfather to Walker's daughter and naming his own daughter Pauline in honour of Walker after his death.

# References

Beltrán, M. (2005), 'The New Hollywood Racelessness: Only the Fast, Furious, (and Multiracial) Will Survive', *Cinema Journal*, 44 (2): 50–67.

Beltrán, M. (2013), 'Fast and Bilingual: *Fast & Furious* and the Latinization of Racelessness', *Cinema Journal*, 53 (1): 75–96.

Bloomer, J. (2019), 'The *Fast and Furious* Movies Have Always Been Gay', *Slate*, 9 August. Available online: https://slate.com/culture/2019/08/fast-furious-movies-gay-hobbs-shaw-subtext.html (accessed 24 April 2022).

Brook, H. (2015), 'Bros before Ho(mo)s: Hollywood Bromance and the Limits of Heterodoxy', *Men and Masculinities*, 18 (2): 249–66.

Collin, R. (2015), '*Fast & Furious 7*: the Bisexual Blockbuster', *The Telegraph*, 2 April. Available online: https://www.telegraph.co.uk/culture/film/10061731/Fast-and-Furious-6-the-bisexual-blockbuster.html (accessed 24 April 2022).

Diesel, V. (2016), [Instagram] 'The Channelling of Dom Begins Here', 28 April. Available online: https://www.instagram.com/p/BEujWQehPLO/?utm_source=ig_embed&utm_campaign=embed_video_watch_again (accessed 24 April 2022).

Evers, C. (2010). 'Queer Waves', *The Inertia*, 11 November. Available online: https://www.theinertia.com/business-media/queer-waves/ (accessed 24 April 2022).

*Hand to Hand Fury* (2017), [Blu-ray] *Fast and Furious 6*, Dir. Justin Lin, USA: Universal Home Video.

Hansen-Miller, D. and R. Gill (2011), 'Lad Flicks: Discursive Reconstructions of Masculinity in Popular Film', in H. Radner and R. Stringer (eds), *Feminism at the Movies*, 36–50, New York: Routledge.

Lane, C. (1998), 'From *The Loveless* to *Point Break*: Kathryn Bigelow's Trajectory in Action', *Cinema Journal*, 73 (4): 59–81.

Mitchell, R. (2013), 'How Paul Walker Helped Create a *Fast and Furious* Box-office Franchise', *CNN Business*, 6 December. Available online: https://edition.cnn.com/2013/12/06/business/paul-walker-fast-furious-franchise/index.html (13 May 2022).

Modleski, T. (2007), 'Misogynist Films: Teaching *Top Gun*', *Cinema Journal*, 47 (1): 101–5.

Mumford, G. (2017), 'Michelle Rodriguez Threatens to Leave *Fast and Furious* Over Limited Female Roles', *The Guardian*, 28 June. Available online: https://www.theguardian.com/film/2017/jun/28/michelle-rodriguez-threatens-to-leave-fast-and-furious-over-limited-female-roles (accessed 24 April 2022).

*The Other Guys* (2010), [Film] Dir. Adam McKay, USA: Sony Pictures Releasing.

*Point Break* (1991), [Film] Dir. Kathryn Bigelow, USA: Warner Bros. Pictures.

Schuckmann, P. (1998), 'Masculinity, the Male Spectator and the Homoerotic Gaze', *Amerikastudien/American Studies*, 43 (4): 671–80.

*Step Brothers* (2008), [Film] Dir. Adam McKay, USA: Columbia Pictures.
Tait, R. C. (2016), 'The Screwball Bromance: Regression, Bisexuality, and Reconfigured Masculinity in *Step Brothers*', *Journal of Men's Studies*, 24 (1): 1–18.
Tasker, Y. (1993), *Spectacular Bodies: Gender, Genre and the Action Cinema*, London: Routledge.
*Top Gun* (1986), [Film] Dir. Tony Scott, USA: Paramount Pictures Studios.
Yamato, J. (2017), 'How *the Fast and the Furious* Took Over the World', *The Daily Beast*, 12 July. Available online: https://www.thedailybeast.com/how-the-fast-and-the-furious-took-over-the-world?ref=scroll (accessed 24 April 2022).

7

# 'What's real is family': Maternal bodies, paternal labour and parenting roles in *Fast & Furious*

Bianca Batti

At the beginning of *The Fate of the Furious* (2017; hereinafter *Fast Eight*), Dominic Toretto (Vin Diesel) and Letty Ortiz (Michelle Rodriguez) are on their honeymoon in Cuba, perusing the custom cars on display at a street racing event. They find a young man and his father working on the engine of the Ford truck that the young man tells them has been passed down in his family. Dom celebrates this family and their generational hard work, calling it the 'Cuban spirit', and tells the young man and his father, 'Don't ever lose that!' Shortly after, Dom wins a drag race (an action-packed sequence through the streets of Havana); and once he crosses the finish line, a cheering group of Cuban children surround him. Dom lifts a young girl up onto his shoulder, smiles over at Letty and shrugs. This opening sequence sheds light on the *Fast Saga*'s strong emphasis on family. The Cuban spirit that Dom lauds in this sequence is domestically reified through the kinship ties of the young man and his father scrappily working together on their car (because, just as the *Fast & Furious* franchise is all about family, so too is it all about cars). This sequence reveals what the *Fast & Furious* franchise celebrates about Dom – his paternalistic moral code. He celebrates father-son bonding and gains the admiration of the children of Cuba. Dom is represented, here, not just as a man of the people but as the *father* of the people.

Letty, by his side the entire time, is represented peripherally as his supportive wife who reinforces Dom's paternalistically rendered heroism – or, as Nathalie Emmanuel's character Ramsey explains in *Furious 7* (2015), Dom is 'Alpha' and Letty is 'Mrs. Alpha'. In short, the opening of *Fast Eight* demonstrates the heteronormative familial frameworks of the *Fast & Furious* franchise. This chapter examines these frameworks as an inroad into interrogating the *Fast Saga*'s continuing pop culture reification of the paterfamilias as idealized contemporary action hero and 'action babes' as figures who recentre paternalistic, masculine strength in action cinema (O'Day 2004; Shary 2013).

The idealized cinematic masculinity of the paterfamilias is something Hannah Hamad (2014: 1) characterizes as a 'dominant cultural trope of postfeminism, and a structuring paradigm of mediated masculinity'. The paternal cinematic hero is increasingly prevalent in the early twenty-first century, during which 'Hollywood has produced a proliferation of distinctly identifiable cycles and sub-cycles of films that discursively prioritize fatherhood'. What's more, the idealized postfeminist paterfamilias *continues* to be centred in contemporary Hollywood films that 'perpetuate extant discourses of fatherhood and develop the cycle such that it continues to remain culturally viable' (Ibid: 6). The figure of the father is a key site for interrogating gender in postfeminist cinema, and Dominic Toretto – the postfeminist paterfamilias of the *Fast Saga* – is a relevant case study for Hollywood cinema's continued prioritization of fatherhood.

Kenneth MacKinnon (2003) explains that, during the 1990s, cinematic representations of masculine strength became 'associated with internal, personal values demonstrated through men's relations with their families'. In post-1990s Hollywood action films, men 'find their salvation in a reassertion of sensitivity and the value that they place on family commitment. Their strengths must now be used in defence of family' (Ibid: 55–63). Thus, films such as *Lethal Weapon 3* (1992), *Die Hard with a Vengeance* (1995) and *Con Air* (1997) feature protagonists whose fatherhood provides a representational framework for their heroism. Following the 1990s, films like *War of the Worlds* (2005) and *San Andreas* (2015) further solidify the centring of the paterfamilias as action hero. The *Fast & Furious* films are therefore part of a cycle of US 'muscular cinema' that increasingly privileges fatherhood through heroes that 'play the figure of the father' (Tasker 1993: 128).

The *Fast Saga*'s Dominic Toretto is a particularly relevant case study for exploring the primacy of the post-millennium, postfeminist paterfamilias in the contemporary US action film. Dom consistently plays the figure of the father, often referring to his motley crew of street racers-cum-superheroes as 'family'. The strength of the bonds among Dom's surrogate family is consistently celebrated as the reason for their ability to successfully vanquish their foes. At the same time, Dom's family perpetuates patriarchal reifications of familial labour, especially in the *Fast Saga*'s depiction of parenthood. This reification becomes especially apparent in the later films of the saga, with the events of *Fast Five* (2011) catalysing the franchise's increasing emphasis on family and the domestic sphere. While *The Fast and the Furious* (2001) establishes Dom as a symbolic father figure through the film's model of chosen family, it is not until *Fast Five* – during which Mia (Jordana Brewster) and Brian (Paul Walker) discover they are going to have a child, and Dom is thus also about to become an uncle – that the domestication of Dom becomes a dominant theme. *Fast & Furious 6* (2013) and *Furious 7* further explore Mia and Brian's roles as parents, while Dom himself becomes a father in *Fast Eight*. As these characters shift into their new parenting roles, so too does the *Fast Saga* shift its representation of familial labour, which depicts maternal and paternal labour in drastically different ways.

This chapter explores the franchise's increasing centring of maternal and paternal bodies. Taking *Fast Eight* as its central case study, it examines the evolving representations of Dom, Letty, Mia and Elena Neves (played by Elsa Pataky), charting these characters' embodiment of patriarchal family and domestic labour. I argue that, from *Fast Five* on, Dom's role as the true patriarch and idealized paterfamilias of *Fast & Furious* becomes solidified through biological fatherhood, and that this shift to paternal action hero is a cinematic effort to rehabilitate Dom's character through domestic authority – he plays the figure of the father for his family, for cinema, for the world. What is more, Dom's rehabilitated fatherly image becomes even more apparent through the representation of women in the *Fast Saga*. Women like Mia, Elena and Letty are relegated to the sidelines of not just these films but also their roles as mothers, because their true representational purpose is to bolster the centrality of Dom's role as *Fast & Furious* father.

## Hard daddies and action babes: Cinematic frameworks for analysing the *Fast Saga*

Film scholars like Susan Jeffords (1994) have argued that action hero fathers become prevalent in action films of the 1980s and 1990s, during and in the wake of the Reagan Era. Jeffords argues that the films of the Reagan Era rearticulate 'masculine strength and power through internal, personal, and family-oriented values' via the intersection of the 'hard body and the "sensitive family man"' (Jeffords 1994: 13). Anne Gjelsvik (2013: 102) argues that the nationalistic hard body of the action genre centres 'a patriarchal and individualistic heroic male' figure, resulting in the action genre being thought of as 'a conservative genre'.

She refers to this figure as 'the new father-hero', whose 'heroic masculinity is less a matter of muscles and is more a matter of inner strength, or an internal masculinity' (Ibid: 99–102).

Andrea Schofield (2016) similarly examines the 'hard daddy', or the 'extremely muscled men' who take on the role of father in contemporary action films. While the hard bodies of the 1980s stem from Reagan Era constructs of idealized masculinity, the muscled hard daddies of post-millennium cinema 'can be linked to post 9/11 politics in the United States' because the 'superhumanly hard body' of the post 9/11 action hero is 'coupled with the theme of paternal protection of the family and nation'. The emergence of the hard daddy is thus 'slippery precisely because it allows the model to change slightly … without any change to the traditional, conservative American family values underlying it and that it serves to uphold' (Ibid: 125–8). Much of Gerard Butler and Dwayne Johnson's respective cinematic oeuvres fit this bill; for example, in *Geostorm* (2017), Butler plays a father and scientist motivated by his young daughter to save the world from both climate change *and* greedy politicians. In *Skyscraper* (2018), Johnson plays an FBI-agent-turned-security-consultant who must save his family trapped in a burning skyscraper that has been taken over by terrorists. Both Johnson and Butler embody the role of the hard daddy in these films (and many others). These father-heroes use their hard bodies to protect their families, the nation and the world.

Conversely, pop culture and cinematic representations of women's maternal roles and familial labour face a different set of discursive tensions. According to Milestone and Meyer (2012), pop culture representations of womanhood often construct women as being 'relational in the sense of being tied to and defined by others, most notably men and children, in their capacities as lovers, partners, wives or mothers' which 'contributes to the maintenance of a culture in which autonomous and full selfhood is not immediately or easily available to women'. This relationality results in motherhood being 'the key role which continues to tie femininity to the domestic sphere' because 'bringing up children is a woman's job' (Ibid: 92–105).

Schofield (2016) explains that women's relationality is pervasive in action films because these films 'maintain an unwavering devotion to a heteronormative notion of family' in which the hard daddy is 'paired with a classically beautiful woman in every case'. Often, these beautiful mother figures 'disappear, fade into the background, or are absent altogether, a common feature of a millennial and postfeminist focus on fatherhood' that centres the parental figure of the hard daddy. The absence of maternal bodies in post-millennium action films 'problematically place[s] the emphasis on the father as nurturer at the expense of the mother, promoting the view that fathers are the ones who should now be doing it all' (Ibid: 134–6). As Yvonne Tasker (1993: 17) contends, this emphasis occurs because the action film 'operates as an almost exclusively male space' in which heroines 'tend to be fought over rather than fighting, avenged rather than avenging. In the role of threatened object they are significant, if passive, narrative figures'. Maternal heroines are especially passive and peripheral in action films because their domestic relationality bolsters the centrality of the hard daddy as action hero, reinforcing action cinema's almost exclusively male spaces.

In Hollywood films of the early 2000s, the relationality and peripherality of the contemporary maternal action hero are complicated by the emergence of characters Marc O'Day (2004: 201) calls *action babes*, or 'attractive women [starring] as hugely capable heroines "kicking ass"'. Action babe movies – like *Æon Flux* (2005) and *Ultraviolet* (2006) – emphasize 'beautiful feminine bodies combined with active masculine strength', and while 'it remains the case that in patriarchy it is often men who look at women and women who are looked at, both the action hero and heroine can increasingly be viewed as simultaneously active and passive, both in action and on display' (Ibid: 203–4). Action babes – including *maternal* action babes – combine conventional, heteronormative beauty with active strength (often deemed the domain of the masculine). They are liminal figures in action cinema, paradoxically both active and passive.

Acknowledging the roles of mothers and fathers is needed when analysing the *Fast Saga*'s representational impact because a 'full understanding of representations of women can also only be gained in conjunction with an analysis of representations of men, and the ways in which they compare' (Milestone and Meyer 2012: 112). There are, of course, limitations to the kind of analysis that compares representations of men and women, masculinities and femininities. Such analysis can fall into the limited trappings of gendered binaries and heteronormativity, instead of making space for a spectrum of gender roles, identities and relationships. That said, *Fast & Furious* itself perpetuates such binaristic constructions of gender and labour. Interrogating these binaries in the *Fast Saga* thus allows for an engagement with the limitations of heteronormative gender roles and the representation of these roles in a popular cultural phenomenon like the *Fast & Furious* family.

## 'Salud, mi familia': Dominic Toretto as *Fast & Furious* paterfamilias

The *Fast Saga* centres Dominic Toretto as the true patriarch of the *Fast & Furious* family. From the first film, Dom acts as paternal moral centre not solely for his biological family but also for the chosen, surrogate family surrounding him. In *The Fast and the Furious*, Mia describes Dom as being 'like gravity' because of his propensity for drawing people into his surrogate family and looking after them. This propensity only accelerates throughout the saga as Dom continues to draw in and nurture new family members from all over the world. Dom is the centre of this familial network; as such, this family functions as a reflection of Dom and what drew these people to him in the first place – his paternal moral code based in loyalty and the uncompromising goal of taking care of one's own (or, as Dom puts it in *Fast & Furious* 6, 'You don't turn your back on family'). Because this family is a reflection of Dom, it also serves to define Dom's paternal masculinity as one that is open to loving relationships with the people in his life. The action hero as true patriarch is thus capable of emotional connectivity, and Dom's connection to his family is what typically catalyses him to action.

Dom's idealized paternal morality is complicated, however, by the fact that he is initially a sort of antihero in the first film. He begins the *Fast Saga* as a street racer in Los Angeles who leads a crew of fellow racers not only in illegal street racing competitions but also in robbing semi-trucks of the goods they transport. As an antihero, Dom is oppositional – he is a man who cannot be tied down, who lives by his own moral code. The first film of the *Fast Saga* thus establishes and celebrates Dom's ethos as a man who lives by his own code of masculinity.

The first film further idealizes Dom's code by grounding it in his relationship with his (now deceased) father. Dom's father shared his love of car culture with his son; Dom's father was a skilled racer 'coming up in the pro stock car circuit' and who helped Dom build his Dodge Charger. Dom's father is his role model who died tragically in a car crash during a race. In his grief, Dom violently assaults the man who caused his father's car to crash on the track: 'I had a wrench. And I hit him, and I didn't intend to keep hitting him, but by the time I was done, I couldn't lift my arm.' The influence of Dom's father is twofold. First, his paternal influence inspires Dom's ultimate occupational path as racer, mechanic, and car expert. But his death also results in Dom's violence, anger, and criminality. Dom brutally assaults a man because his antiheroic, oppositional masculine code requires him to seek justice on his own terms. At the same time, though, Dom does seem to express remorse, which solidifies his antiheroism – yes, he behaved violently, but the audience is asked to empathize with his violent response to his father's death. Because he acted impulsively out of grief, his actions are meant to be justified, or at least forgiven. This father/son framework is thus the justification for Dom's masculinist violence.

However, this framework shifts in *Fast Five*, as the franchise develops Dom's backstory including his relationship with his father. In *Fast Five*, Dom's father is referred to as a paternal role model – someone who went to church, supported his community and took the time to help his daughter with her education alongside providing for his family. This shift from posthumous justification for Dom's youthful, rebellious violence to paternal role model parallels Dom's own shifting representation throughout the saga; Dom too shifts from wayward antihero who lacks a strong male role model to a world-wise paternal role model in his own right as he replicates the family-focused moral code he learned from his deceased father.

Dom's relationship with his father is thus crucial to how Dom is (re)cast in the later films of the *Fast & Furious* franchise. Dom is not even present in the second or third films of the franchise, but upon his return, he is remodelled and recentred in the franchise through his playing the figure of the father. From *Fast Five* on, Dom acts off his memory of his father's work ethic, domesticity and paternal moral code. The father/son relationship that anchors Dom to the domestic sphere speaks to Jeffords's (1994: 170) argument that action films privilege 'the world of the family' as a response to 'declining workplace and national structures as sources of masculine authority and power'. By centring the power of the father in the domestic sphere, action films are not required to 'acknowledge a point at which masculinity must recognize its own negation' because action films instead allow audiences to admire action heroes' 'emotional commitment' (Ibid: 172). In the *Fast Saga*, audiences are asked to admire Dom's emotional commitment to his family, which allows his idealized post-millennium masculinity to remain intact, rehabilitated through the father/son relationship.

All this comes to a head in *Fast Eight* when Dom himself becomes a biological father. The villain Cipher (played by Charlize Theron) has kidnapped Elena Neves, with whom Dom had a romantic relationship in *Fast Five* and *Fast & Furious 6*. Dom also discovers that Cipher has kidnapped Elena and Dom's infant son – a son Dom did not know he had prior to Cipher's kidnapping him. Elena, restrained in a cell, tells Dom, 'Whatever happens, just save our son. *Your* son.' Elena's call catalyses Dom into action: he performs feats of heroism to save *his* son. Moreover, Elena's emphasis on '*Your* son' prioritizes Dom's fatherhood. In this scene, then, Dom is the father-as-saviour while Elena is the mother who requires salvation.

While Dom's newfound role as biological father gives him the paternal impetus for fighting back against Cipher's villainy, it also results in a new set of vulnerabilities. Indeed, Cipher is able to coerce Dom into working for her by threatening to harm his child. On the surface, it seems as though Dom must make a choice. Either he must work for Cipher to save his son, thereby turning his back on the rest of his surrogate family (which we know all too well does not square with Dom's moral code), or he must reject Cipher's offer, thereby putting Elena and his son at risk. Cipher calls Dom's paternal moral code into question and tells him he is 'a man who lives by his own rules' who should not be tied down by family. In other words, Cipher believes Dom's prioritization of family is at odds with his original status as street-racing antihero. *Fast Eight*, through Cipher, renders precarious Dom's kinship bonds, also evidenced in some of the film's taglines, like 'Family will be broken' and 'Family no more'. *Fast Eight* brings these tensions to the fore because Dom's central conflict occurs through the need to reconcile the responsibilities he has taken on by playing the figure of the father with the risk he continually asks his family members to take on.

Dom's role as post-millennium paterfamilias ultimately provides the framework through which to resolve these tensions. Dom asks Cipher, 'You want to see the old Dom? Watch.' The audience, too, watches as Dom wields the furious violence of his antiheroic roots to take down Cipher and save his son. Just as Dom's love for his father drove him to violence years ago, so too does his love for his newfound son return him to violence – the old Dom is born anew when his role as father is literalized through the appearance of his biological son. Dom's biological fatherhood thus functions as the film's narrative motivation for his violent actions throughout the film; his literalized fatherhood gives audiences a reason to continue to root for him because his violence is framed as a heroic act of justice in the name of his son.

Karen Schneider (1999: 4) refers to this (re)centring as the 'spectacular rearticulation' of the heteronormative nuclear family, in which the action hero's story is 'the story of the family, tortured and triumphant'. *Fast Eight* (and the *Fast & Furious* franchise more broadly) fits this bill, for it 'violently enact[s] the centrality of the family to the structuring of contemporary American experience' (Ibid: 4). Dom puts his family at risk so that he can save them. Indeed, he's able to reassemble the family unit through violence precisely because he is the hard daddy who protects 'protect the family, the community, the nation, and even the world' (Schofield 2016: 128). While Dom's violence, in the beginning of *Fast Eight*, seems to tear his family apart, it is also what ultimately brings them (at least, those left alive) together again by the end of the film. Dom's oppositional, violent masculinity is rehabilitated because it allows him to bring his family back together, stronger than before.

What complicates Dom's rehabilitated, oppositional masculinity is its paradoxical oppositionality towards the capitalist structures undergirding a big-budget Hollywood action franchise like *Fast & Furious*. Dom's paternalistic moral code is constructed in opposition to the capitalist prioritization of wealth accumulation. Perhaps the clearest demonstration of this occurs in a toast Dom gives in *Fast Five*: 'Toast! Money will come and go. We know that. But the most important thing in life will always be the people in this room. Right here. Right now. Salud, mi familia.' This oppositional posturing is paradoxical because Dom and his family are working together to steal millions of dollars from a Brazilian drug cartel in *Fast Five*. They are thus (like the franchise itself) labouring together towards the attainment of capital – the very money that Dom says will come and go. Dom's rehabilitated paternalism requires him to discursively deprioritize such monetary gain even while seeking it; he is no longer the thieving antihero of *The Fast and the Furious* but is now, from *Fast Five* on, the strong, paternal everyman who centres family and loyalty.

This shift in Dom's depiction allows *Fast & Furious* to tidily avoid challenging the inequities that occur within the capitalist systems in which the franchise is located; indeed, the centring of family allows the franchise to sidestep systemic concerns and continue profiting from them. Dom, the heroically paternal everyman, promotes a homogenizing ethos that deprioritizes the kind of financial stability that is hard to come by for most people existing within capitalist systems of labour and power (and thus much of the *Fast Saga*'s audience itself). Dom hosts backyard barbecues at his home in Los Angeles, he knows his way around the favelas of Brazil, and he is beloved by the children of Cuba. Dom, the paternal everyman, is a hero the *Fast Saga*'s audience can root for without having to acknowledge the capitalist systems that exploit them while the franchise itself simultaneously profits from their spectatorship. Dom's representation as post-millennium paterfamilias is thus both a paradoxical and conservative one; the centring of Dom's paternal heroism retains the status quo of capitalism *and* masculinity while superficially posturing in opposition to the very systems of power the *Fast Saga* continues to uphold.

## 'You ride, I ride': The maternal action babes of the *Fast Saga*

Dom's centring as paternal action hero happens at a cost, and women (especially those who are mothers and mother figures) bear the brunt of that cost. Andrea Schofield (2016: 137) explains that maternal peripherality in action films 'reinforces the dominance of the American male at the head of the household, and the idea that his happiness is paramount'. Their peripherality also reinforces heteronormative models of family 'with strong gender stereotypes at their cores, reasserting the status quo' (Ibid). The heteronormative peripherality of the women in Dom's orbit ultimately serves to reinforce the status quo of Dom's centred and idealized masculinity.

For example, the women of *Fast & Furious* often function as representational figures who reinforce Dom's ethos and worthiness as an action hero. If Dom is the paternal everyman, Mia is the maternal everywoman who reaffirms Dom's masculinity through her idealized femininity as it manifests in the domestic sphere. Dom hosts the barbecues, but Mia does the dishes afterwards. At the same time, Mia does the grocery shopping and reminds Dom to say grace. In *The Fast and the Furious*, when Brian tells Mia that the 'only thing that ever pulled [him] in was [her]', she acknowledges her peripherality in relation to Dom in responding, 'It's nice to come first every once in a while.' Mia's only venue for centrality as a woman in the franchise is through heteronormative romantic love. But even then, her centrality only goes so far because Brian's relationship with (and ultimate marriage to) Mia functions as *his* inroad into *Dom's* family. As an idealized heteronormative woman, Mia is always relational, whereby many of her actions serve to bolster Dom's centrality the *Fast Saga*'s hero.

Similar claims can be made for the role of Letty Ortiz. Letty starts off in *The Fast and the Furious* as Dom's girlfriend and fellow street racer who is consistently objectified and fetishized: Dom refers to Letty as 'my trophy', for example, while other characters say they want to race Letty 'for that sweet little ass'. While Letty is fetishized in street racing's masculinist subculture, she is also depicted as a competent driver and someone unafraid to stand up for herself. Letty's liminality – the fact that she combines agency with objectification – results from her existing as a woman in a patriarchal subculture. Letty must navigate the male-dominated subculture of the street-racing scene: she must navigate a culture that sees her not as an expert street racer or central member of their community but instead as a peripheral trophy, a pretty face who is expected to sit on the sidelines instead of in the seat of a car. Letty pushes back against her objectification and marginalization, but she also accepts the gendered rules of street racing. Her acceptance of these norms allows her, liminally and problematically, to empower herself and claim space with that masculinist subculture. In this sense, Letty is indicative of cinematic character type that Marc O'Day (2004: 216) refers to as the action babe who 'produce[s] potent fantasies of female empowerment'. Letty embodies the role of the action babe – a liminal, paradoxical figure who is 'both vulnerable and strong and, above all, who survive[s] and win[s], often in great style' (Ibid). The action babe is a paradoxical cinematic character because she unsettles traditional gender binaries while simultaneously upholding them. Letty, too, is a paradox. She is both strong and vulnerable, upsetting gender norms; but she also empowers herself so that she can exist within and thus perpetuate the masculinist subculture of street racing, thereby upholding the gendered centrality of patriarchy and masculinity.

Letty's cinematic relationality to Dom further complicates her role as action babe and her representational ability to unsettle heteronormative gender binaries. Her relational status as Dom's girlfriend often provides narrative grounding for Dom's actions. For example, Letty's murder in the fourth film, *Fast & Furious* (2009), narratively justifies Dom's violent efforts to seek justice and revenge. Letty's reappearance in *Fast & Furious 6* (in which it is revealed that she survived the attack on her life but suffered substantial memory loss) affords Dom similar narrative justification for his violent efforts to save her and reassimilate her back into his family. Letty's erasure and subsequent re-emergence thus reiterate Dom's position in the franchise.

What's more, Letty's apparent death in the fourth film allows Dom to justify his coupling with Elena Neves in *Fast Five*; with Letty out of the picture, Dom is a free agent. Elena, a police officer in Rio de Janeiro, lends an international dimension to Dom's paternal everyman status. She is idealized (in true action babe fashion) as a tough, competent officer and an understanding and beautiful woman who wants to help those around her. She too is an everywoman in her own right, which makes her representationally worthy of Dom's love and trust because her moral code aligns with his. But her worthiness also underscores Dom's, reinforcing his representational centrality in the franchise. Further, because Elena was previously married to a fellow police officer who died in the line of duty, she is tethered domestically to a man even in her occupation. Her domesticity ultimately helps justify Dom's return to Letty when she re-emerges in *Fast & Furious 6*. Elena says to Dom, 'If that was my husband, if there was a chance, no matter how small, I would go.' Like Letty, Elena is a paradoxical action babe. She is both a tough cop *and* a loving wife, and the intersection of these traits is what provides Dom the narrative justification for leaving her. She tells Dom to go because it is what she, the idealized action babe, would do. In other words, Elena's moral code reinforces Dom's, while also providing justification for Dom's non-monogamy, which allows Dom to retain his idealized paternalistic masculinity.

When Letty and Elena finally meet at the end of *Fast & Furious 6*, they diffuse any possibility for romantic tension or conflict; they thank each other for trying to 'keep [Dom] out of trouble', saying that it 'takes an amazing woman' to be with such 'an amazing guy'. On the surface, their mutual respect and understanding make space for reimagined alternatives in what is deemed socially acceptable in constructions of family, which aligns with the action babe's potential for unsettling gender norms. However, it also, paradoxically, allows Dom to sidestep what could have been a complicated situation because Elena and Letty's tidy resolution functions as little more than a reflection of Dom himself – they are amazing women *because* Dom is an amazing man. They are worthy action babe protagonists *because* Dom is a worthy masculine action hero. Thus, while Elena and Mia have the potential to representationally disrupt heteronormative family structures, they never achieve that potential because the post-millennium action babes of the *Fast Saga* are conservative postfeminist figures who bolster the centrality of the patriarchal status quo.

Further, when Mia, Elena and Letty become mothers and maternal figures, their maternal bodies continue to function as embodied reinforcements for Dom's paternal masculinity. Mia's pregnancy in *Fast Five* begins Dom's transition to hard daddy. When Mia tells Brian and Dom she is pregnant, Dom says, 'Our family just got bigger.' Brian may be the biological father, but in saying '*Our* family' Dom centres himself as the true patriarch of their family. More than this, Dom acts as paternal mentor to Mia and Brian as they navigate the world as new parents, solidifying his status as surrogate father. When Mia tells Dom she is pregnant with her second child but has not yet told Brian, being afraid he will be 'disappointed with his life', Dom reaffirms her idealized domesticity and femininity by reaffirming that she is 'the best thing that's ever happened to [Brian].' Referring to Mia as the best *thing* in Brian's life is telling – she may be a *good* thing but she is a thing nonetheless. Mia is a conservative, heteronormative maternal prop for both Brian and Dom. She connects them to each other by blood and acts as a domestic catalyst for both men's heroic violence.

In *Fast Eight*, Elena also becomes a maternal prop, which further demonstrates the limitations in her potential to disrupt gender binaries as action babe. When

Cipher captures Elena and her infant son, the threat to Dom's family catalyses him to action. While Elena has shown herself to be both strong and vulnerable as an action babe of the franchise, her (re)construction as vulnerable mother returns her to the status quo of representational gender binaries; she is the passive, captured mother who must be saved and Dom is the active, heroic father who strives to save her. Her passive maternity centres Dom's paternity, which is evidenced when she tells Dom of their child, 'I call him Marcos. But that's his middle name. I thought his father should give him his first name.' Even in the act of naming their son, Dom's fatherhood takes primacy over Elena's motherhood. Dom's paternal precedence erases Elena's maternal significance. Elena's maternity is further erased through her absence; we never see the lived, bodily experience of her pregnancy or labour, or the challenging work of raising an infant as a single, working mother. We see none of Elena's lived maternal experience or domestic labour. We only see her capture – the conservative relational catalyst for Dom's paternal violence.

Elena's role as mother is thus *fully* erased when Cipher murders her. Elena's murder occurs off-screen – a representational erasure – but we see the muzzle flashes, hear Marcos cry and focus on Dom's face as grief and rage play out across it upon witnessing Elena's murder. Because the camera focuses on Dom's reaction, his paternity is centred while Elena's maternity is erased cinematically (her death occurs off-screen) *and* materially (she is erased when murdered). Her death justifies Dom's violent heroism, just as her motherhood solidifies Dom's role as true patriarch by literalizing it through biological fatherhood. Thus, while Elena enters the franchise in *Fast Five* as an action babe with the potential to challenge traditional gender roles, the franchise ultimately recasts her as a martyred mother in *Fast Eight* whose primary representational value is to prop up Dom's paternal ethos.

Like Elena, Mia's maternity is rendered peripheral through the erasure of her maternal body. Mia gives birth in *Fast & Furious 6*, but as with Elena we do not see the work of that labour. The messy, difficult work of pregnancy and motherhood is not visible in the *Fast Saga*. Even Mia's birth scene focuses on Brian and Dom's efforts to race each other to the convent hospital in which Mia begins her labour. This focus not only centres Brian and Dom's heroic fatherhood through the passive peripherality of Mia's waiting maternal body, but it also, through its location at a *convent* hospital, idealizes Mia's maternal femininity through the piety that the convent setting implies. Mia's maternal piety reflects onto Brian and Dom, rehabilitating *both* men as worthy and good fathers. Just as Mia's maternal labour is visually erased from the *Fast Saga*, so too is her maternal role *narratively* erased. After Paul Walker's death, Brian is absent from the franchise. Because Mia's character is attached to his, the franchise writes Mia out of some of the later films of the *Fast Saga*, a testament to just how relational her character is. Mia is barely in *Furious 7* and is not in *Fast Eight* at all – a narrative death that demonstrates that Mia's representational role is to orbit and reflect Brian (instead of existing in her own capacity).

Similarly, Elena's murder narratively makes room for Letty to become representationally reborn as adoptive mother to Marcos. The groundwork for Letty's transition into a maternal figure is laid at the beginning of *Fast Eight*, as a postcoital Letty discusses the possibility of having a child with Dom: 'I couldn't help but to imagine what you'd be like if you were a dad.' Letty here reveals that the underlying motivation for having a child is so Dom can be a father; this statement centres what fatherhood would mean for Dom and says nothing about what motherhood would mean for Letty. Letty never states whether or not *she* wants a child, an omission that centres Dom's fatherhood as being of primary domestic importance in the potential of Letty's pregnancy. Here again the later films of the *Fast Saga* return to the patriarchal status quo by centring fatherhood at the expense of motherhood and hierarchically casting the power of the father as being more important than the power of the mother.

Interestingly, the franchise's efforts to rehabilitate Dom as hard daddy *require* his domestic connections to Letty. Letty, unlike Elena, is married to Dom, so when Letty takes Elena's maternal place after her death by becoming Marcos's adoptive mother, she returns Dom and Marcos to the conservative, heteronormative status quo of the nuclear family. Dom resides at the head of this nuclear family, a hierarchical domesticity that Letty reinforces in her wedding vows to Dom: 'You will never be alone again. I vow wherever you go, I go. You ride, I ride' (*Furious 7*). Dom's needs go first because he is narratively prioritized at Letty's expense. We never see Letty have any say in her newfound adoptive mother status; instead, motherhood is something she passively receives. In many ways, Letty's trajectory towards motherhood demonstrates the representational limitations of the franchise's action babes. Letty, Elena and Mia have been recast as prescriptive, postfeminist mothers, a step backward from the already problematic status the action babe occupies. Through their passive relationality as mothers and wives, Letty, Mia and Elena are limited in their capacity to unsettle gender binaries as action babes. The post-millennium, postfeminist ethos of the *Fast & Furious* franchise instead uses their roles as women and mothers to reinforce Dom's paternal primacy.

## Conclusion: New (domestic) frontiers for the *Fast Saga*

In the *Fast Saga*, the masculinities of characters like Dominic Toretto are increasingly manifested through fatherhood, while, simultaneously, the femininities of characters like Elena Neves, Mia Toretto and Letty Ortiz are increasingly manifested through motherhood. The paternalism that Dom demonstrated as surrogate father of his chosen family in the early films of the franchise is now literalized in his biological role as Marcos's father after *Fast Eight*, which renders Dom a father now of both Marcos and the *Fast & Furious* franchise writ large. Examining Dom's fatherhood thus sheds light on the father-hero's perpetuation of the heteronormative, masculinist centrality of patriarchal power in post-millennium action films. Simultaneously, the *Fast Saga* has marginalized the maternal roles and labour of Elena, Mia and Letty to reinforce Dom's paternal power. Examining Mia, Letty and Elena's roles as mothers sheds light on the ways (maternal) action babes continue to be overlooked, erased and made peripheral in post-millennium action films' cinematic imaginings of family. My efforts to examine these women are thus an effort to counter their representational peripherality in the franchise. My effort to examine Dom as *Fast & Furious* paterfamilias is an effort to shed light on action cinema's continued post-millennium, postfeminist centring of heteronormative masculinities.

It will be interesting to see how the future films of the *Fast & Furious* franchise navigate the continuing parenting roles of its central characters. Whatever transpires, it does seem likely that Dom's fatherhood will continue to have increasing importance for the future of the franchise. Cinematic, masculine heroes like Dominic Toretto 'can no longer ride off into the sunset with just a horse for company. The frontier is closed. Or else new frontiers have to be found – in space, or foreign wars – to replace the alibi for male violence that the frontier once provided' (MacKinnon 2003: 63). Space, as a new frontier for male violence and action, is indeed a venue for *F9* (2021) – but fatherhood, too, is a new frontier increasingly explored (at the expense of motherhood) in the *Fast Saga*.

## References

*Æon Flux* (2005), [Film] Dir. Karyn Kusama, USA: MTV Films.
*Con Air* (1997), [Film] Dir. Simon West, USA: Touchstone Pictures.
*Die Hard with a Vengeance* (1995), [Film] Dir. John McTiernan, USA: Cinergi Pictures.

*F9* (2020), [YouTube] 'Official Trailer', 31 January. Available online: https://www.youtube.com/watch?v=aSiDu3Ywi8E (accessed 3 June 2021).

*Geostorm* (2017), [Film] Dir. Dean Devlin, USA: Warner Bros. Pictures.

Gjelsvik, A. (2013), 'From Hard Bodies to Soft Daddies: Action Aesthetics and Masculine Values in Contemporary American Action Films', in K. Aukrust (ed), *Assigning Cultural Values*, 91–106, New York: Peter Lang.

Hamad, H. (2014), *Postfeminism and Paternity in Contemporary U.S. Film: Framing Fatherhood*, London: Routledge.

Jeffords, S. (1994), *Hard Bodies: Hollywood Masculinity in the Reagan Era*, New Brunswick: Rutgers University Press.

*Lethal Weapon 3* (1992), [Film] Dir. Richard Donner, USA: Silver Pictures.

MacKinnon, K. (2003), *Representing Men: Maleness and Masculinity in the Media*, London: Arnold.

Milestone, K. and A. Meyer (2012), *Gender and Popular Culture*, Cambridge: Polity.

O'Day, M. (2004), 'Beauty in Motion: Gender, Spectacle and Action Babe Cinema', in Y. Tasker (ed), *Action and Adventure Cinema*, 201–18, London: Routledge.

*San Andreas* (2011), [Film] Dir. Brad Peyton, USA: New Line Cinema.

Schneider, K. (1999), 'With Violence: Rearticulating the Family in the Contemporary Action Thriller', *Journal of Popular Film and Television*, 27 (1): 2–11.

Schofield, A. (2016), 'Hard Bodies, Soft Hearts: Mixed-Race Men as Muscular Daddies in the Films of Vin Diesel and Dwayne Johnson', in E. Podnieks (ed), *Pops in Pop Culture: Fatherhood, Masculinity, and the New Man*, 125–40, New York: Palgrave Macmillan.

Shary, T. ed (2013), *Millennial Masculinity: Men in Contemporary American Cinema*, Detroit: Wayne State University Press.

*Skyscraper* (2018), [Film] Dir. Rawson Marshall Thurber, USA: Legendary Pictures.

Tasker, Y. (1993), *Spectacular Bodies: Gender, Genre, and the Action Cinema*, London: Routledge.

*Ultraviolet* (2006), [Film] Dir. Kurt Wimmer, USA: Screen Gems.

*War of the Worlds* (2005), [Film] Dir. Steven Spielberg, USA: Amblin Entertainment.

8

# 'I never want to lose a fight': Masculinity, machismo and high-octane action in the *Fast & Furious* franchise

Rebecca Feasey

*The Fast and the Furious* (2001) is both reviled and revered as a remake of the classic action film *Point Break* (1990). However, while popular commentary identifies clear similarities in terms of characters and plot (Jhaveri 2018), the bodies that appear on screen in the two films are starkly different. Whereas Patrick Swayze's charismatic gang-leader Bodhi brings physical grace, agility and strength to the earlier film (Feasey 2023; Tasker 1993a), his contemporary equivalent Dominic Toretto represents a far more rigid and retro iteration of the action hero, owing largely to the muscular physique of actor Vin Diesel. Diesel's hero has since been joined by other equally muscular and macho men within the gear-shifting franchise – namely, Dwayne 'The Rock' Johnson as Luke Hobbs and Jason Statham as Deckard Shaw, two characters who started out as antagonists (in *Fast Five* [2011] and *Fast & Furious* 6 [2013], respectively), before being integrated into the main cast. Although there are various other masculinities on offer in the *Fast & Furious* franchise – from blond-haired, all-American Brian (Paul Walker) to the tomboyish figure of Letty (Michelle Rodriguez) – the ripped and muscular bodies of Dom/Diesel, Hobbs/Johnson and Shaw/Statham are worthy of further attention. After all, these physiques hark back to earlier performances of aggressively macho power and posturing more routinely associated with 1980s action stars such as Arnold Schwarzenegger and Sylvester Stallone, while simultaneously offering a space for negotiating such representations. On one level, this hard-bodied tradition is maintained and circulated by *Fast & Furious*, whereby the films and their supporting media commentary draw attention to the physicality and potent masculinity of Diesel, Johnson and Statham. And, yet, there remains another reading and reception of these actors' herculean bodies both within and beyond the screen space, a reading which sees these men struggling for hegemonic credibility.

Action films are committed to the display of male bodies, be they dancing, driving, fucking or fighting (King 2000; Tasker 1993a). Indeed, 'the role of narrative is strictly secondary' to the hard bodies on offer in these films (Barker and Brookes 1998: 113). And this is particularly true of the films in the *Fast & Furious* franchise, where the bodies of Diesel, Johnson and Statham loom large. It is the multiplicity of male bodies on offer within the franchise that simultaneously upholds and challenges earlier iterations of the hard-bodied hero. After all, while the genre has routinely presented a singular muscular action figure looking to save a city, town or global stage, *Fast & Furious* has scaled up the number of star bodies on display, allowing these bodies to work together while being simultaneously pitted against one another. The notion of ensemble action is relatively new in the genre in question; and while it affords many and multiple opportunities for physical excess, it does so at the expense of presenting a stand-alone hero or a clearly structured hegemonic hierarchy.

With the importance of such bodies in mind, Erich Schwartzel (2019), writing for *The Wall Street Journal*, introduces *Fast & Furious* fans (and those less invested in the franchise) to Diesel, Johnson and Statham's contractual requirements. Audiences are used to hearing about A-list demands in relation to credits, percentage of profits, screen time and script approval, but Schwartzel has heard from *Fast & Furious* producers and crew members about agreements with the studio to carefully balance punches, blows and kicks for the male stars in question (see also Bakare 2019). The story became the focal point for popular and professional commentaries and subsequent mocking of masculinity in relation to hard bodies, fragile egos and broader debates about contemporary male anxiety and masculine insecurity. Having to choreograph the performers so as to afford each equal 'muscle time' in the franchise, reminds us of the hegemonic hierarchy that equates successful masculinity with physical strength and stamina both on and off screen (Schwartzel 2019; see Connell 2005). With this in mind, the following analysis will draw attention to Schwartzel's article and broader press reception materials that foreground notions of age, appearance, power and potency, in order to make sense of the masculinities, machismo and muscular bodies that are on display in the *Fast & Furious* franchise. The goal is to consider the ways in which these hard-bodied action heroes can be seen to both uphold but also disavow their hegemonic credentials in line with earlier iterations of masculine action. These men are keen to secure and maintain their stoic, heroic and authoritative stature by way of their hard-bodied actions, and yet there exists a fine line between maintaining physical power and performing a parody of that self-same prowess.

## Hard bodies and hegemonic masculinities

Feminist film theory has long been interested in the representation of hard, muscular and/or hysterical male bodies. Drawing on Laura Mulvey's (1975) psychoanalytic work on sexual difference in the cinema, Steve Neale (1983/1994) examines the representation of male bodies in masculine-defined genres ranging from action films to westerns. His central thesis is that male bodies are put on display as a site of spectatorial pleasure. Although the object of the spectatorial gaze is routinely associated with feminine lack, as per a binary split between the active/male and the passive/female, Neale notes how on-screen male heroes typically have to *prove* their masculinity despite, and indeed, in part due to their spectacular bodies. Neale reminds us that active males in the action genre are routinely tested and qualified. These characters have to prove their strength, character and resourcefulness over other men in the screen space in order to earn their status as heroic, and indeed hegemonic, figures of masterful spectatorial identification. In line with Neale's (1983/1994) central thesis, action films and franchises from the 1980s to the present routinely depict their hard-bodied heroes being tormented as plot and story demands. Yvonne Tasker (1993a: 39) likewise argues that the genre routinely depicts muscular bodies experiencing torture and suffering, whereby the boundaries of the hard male body 'are repeatedly violated [and] penetrated'. It is the ability to fight through these ritualized scenes of conflict and suffering that enables the hero to show their resolve, determination and omnipotence. According to both Neale and Tasker, these heroes need to be tested and found wanting prior to their later physical victories, in order to earn audience investment in their journey and underline their masculine dominance at narrative closure. Men continue to be put in opposition to other men in the action genre. Strained and straining male bodies are routinely presented as a site of spectacle, display and agency. Characters and, by extension, star actors are routinely held up as hard-bodied figures to emulate, their heroic and stoic efforts having been inextricably linked with the genre in question. Thus, a link seems to exist between the herculean body as capable of withstanding physical trauma, on the one hand, and broader questions around male power and masculine potency as it relates to an oft-valued and valuable iteration of manhood, on the other.

Outside of film studies, the work of Raewyn Connell (2005) provides a valuable framework for exploring the flexible and agile nature of masculine identity. Connell notes that there are many ways of expressing and experiencing masculinity, pointing to a hierarchy of masculinities rather than a fixed, monolithic iteration of manhood. And yet, the hegemonic hierarchy is said to point to a correct or preferred iteration of traditional masculinity that maps onto laconic hard-bodied action figures of earlier generations. The pinnacle of hegemonic masculinity has long been associated with the genre wherein machismo, stoicism, physical prowess, agency, activity, self-reliance and independence, are routinely championed above more domestic and connected iterations of manhood. However, even the toughest of these hard-bodied fictions have to earn and continue to earn their hegemonic credentials, film after film, sequel after spin-off in the franchise. Men do not reach the hegemonic pinnacle and remain in that lofty position; rather, they have to be tested and qualified at each big-budget outing and beyond. This positioning is problematic because while society asks for 'New Men' to replace more traditional/regressive iterations of masculinity, looking to men as caregivers not just authoritative providers, the hegemonic hierarchy continues to hold sway. In short, our action heroes are presented to audiences as 'retro' models of masculinity to emulate or admire (Martin 2015).

Therefore, although the lacerated, bleeding and penetrated male body of the action cinema indicates 'that the hard body can be wounded, that it isn't invulnerable or invincible … the ability to endure severe pain underscores how truly hard these bodies are' (Jeffords 1994: 50). The hard, built, forceful and dominating body of the male is central to both the hegemonic hierarchy and the action genre. Such bodies, once tested, are sold to audiences as heroic and masterful, each stunt, drive or fight is a display of strength, stamina and potency. That said, these visibly worked-on bodies call into question that self-same power. The suggestion here then is that the hard-bodied male speaks to an anxious and threatened iteration of masculinity, a sort of protesting too much of power and authority (Creed 1987). Indeed, their 'hysterical excesses' are said to expose 'a version of masculinity in crisis' whereby muscularity itself is read as 'an act of desperation that lays bare its artificiality' (King 2000: 112). In short, it has been argued that the action genre speaks less of male authority, control and mastery, and more of crisis, weakness and a loss of social power.

In relation to the *Fast & Furious* franchise, we are asked to consider if the ageing muscularity of the cinematic universe stands in for masculine power or parodic performance. After all, Diesel, Johnson and Statham are not just any male bodies in action; they are spectacularly hard(ened) bodies that draw attention to their cars, muscles and, by extension, their very masculinity. The assumption here is that a man in, with and of power, should not need to concern himself with the potential potency of his contemporaries, meaning that any posturing on the topic could be taken as a sign of male fragility rather than active hegemonic agency (Kimmel 2004: 186).

## Hierarchies of masculinity in the *Fast & Furious* franchise

The muscular Diesel plays the elite street racer, auto mechanic and convict Toretto, who appears in the majority of films in the series. Although at various points Toretto is presented as a brother, brother-in-law, husband, uncle and father, it is his efforts as a high-stakes hijacker and, later, explosive government recruit that loom large on screen. In *Fast Five*, the former pro-wrestler Dwayne 'The Rock' Johnson is introduced as Hobbs, a Diplomatic Security Service agent and bounty hunter. Hobbs is tasked with arresting Toretto's racing crew for the murder of Drug Enforcement Administration agents, but tensions between the two men are put on hold when Hobbs learns of Toretto's innocence. Toretto and Hobbs shift from arch rivals to begrudging teammates, becoming something akin to friends as the franchise progresses. Last but not least, we are introduced to Jason Statham as he plays the macho and posturing Shaw, a former British special forces soldier and MI6 agent turned mercenary. Shaw appears as an overarching antagonist in *The Fast and the Furious: Tokyo Drift* (2006) and *Fast & Furious 6* (2013), before taking on the role of Toretto's central antagonist in *Furious 7* (2015). Although Shaw seeks revenge on Toretto and his team for hospitalizing his brother, the two evolve into something resembling allies. In the somewhat predictable, but no less enjoyable tradition of a buddy-cop movie, Hobbs and Shaw move from hostile muscle-bound adversaries to brothers in arms in the *Fast & Furious* spinoff, *Hobbs & Shaw* (2019).

Cars and drivers are both watched and judged for their size, speed, strength, stamina, power and performance in the franchise (Martin 2015). Just as the cars jostle for pole position, so too the hard bodies jostle for a spot at the top of the hegemonic hierarchy. The racing circuit appeals precisely because it can be read as the last bastion of hegemonic masculinity, with racers lining up both on the streets and in the rankings of male power. With hard bodies and hierarchies in mind then, it is worth noting that Johnson and Diesel stand at 1.96m and 1.82m, respectively, while former Olympic diver and model Statham – at 1.78m – is the shortest of the three actors. While the average adult male stands at 1.75m in both the UK and the United States, it is clear that all of these performers stand above the average male, albeit some from a loftier position than others.

Even a cursory glance at the films makes it clear that the physically masterful characters of Toretto, Hobbs and Shaw are presented as sites of physical spectacle. Their hard bodies are repeatedly put on display in scenes and sequences that ask us to view and champion the stamina and resilience of each man in turn. While altercations between the men routinely end without victor or victory, other sequences in the franchise seek to demonstrate physical prowess without a direct face-off. By way of an example, the prison fight scene from *The Fate of the Furious* (2017) is a hard-bodied, ensemble set piece that encourages us to gaze at the physical prowess of both Hobbs and Shaw as they break out of a maximum security prison. Even though the scene begins with macho banter and verbal sparring, teasing audiences with the possibility of a 'straight-up, old-fashioned fight fight' between the two characters, we are soon left watching the herculean efforts of these men separately but simultaneously as they escape their cells. Both bodies are depicted as active, potent and masterful, both looking to take their place at the pinnacle of the hegemonic hierarchy. As such, the fight (like many others in the franchise) appears to deflect and negotiate genre conventions that routinely award a singular figure as victor and hero. All three male stars of the franchise can be seen to construct and maintain their power and potency against the other men in the screen space, therefore; but they do so in a way that appears to lock them in a curious form of stasis, as equally active and alpha males operating within the ensemble action structure. The various ways in which *Fast & Furious* negotiates the hegemonic hierarchy can be seen to extend outwards from the films and into the press reception and commentary, as the franchise intersects with wider debates about gender, masculinity, sexuality and ageing.

The *Fast & Furious* franchise can be understood as a crucial site for debating and negotiating ideas around contemporary masculinity and appropriate machismo on screen and off. Even before Statham joined the 'manchise', *Essence* (2011) was talking about Diesel and Johnson as the 'eye candy' of the film series. Elsewhere, Diesel is singled out as a 'musclehound' for audiences to admire (Eschrich 2015) while Johnson is swooned over for this 'square jaw and gorgeous girth' (Essence 2011). Indeed, the franchise as a whole is championed for its 'prodigious displays of musculature' (Bloomer 2019), 'macho melodrama' (Puchko 2020) and 'testosterone-soaked action' (Martin 2015). Since Statham joined, these films have been said to house 'three of the biggest, beefiest actors in Hollywood' (Millar 2019). These men are not just presented to us as muscular frames to admire, but rather, they are routinely held up as figures, and 'shredded' physiques to emulate (Banham 2015; Jussim 2018). Their bodies are hard, built, 'taut' and 'ready for action' (Dyer 2002: 129), and it is this physicality and hard-bodied agency that drives the on- and off-screen hierarchies of masculinity. Commenting on the proposed *Hobbs & Shaw* sequel, we are told that there are 'two solid facts that can be confirmed: Dwayne "The Rock" Johnson keeps growing more muscles, and Jason Statham's beard stubble gets coarser and manlier every time he punches a baddie in the face' (Tye 2022). In short, muscles and machismo are central to the *Fast & Furious* cinematic universe, forming a key part of both its film/star brand and identity.

## From formidable to fragile masculinity

Seminal work from the field of feminist film studies makes it clear that the appeal of the action hero lies in the new and diverse ways in which their strength, physicality and, by extension, masculinity are tested within the narrative (Neale 1983/1994). In Tasker's (1993b: 233) work on the genre we are reminded of the 'expansive landscapes' and the 'staggering obstacles' that the hero 'must overcome'. Whether it is a terrified looking Schwarzenegger/Dutch being hunted in *Predator* (1987), Stallone/Rocky as the perennial underdog in the movies of the same name or even Tom Cruise/Ethan Hunt being *almost* killed in the *Mission: Impossible* franchise, these men are all pushed to their breaking point before they earn, or reclaim, their heroic credentials. Indeed, John Beynon (2001: 65) argues that while hard and muscular physiques are important to the action hero, it's ultimately their 'determination ... to survive' that sets them apart within the filmic narratives. Thus, the hero's suffering is a central trope in the action genre, one of several 'masochistic spectacles' that allows for the 'eroticisation of the male body, through physical punishment and near-destruction', while also offering the opportunity for 'regeneration and remasculinization' (Fradley 2004: 239).

The men of *Fast & Furious* do battle with rocket launchers and robot cars, and, as such, their ability to withstand pain, suffering, torment and torture is clear and noted. However, rather than continue to present these hard bodies as sites of power and potency, the characters of Toretto, Hobbs and Shaw – and, by extension, the actor, wrestler and diver – could alternatively be read more in line with Barbara Creed's (1987) notion of anxious and hysterical masculinity than hegemonic hard-bodied heroes. According to Creed, the drive to construct and maintain a gym-honed muscular physique speaks to a man's desire to be read as assertive and authoritative rather than as evidence of any innate or assumed power or potency behind that labour. The time and energy dedicated to bulking up in line with the action body can be seen to challenge masculine potency in the sense that genuine male power would not demand such painstaking efforts. Picking up on Creed's seminal thesis, much popular and professional news and review media questions the ostensible mastery of the men behind the franchise.

Schwartzel's (2019) article on the fragile egos of these muscular action heroes was soon picked up by a range of mainstream news and magazine titles keen to mock the seemingly macho stars for their hard-bodied insecurities. The on-set stories revealed to *The Wall Street Journal* and circulated through surrounding channels of discourse coincided with the latest release in the franchise, so that the media reporting of the 'evenly matched' fight scenes became part of and intertwined with the more formulaic and orchestrated press junket that was scheduled to assist in marketing the film (Di Placido 2019). The much-repeated commentaries about physical parity and the matching of threats, punches and prowess meant that reviewers, commentators and critics alike veered between humour and hostility when they spoke about the 'perfectly balanced tedium' of fights between the action men (Heritage 2019).

Criticisms and commentaries spanned countries, contexts and interest groups ranging from automobile-leaning publications, entertainment and pop culture websites, to investigative news titles and business sites. Irrespective of the title in question, they shared a dismissive and derisory tone in their consideration and condemnation of the bulky men in the franchise, drawing attention to the bulging biceps and ripped bodies while highlighting the gulf between their assumed bodily power and their fragile egos. If the hegemonic hierarchy demands that men be forceful, dominant, assertive and victorious in the public realm, we are being told that the big name and bulky stars of the franchise only have the appearance rather than the substance of men in, with and of power. As one Universal spokesman put it, 'every character has their moment … all are seen as formidable opponents' (Schwartzel 2019). Formidable opponents indeed. It is rare that Toretto, Hobbs or Shaw ever win a fight in the franchise. Rather, there is a 'strange symmetry that afflicts the fight scenes' (Di Placido 2019), whereby 'everyone comes out the victor' (Barfield 2019). It is noted that in order 'to appease the demands of all this fragile masculinity' fights between the big name and bulky performers 'tend to end as draws, usually stopped by miraculous outside forces' (Heritage 2019). Dani Di Placido (2019) echoes this point when he states that a 'firm resolution to physical conflict is almost always interrupted by a deus ex machina' in the franchise.

Michael Ballaban (2019) comments that 'given the advanced state of musculature, experience, and career level of action stars like The Rock, Jason Statham, and Vin Diesel' you would assume 'that all three would feel very secure and self-actualized', before adding: 'You would, reportedly, be wrong.' He goes on to note that all three men 'have such massive egos that entire scenes have to be stroked and massaged around them'. Likewise, Alexander Pan (2019) tells us that '[p]itting three protein-chugging bros on a *Fast and Furious* movie set was always going to end in tears' because the last few films have 'essentially consisted of trying to not make either Diesel, Johnson or Statham look, ahem, weak'. Review literature leaves little to the imagination when it describes *Hobbs & Shaw* as 'the most hilariously brittle willy-waving contests in living memory' (Heritage 2019). In short, Schwartzel's (2019) news story became the central focus for the contested and fraught nature of the masculinities offered up in the franchise. Crucially, critics often sought to shift the emphasis from physicality and fighting to sex and performance, with one contemporary article suggesting: 'perhaps it would be a good idea to expand the contractual clauses to other, non-violent aspects of their work … it would be wise to add a sex scene clause … make each sex scene last for exactly three thrusts, during which the female actor yawns distractedly, before the male actor cries and apologies' (Heritage 2019). A lack of sexual stamina and disappointing bedroom performance are indicating a split between hard bodies and hegemonic credibility here. As stated from the outset of the franchise, 'It's not how you stand by your car, it is how you race your car that counts'; and the mocking tone of the commentary makes it clear that the action stars are lacking sexual potency, routinely linked to male mastery. Indeed, hard and built gym bodies can be chided for their interest in appearance and attractiveness over health and fitness. Thus, it is more agile and less bulky figures such as Keanu Reeves who are regularly being championed as the new face of action cinema, as their lightly-toned physiques speak of a quiet-but-powerful masculinity that starkly contrasts the excesses of the hard-bodied men who continue to perform in *Fast & Furious* (Feasey 2023).

Review media is openly chiding in their reading of hard bodies as muscular yet hysterical masks for anxious and fragile masculinities in action. There remains a question here about the ways in which audiences view the muscular masquerade as either reinforcing hegemonic power relations or undermining them. Although one might suggest that the *Fast & Furious* franchise and its surrounding media texts go some way towards denouncing the hegemonic hierarchy, we are reminded that such muscular posturing – or what might be termed the masculine masquerade – remains 'eminently popular, and undeniably potent' with audiences and fans alike (Holmlund 1994: 226). Indeed, while criticisms and commentaries are at turns dismissive and disparaging of the hysterical bodies and their fragile heroics both on and off screen, there remains an equally popular discourse that reads these bodies as beacons of macho strength, prowess and potency, where the physical site of excessive labour is watched, monitored, championed and revered (Leydon 2019; Langberg 2015). Much like the cars of the franchise whose bodies are buffed, polished, monitored and exalted, these hard male bodies are worked on and over, routinely and repeatedly. The men in question share their workouts with a willing audience via men's health magazines and broader social media posts and commentaries (Banham 2015). Even Diesel who has had to deal with speculation over his fluctuating weight and muscle tone befits the action star who always, like the action men of Neale's (1983/1994) foundational thesis, come back harder, firmer and ready to fight another day. In short, these herculean bodies can be understood as negotiated sites of male power, and potency for the actors, characters, creatives, audiences and reviewers within and beyond the franchise.

As noted, seminal scholarship on the action genre makes it clear that a hero needs to be tested in order to prove his masculine credentials for the characters on screen and the invested audience. However, what's interesting here is how popular critics and commentators echo this need for trial and investigation in their accounts of *Fast & Furious*' male stars. We are reminded that it is compelling to 'see one's favourite action hero fall, be beaten to a pulp, only to rise against his aggressor later. Failure is, after all, absolutely integral to the hero's journey' (Di Placido 2019). Although contemporary 'action movies are all about stakes and vulnerability … we need to see them fail so that they can pick themselves up again' (Chatterjee 2019). The *Wall Street Journal* revelations make it clear that the men of the *Fast & Furious* franchise are not prepared to put themselves in these positions of vulnerability up against a potentially hard/er co-star, irrespective of the more routine genre conventions or the hegemonic rewards that are associated with a hero's recovery from pain and torture. While tortured hard bodies are remembered for their heroics, earned over the protagonist's narrative journey, the ostensibly hard bodies of *Fast & Furious* are singled out for their inability to lose a fight, not in a way that garners respect or approval from audiences, industry or reviewers, but in a way that is said to signal their 'crippling fear of emasculation' (Di Placido 2019).

Seminal work on masculinity as spectacle talks about a relatively clear-cut struggle between a hero and villain, referring to the plight of a singular hero suffering at the hands of his nemesis before overcoming and overpowering the inferior masculine threat (Neale 1983/1994). In the action films of the 1980s and 1990s, the hero's physical strife was an engaging and entertaining way of proving their masculine, alpha credentials against other men in the screen space. And yet, while such hard-won mastery makes sense for earlier westerns, war films and historical epics, it doesn't necessarily take into account the ensemble casting of *Fast & Furious*. Although the stars are happy to jostle with their role as either protagonist or antagonist, they are less flexible when it comes to their prowess and primacy. While the literal superheroes of the Marvel Cinematic Universe are regularly seen 'absorbing, and distributing, devastating blows to one another', the men of *Fast & Furious* have no superhero credentials to fall back on (Di Placido 2019). It's as if their very masculinity is, in line with the hegemonic hierarchy, only as good as their last fight or drive, meaning that they cannot let their characters or their star images be tainted by anything less than a bulky draw. That said, the male heroes of *Fast & Furious* are heading towards 'geri-action' territory, and, as such, it is useful to consider the ways in which they might be received in future instalments.

## Fifty is the new ... action hero

Late forty and fifty-something action stars are neither new, nor a novelty in Hollywood (Feasey 2011). While Sean Connery returned to the role of James Bond in *Never Say Never Again* (1983) aged fifty-two, Roger Moore kept performing in that role until *A View to a Kill* (1985), aged fifty-seven. Likewise, action stars such as John Wayne, Burt Lancaster, Steve McQueen and Clint Eastwood, have all performed middle-aged or more mature heroic roles (Tasker 2010). Virginia Wexman (1993: 69) makes the point that the careers of many western stars 'blossomed as their youthful allure faded', while 'a number of classic westerns made in the late 1950s to mid-1970s take the ageing of these stars as their narrative focus' (Holmlund 2002: 143). However, although these ageing stars were performing images of the tough male hero, they were not having to present their bodies as hard, potent spectacles. In fact, it is only recently that we have seen the trend for older actors reprising earlier heroic and hard-bodied action roles, be it Bruce Willis (fifty-two) in *Die Hard 4.0* (2007), Dolph Lungdren (fifty-three) in *The Expendables* (2010) or Sylvester Stallone (sixty) in *Rocky Balboa* (2006). In order to understand the popular appeal of such performances, it has been suggested that 'the ageing body can work as an asset, just another challenge that our battered hero has to overcome' (Tasker 2010). In this way, ageing masculinity is not read as unreliable or failing, problematic or powerless because it is 'skill, toughness and endurance' rather than appearance that is 'valorized' in the genre in question (Beynon 2001: 65). These ageing bodies are still hard bodies, capable of withstanding pain and punishment, and as such they maintain their hegemonic credentials. Any receding hair-lines merely reinforce the notion of power and potency as these men continue to fight, scuffle and come back victorious against younger, ostensibly more virile counterparts.

Ideas of ageing masculinity and/or appearance are directly relevant to a consideration of the *Fast & Furious* franchise. After all, at the time of writing this chapter – just prior to the release of *F9* (2021) – Johnson (forty-nine), Diesel (fifty-four) and Statham (fifty-four) are well past their youth and firmly into middle age. However, seventy seems to be the new fifty in the action movie, with a number of older action icons continuing to perform in the genre at an age when we might previously have expected them to retire - namely, Harrison Ford (seventy-one) in *The Expendables 3* (2014), Arnold Schwarzenegger (seventy-two) in *Terminator: Dark Fate* (2019) and Sylvester Stallone (seventy-three) in *Rambo: Last Blood* (2019). In comparison to these septuagenarians, the late forty-something Johnson and his fifty-something co-stars, Diesel and Statham, appear relatively youthful. From this perspective, then, the bold, bald look of the *Fast & Furious* leads would seem to be unconnected with notions of ageing masculinity.

The close-cropped hair should be read as an extension of their sleek, well-oiled physiques and/or the turbo-boosted cars that they race. These men demand our gaze due to their strong jaws and gym-built bodies, meaning hair styles and styling are often deemed superfluous to any discussion of Johnson, Diesel and Statham as action stars. The hair, like their hard bodies, appears ageless, challenging any decline in virility, potency or visibility that often accompanies later decades. Indeed, their lack of hair is read as an external sign of their testosterone-fuelled masculinity rather than a commentary on their ageing or appearance over the course of the franchise. When Kirsty Puchko (2020) speaks of Diesel's return to the franchise in an upcoming eleventh film, she refers to the star in question as the 'premiere bald badass' of the franchise. The commentary says nothing about age or ageing, rather, we are being asked to consider the interlinking of hard, heroic and hairless masculinity here. Indeed, while the 2012 headline 'Are Bald Men More Virile' is accompanied by a stern looking Willis (Hammond 2012), the more recent 'Bald Men Are More Confident and Attractive' is accompanied by a photo of Statham, with reference also to Diesel (Petter 2017). In a recently published feature in *GQ*, entitled 'Studies Say Bald Men Are More Dominant and Attractive Than Their Thick-Haired Brothers', the article is anchored by a photo of Diesel, Statham and Johnson (GQ 2019). Thus, when their lack of hair is commented on, it is only ever championed and applauded in line with assertive masculinities. In her review of *The Fate of the Furious*, Shani Silver (2017) goes as far as to suggest that the franchise is 'where attractive bald men come to thrive'. The baldness of Diesel, Johnson and Statham, is not framed as evidence of their diminishing powers or the frailties that might normally be seen to come with ageing. Instead, it is held up as further indication of their power and their worked-on bodies which are primed and ready for spectacular action, to be gazed at and upon.

One might assume that a dialogue about age/ing and accompanying questions around power and authority are relevant for the bald, fifty-somethings that dominate *Fast & Furious*. But it's the bodies rather than the hairlines or wrinkled visage of these men that is presented as worthy of their hegemonic credentials and, by extension, the continued success of the franchise. It is as if these men have become a touchstone for ideas of bald beauty, attached to virility and potency. The images of Diesel, Johnson and Shaw can help audiences make sense of the hegemonic hierarchy, considering the role of bodies, hairlines, virility and action to the ranking of contemporary machismo. However, even though one can look at these men as sites of herculean power in a fast and furious universe, the fact that they remain unwilling to show weakness or vulnerability in the face of an alpha threat demonstrates their tenuous grip on masculine power.

## Conclusion: Multiple readings and star images

There is no single, monolithic or fixed reading of the hard-bodied men of *Fast & Furious*. Rather, audience reception can be constructed and circulated by the stars themselves who are keen to ensure their on-screen potency, the filmmakers who ensure and enable the carefully balanced fights and theatrics (Schwartzel 2019), by men's health media who position the performers as empowered role models of physical strength, training and endurance, by popular commentators who fawn over the beauty of the men in motion or by a wider set of professional review commentaries who situate these men as the pinnacle of anxious, fragile overworked and excessive manhood. These men are held up as figureheads of hard and assertive hegemonic masculinity, while simultaneously foregrounding the challenges that accompany excessive and laboured bodies. In short, the franchise can be understood as a space for contested and indeed contradictory readings as they relate to masculinity, machismo, power and potency in contemporary action.

If we were to think about the role of star images to career longevity, Diesel, Johnson and Statham might be looking to maintain their hegemonic credentials so as to afford continued employment in mainstream Hollywood. That said, beyond the *Fast & Furious* franchise, these built performers are seen to play to the more routine codes and conventions of action cinema whereby their bodies and their masculinities can be challenged, tried and tested.

It is the 'alpha' credentials of the *Fast & Furious* ensemble that finds Diesel, Johnson and Statham refusing to be perceived as weaker or weakened at the hands of the other male stars of the franchise. Writing about the shifting nature and social construction of manhood, Michael Kimmel (2004: 186) noted that 'other men watch us, rank us [and] grant our acceptance into the realm of manhood'. And this sense of men in competition with other men – sizing them up, judging, challenging and finding them wanting – is particularly evident in both the *Fast & Furious* films and the promotional discourse surrounding them, where the hard-bodied performers each compete to carefully balance atop the hegemonic hierarchy, a place routinely saved for a single figure elsewhere in action cinema.

# References

Bakare, L. (2019), 'Jason Statham and The Rock Refuse to Lose Fights against One Another', *The Guardian*, 2 August. Available online: https://www.theguardian.com/film/2019/aug/02/fast-furious-stars-contract-demand-not-lose-fights-jason-statham-dwayne-johnson (accessed 23 April 2022).

Ballaban, M. (2019), 'The Big Strong *Fast and Furious* Men Have Very Fragile Egos: Report', *Jalopnik*, 2 August. Available online: https://jalopnik.com/the-big-strong-fast-and-furious-men-have-very-fragile-e-1836909726 (accessed 23 April 2022).

Banham, T. (2015), 'Build *Fast and Furious* Muscle', *Men's Health*, 30 March. Available online: https://www.menshealth.com/uk/building-muscle/a754024/build-fast-and-furious-muscle/ (accessed 23 April 2022).

Barfield, C. (2019), 'The Macho, Muscle-bound Stars of *The Fast & Furious* Series Are Reportedly Insecure about Looking Bad in the Fight Scenes', *The Playlist*, 2 August. Available online: https://theplaylist.net/fast-furious-fight-contracts-20190802/ (accessed 23 April 2022).

Barker, M. and Brooks, K. (1998), *Knowing Audiences: Judge Dredd, Its Friends, Fans, and Foes*, Luton: University of Luton Press.

Beynon, J. (2001), *Masculinities and Culture*, Buckingham: Open University Press.

Bloomer, J. (2019), 'The *Fast and Furious* Films Have Always Been Gay', *Slate*, 9 August. Available online: https://slate.com/culture/2019/08/fast-furious-movies-gay-hobbs-shaw-subtext.html (accessed 13 May 2022).

Chatterjee, P. (2019), 'Fast But Not So Furious? Vin Diesel, Jason Statham, Dwayne Johnson Are Afraid to Look Weak on Screen', *Mashable India*, 2 August. Available online: https://in.mashable.com/entertainment/5397/fast-but-not-so-furious-vin-diesel-jason-statham-dwayne-johnson-are-afraid-to-look-weak-on-screen (accessed 23 April 2022).

Connell, R. (2005), *Masculinities*, Berkeley: University of California Press.

Creed, B. (1987), 'From Here to Modernity: Feminism and Postmodernism', *Screen* 28 (2): 47–68.

*Die Hard 4.0* (2007), [Film] Dir. Len Wiseman, USA: 20th Century Fox.

Di Placido, D. (2019), 'The Fragility of *The Fast & Furious* Stars', *Forbes*, 4 August. Available online: https://www.forbes.com/sites/danidiplacido/2019/08/04/the-fragility-of-the-fast-furious-stars/?sh=596886de6d75 (accessed 23 April 2022).

Dyer, R. (2002), *Only Entertainment*, London: Routledge.

Eschrich, J. (2015), 'Vin Diesel is Not a Macho Lunkhead. He's So Much More', *Slate*, 6 April. Available online: https://slate.com/culture/2015/04/vin-diesel-in-furious-7-the-actor-is-not-a-macho-lunkhead-he-s-so-much-more.html (accessed 23 April 2022).

Essence (2011), 'Eye Candy: The Men of *The Fast and Furious*', *Essence*, 6 May. Available online: https://www.essence.com/love/eye-candy-men-fast-and-furious/ (accessed 23 April 2022).

*The Expendables* (2010), [Film] Dir. Sylvester Stallone, USA: Lionsgate.
*The Expendables 3* (2014), [Film] Dir. Patrick Hughes, USA: Lionsgate.
Feasey, R. (2011), 'Mature Masculinity and the Aging Action Hero', *Groniek*, 190: 507–20.
Feasey, R. (2023), 'From the One to John Wick: Keanu Reeves and the Action Genre', in R. Middlemost and S. Gerrard (eds), *Gender and Action Films (1980–2000): Beauty in Motion*, London: Emerald Publishing.
Fradley, M. (2004), 'Maximus Melodramaticus: Masculinity, Masochism and White Male Paranoia in Contemporary Hollywood Cinema', in Y. Tasker (ed), *Action and Adventure Cinema*, 235–51, London: Routledge.
GQ (2019), 'Studies Say Bald Men Are More Dominant and Attractive Than Their Thick-haired Brothers', *GQ*, 19 March. Available online: https://www.gq.com.au/grooming/hair/studies-say-bald-men-are-more-dominant-and-attractive-than-their-thickhaired-brothers/news-story/d5369e712083818cf49882954aa9af1d (accessed 23 April 2022).
Hammond, C. (2012), 'Are Bald Men More Virile?', *BBC.com*, 11 December. Available online: https://www.bbc.com/future/article/20121210-are-bald-men-more-virile (accessed 23 April 2022).
Heritage, S. (2019), 'Fragile Masculinity: Why No One in the *Fast and Furious* Films Can Lose a Fight', *The Guardian*, 2 August. Available online: https://www.theguardian.com/film/2019/aug/02/fast-and-furious-dwayne-johnson-jason-statham-rock-lose-fight (accessed 23 April 2022).
Holmlund, C. (1994), 'Masculinity as Multiple Masquerade', in S. Cohan and I. R. Hark (eds), *Screening the Male: Exploring Masculinities in Hollywood Cinema*, 213–29, London: Routledge.
Holmlund, C. (2002), *Impossible Bodies: Femininity and Masculinity at the Movies*, London: Routledge.
Jeffords, S. (1994), *Hard Bodies: Hollywood Masculinity in the Reagan Era*, New Jersey: Rutgers University Press.
Jhaveri, H. (2018), 'Brilliant Flowchart Proves *Point Break* and *The Fast and the Furious* Are Basically the Same Movie', *USA Today*, 15 August. Available online: https://ftw.usatoday.com/2018/08/whoa-point-break-fast-and-the-furious-are-basically-the-same-movie (accessed 23 April 2022).
Jussim, M. (2018), '37 Ways the *Fast and the Furious* Cast Builds Muscle and Trains', *Men's Journal*, n.d. Available online: https://www.mensjournal.com/entertainment/37-ways-fate-furious-cast-builds-muscle-and-gets-shredded/ (accessed 23 April 2022).
Kimmel, M. (2004), 'Masculinity as Homophobia: Fear, Shame, and Silence in the Construction of Gender Identity', in P. Murphy (ed), *Feminism and Masculinities*, 182–99, Oxford: Oxford University Press.
King, G. (2000), *Spectacular Narratives: Hollywood in the Age of the Blockbuster*, London: I. B. Tauris.

Langberg, E. (2015), 'Men, Muscle Cars, and Melodrama: The *Fast and Furious* Franchise's Quietly Radical Embrace of Emotion', *Medium*, 13 April. Available online: https://medium.com/everythings-interesting/men-muscle-cars-and-melodrama-the-fast-and-furious-franchise-s-quietly-radical-embrace-of-emotion-4f6643e573e7 (accessed 23 April 2022).

Leydon, J. (2019), '*Fast & Furious* Films Ranked from Best to Worst', *Variety*, 2 August. Available online: https://web.archive.org/web/20191001025112if_/https://variety.com/gallery/fast-furious-films-ranked-worst-to-best-paul-walker-vin-diesel-testosterone/ (accessed 23 April 2022).

Martin, J. (2015), 'The *Fast & Furious* Macho, Macho Men', *Good*, 4 March. Available online: https://www.good.is/articles/fast-and-furious-men (accessed 13 May 2022).

Millar, J. (2019), 'Jason Statham and The Rock Have Contracts That Stipulate They Can't Lose in Fight Scenes', *GQ*, 8 August. Available online: https://www.gq.com.au/entertainment/celebrity/jason-statham-and-the-rock-have-contracts-that-stipulate-they-cant-lose-in-fight-scenes/news-story/459133902ac44957819fb2f93b6e29ef (accessed 23 April 2022).

Mulvey, L. (1975), 'Visual Pleasure and Narrative Cinema', *Screen*, 16 (3): 6–18.

Neale, S. (1983/1994), 'Masculinity as Spectacle: Reflections on Men and Mainstreapanm Cinema', in S. Cohan and I. R. Hark (eds), *Screening the Male: Exploring Masculinities in Hollywood Cinema*, 9–22, London: Routledge.

*Never Say Never Again* (1983), [Film] Dir. Irvin Kershner, USA: Warner Bros. Pictures.

Pan, A. (2019), 'Toxic Masculinity Went Full Throttle on *Fast and Furious* with the Stars' Pathetic Demands', *GOAT*, 2 August. Available online: https://goat.com.au/movies/toxic-masculinity-went-full-throttle-on-fast-and-furious-with-the-stars-pathetic-demands/ (accessed 23 April 2022).

Petter, O. (2017), 'Bald Men Are More Confident and Attractive, Study Finds', *The Independent* (UK), 13 December. Available online: https://www.independent.co.uk/life-style/love-sex/bald-men-more-confident-attractive-male-female-rate-photographs-study-pennsylvania-a7946466.html (accessed 23 April 2022).

*Point Break* (1991), [Film] Dir. Kathryn Bigelow, USA: Warner Bros. Pictures.

*Predator* (1987), [Film] Dir. John McTiernan, USA: 20th Century Fox.

Puchko, K. (2020), 'How *Fast & Furious* Became the Baldest Action Franchise of all Time', *Mel Magazine*, n.d. Available online: https://melmagazine.com/en-us/story/how-fast-furious-became-the-baldest-action-franchise-of-all-time (accessed 23 April 2022).

*Rambo: Last Blood* (2019), [Film] Dir. Adrian Grünberg, USA: Lionsgate.

*Rocky Balboa* (2006), [Film] Dir. Sylvester Stallone, USA: MGM / Sony.

Schwartzel, E. (2019), '*Fast & Furious* Stars' Complicated Demand – I Never Want to Lose a Fight', *The Wall Street Journal*, 1 August. Available online: https://www.wsj.com/articles/fast-furious-stars-complicated-demandi-never-want-to-lose-a-fight-11564673490 (accessed 23 April 2022).

Silver, S. (2017), '4 Attractive Bald Men aka *The Fate of the Furious*', *Movie Time Guru*, 23 April. Available online: https://movietime.guru/4-attractive-bald-men-aka-the-fate-of-the-furious-70ab636984ef (accessed 23 April 2022).

Tasker, Y. (1993a), *Spectacular Bodies: Gender, Genre and the Action Cinema*, London: Routledge.

Tasker, Y. (1993b), 'Dumb Movies for Dumb People: Masculinity, the Body and the Voice in Contemporary Action Cinema', in S. Cohan and I. R. Hark (eds), *Screening the Male: Exploring Masculinities in Hollywood Cinema*, 230–44, London: Routledge.

Tasker, Y. (2010), 'Ageing and Action Authenticity', *In Media Res: A Media Commons Project*, 12 August. Available online: http://mediacommons.org/imr/2010/08/05/aging-and-action-authenticity (accessed 23 April 2022).

Tye, S. (2022), '*Hobbs & Shaw 2* Release Date, Cast, Plot and Trailer – What We Know so Far', *Looper*, 21 January. Available online: https://www.looper.com/246491/hobbs-shaw-2-release-date-cast-plot-trailer/ (accessed 23 April 2022).

*A View to a Kill* (1985), [Film] Dir. John Glen, USA: MGM / UA Entertainment.

Wexman, V. W. (1993), *Creating the Couple: Love, Marriage and Hollywood Performance*, Princeton: Princeton University Press.

# 9

# The on- and off-screen bromances of *Fast & Furious*

Jackie Raphael and Celia Lam

Authenticity and sincerity are questions common to the field of celebrity studies, which interrogates the meaning and function of celebrity figures in a multitude of cultural contexts. The increasing commodification of celebrity culture (a culture built on the practice of promotion within consumer cultures) further highlights questions of genuineness as we question whether celebrities really are who they claim to be. Claims to sincerity are complicated in contemporary digital environments that encourage highly cultivated performances of personhood authenticated by ordinariness in private spaces.

This chapter considers how on-screen and off-screen presentations influence the 'reading' of the bromance between Paul Walker (Brian O'Conner) and Vin Diesel (Dominic Toretto). This particular bromance is created, like many other contemporary celebrity bromances, as a result of character dynamics emerging from the *Fast & Furious* franchise and is utilized for promotion. Indeed, creating synergies between stars in ensemble casts has become a key feature in both the production and marketing of action films within contemporary Hollywood (Gutiérrez 2015: 39). In this sense, the authenticity of the bromance is already questionable, as there is an ever present framework of advertising.

The *Fast & Furious* franchise shares many similarities with ensemble films with strong action elements. Like films in the Marvel Cinematic Universe (MCU) or *X-Men* franchises, character dynamics feature heavily in both the on- and off-screen contexts of *Fast & Furious*, with intimacy (or friendly antagonism) between characters often replicated in off-screen contexts during promotional runs or displayed in the online interactions between cast members. Unlike the films of the MCU or *X-Men*, which place equal emphasis on the expansion of a narrative universe and development of character dynamics, it could be argued that the *Fast & Furious* franchise capitalizes most on its presentation of character dynamics, centring on the two main character/actor dyads of Walker/Brian and Diesel/Dom.

While sitting within the action genre more broadly, the *Fast & Furious* franchise specifically draws on a spate of buddy cop films from the 1980s and 1990s (inspired by television series of the 1970s), including *48 Hours* (1982), *Beverley Hills Cop* (1984), *Lethal Weapon* (1987) and *Bad Boys* (1995). In many of these relationships, the characters bicker throughout the film until they unite on a mission and a friendship forms. This is similar to the initial plot of *The Fast and the Furious* (2001), which many argue is almost a direct copy of *Point Break* (1991). Indeed, both films centre on an undercover police officer who bonds with a gang of criminals, after losing himself in the criminal subculture that he was supposed to investigate. Through this process, the two leading men (hero cop and lead criminal) develop a bromance, which is presented as far more significant than the romances in the films. These films go beyond the buddy-cop genre, taking the male friendship into a more intimate space. These films can be categorized as a subgenre of buddy-cop films, noted as an action bromance genre.

This bromance action film is significantly different from the bromance genre films of the early 2000s, exemplified by John Hamburg's *I Love You Man* (2009), which examine questions of manhood and expressions of male homosocial intimacy. This genre is considered to be a contemporary manifestation of the explorations of masculinity that started in 1970s American buddy films (DeAngelis 2014: 1). While male homosocial relationships are explored in action films like *Fast & Furious*, it is done so within the hypermasculine framework of an action-heist narrative. Homosocial bonding is both a subtext for the action in the film, as well as constant undercurrent (or subplot) connecting the various films in the franchise. In *Fast & Furious*, the bromance element was introduced in the first film and intensified through subsequent films, culminating in a touching on-screen send-off in *Furious 7* (2015).

A key element distinguishing this franchise from others in the action bromance genre is the fact that much of the more recent iterations of the bromance are posthumous. Both Walker/Brian's on-screen send off and Diesel's accounts of his relationship with Walker take place after Walker's death. Kasey Hudak (2014: 390–4) notes that images of deceased celebrities are akin to 'artefacts preserved in media', which creates a 'memory-image' of the individual and provoke related emotions (such as nostalgia). Hudak highlights how the image of celebrities can be preserved in the cultural zeitgeist, 'possibly forever. But only if their presence is (re)presented to audiences'. Diesel's social media use constitutes part of the (re)presentation of Walker's image and directly engages in the memory-image and nostalgia, while recasting Walker's image within a relationship of Diesel's own telling. Thus, the posthumous nature of the bromance may also influence its ongoing presentation. This chapter considers how the central bromance in the *Fast & Furious* franchise is expressed on-screen, off-screen and posthumously. It argues that the off-screen bromance is legitimated through parallels to the on-screen relationship and the presentation of specific markers of sincerity and authenticity. Finally, it reflects on how questions of commodification complicate the reading of the bromance off-screen.

## Celebrity, authenticity and bromance

Gaston Franssen (2019: 315) noted 'celebrity culture can be understood as an endless quest for the sincere and the authentic'. Paradoxically, this quest occurs in a culture comprised of 'make-believe, artificiality and image control, in which it is profoundly challenging to determine what truly is sincere or authentic' (Ibid). Franssen highlights the conceptual conundrum and source of intellectual stimulation for scholars, media commentators and audiences engaging with celebrity culture. That is, a fascination with seeking reality within highly constructed environments in which ambiguity is common and speculation is normal. Authenticity is located (or sought) in the sincere, genuine, 'real' side of the famous individual, juxtaposed against the performativity of their public personas.

The conceptual bind of determining the validity of that which, by definition, is hidden from sight is acknowledged by scholars, who highlight the paradoxical need to perform authenticity in order to generate a sense of credibility (Fillitz and Saris 2013; Holmes and Redmond 2006). For Richard Dyer (1991: 141), the 'markers of authenticity' are located in a 'lack of control, lack of premeditation and privacy', yet are expressed in the management of the star's public image through incorporation into works featuring the star or retrofitted in subsequent interpretations after private details emerge. Dyer argues the processes of authentication are, like the production of the star image, inherently unstable ones because the boundary between sincerity and authenticity, star-as-image and star-as-person, performance and non-performance blur in the very generation of the star itself.

Subsequent scholars further problematize the authenticity of the private by demonstrating how equally performative the private is in a social media context (Marwick and boyd 2010). Writing of a shift from 'representational' to 'presentational culture', P. David Marshall (2010) highlights the emergence of a public/private self that celebrity figures present (perform) on social media platforms. The public/private self is manifest through displays of the private in highly performative and codified online presentations that directly challenge notions of truth in private spaces. The 'inner self' may still exist as a state of being, but whether it can be located in the 'backstage' of the private is questionable. This chapter aims not to provide a definitive answer to what is authentic but considers how the presentation of the bromance influences appearances of authenticity.

We have elsewhere argued that celebrity bromances are grounded in dual notions of performativity and authenticity, which are complicated when read against a promotional context (Lam and Raphael 2018). As an external expression of intimacy, the bromance is highly performative, feeding speculations around the sincerity of celebrity figures. However, rather than questioning the authenticity of whether a celebrity 'really is what she or he appears to be' (Dyer 1991: 10), the genuineness of the closeness between celebrities is interrogated as the performative intimacy of the bromance is deconstructed. Unsurprisingly, the interrogation intensifies when celebrity bromances gain prominence during promotion runs for feature films or television series.

## Markers of authenticity

A means to interrogate the complexity of the performative intimacy of bromances is located in Dyer's (1991: 141) aforementioned 'markers of sincerity and authenticity'. Proposed as a means to deconstruct the authenticating processes of stars, Dyer's markers are grounded in notions that the 'real' individual can be found 'behind or beneath the surface' of performance or packaging. He suggests that authenticity and sincerity can be implied through 'lack of control, lack of premeditation and privacy' (Dyer 1991: 141). It is conceptualized that the 'real' individual can be identified through behaviours such as speech patterns, gestures and unscripted (improvised) moments. The interactions between actors can also be interrogated through markers of authenticity and sincerity.

However, unlike Dyer's analysis of authenticating processes of individual stars and celebrities, the markers active within a bromance need necessarily to take into consideration dynamics within a dyad. To this end, we extend Dyer's three markers to account for how the 'truth' of a relationship (rather than individual) could be conceptualized. Building on the notion of unplanned expression suggested in Dyer's lack of control and premeditation, verbal and physical interaction becomes the point of focus for bromance pairs. Verbal banter may appear planned, especially if jokes and anecdotes are repeated in successive media appearances. However, a friendly (even intimate) dynamic is fostered through interactions that create a sense of fun and levity, a lack of premeditation adding to a sense of genuineness. Spontaneity thus characterizes the first marker of authenticity related to celebrity dynamics. If interactions are perceived as spontaneous and not planned or rehearsed (i.e. lacking control), the likelihood of interpretations that they are genuine increases.

Dyer's marker of privacy translates, in the context of a relationship, to continued off-screen contact and involvement in personal milestones. Likewise situating authenticity in the conceptual reality of the private space, continued off-screen contact implicates a desire to interact without external pressure (such as contractual promotional interviews). Involvement in personal milestones is similarly situated in the private realm of the 'real' individual behind the public persona. Grounded in the social tendency to involve those important to oneself in personal milestones, the presence of celebrities at occasions such as engagement or weddings reinforces a sense that the individuals are important to each other, contributing to a sense of genuineness.

An additional marker is a history of association which is established either through continuity between on- and off-screen dynamics, or off-screen. At the same time, the ongoing display of the bromance and in particular the consistency of its presentation constitutes part of the authenticating process. On-screen bromances follow clear, logical and coherent narrative trajectories that investigate homosocial intimacy while maintaining heteronormative boundaries (see DeAngelis 2014). Indeed, the development of the relationship between the bromance pair is of primary concern to the plots of bromance films. While bromance action films may feature alternative central plots (for instance a heist), the bromance between the characters forms a strong subplot that can extend over a number of films. Off-screen bromances do not have the benefit of clear plot development; however, they nonetheless constitute an ongoing narrative. This narrative is expressed through fragmented media, social media and fan accounts that are ultimately pieced together by the viewer, although they are also occasionally summarized by the press when talking of bromances with celebrities. The consistency of this ongoing performance thus both contributes to the generation of a genuine relationship between the bromance pair, and is a means to assess this genuineness.

As external expressions of interpersonal dynamics, the bromance is by definition performative. Sincerity is expressed through markers or a rhetoric of authenticity that is effective so long as it is not 'perceived as a rhetoric' (Dyer 1991: 141). Building on Dyer, we thus propose four markers of authenticity: History, Privacy, Spontaneity and Consistency. The following discussion will engage with these markers to interrogate the formation of the Walker/Diesel bromance and reflect on its sincerity. To narrow our focus, the intersections between on- and off-screen presentations of the bromance will be the primary site of discussion.

## Markers of authenticity: The Walker/Diesel bromance

Bromances have a variety of origins, with some associations starting early on in celebrities' journey to fame and others derived from on-screen dynamics between characters. For those celebrity pairings who are known to have interacted prior to becoming famous, this establishes a bromance narrative based in relative youth, where the relationship was forged at, say, a school or training institutions, and before formally entering the industry. These 'pre-success bromances' (Lam and Raphael 2022) implicate a long history of association that precedes the 'manufactured mask of fame' associated with celebrity images (Holmes and Redmond 2006: 4), lending a degree of genuineness to the bromance narrative. Conversely, bromances dynamics established on-screen can flow off-screen to reinforce continuity between fictional and real-world contexts. The presentation of the off-screen bromance is grounded in confluence between on- and off-screen dynamics and relies more heavily on a continuation of the on-screen dynamics to ensure the plausibility of that which is presented off-screen.

Having met through signing up to be in *The Fast and the Furious*, the Walker/Diesel bromance is established on-screen, with the film franchise providing the basis of their bromance history and helping to shape its ongoing narrative. The *Fast & Furious* franchise is set in the drag racing subculture, pitting the main characters Brian (Walker) and Dom (Diesel) against each other as law enforcement and outlaw. While often at odds with one another, the characters share a special bond, which creates tensions, intrigue and drives much of the plot. The bromance itself is situated within a broader familial context, with a romantic relationship between Dom's sister Mia, and Brian, as well as the characterization of connections between the various casts of the films as part of a larger crew, or family. Helping family members in danger is a common theme that drives the plots of the films, such as in *Fast & Furious 6* (2013) when Brian leaves Mia and their child to help Dom battle Owen Shaw (Luke Evans). Again in *Furious 7*, Brian leaves his family to help Dom.

However, as the final scene of *Furious 7* illustrates, it is ultimately the Brian/Dom bromance that is featured as the central relationship in the films. The scene depicts the reactions of all main characters to the news of Brian's retirement, with close-ups illustrating they will miss Brian and his family. It then cuts to Dom and Brian for a bromantic moment. Brian says to Dom 'Hey, thought you could leave without saying goodbye?' The characters share glances from their cars as 'See You Again' by Charlie Puth and Wiz Khalifa plays, followed by Dom's voice over about being 'brothers'. Since Walker's death, the franchise has kept Brian in the narrative by making mentions to his character and using his car as a representation of his character.

The Brian/Dom bromance is thus established in hypermasculine terms, situated as it is within the racing subculture and expressed through narrative conditions where the characters risk their lives for one another during action and fight sequences. All the while, the pair maintain a sense of competitiveness, bantering throughout. However, the closeness of the relationship is emphasized through heart-to-heart moments between the two. Presented as it is within an overall familial dynamic, the on-screen bromance adopts 'brotherhood' as the main means to express the intimacy between the two male characters. This characterization becomes the foundation of the off-screen bromance, which emphasizes both the hypermasculine context and the familial expression.

While Diesel himself has acknowledged that he and Walker did not get along all the time (Diesel 2020), the media continues to portray them as having an off-screen bromance. Over the years this bromance was reinforced by both actors in interviews by calling one another 'brothers'. Diesel and Walker began their journey as they prepared for *The Fast and the Furious*. In a 2011 interview, Walker summarized their experience: 'When I was first working with Vin it was about hooking up with girls and going out and partying … And now it's like, yeah man I'm having another kid … It's changed a little bit' (Larkin 2014).

Explaining how they shared significant moments together, establishes that an off-screen bond exists. Interestingly, both their on-screen and off-screen relationship reflects a close friendship that is always framed in terms of masculine norms. However, this statement also shows how time has passed between films. The first film was released in 2001 and a new film in the franchise has been released approximately every few years since then. However, in between working on the first film and Diesel's return, several years passed where the actors did not appear publicly together to express their bromance. While their on-screen relationships are attached through romances, siblings and friendships, their off-screen bond is built through filming, promoting and reconnecting frequently for the next instalment.

In 2014, Diesel posted a compilation video of himself with Walker in tribute, which various media outlets reported on and referred to the video as being evidence of their 'off-screen bromance' (Extra 2014; Larkin 2014; Nessif 2014). A significant moment in the video is when Walker gives Diesel a hug while everyone sings happy birthday, showing an intimacy. However, this was captured on set with other cast and crew. Whether Diesel and Walker spent much time together outside of work is difficult to authenticate, as it probably was not captured on camera. However, the concept of Walker and Diesel having an off-screen bromance certainly added value to the franchise.

In a 2011 interview, Walker was asked about the parallel of his on-screen and off-screen relationship with Diesel to which he called Diesel a 'good friend' and then stated: 'I'm a backpacker, trekker, hunter, fisherman … he's more of a city guy … our personality and how we are so different, I think that's what people have found complimentary … and we bring it together. And as opposed to it being a clash … people clicked with it' (Enterainment.ie 2011). Thus, Walker acknowledges they have opposing personalities both on-screen and off-screen but claims audiences 'click with' the on-screen relationship. This comment reflects their macho personalities and competitive bravado, which was consistently expressed when they were asked who was better at racing cars. Their friendship is further reinforced in a 2013 interview when Walker stated: 'There's times when it's really not a scene anymore. Vin coming up and you know playing uncle Dom, we do that in our real life. So it's funny we've grown with it' (The World of Movies 2013). While this comment could be intended as a promotional strategy, as it is directly attached to discussing the film, there are various photos of them with each other's family members, creating a sense of authenticity.

## Privacy

The display of moments with families aligns with conceptualizations of the private space as more authentic due to its contrast with the Goffmanian notion of the performative public space, and also to savviness regarding the constructed nature of the public images. Erving Goffman's (1956) dramaturgical allegory for social interactions likens individuals to actors performing on stage. The public 'front stage' self is considered and planned, wherein performative elements such as body language, dress and vocal delivery are modulated to address the anticipated 'audience'. In contrast to this considered on-stage self, the private 'backstage' self is devoid of the accoutrement of performance, revealing the 'actor' as they are. Scholarly critiques of the authenticity of the private have already been highlighted early in the chapter; however, the conceptual authenticity of the 'backstage' lends to presentation (and accounts) of the private powerful connotations of genuineness.

The presentation of images with family members not only reinforces the familial bond expressed in the on-screen dynamic, it also highlights interactions in the perceived authentic spaces of the private. Devoid of any contractual need to emphasize a bond during public promotional interviews, celebrities choosing to spend time together in private suggests a genuine desire to interact. Similarly, sharing stories of interactions with extended family reinforces a sense of interaction that extends beyond collaboration on film productions and public appearances.

On 21 April 2014, Diesel posted an image of himself with Walker's brothers on Facebook and wrote about when he first heard of Walker's death: '[Walker's] father said, Paul loved you Vin … I awkwardly and nervously said, aw come on … then he said … you don't have to get along every second to love each other … so true' (Diesel 2014). Thus, Walker's father and Diesel both admitted they did not always get along. While the claim that Walker loved Diesel does reinforce a genuine friendship, the story was told from Diesel's perspective. This post also worked as a promotion for the film, as Walker's brothers were helping to finish *Furious 7*.

Diesel had already quoted Walker's mother in a Facebook post in 2013 (Nessif 2013). However, in 2017 Diesel chose to share more details of the conversation in an interview while promoting the eighth film of the franchise (the first without Walker). This appears to have a different motive. Diesel explained that after giving condolences to Walker's mother she returned it: 'I said, "Why? Why are you saying you're sorry to me?" She said, "Because you lost your other half"' (SirusXM 2017). Using the term, 'other half', adds to the portrayal of a bromance, as it is usually used for romantic partners. Diesel went on to share another story of Walker's mother saying to his mother to 'love your child' (Ibid). This shows a connection between their parents, reinforcing an authenticity of their closeness. In the same interview he confessed: 'We didn't have to see each other every day' (Ibid). Hinting, proximity did not affect closeness. However, it could suggest they were not that close outside of filming.

Diesel has also posted about his children and Walker's daughter Meadow, claiming that they are friends (Parker 2019; Wallis 2019). In sharing these personal photos, it creates a sense of credibility behind the online narrative portrayed. While such imagery is rare, it could be to maintain privacy, as Meadow herself has also posted about being close to Diesel's family (McRady 2020). Cynically, it could also be a way of Meadow gaining media attention for her modelling career.

The involvement of bromance partners in personal milestones is also a marker of authenticity grounded in privacy. As mentioned earlier, inclusion of people in important personal milestones is a reflection of the importance of the individual and reinforces the degree of closeness. For instance, to name a child after an individual suggests a special type of connection.

The Walker/Diesel bromance demonstrates both on and off-screen instances of this level of intimate connection. On-screen this occurs in *The Fate of the Furious* (2017, hereinafter *Fast Eight*), when Dom announces he named his child Brian. Off-screen Diesel announced in 2015 that he named his daughter Pauline, claiming Walker as the namesake. Diesel later mentioned it repeatedly during the promotion of his film *Bloodshot* (2020), while also discussing the upcoming *Fast & Furious* film (Hines 2015). It is worth noting Diesel's twin brother also shares the name Paul and it may not have been exclusively the rationale. Regardless of the sincerity in sharing this story and linking it to Walker, it generated media attention. As a result, it appears that Diesel utilized Walker's death to promote a film that does not relate to him. However, it did link back to the *Fast & Furious* film that was later released, where art imitated life, having Dom name his child after Brian. Thus, there is some ambiguity behind Diesel's intentions, impacting on the authenticity of the off-screen bromance between Diesel and Walker.

## Spontaneity and consistency

Walker and Diesel demonstrate fewer instances of spontaneous interactions, based on materials gathered thus far. Rather, the authenticating processes of their off-screen bromance rely more heavily on their history in the *Fast & Furious* franchise and sharing private moments on social media. Their bromance is characterized in a similar fashion to their on-screen counterparts as hypermasculine and familial. This characterization is reinforced through consistent accounts on different mediums, of their shared experiences with the film franchise, their hobbies and knowledge of each other's families. Walker's 2013's references to Diesel 'playing uncle Dom … in our real life' highlights the familial connections spanning on- and off-screen contexts (The World of Movies 2013). Thus, over a number of years and through a number of media platforms, Walker and Diesel's account of their relationship consistently emphasizes a bond that is expressed in familial terms.

Consistency can also manifest in the maintenance of an ongoing bromance narrative. Walker's references to growth and change during press interviews highlight an ongoing connection between the two that is mirrored in their characters' development. Walker's 2011 summation of his ten years with Diesel reinforces both the continuity between actor and character, and parallels between the two actors. From 'hooking up with girls' to 'having another kid' (Larkin 2014), both Walker and Diesel have matured over the span of (in 2011) five films, with the maturation reflected on-screen through the formation of nuclear family units in *Fast Five* (2011). The framework of regular reunions for subsequent installations of the *Fast & Furious* franchise also provides the off-screen bromance with a sense of stability. Media references to the films, such as Diesel's 2015 performance of 'See you again', contribute to a consistent presentation of the ongoing bromance. After Walker's passing, Diesel maintained the narrative of their bromance through references that characterize Walker in similar familial terms to their on-screen bromance. He thereby contributes both to Walker's posthumous image and their ongoing bromance narrative.

While bromances are by no means monogamous, the presence of other bromances could affect the reading of the central bromance, especially when they occur within the same franchise. Paul Walker and Tyrese Gibson also presented a public bromance. While Walker often showed a resistance in making more of the *Fast & Furious* films, he stated in several interviews that he would return to make a fifth movie 'pending Tyrese is in it' (MsFastFurious1 2014). This was after Gibson had not been included in the fourth film. Various other interviews and Gibson's reaction to Walker's death also reinforced that perhaps their bromance was stronger than the Walker/Diesel relationship (Ibid). Furthermore, Gibson appeared in the documentary, *I am Paul Walker* (2018), while Diesel and the rest of the *Fast & Furious* cast did not. Moreover, Gibson and Rodriguez presented the posthumous Nobel prize to Walker in 2015 (Ibid). Their involvement and closeness to the Walker family add a sense of credibility behind their bond. Diesel's absence from the award ceremony and documentary may have been due to scheduling or it could be by choice. It is difficult to know the authenticity behind a bromance; however, the ambiguity of their relationship and timing of Diesel's stories create the impression that he is capitalizing on their apparent bromance.

Walker and Gibson's bromance also has similar characteristics to Walker/Diesel with intimacy expressed in familial terms and connections to the on-screen and public discussion. Yet, some small examples of more seemingly spontaneous expressions of emotions suggest that the Gibson/Walker bromance is genuine. Fans and celebrities mourned Walker globally through social media (Raphael 2018). However, Diesel was perhaps the most public and frequent. First, with his initial social media post, which was followed by a public appearance at a fan gathering. On 3 December 2013, Diesel posted a Thomas Campbell quote followed by: 'Pablo, I wish you could see the world right now … and the profound impact, your full life has had on it, on Us … on me … I will always love you Brian, as the brother you were … on and off screen' (Diesel 2020). By using the nickname 'Pablo', it somewhat reinforces a closeness. While he only started using this name on Facebook after Walker's death, he had also sung it in the birthday video. Choosing to use it publicly implies an attempt to emphasize their relationship. Furthermore, by using the name 'Brian' it links back to their franchise, which is unnecessary considering the circumstances, thus working as a promotion. Diesel also calls Walker a brother 'on- and off screen', drawing connections between their character bromance and real-life relationship.

When attending a fan gathering at the Walker crash site, Diesel used a police car's PA system to thank fans for attending and referred to Walker as an 'angel' (CNN 2013). In contrast, Gibson was seen crying at the crash site at a different time but did not draw attention to himself. Gibson did, however, share a lot of personal tweets, including a screen grab of Walker's last message to him. Contrasted to this seemingly 'private' expression of affection and grief, Diesel's more strategically timed expression of intimacy could decrease its level of authenticity.

## Capitalizing, authenticity and ambiguity

The authenticity of bromances can be hard to determine due to the highly performative nature of the bromance, public visibility that coincides with (and are incorporated into) marketing campaigns for works and questions surrounding the motivation behind any confluence between on- and off-screen dynamics. The spectre of capitalization looms large over the presentation of the bromance, especially when it is suspected that individual celebrity figures leverage the celebrity capital of other celebrities in order to increase their own popularity. In the case of the Walker/Diesel bromance, a number of factors complicate the interpretation of the relationship as genuine.

First, the timing of Diesel's posts referring to Walker coincided with the promotion of films within the *Fast & Furious* franchise. In order to analyse the authenticity of their off-screen bromance further, screen grabs of Diesel's Facebook page were collected (from 13 March 2009 when Diesel joined Facebook to 17 April 2020). Using the search function, key words relating to Walker were entered – 'Pablo', 'Paul', 'Brian' and 'Paul Walker'. Diesel only mentioned him directly online roughly five times prior to Walker's death in 2013. Posthumously, he mentioned him frequently by name (approximately twenty-six times); however, in most instances it linked to some promotion for the new *Fast & Furious* films. Even the posts prior to his death were usually in promotion for their films. Although, one was in promotion for Walker's charity, Reach Out WorldWide (ROWW). Diesel has continued to show support for ROWW, with one video posted 2 October 2018 of himself with Cody Walker advertising the charity. By continuing Walker's legacy and maintaining a relationship with his brother, this adds authenticity. It also produces positive publicity for Diesel.

This could be viewed as an extension of marketing techniques that seek to 'help foster a synergy' between headline stars in ensemble casts that Peter Gutiérrez (2015: 39) argues has become a feature of action films. As the promotion ultimately services the film, and by extension the cast who are characterized as 'quasi-families' in the film and marketing thereof (Ibid), Diesel's references to Walker can be considered within a continuum of social media posts that benefit the collective effort more than his individual public image. Conversely, speaking about his relationship with Walker during promotion of films unrelated to the franchise challenges the genuine intention, as it is potentially self-serving. Diesel's references to Walker during promotion of *Bloodshot*, whether prompted by journalists or not, add little to public awareness of the franchise nor does it develop the on- and off-screen dynamic between Walker and Diesel. Instead, it draws associations to an unrelated cast dynamic, seemingly motivated by a desire to capitalize on the emotional capital of another ensemble. As Peter Turner (2019: 477) argues, Diesel's use of social media creates an elite 'interstellar community comprised of the *Fast & Furious* cast that use their posts to signify their position within the group'. Diesel's references to Walker in his social media posts and interviews recall this elite interstellar community and reinforces his own position as a member of the group.

Second, the Walker/Diesel bromance is a central, but not singular, intimate dynamic. The intertextual relationship between on- and off-screen bromances often reinforces the authenticity of both on-screen and off-screen relationships due to a confluence between 'scripted' character dynamics and 'real' emotional connections between actors who demonstrate similar dynamics off-screen. The Walker/Diesel bromance is not presented as a straightforward dyad, due to the aforementioned trend noted by Gutiérrez (2015: 39) to characterize the ensemble casts of action films as 'quasi-families'. Rather than focusing on a single star pairing, action films like the *Fast & Furious* franchise offer a diverse cast from which to attract audience attention, and on whom to build marketing campaigns. The Walker/Diesel relationship is one of a number of on- and off-screen relationships that feature in the narrative and promotion of the films. Whether being a member on an ensemble dilutes the on-screen bromance is questionable, as the final scene in *Furious 7* clearly emphasizes the Brian/Dom relationship through its use of sentimental soundtrack and montage editing. However, the fact they are one of a number of possible close cast mates within the 'family' potentially minimizes the potency of the Walker/Diesel bromance off-screen. At the very least, there is ambiguity whether the closeness between them is genuine or strategically played-up.

Third, the presentation of the bromance potentially suggests a lack of authenticity as it plays out through retrospective anecdotes from Diesel. Our previous examination of pairings in the *X-Men* franchise considered interactions that were widely documented either visually through videos of interviews (Lam and Raphael 2018) or online interactions on social media (Lam and Raphael

2019). The Walker/Diesel bromance is recounted mostly through interviews or posts by Diesel, providing less interaction to observe and from which to make determinations about how closely external expression matches internal feelings (or on-screen dynamics). The public presentation of actor dynamics is likely to contain performative elements; however, characteristics unique to the relationship work to legitimize the dynamic and add credibility to the bromance. Markers of 'sincerity and authenticity' (Dyer 1991: 141) manifest in reciprocal references to shared history, or in-situ interactions (use of humour, banter and physical proximity) that provides visual 'evidence' to suggest what is witnessed is in some way genuine. The untimely passing of Walker in 2013 prevents the construction of ongoing social media interactions through which to assess his bromance with Diesel, and although there are recorded interviews wherein both mention their 'brotherhood' with the other, these are predominantly conducted individually with less opportunity to preserve actual interactions. Diesel's recounting of their history is one-sided and conveyed from his position as producer of the *Fast & Furious* franchise, thus appearing premeditated to ensure the core relationship of the films remains active in public consciousness.

Finally, while Diesel's public presentation of their bromance sustains fans' affective connections to the *Fast & Furious* franchise, it also prolongs Walker's image posthumously and contributes to the building of his legacy. Therefore, regardless of the sincerity behind his actual relationship with Walker, Diesel is helping to preserve his memory through the franchise and promotion of ROWW.

## Conclusion

The intertextual connections between on-screen and off-screen bromances operate to legitimate and authenticate the relationship between character/actor dyads. However, reference to bromances devoid of conditions that present markers of authenticity, or which implicate the promotion of works unrelated to an on-screen bromance threaten the stability and credibility of the bromance. Grounding the history of the bromance in the on-screen representation provides it with a solid foundation from which to build an ongoing bromance narrative, intertextual references to the on-screen helping to reinforce the credibility of the off-screen dynamic. References to private moments also help to reinforce the off-screen presentation. However, a lack of opportunity to observe the bromance results in a lack of spontaneous markers of authenticity through which to assess the dynamic. Compounding the notion that Diesel is capitalizing on his bromance with Walker is the fact that Walker's passing means no 'new' examples of their bromance can be offered for scrutiny; the Walker/Diesel bromance can only be expressed retrospectively. Yet, Diesel's references to their bromance serve to prolong Walker's public image as much as it helps him to maintain his own. It also enables Diesel to more effectively maintain the consistency of their bromance narrative. The question of capitalization therefore needs to be considered within contexts that are influenced as much by on-screen representation as it is by the highly mediated presentations of celebrity identity, relationships and (posthumous) legacy.

# References

*48 Hours* (1982), [Film] Dir. James Horner, USA: Paramount Picture Studios.
*Bad Boys* (1995), [Film] Dir. Michael Bay, USA: Columbia Pictures.
*Beverly Hills Cop* (1984), [Film] Dir. Martin Brest, USA: Paramount Picture Studios.
*Bloodshot* (2020), [Film] Dir. David SF Wilson, USA: Columbia Pictures.
CNN (2013), [YouTube] 'Vin Diesel Thanks Fans at Paul Walker's Crash Site', 3 December. Available online: https://www.youtube.com/watch?v=gU6PSvuK-aY (accessed 3 July 2020).
DeAngelis, M. (ed) (2014), *Reading the Bromance: Homosocial Relationships in Film and Television*, Detroit: Wayne State University Press.
Diesel, V. (2014), [Facebook] 14 April. Available online: https://www.facebook.com/VinDiesel (accessed 9 July 2021).
Diesel, V. (2020), [Facebook] 17 April. Available online: https://www.facebook.com/VinDiesel (accessed 17 April 2020).
Dyer, R. (1991), 'A Star Is Born and the Construction of Authenticity', in C. Geraghty (ed), *Stardom: Industry of Desire*, 136–44, London: Routledge.
Entertainment.ie (2011), [YouTube] 'Fast & Furious 5 Interviews: Paul Walker', *Entertainment.ie*, 21 April. Available online: https://www.youtube.com/watch?v=cfFkrqk1hvE (accessed 3 July 2020).
Extra (2014), 'Vin Diesel Honours Paul Walker with Heartwarming Video', 8 January. Available online: https://extratv.com/2014/01/08/vin-diesepaul-walker-vin-diesel-honors-fast-and-furious-co-star-with-heart-warming-video/ (accessed 3 July 2020).
Fillitz, T. and J. A. Saris (2013), 'Introduction: Authenticity Aujourd'Hui', in T. Fillitz and J. A. Saris (eds), *Debating Authenticity: Concepts of Modernity in Anthropological Perspective*, 1–26, Oxford: Berghahn Books.

Franssen, G. (2019), 'Sincerity and Authenticity in Celebrity Culture: Introduction', *Celebrity Studies*, 10 (3): 315–19.
Goffman, E. (1956), *The Presentation of Self in Everyday Life*, Scotland: Doubleday.
Gutiérrez, P. (2015), 'Safety in Numbers: The Staggering Success of the "Ensemble Action Movie"', *Screen Education*, 79: 38–45.
Hines, R. (2015), 'Vin Diesel Reveals His New Baby's Very Special Name, a Tribute to Paul Walker', *Today*, 14 March. Available online: https://www.today.com/parents/paul-walker-tribute-vin-diesel-reveals-his-new-babys-name-t10586 (accessed 3 July 2020).
Holmes, S. and S. Redmond (eds) (2006), *Framing Celebrity: New Directions in Celebrity Culture*, Oxon: Routledge.
Hudak, K. C. (2014), 'A Phantasmic Experience: Narrative Connection of Dead Celebrities in Advertisements', *Culture, Theory and Critique*, 55 (3): 383–400.
*I am Paul Walker* (2018), [Film] Dir. Adrian Buitehuis, USA: Paramount Network.
*I Love You Man* (2009), [Film] Dir. John Hamburg, USA: Paramount Picture Studios.
Lam, C. and J. Raphael (2018), 'X-Men Bromance: Film, Audience and Promotion', *Celebrity Studies*, 9 (3): 355–74.
Lam, C. and J. Raphael (2022), *Celebrity Bromances: Constructing, Interpreting and Utilising Personas*, London: Routledge.
Larkin, M. (2014), '"I Wish He Could See What We Have Created": Vin Diesel Shares New Photo Featuring Tragic Co-star Paul Walker in *Furious 7*', *Daily Mail*, 24 September. Available online: https://www.dailymail.co.uk/tvshowbiz/article-2767556/Vin-Diesel-shares-new-photo-featuring-tragic-costar-Paul-Walker-Fast-And-Furious-7.html (accessed 3 July 2020).
*Lethal Weapon* (1987), [Film] Dir. Richard Donner, USA: Warner Bros. Pictures.
Marshall, D. P. (2010), 'The Promotion and Presentation of the Self: Celebrity as Marker of Presentational Media', *Celebrity Studies*, 1 (1): 35–48.
Marwick, A. and d. boyd (2010), 'I Tweet Honestly, I Tweet Passionately: Twitter Users, Context Collapse, and the Imagined Audience', *New Media & Society*, 13 (1): 114–33.
McRady, R. (2020), 'Paul Walker's Daughter Meadow Snaps Selfie with Vin Diesel's Kids', *ET*, 29 June. Available Online: https://www.etonline.com/paul-walkers-daughter-meadow-snaps-selfie-with-vin-diesels-kids-148900 (accessed 3 July 2020).
MsFastFurious1 (2013), [YouTube] 'Paul Walker Proud of Tyrese Gibson During *Fast Five* Interview', 18 October. Available online: https://www.youtube.com/watch?v=fAEDzk8ziEU (accessed 3 July 2020).
MsFastFurious1 (2014), [YouTube] '*Fast 4* and *Fast 5* Cast Interviews', 1 January. Available online: https://www.youtube.com/watch?v=PLmueGun5t8 (accessed 3 July 2020).
Nessif, B. (2013), 'Vin Diesel Visits Paul Walker's Mom, Talks about Breaking Down and Losing His "Other Half"', *E News*, 7 December. Available online: https://www.eonline.com/news/488475/vin-diesel-visits-paul-walker-s-mom-talks-about-breaking-down-and-losing-his-other-half (accessed 3 July 2020).

Nessif, B. (2014), 'Vin Diesel Shares Epic Paul Walker Video: Watch Their Best Offscreen Bromance Moments Right Here', *E News*, 8 January. Available online: https://www.eonline.com/au/news/496762/vin-diesel-shares-epic-paul-walker-video-watch-their-best-offscreen-bromance-moments-right-here (accessed 3 July 2020).

Noble Awards (2015), [YouTube] 'Paul Walker Tribute the Noble Awards 2015 (Official/Original)', 6 April. Available online: https://www.youtube.com/watch?v=tMTZcnrat90 (accessed 3 July 2020).

Parker, B. (2019), 'Paul Walker and Vin Diesel's Daughters are Just as Close as Their Famous Dads Were', *Channel24*, 31 August. Available online: https://www.news24.com/channel/Gossip/News/pic-paul-walker-and-vin-diesels-daughters-are-just-as-close-as-their-famous-dads-were-20190831-2 (accessed 3 July 2020).

*Point Break* (1991), [Film] Dir. Kathryn Bigelow, USA: Warner Bros. Pictures.

Raphael, J. (2018), 'Paul Walker: The Facts and the Fiction', in C. Lam, J. Raphael, and M. Webber (eds), *Disassembling the Celebrity Figure*, 149–70, Boston: Brill.

Raphael, J. and C. Lam (2019), 'True Bromance: The Authenticity behind the Stewart/McKellen Relationship', *Celebrity Studies*, 10 (2): 153–73.

*Rush Hour* (1998), [Film] Dir. Brett Ratner, USA: New Line Cinema.

SirusXM Entertainment (2017), 'Vin Diesel Reveals a Never-Before-Heard Conversation between His Mom and Paul Walker's Mother', *SoundCloud*. Available online: https://soundcloud.com/siriusxmentertainment/vin-diesel-reveals-a-never-before-heard-conversation-between-his-mom-and-paul-walkers-mother (accessed 3 July 2002).

*Stakeout* (1987), [Film] Dir. John Badham, USA: Touchstone Pictures.

Turner, P. (2019), 'Fast Marketing, Furious Interactions: An Interstellar Community on Instagram', *Celebrity Studies*, 10 (4): 469–78.

Wallis, T. (2019), 'Vin Diesel Sends Sweet Message to Paul Walker's Daughter on Her 21st Birthday', *Mirror*, 6 November. Available online: https://www.mirror.co.uk/3am/celebrity-news/vin-diesel-sends-sweet-message-20822075 (accessed 3 July 2020).

*The World of Movies* (2013), [YouTube] '*The Fast and the Furious 6* – Fastest Cars – Behind the Scenes Making of's', 1 October. Available online: https://www.youtube.com/watch?v=0oZp4qxsXQs (accessed 3 July 2020).

# 10

# 'It's so so so so so so important': China's role in shaping the *Fast & Furious* franchise

Fraser Elliott

On their releases in 2015 and 2017 respectively, *Furious 7* and *The Fate of the Furious* (hereinafter *Fast Eight*) broke box office records for international films in Mainland China.[1] *Fast Eight*, in particular, managed to recoup an impressive near $60 million USD[2] by the end of its opening Friday alone, setting record highs for 'biggest opening day and single day ever' (Brzeski 2017). Outside of *Avengers: Endgame* (2019), these two *Fast & Furious* films currently occupy the highest spots for international releases at the Chinese box office; and they continue a trend that started with *Fast Five* (2011) whereby every film in the franchise has made more money in China than any other single territory, including, perhaps surprisingly, the United States.

China is now the primary marketplace for *Fast & Furious*. As a testament to this new global economy, *Fast 9* (2021) was released in China, Russia and South Korea on 21 May 2021, a full month ahead of its release in North America and most of Europe on 25 June. Partly driven by the impacts of the Covid-19 pandemic, where Chinese cinemas were quicker to reopen than those in North America, this international rollout nevertheless follows Hollywood's turn to China over the last decade which I document below. This new direction has not been without challenges, however; and the release of *Fast 9* shows us just how precarious and unstable the pursuit of Chinese revenues can be. Although the film opened to an impressive $135 million in China on its opening weekend – a record for pandemic releases (Shafer 2021) – its healthy reception wavered almost immediately. After eight days in cinemas, the gross for *Fast 9* dropped 90 per cent through the combined effect of poor word-of-mouth and a political *faux pas* from star John Cena (Clark 2021). During a press tour ahead of the film's release, Cena excitedly told a Taiwanese broadcaster that Taiwan would be 'the first country that can watch *F9*' (Ni 2021) and unwittingly stepped into a geopolitical debate over the contested status of Taiwan as a country distinct from the People's Republic of China. For this statement, Cena was admonished by patriotic netizens in China who rallied for a boycott of the film's release and earned a swift and protracted apology from the star himself.

*Fast & Furious* provides a valuable insight into the opportunities and pitfalls of targeting the Chinese box office. Indeed, in its ongoing expansion into this market, the franchise must negotiate with a complex set of forces and conditions, which derive not just from the preferences of Mainland China's audiences, but also from the region's distinctive industrial and political processes. These conditions and forces have undoubtedly shaped the development of *Fast & Furious* into what we know it as today. However, while much has been made, among critics and fans, of the significant aesthetic changes across the franchise – its transformation from a relatively taut street racing crime film set in Los Angeles to increasingly bombastic globe-trotting, technophobic, superhero narratives – less attention has been paid to the equally radical shift at the level of circulation and production. On the release of the first film in 2001, few would have predicted that a film steeped in the mythology of Los Angeles and Hollywood's genre cinema would go on to become the transnational behemoth it has. It would certainly have been surprising to hear that, starting with *Fast & Furious 6* (2013), each entry in the franchise would be made in collaboration with China Film Group, a state-run distribution company which holds a monopoly on imported films (every foreign film that seeks a release in China must pass through the China Film Group).

This shift in the production and circulation of the *Fast & Furious* films is representative of developing trends in the contemporary blockbuster at large, mostly regarding the franchise film and the exact nature of Hollywood's reliance on the international markets. In this chapter I consider the importance of these contextual trends for the formal development of *Fast & Furious*, paying attention to how the increasingly global (specifically Chinese) ambition of the franchise has fed into the aesthetic developments of the series. Such work is useful because textual analysis can only take our understanding so far. For every explanation and analysis of a trend based on the films and their form alone, there are equally compelling contextual justifications that result from the franchise's increasingly global interconnectedness, its collaborative labour with Chinese production companies and its carefully considered targeting of new international audiences.

The aesthetic and narrative developments seen in the franchise since *Fast Five* appear as they do because they are well suited to the Chinese market. Although this market is vast and certainly diverse, there are preferences among what Xu Song (2018: 185) understands as the 'general movie going public' in China which *Fast & Furious* almost uniquely appeals to. There is, for example, a general desire for 'large-scale action/science fiction blockbusters and 3D-effect foreign films'. This is a type of filmmaking that Hollywood has perfected in recent decades which, until relatively recently, Chinese studios were unable to match technologically. It's also one that *Fast & Furious* – perhaps the 'biggest, loudest, dumbest' film around – excels at (De Semlyen 2011). Vitally for *Fast & Furious*, though, is the balancing of this bombastic action with sentimentality, and its almost saccharine depiction of themes of family and loyalty. Patrick Brzeski (2021a) notes, 'a little sentimentality rarely hurts' in the Chinese market. Reports abound of films with 'emotional or heart-warming content' at their core earning huge returns at the box office (Shackleton 2021). While other Hollywood films have been dismissed by Chinese film-goers as 'too commercialized' and lacking heart (Wang 2018), *Fast & Furious* has managed to maintain a Chinese fanbase through its marriage of over-the-top action and sentimentality.

This defining characteristic of the franchise has developed alongside its targeting of Chinese audiences and is but one example of how market trends in this region have encouraged the franchise to move in a specific direction. Across this chapter I explore the success of *Fast & Furious* in China as a means of contextualizing our understanding of the *textual* characteristics of the franchise's later films. The edited collection this chapter sits in is an attempt to incorporate recognition of *Fast & Furious* into discussions of the ongoing 'Franchise Era' (Fleury, Hartzheim and Mamber 2019) in general and, for this to be comprehensive, we need to consider the aesthetic, formal changes ushered in by an increasingly global marketplace for Hollywood films. Through a focus on the function of stardom in *Fast & Furious*, and a case study of *Furious 7* (2015) in particular, I seek to challenge some dominant ideas about the circulation and reception of franchise films globally, showing how the modes of spectatorship we understand these films to offer audiences in Euro-American contexts do not necessarily function in the same way in countries like China. The chapter argues for a more context-/region-specific approach that is more able to capture the distinctive appeals these films hold for different audiences. *Fast & Furious* illustrates the need for such films to embody a 'multi-perspective approach' (Manning and Shackford-Bradley 2010: 36), in production and form, whereby the aesthetic strategies of these films must provide a range of possible avenues for engagement to heterogeneous, international audiences. It is a franchise which also shows us that the returns of such strategies are by no means assured and the contemporary marketplace is a precarious one for Hollywood's stakeholders.

## An international franchise

The growth of the international box office of the *Fast & Furious* franchise has been striking. *The Fast and the Furious* (2001) took $207 million globally. The majority of this figure – $144 million – came from domestic US audiences, with fourteen other countries providing the international income. Despite relatively large returns from European nations, Australia and Mexico, the domestic box office accounted for 70 per cent of the total revenue for the film.[3] This contrasts sharply with the picture fourteen years later when *Furious 7* not only earned $1.5 billion globally – an eightfold increase from the first film – but also did so across a far larger number of territories. For this release, domestic US audiences accounted for $353 million, roughly 23 per cent of the total box office, while the remaining 77 per cent came from international locations. A total of sixty-seven countries contributed, with several territories providing upwards of $40 million individually including Brazil ($47 million), Mexico ($51 million) and the UK ($60 million). Most important though, was the $390 million that came from China, beating out domestic receipts by close to $40 million.

Before turning to China, it's important to acknowledge the vast increase in territories in general, as over half of *Furious 7*'s total box office came from a diverse spread of countries beyond China and the United States. These sixty-five other locations speak to the globalization of contemporary Hollywood and the desire for such films to travel as easily as possible across borders to heterogeneous audiences (Song 2018: 179). There are two ways to read these statistics. On one level, they illustrate Hollywood's dominance of the global film market. This is an understanding laid out by Kailash Koushik and Jennifer M. Proffitt (2019: 30) in their examination of the circulation of blockbuster franchises like *Fast & Furious* in the wider context of transnational capitalism and North America's continued 'exploitation of labour, audiences and environments' the world over. However, on another level, these statistics represent something of a softening of Hollywood's agency, an argument I develop below. These territories provide a plethora of audiences with diverse viewing preferences and habits, so any desire to appeal across all will inevitably require compromise and the integration of what has been called a 'multi-perspective approach' to the films themselves (Manning and Shackford-Bradley 2010: 36).[4] This term refers to aesthetic devices – how filmmakers consciously mediate their films for different global audiences – but the dispersal of power from Hollywood to other regions implied in this multi-perspective approach extends to considerations of production and circulation. As films like *Fast & Furious* become more prominent internationally, they must not only accommodate a wider range of audience tastes, but their creators must collaborate with those international stakeholders, creatives and agencies who possess expertise and knowledge of their respective regions. The leverage of China within this space, in particular, gives us a vital route into understanding the function of these non-US markets in contemporary blockbuster film culture.

The success and growth of *Fast & Furious* films in China are all the more significant when we consider their nature as sequels in a long-running franchise. Franchise films rely, though not exclusively, on viewer familiarity: a pre-existing audience with in-built knowledge is a necessity for Hollywood studios to reap the rewards of the franchise formula. This is explored in much contemporary franchise scholarship – from Henry Jenkins (2006) through to James Fleury, Bryan Hikari Hartzheim and Stephen Mamber (2019) – which observes the rise of transmedia strategies in studios like Disney and Warner Bros. The transmedia, cinematic universes crafted by these corporations are designed to increase audience engagement, encouraging more interaction by stretching narratives and characters across multiple media forms and tie-ins. This has been a successful risk management strategy in the United States, where such viewer-bases have been cultivated over decades of exposure to the intellectual properties in question.

The same consumer base for these franchises does not, however, exist in China, posing problems for this core strategy of contemporary production. The films in the final trilogy in the *Star Wars* 'Skywalker Saga' are among the most famous examples of films to 'bomb' in China. Following a relatively long absence from cinemas, the marketing of these films was built around a long-anticipated return of the franchise, with promotional materials seeking to exploit audience nostalgia for the earlier films in the original trilogy (1977–83) and the prequels (1999–2005). While this strategy worked for US audiences, where the first film of this trilogy instalment – *Star Wars: The Force Awakens* (2015) – earned just shy of $1 billion, it was far less successful in China. The Chinese box office for *The Force Awakens* totalled 'just' $52 million– significantly less than the likes of *Fast & Furious 6* and *Furious 7*, for example – and the returns decreased with each release thereafter, leading to a final $12 million in cinema ticket sales for the finale, *Star Wars: The Rise of Skywalker* (2019). The tepid and diminishing response from Chinese audiences can be attributed to the fact that these films did not mark a 'return' to *Star Wars* for Chinese audiences. The original trilogy of films barely made it to the territory due to their release just after China's Cultural Revolution and, as such, there is no equivalent nostalgia for Chinese audiences in *Star Wars* and many viewers see the lore as too impenetrable to engage with (Yuhas 2020).

The *Star Wars* example suggests that the pleasures afforded a spectator by the sequel in contemporary franchise cinema do not always apply to China where many of the audiences are newcomers to these decades-old narratives. This is a much bigger phenomenon than one bound to the social and political turmoil China underwent during the second half of the twentieth century. Indeed, familiarity with film franchises is as much a question of access to cinema screens as it is political disruption. While there has long been a robust home media circuit in China, wide-reaching theatrical exhibition is a much more recent development. The statistics here are staggering; and, if we chart them alongside *Fast & Furious*' development, the correlation proves telling. In 2002, the year after the franchise began, there were only 1,581 cinema screens in China. This had already increased to 4,723 in 2009 at the time of the release of *Fast Four*. The pace then began to pick up significantly so that, by 2017, when *Fast Eight* hit cinemas, there were a total of 51,000 cinema screens in the country (Song 2018: 178). By the time of *Fast 9*'s release, the figure sat at 75,000 screens (Davis 2021), suggesting that the growth is not yet starting to plateau. These statistics represent a nearly 5,000 per cent increase in cinema screens, opening up a much larger potential market to Hollywood studios: one comprised, crucially, of entirely new theatrical audiences altogether.

The question, then, is how Universal has been able to successfully attract these audiences with a franchise as expansive as *Fast & Furious* when Disney were unable to with *Star Wars*, despite the latter's huge media campaigns. The iterative increase in audiences for *Fast & Furious* has bucked the trend of sequels here to such an extent that, as a result, some scholars have suggested that 'the Hollywood sequel has a *greater impact* on Chinese audiences than in the USA' (Chiu et al 2019: 1018, emphasis added). Hollywood sequels have the potential to carry a certain capital for Chinese audiences, but the failure of *Star Wars* suggests there must be other factors at play here. How exactly has *Fast & Furious* navigated this space, and what effect has this pursuit had on the form of the films themselves?

## *Fast & Furious* and Hollywood's turn to China

One of the key ways in which *Fast & Furious* has been able to gain a competitive advantage in Mainland China is through Universal's direct collaborations with Chinese corporations such as China Film Group. There are currently two dominant methods for Hollywood studios to access the Chinese market: revenue sharing and co-production, with the former being most common. Co-productions can be more lucrative for studios, but they are rarer due to their strict regulation policies and 'burdensome' production restrictions that outweigh the possible benefits of the relationship (Song 2018: 179). Co-productions must contain at least one scene shot in China and one Chinese actor; one-third of their investment must come from Chinese companies; and, most controversially, they must contain 'positive Chinese elements' (O'Connor and Armstrong 2015: 9). *Fast & Furious* is no stranger to this kind of production arrangement. Universal has worked with the British Film Institute (BFI) in the UK to secure tax relief on its films for the inclusion of various stars like Jason Statham, and prominent use of filming locations in London and Edinburgh. Deemed to be significantly 'British' due to these creative choices, *Fast & Furious* 6 passed the BFI's 'cultural test' and earned a 25 per cent tax relief on all production expenditure (Presence 2017). The results of this collaboration have been clear on the franchise with Statham's Shaw and his family playing a prominent role in the main series and its spinoffs. In contrast, the results of Universal's efforts to engage China are less visible, tending to operate beneath the surface of the texts themselves.

As of the release of *Fast 9*, none of the *Fast & Furious* films have been set in China in a meaningful way – beyond a brief nod to Hong Kong and Macau in the sixth film – and no Chinese stars have yet joined the 'family'. Instead, Universal has pursued the other, more common, form of partnership with China: revenue sharing. In this model, Hollywood studios work with Chinese distribution and exhibition partners in a more behind-the-scenes mode: these partners cover local tax and promotion costs in exchange for a large percentage of a given film's Chinese box office. Revenue sharing has ushered in some of the highest profile success stories of Hollywood in China, including *Transformers: Age of Extinction* (2014) and its $320 million box office, the highest in China for that year. The collaboration helped *Furious* 7 to a vast release on more than 70 per cent of China's screens – over 90,000 showings per day (Song 2018: 88). It also led to the film receiving a 'stellar marketing campaign' across China through coordination with the China Film Group and China's State

Administration of Radio, Film and Television (Cain 2015). In return, China Film Group took 10 per cent of the film's Chinese revenue.

This cooperation with China Film Group clearly played a significant role in facilitating the success of *Fast & Furious* in China. However, this kind of collaboration also taps into broader, contentious questions around China's influence and command over the form and content of Hollywood productions. All imported films to China are subject to censorship from the Propaganda Department of the Communist Party's Central Committee, an organization whose official role is 'to protect [China's] national culture while resisting conflicting Western values in the context of film globalisation' (Song 2018: 181). Furthermore, China has no tiered classification system so films must be considered suitable for all audiences and avoid explicit representations of sex, violence, profanity and political dissent. Historically, this meant that China would receive a different edit of a Hollywood film to cinemas in other territories. Often, this played out in quite benign ways like the additional inclusion of star Fan Bingbing in the Chinese version of Marvel's *Iron Man 3* (2013) or extended sequences of Shanghai in the Chinese release of *Looper* (2012), a change from the Parisian setting of its novel. Yet the vagaries of this system have posed numerous challenges for Hollywood studios, including concerns that the Chinese Communist Party (CCP) is manipulating the market for economic and political gain (McMahon 2020: 8).

Since these occurrences in the mid-2010s, it has become rarer for the Chinese market to receive a noticeably different version of a Hollywood film to its North American and European release. A key reason for this shift is the negative reputational impact the edits can have for both Chinese audiences – who lose enthusiasm for the version available at Chinese cinemas – and international pundits, who decry Hollywood as 'kowtowing' to the Chinese government (Lukinbeal 2019). Instead, edits have become pre-emptive, moving to form part of the production process. Right from the screenwriting stages of pre-production, studios are targeting China but also engaging in self-censorship, specifically tailoring their scripts/concepts for both Chinese tastes and regulations. The result is that the version of a film released in China is now largely the same as the version released elsewhere around the world.

This workaround has not always proved seamless, however, and there continue to be moments of controversy when the self-censorship is transparent. A particularly notable example was the response to Marvel's re-writing of a character – the Ancient One – in *Doctor Strange* (2016). The character, who is a Tibetan monk in the original comics, was re-written as a Celt by screenwriter C. Robert Cargill fearing, as John Cena has learned, that acknowledging Tibet as a country would have alienated the Chinese government and the region's audiences (Double Toasted 2016). As a result of the alteration and the casting of white British actor Tilda Swinton, *Doctor Strange* was criticized both for appeasing the CCP *and* for resurfacing problematic trends of 'whitewashing' and regressive casting choices for Asian film roles (Evans 2016). More recently, fans noticed the removal of Japan and Taiwan flags from a character's jacket in *Top Gun: Maverick* (2022), leading to similar accusations of political compromise (Shen 2020).

These assessments complicate current understandings of Hollywood's reach into the Chinese market. They question the extent to which these are processes which maintain the historical power dynamic of American dominance over global film cultures. Koushik and Proffitt (2019: 28) make a compelling case that the strategies listed above represent a covert shift in Hollywood that now 'operates, exploits and maintains its economic and cultural dominance' in global markets: that international collaborations work to conceal Hollywood's global dominance through 'production, financing, marketing and distribution business practices'. While there is a great deal of truth to this, we could equally suggest that the processes Hollywood studios must engage in to enter this market limit their dominance through compulsory aesthetic, political, formal, promotional and circulation compromises with the Chinese state apparatus.

The complexity of these processes is particularly apparent in the case of *Fast & Furious*. We can see the impact of these compromises and collaborations within the texts themselves, evident in the formal approaches and adaptations that have been incorporated to ensure the franchise remains a strong commercial prospect in China. Indeed, the distinctive formal and aesthetic characteristics of *Fast & Furious* align very closely with the conditions of the Chinese market: the franchise is almost uniquely free of sex, generally apolitical, and any moral deviance contained within the criminal behaviour of the main cast is softened by the sentimental focus on 'family' and the honourable, censor-friendly, intentions therein. Each of these elements – while not specifically aimed at China alone – renders *Fast & Furious* a strong property for export to that specific territory, allowing it to negotiate the distinctive network of industrial conditions, audience tastes and political processes therein.

Thanks to *Fast & Furious'* deft negotiation of the complexities of the Chinese marketplace, many of these contextual factors and drivers of aesthetic developments are not always apparent or immediately visible. Entries like *Furious 7* have been understood by experts on Sino-American collaboration as the archetypal example of 'Chinese corporate investments in Hollywood studio films' (Kokas 2017: 169).[5] Unlike those studios mentioned above, Universal has thus far avoided any significant backlash by cultural commentators to the substantial involvement of China Film Group in the films' production, distribution and exhibition. We might attribute this to the lack of overtly noticeable Chinese elements in the films themselves. The franchise is, as Kokas (2017: 164) suggests, not an example of 'Hollywood made in China' but one that showcases the *structural* changes ushered in by these trends: an indicator of how 'Hollywood studio productions will also increasingly be made by China – or rather, by Chinese companies investing in Hollywood.' Learning from the stumbles of the early 2010s, this is a much less noticeable form of Chinese involvement or targeting than, say, *Iron Man 3* was, but it is one that remains vital to the American studios concerned.

China is mostly absent in the diegetic world of *Fast & Furious*. However, this may not be true for much longer if the assurances of members of the *Fast* family are to be believed. At a 2019 event in Beijing, Dwayne Johnson assured audiences that Chinese action star Wu Jing (an actor particularly associated with promoting state politics) will star in the *Hobbs and Shaw* (2019) sequel. Franchise screenwriter Chris Morgan claimed in the same event that he would 'like to see, down the road, if [they] are able to do a giant portion or even the entire movie here in China' (Rui 2019). Diesel made similar assurances to a crowd in China's capital at a *Furious 7* event, stating 'If we ever made another *Fast & Furious* film, we will film in China!' (Loh 2015). At the time of writing, these seem to be broken promises, but they are not unreasonable suggestions and represent a logical next step in the franchise's ongoing approach to Chinese collaboration. After all, Diesel himself has previously led projects where this collaboration is more visible to audiences from within the films themselves, including *xXx: Return of Xander Cage* (2017). Produced by Diesel's One Race Films, a studio responsible for all post-2009 *Fast & Furious* releases, *xXx* featured an international roster of stars, including Hong Kong/Chinese megastars Donnie Yen and Kris Wu, which partly explains its success in the region (Koushik and Proffitt 2019).

Even if these promises remain broken, such assurances show us how *Fast & Furious* has been able to access the Chinese market without damaging its reputation in other territories. While many of their savvy strategies have been invisible to international viewers, they are vital to acknowledge here because they do appear to inform the films themselves and their modes of address in addition to simply shaping promotional tours in discrete territories. We can see this most clearly by interrogating how the star personas of *Fast & Furious*' cast function within the films themselves. The star personas of Diesel, Dwayne Johnson and their colleagues are a way in to understanding the franchise's targeting of a diverse spectatorship and the ways in which it offers a means of engagement to international audiences, including those in China.

## Stardom as part of *Furious 7*'s fractured appeal

The cast events discussed above show how much, when it comes to engaging with Chinese audiences, Universal retains an investment in the stardom of the *Fast & Furious* cast. The emphasis on stars in the marketing and production of *Fast & Furious* is something of an outlier in the 'franchise era' when the importance of stardom is seen to have paled in importance against the rise of brands and cinematic universes. In their compelling introductory summary to *The Franchise Era*, Fleury, Hartzheim and Mamber (2019: 8) observe how the 'global star-centric economy' has been reconfigured in the age of big-budget blockbusters thanks to 'the displacement of mid-budget films'. In this understanding, Hollywood has transitioned away from a star-based economy towards a character-based model: film studios are less interested in owning 'talent' than they are 'brands', and many actors still invested in star vehicles have migrated to television and other media (Ibid 2019: 9). The *Avengers* films may cast a roster of notable actors including many A-list names, but here 'Marvel is the star' and Black Widow and Iron Man carry more currency than Scarlet Johansson and Robert Downey Jr. who depict them (Wesley Morris, quoted in Fleury, Hartzheim and Mamber 2019: 9).[6]

Looking at *Fast & Furious* from the perspective of its circulation in China, we can see that, actually, the stardom of its cast remains central to its success in the region. Seen as a particularly astute part of China Film Group and Universal's marketing campaigns, promotional cast events across China – often in Beijing – have been crucial in attracting Chinese audiences to the franchise and are 'believed to be a big contributor to the success of *Furious 7* in China's cinema market' (Cunningham 2015). They capitalize on a particularly Chinese phenomenon whereby the success of a film is often inextricably linked with how well maintained the relationship is between its cast and Chinese fan communities: such relationships have been known to significantly 'boost box office performance' (Song 2018: 186). These cast events in Beijing, Shanghai and other cities and administrative regions around China have scaffolded the release of every *Fast & Furious* film since *Fast & Furious 6*. For example, both Jason Statham and Dwayne Johnson made stopovers in Shanghai and Guangzhou to promote *Hobbs & Shaw* (2019), the series' first spinoff which traded on the star power and leverage of its leading pair.

It is notable that, in their summary of the franchise era and its shift in focus from stardom to character, Fleury, Hartzheim and Mamber (2019: 10) allude to the instability of star-vehicles by citing the failure at the US box office of Dwayne Johnson's non-franchise release *Skyscraper* (2018). While true from a North American perspective, the same does not apply to China. Despite its lukewarm domestic reception of $68 million, the Hong Kong-set *Skyscraper* earned a reasonable $98 million at the Chinese box office. Importantly, it provided an opportunity to consolidate Johnson's stardom with Chinese audiences, building on his success with the *Fast & Furious* films. Johnson has been open about his conscious turn to China in the early 2010s as a response to not getting cast in superhero films. Speaking to Chinese magazine *STYLE*, Johnson told readers in 2018 that he thought 'the best and most important thing that [he] could do was establish a relationship with the Chinese audience' (Tie 2018). Just as Universal had with *Fast & Furious*, Johnson saw a developing market in China and worked to specifically target audiences there on their own terms of in-person promotional tours and starring roles in co-productions like *Skyscaper* with a visible 'Chinese' influence.

From this perspective, *Skyscraper* stands out as less of a flop and more of a strategic investment on the part of Johnson and other stakeholders. Indeed, outside of *Fast & Furious*, *Skyscraper* represents the pinnacle of Johnson's efforts to break into the Chinese market. It was the world's top-grossing film when it opened in China and its release was supported by a promotional tour of Shanghai (and Hong Kong) by Johnson himself. What's more, the film was a co-production with Legendary Entertainment, a company owned by Wanda, a Chinese conglomerate. Their involvement was deemed meaningful enough for *Skyscraper* to be considered a Chinese film by the state apparatus so it could be released in summer during a 'blackout' month where no foreign films can open (Guerrasio 2018). As such, it's not unreasonable to suggest that *Fast & Furious* spinoff *Hobbs & Shaw* (2019) would not have been made were it not for the star leverage of Johnson in China. Through the China example, we can see that, vitally, stardom offers a 'way in' to a franchise like *Fast & Furious* for new audiences. Here, the casting of a global megastar such as Johnson provides a familiar presence, acting as scaffolding to help audiences navigate the surprisingly complex lore and character relations of the later *Fast & Furious* films.

A key example of the significance of stardom, in this regard, is *Furious 7*. This entry remains the series' highest grossing in China, but it also represents a particularly hard sell to newcomers. It has a first act which is laden with a complex amnesia plot that relies on an intimate knowledge of the franchise, its characters Letty and Dom, and the surprisingly circuitous series timeline. That it managed to attract more Chinese audiences than ever before – including a significant amount who only just gained access to film exhibition spaces – is perhaps surprising. It would be a stretch for me to suggest that this was entirely down to the appeal of the *Fast* family's star personas as those previously mentioned themes of 'family, loyalty and integrity' certainly serve as ways in to the film, particularly for audiences in China (Dergarabedia, qtd in Brennan 2015). The assurance of action spectacle holds similar appeal. However, considering the importance of cast events in the region, I would attest that an equal appeal must come from the stardom of Diesel, Statham, Johnson and, in the case of *Furious 7*, Paul Walker. The various narratives constructed around their star personas provided another entry point into the film, helping to structure the viewing experiences for international audiences less familiar with the complex lore of the six previous films.

Walker died in a car crash during the production of *Furious 7* and the film's narrative had to be re-written to accommodate for this unexpected loss. Prospective audiences bought into *Furious 7* to see how the franchise would write out one of its lead stars, and nowhere was this as strong as in China. Lily Kuo (2015) notes that Walker's death struck a chord with audiences there as shown by an outpouring of mourning over the social media platform Weibo, suggesting that the associations this brought to *Furious 7* chimed with the general Chinese audiences' engagement with sentimental narratives that were popular at the time of its release. Rob Cain (2015) leans equally into Chinese social media – which can 'instantly make or break a movie' in China – and Walker's ubiquity on the WeChat platform following his death. A telling phrase in Cain's discussion of *Furious 7* is how 'curiosity to see the final ride into the sunset of the well-liked actor who was in many ways the heart of this franchise drew numerous *Fast & Furious newbies* to Chinese multiplexes' (emphasis added). As it did all over the world, Walker's death brought new audiences into the franchise by offering a number of parallel avenues of engagement through the film's negotiation of his star persona. Viewers lost in the density of the character exposition elsewhere could anchor their spectatorship on the lingering threat of Walker's (and his character, Brian's) departure from the franchise. It is noted elsewhere in this collection that Brian's exit in *Furious 7* makes little diegetic sense: the viewer is told he is leaving to spend time with his family, but the emotional weight ascribed to his exit through the film form is incongruous to a viewer unaware of Walker's death. In other words, Walker's stardom is vital in understanding *Furious 7* as a cohesive narrative and an engagement based entirely on Brian's character alone does not quite work.

Whether through the unexpected tragedy of Walker's death or the carefully curated bolstering of Johnson's Chinese career, *Furious 7* and later films in the *Fast & Furious* franchise in general promote a mode of spectatorship that gestures back to more historical understandings of stardom and its function in earlier decades of Hollywood cinema. *Fast & Furious* complicates the neatness of the franchise film's functioning in a purely Euro-American circulation context by maintaining stardom and star personas as necessary avenues for engagement with the films in international spaces. While by no means exclusive to China, the ways in which these films and their stars have navigated and been honed to succeed within the Chinese marketplace offer a useful way through which to understand these, perhaps unexpected, qualities of the contemporary franchise and reiterate the importance of China to Universal's global ambitions.

## An unstable future for the franchise

The influence of stardom on *Fast & Furious* in China is so great that it can carry equal leverage in alienating viewers, as it does in attracting them. As noted above, *Fast 9* was released in parts of Asia – including China, Taiwan and South Korea – over a month before the United States. Following the tried-and-tested press gambit from previous releases, the stars of *Fast 9* conducted various interviews and cast events for audiences in these regions. During one such interview with the Taiwanese broadcaster TVBS, *Fast 9* star John Cena excitedly told viewers that 'Taiwan is the first country that can watch *F9*' (Ni 2021). The actor-wrestler who can speak Mandarin and has spent recent years cultivating a fan base in China, was quickly admonished by patriotic Chinese netizens for acknowledging Taiwan as a country separate to the PRC. Cena immediately posted a video, speaking in Mandarin, on his Weibo account, apologizing: 'I made a mistake, I must say right now. It's so so so so so so important, I love and respect Chinese people. Sorry. Sorry. I'm really sorry. You have to understand that I love and respect China and Chinese people.' In the days after Cena's *faux pas*, *Fast 9*'s box office takings in China fell 85 per cent and its user score on taste-making social network Douban sat at 5.5, lower than the other major releases of the year. As a result of this steep decline, *Fast 9* made significantly less at the Chinese box office than Universal expected, and though it would be irresponsible to attribute this to Cena's comments alone – the film received lukewarm reviews in the territory still recovering from Covid-19 – they certainly appear to have played a role (Brzeski 2021b).

What the stumbles of *Fast 9* do show with certainty is that Hollywood's current reliance, and navigation of, the Chinese market is a precarious one. While I have articulated this through a focus on stardom and its function in contemporary franchise cinema, the impact and repercussions are much broader. *Fast & Furious* could not have expanded in the ways it has without China. As a prototypical example of Koskas' understanding of Hollywood made *by* (rather than *in*) China, *Fast & Furious* has developed across its recent instalments through a desire to appeal to audience tastes in China and across the globe. Perfecting a formula since *Fast Five*, Universal has played to the desires of Chinese audiences through its stars and increasingly bombastic set pieces – targeting an audience understood to enjoy this kind of 'large-scale action'. *Fast & Furious* has functioned as one arm of Hollywood's expansionism and its desire to try and 'strengthen Chinese audience's trust and confidence in Hollywood movies [and] reintroduce the blockbuster consumerism culture to them' (Song 2018: 185). Thanks to the huge income provided by the Chinese box office, *Fast & Furious* has been able to expand its production budgets and incrementally increase the scale and spectacle of the set pieces in each subsequent release – something that is at the core of its brand as one of contemporary Hollywood's biggest and most outrageous cinematic properties.

The challenge now is two-fold. In addition to the political precarity of the marketplace, the Chinese film industry is now producing equally high-budget, 'large-scale action' blockbusters that are becoming more popular with Chinese audiences than their Hollywood counterparts. Any hope that appealing to Chinese audience preferences would strengthen that audience's confidence in Hollywood has not materialized with any geographical exclusivity: the audience's trust and confidence in 'blockbuster consumerism culture' have been bolstered, but there is no allegiance to Hollywood therein. I started this chapter noting that *Furious 7* and *Fast Eight* occupy second and third place for the highest grossing international films in China. While this is true, they occupy the much less impressive fifteenth and eighteenth positions if we include domestic releases in the list (Endata 2021). Recent releases like *The Eight Hundred* (2020), *The Wandering Earth* (2019) and *Wolf Warrior 2* (2017) are giving audiences not 'Hollywood made by China', nor even 'Hollywood made in China', but a wholly domestic blockbuster offering that is proving more and more popular with Chinese audiences. This aspect of the Chinese marketplace poses a major threat to Hollywood studios, as Aynne Kokas warns: 'If China doesn't need US movies, Hollywood studios will have to dramatically reduce their spending on big budget blockbusters' (Pallotta 2021).

The vast Chinese box office has supported *Fast & Furious* and its move into new spaces of bombastic action that would not have been possible without this new source of income. While it's tempting to point to *Fast & Furious* as an example of Universal and Hollywood's continued exploitation of the global market, I have suggested that the mechanisms of this process belie a much more equal power dynamic. China continues to be a thorny space for Hollywood studios to navigate aesthetically and politically, but *Fast & Furious* has been largely successful at appealing to audiences in China without enduring the same criticisms – and suffering the same pitfalls – that have befallen other popular franchises. Yet, *Fast 9*'s rapid decline at the Chinese box office is just one incident that poses grand questions for the remaining two films in the franchise: if China is no longer interested in these films, will *Fast & Furious* be able to afford the ostentatious finale and provide the types of big-screen spectacle that are so central to its brand? China remains so so so so so so important to *Fast & Furious* and Hollywood, but if the reverse is no longer true, these films will start to look drastically different in the coming years for audiences the world over.

# Notes

1 Throughout this chapter, 'China' is used to refer to Mainland China – the People's Republic of China – specifically.
2 All box office statistics discussed in this chapter are in US Dollars.
3 All references to box office figures for *Fast & Furious* are from Box Office Mojo. Cited in the references section.

4   See Jones and Gulam's chapter in this collection for more information on the multifaceted representational politics of *Fast & Furious*.
5   I would assume that Kokas (2017) would consider *The Fate of the Furious* (2017), which was released after her study was published, equally representative.
6   Whether this collapsing is as true for *Fast & Furious* is debatable. Before the arrival of Johnson in *Fast Five*, few of the cast were particularly well known outside of the franchise. As noted elsewhere in this collection, the personas of Walker and to some extent Diesel have become inextricably linked with those of their on-screen Brian O'Conner and Dominic Toretto; the same could be said for Michelle Rodriguez (Letty), Sung Kang (Han) and others.

## References

*Avengers: Endgame* (2019), [Film] Dir. Anthony and Joe Russo, USA: Walt Disney Studios Motion Pictures.
Box Office Mojo. (No Date), 'Franchise: *The Fast and the Furious*', Available online: https://www.boxofficemojo.com/franchise/fr3628568325/ (accessed 26 July 2021).
Brennan, J. (2015), 'What Do China and *Furious 7* Have in Common? Machine Porn', *Forbes*, 30 April. Available online: https://www.forbes.com/sites/judebrennan/2015/04/30/what-do-china-and-furious-7-have-in-common-machine-porn/?sh=6688a17a76fe (accessed 19 July 2021).
Brzeski, P. (2017), 'China Box Office: *The Fate of the Furious* Races into Record Books with $190M Opening', *The Hollywood Reporter*, 16 April. Available online: https://www.hollywoodreporter.com/movies/movie-news/china-box-office-fate-furious-races-record-books-190m-opening-994404/ (accessed 6 August 2021).
Brzeski, P. (2021a), 'China Box Office: *Hi, Mom* Surges Past *Detective Chinatown 3* with $90M+ in Daily Revenue', *The Hollywood Reporter*, 16 February. Available online: https://www.hollywoodreporter.com/movies/movie-news/china-box-office-comedy-hi-mom-surges-4133423/ (accessed 28 July 2021).
Brzeski, P. (2021b), 'China Box Office: *F9* Falls 85 Percent amid Weak Reviews, John Cena Controversy', *The Hollywood Reporter*, 31 May. Available online: https://www.hollywoodreporter.com/movies/movie-news/f9-china-box-office-poor-reviews-john-cena-controversy-1234961123/ (accessed 28 July 2021).
Cain, R. (2015), 'Why Is China So *Furious*?', *China Film Biz*, 22 April. Available online: https://chinafilmbiz.com/2015/04/22/why-is-china-so-furious/ (accessed 19 July 2021).
Chiu, Y. L., K. H. Chen, J. N. Wang, and Y. T. Shu (2019), 'The Impact of Online Movie Word-of-mouth on Consumer Choice: A Comparison of American and Chinese Consumers', *International Marketing Review*, 36 (6): 996–1025.
Clark, T. (2021), '*Fast and Furious 9* is Soaring at the Box Office in China and Easing Fears about the Future of Hollywood Blockbusters in the Crucial Market', *Insider*,

24 May. Available online: https://www.businessinsider.com/fast-and-furious-9-dominating-china-box-office-analysis-2021-5 (accessed 8 August 2021).

Cunningham, T. (2015), '*Furious 7*'s Massive China Haul Will Exceed Its U.S. Box Office', *The Wrap*, 28 April. Available online: https://fortune.com/2015/04/28/furious-7s-massive-china-haul-will-exceed-its-u-s-box-office/ (accessed 13 May 2022).

Davis, R. (2021), 'China's Cinema Screen Count Leaps Despite COVID Closures', *Variety*, 16 February. Available online: https://variety.com/2021/film/news/china-cinema-screen-count-increased-2020-1234909164/ (accessed 14 July 2021).

De Semlyen, N. (2011), '*Fast & Furious 5*: Rio Heist Review', *Empire*, 14 January. Available online: https://www.empireonline.com/movies/reviews/fast-furious-5-rio-heist-review/ (accessed 22 April 2022).

*Doctor Strange* (2016), [Film] Dir. Scott Dickerson, USA: Walt Disney Studios Motion Pictures.

Double Toasted (2016), [YouTube] 'Exclusive! Doctor Strange Writer C. Robert Cargill – Double Toasted Interview', 23 April. Available online: https://www.youtube.com/watch?v=eEpbUf8dGq0 (accessed 8 August 2021).

*The Eight Hundred* (2020), [Film] Dir. Guan Hu, China: Huayi Brothers.

Endata (2021), '内地总票房排名', *Endata*, (n.d.). Available online: https://www.endata.com.cn/BoxOffice/BO/History/Movie/Alltimedomestic.html (accessed 29 July 2021).

Evans, A. (2016), '*Doctor Strange* "Whitewashing" Row Resurfaces with New Criticism of Swinton Casting', *The Guardian*, 4 November. Available online: https://www.theguardian.com/film/2016/nov/04/doctor-strange-tilda-swinton-whitewashing-row (accessed 6 August 2021).

Fleury, J., B. H. Hartzheim and S. Mamber (2019), *The Franchise Era: Managing Media in the Digital Economy*, Edinburgh: Edinburgh University Press.

Guerrasio, J. (2018), 'How the Rock's Popularity in China Led *Skyscraper* to Rebound and Become the Global Box-office Winner of the Weekend', *Insider*, 23 July. Available online: https://www.businessinsider.com/the-rocks-popularity-in-china-led-to-skyscraper-box-office-rebound-2018-7?r=US&IR=T (accessed 26 July 2021).

*Iron Man 3* (2013), [Film] Dir. Shane Black, USA: Walt Disney Studios Motion Pictures.

Jenkins, H. (2006), *Convergence Culture: Where Old and New Media Collide*, New York: NYU Press.

Kokas, A. (2017), *Hollywood Made in China*, Oakland: University of California Press.

Koushik, K. and J. M. Proffitt (2019), 'Global Capital, Global Labour, and Global Dominance: The Case of *xXx: Return of Xander Cage*', *International Journal of Media & Cultural Politics*, 15 (1): 27–47.

Kuo, L. (2015), '*Furious 7*'s Record-Breaking Debut Confirms China's Love of Bad Action Movies', *Quartz*, 14 April. Available online: https://qz.com/382869/furious-7s-record-breaking-debut-confirms-chinas-love-of-bad-action-movies/ (accessed 19 July 2021).

Loh, G. S. (2015), 'Vin Diesel Hints at *Fast and Furious 8* Movie', *Today*, 26 March. Available online: https://www.todayonline.com/entertainment/movies/vin-diesel-hints-fast-and-furious-8-movie (accessed 14 July 2021).

*Looper* (2012), [Film] Dir. Rian Johnson, USA: Sony Pictures Releasing.

Lukinbeal, C. (2019), 'The Chinafication of Hollywood: Chinese Consumption and the Self-Censorship of US Films through a Case Study of *Transformers: Age of Extinction*', *Erdkunde*, 73 (2): 97–110.

Manning, C., and J. Shackford-Bradley (2010), 'Global Subjects in Motion: Strategies for Representing Globalization in Film', *Journal of Film and Video*, 62: 36–52.

McMahon, J. (2020), 'Selling Hollywood to China', *Forum for Social Economics*, 50 (4): 414–30.

Ni, V. (2021), 'John Cena "Very Sorry" for Saying Taiwan Is a Country', *The Guardian*, 25 May. Available online: https://www.theguardian.com/world/2021/may/26/john-cena-very-sorry-for-saying-taiwan-is-a-country (accessed 28 July 2021).

O'Connor, S. and N. Armstrong (2015), 'Directed by Hollywood, Edited by China: How China's Censorship and Influence Affect Films Worldwide', in *U.S., China Economic and Security Review Commission Staff Report*. Available online: https://www.uscc.gov/sites/default/files/Research/Directed%20by%20Hollywood%20Edited%20by%20China.pdf (accessed 19 July 2021).

Pallotta, F. (2021), 'What if China No Longer Needs Hollywood? That's Bad News for the Film Industry', *CNN Business*, 28 January. Available online: https://edition.cnn.com/2021/01/28/media/china-box-office-coronavirus/index.html (accessed 28 July 2021).

Presence, S. (2017), 'The Finance and Production of Independent Film and Television in the United Kingdom: A Critical Introduction', in Eva Bakoy, Roel Puijk and Andrew Spicer (eds), *Building Successful and Sustainable Film and Television Business: A Cross-National Perspective*, 247–69, Bristol: Intellect Books.

Rui, Z. (2019), 'Wu Jung, Reeves Could Join *Hobbs & Shaw* Sequel', *China.Org.Cn*, 9 August. Available online: http://www.china.org.cn/arts/2019-08/09/content_75082591.htm (accessed 14 July 2021).

Shackleton, L. (2021), 'China Box Office: Local Titles Propel China to Record-breaking New Year's Day', *Screen Daily*, 4 January. Available online: https://www.screendaily.com/news/china-box-office-local-titles-propel-china-to-record-breaking-new-years-day/5155988.article (accessed 8 August 2021).

Shafer, E. (2021), 'Box Office: *F9* Zooming to Huge $160 Million-Plus Debut Overseas', *Variety*, 22 May. Available online: https://variety.com/2021/film/box-office/f9-record-breaking-opening-weekend-international-box-office-1234979423/ (accessed 26 July 2021).

Shen, X. (2020), 'Hollywood is Being Called Out for Appeasing Chinese Censors, but State Media Doesn't See the Problem', *South China Morning Post*, 8 August. Available online: https://www.scmp.com/abacus/culture/article/3096475/hollywood-being-called-out-appeasing-chinese-censors-state-media (accessed 14 July 2021).

*Skyscraper* (2018), [Film] Dir. Rawson Marshall Thurber, USA: Universal Pictures.

Song, X. (2018), 'Hollywood Movies and China: Analysis of Hollywood Globalisation and Relationship Management in China's Cinema Market', *Global Media and China*, 3 (3): 177–94.

*Star Wars: The Force Awakens* (2015), [Film] Dir. J. J. Abrams, USA: Walt Disney Studios Motion Pictures.

*Star Wars: The Rise of Skywalker* (2019), [Film] Dir. J. J. Abrams, USA: Walt Disney Studios Motion Pictures.

Tie, A. (2018), 'Dwayne "The Rock" Johnson and *Skyscraper* Cast in Hong Kong to Promote Film', *South China Morning Post*, 5 July. Available online: https://www.scmp.com/magazines/style/news-trends/article/2153939/dwayne-rock-johnson-and-skyscraper-cast-hong-kong (accessed 6 August 2021).

*Top Gun: Maverick* (2022), [Film] Dir. Joseph Kosinski, USA: Paramount Pictures Studios.

*Transformers: Age of Extinction* (2014), [Film] Dir. Michael Bay, USA: Paramount Pictures.

*The Wandering Earth* (2019), [Film] Dir. Frant Gwo, China: China Film Group Corporation.

Wang, Y. (2018), 'Chinese Moviegoers are Developing Diversified Tastes, Which Doesn't Bode Well for Hollywood', *Forbes*, 5 February. Available online: https://www.forbes.com/sites/ywang/2018/02/05/chinese-moviegoers-are-developing-diversified-tastes-which-doesnt-bode-well-for-hollywood/?sh=7e11d3f57e7f (accessed 8 August 2021).

*Wolf Warrior 2* (2017), [Film] Dir. Wu Jing, China: Kadokawa.

*xXx: Return of Xander Cage* (2017), [Film] Dir. D. J. Caruso, USA: Paramount Picture Studios.

Yuhas, A. (2020), 'Why *Star Wars* Keeps Bombing in China', *The New York Times*, 14 January. Available online: https://www.nytimes.com/2020/01/14/movies/star-wars-china.html (accessed 15 July 2021).

# 11

# Fun for all the family: Adapting *Fast & Furious* as animated children's television

### Sam Summers

As the *Fast & Furious* franchise has grown in scale and scope, both in its storylines and as a force at the box office, so too has it grown as a transmedia franchise. Beginning in 2015, following the immense success of the fifth and sixth entries in the series, *Fast & Furious* has expanded its brand to encompass the kind of big-budget paratextual offshoots perhaps more commonly associated with franchises like *Star Wars* and the Marvel Cinematic Universe (MCU). Indeed, this period has seen the development and release of several such spinoffs, including *Fast & Furious: Supercharged*, a theme park attraction, *Fast & Furious Live*, a touring stunt show and *Fast & Furious: Spy Racers* (herein *Spy Racers*), an animated series created by DreamWorks Animation for Netflix that first aired in 2019. Following the adventures of a gang of young racers led by Tony Toretto, the teenaged cousin of the films' protagonist, Vin Diesel's Dom Toretto, *Spy Racers* presents viewers with a new set of storylines which ostensibly take place in the same fictional world as the live-action movies. This chapter will explore the various ways in which *Spy Racers* adapts the *Fast & Furious* films in order to satisfy, and take advantage of, the unique conditions of television, animation and children's media. In doing so, it will frame *Spy Racers* in terms of a decades-old tradition of film-to-TV animated adaptations, as well as examining how the show's implementation of transmedia storytelling exemplifies a uniquely contemporary approach to franchising.

The existence of *Spy Racers* is the result of the convergence of three distinct entertainment brands: DreamWorks Animation, Netflix and Universal Pictures. One of the biggest names in animated feature production throughout the 2000s, by 2013 DreamWorks faced increased competition and flagging box office returns. In search of a new revenue stream, founder Jeffrey Katzenberg struck a landmark deal with Netflix to produce 300 hours of original children's animated programming – the first original content of its kind to be commissioned by the streamer (Faughnder 2018). The initial wave of DreamWorks programming exploited its existing brand recognition and franchises, spinning off shows from feature films like *Turbo* (2013) and *Madagascar* (2005), before expanding into original properties and licensed adaptations. This expansion coincided with the 2016 purchase of DreamWorks by Comcast, the parent company of Universal Pictures. The studio's partnership with Netflix was retained following the acquisition, and DreamWorks' ability to meet the streaming service's needs was bolstered by its new owners. As Margie Cohn, president of DreamWorks Animation Television, puts it, the studio initially 'didn't necessarily have the resources to put [the Netflix partnership] on its feet the way they needed to … When the acquisition happened, we were suddenly part of a mature company' (quoted in Faughnder 2018). The most tangible example of the impact that this new ownership has had on DreamWorks' Netflix offerings is the production of a series of children's programs adapted from some of Universal's most successful live-action franchises, which at the time of writing comprises *Spy Racers*, as well as *Jurassic World: Camp Cretaceous* (2020–2022).

The adaptation of these film franchises into children's animated programs is a complex process requiring numerous changes from the source material across multiple textual axes. One of the most readily apparent is the need to adapt source material aimed at more mature audiences into a show suitable for young children. While neither the *Fast* nor the *Jurassic* films are explicitly adult-oriented, they generally target an older audience than their respective spin-off series. Each film in both franchises is rated PG-13 by the MPAA, with the *Fast Saga* ratings generally citing 'violence', 'strong language' and 'sexuality' and the *Jurassic* ratings typically attributed to 'intense violence' and 'peril'. By contrast, *Spy Racers* is rated TV-Y7 by the FCC, recommending it for children aged seven and older, while *Camp Cretaceous* is rated TV-PG. While children may or may not have enjoyed the live-action iterations of these franchises, in adapting them for Netflix, DreamWorks have taken steps to ensure that the shows specifically target a generally younger age range than the films.

The challenges of adapting *Fast & Furious* for children have been acknowledged at an executive level. Indeed, in an *LA Times* profile, Cohn acknowledged that 'there's nothing specifically directed toward a kid audience in that franchise [but] we thought we could really make something in that sweet spot that extends the franchise for the younger end of the audience' (Faughnder 2018). In addition to including subject matter generally considered unsuitable for children, it also features next to no child presence. Unlike the *Jurassic Park* films, also the subject of a DreamWorks animated series, there are hardly any children present in the *Fast & Furious* features, aside from the minimal presence of Dom's infant son in the eighth and ninth instalments. Despite this, Cohn's comments indicate that the need to adapt the franchise for children was a core element in the ethos behind the show's production. As I shall discuss in the following section, this is reflective of both presumptions regarding the suitability of animation for a child audience, and of the desire of corporate intellectual property holders to extend the appeal of their brands to children.

This places *Spy Racers* in the tradition of a long line of children's animated series based on live-action films and franchises ostensibly aimed at an older audience. Beginning in the late 1960s with *Journey to the Center of the Earth* (1967) and *Fantastic Voyage* (1968–9), both produced by Filmation and based on 20th Century Fox feature films, the trend escalated in the late 1980s following the immense success of DIC and Columbia Pictures' *The Real Ghostbusters* (1986–1991). A fifteen-year boom in the production of such series followed, resulting in over twenty examples reaching the airwaves. These ranged from adaptations of relatively benign, PG-rated sources like *Back to the Future* (1985; animated series 1991–2) and *Jumanji* (1995; animated series 1996–9) to notoriously violent, hard-R movies like *RoboCop* (1987; animated series 1988) and *Rambo: First Blood Part II* (1985; adapted as *Rambo: The Force of Freedom*, 1986). Far fewer takes on the concept have arisen in the new millennium, with the main exception being the series of successful computer-animated shows set in the *Star Wars* universe, beginning with *The Clone Wars* (2008–).

In both their visual style and their specific intertextual relationship with the films on which they're based, these *Star Wars* shows are the immediate precursors to *Spy Racers*. However, in order to fully assess the adaptive strategies on display in *Spy Racers*, we must view it in the context of the wider history of this trend. For these purposes, I've reviewed a corpus of thirty-two animated series based on live-action film franchises and aimed at a younger audience. Something common to each example is the need to adapt the source material along three core axes: in addition to being adapted for children, the sources must be adapted for animation, and adapted for television as a serialized transmedia extension of the original franchise. Over the remainder of the chapter, I will first take these axes one by one and explore the different strategies employed by my historical examples to meet these purposes. I will then apply these findings to *Spy Racers* to demonstrate how it functions as a contemporary example of the trend.

## Adapting for children

Returning to Cohn's statement on the genesis of *Spy Racers*, it's clear that developing a child audience was a paramount concern in, and indeed one of the core reasons behind, the show's development. But why are these animated adaptions so consistently targeted towards children in the first place? The answer partially lies in the long-held Western cultural belief that animation is primarily a children's medium. This is itself linked to the historical programming of animated series in timeslots associated with child audiences in order to facilitate targeted advertising (Dobson 2018: 84), and indeed the first major wave of animated movie adaptations that began with *The Real Ghostbusters* can be ascribed to the entertainment industry's desire to exploit the cross-demographic potential of certain cinematic franchises for promotional purposes (Wells 2003: 29). Arguably, it is these branding strategies, more than any preconceived notions about animation as children's entertainment, that have carried the trend of adaptations through to the modern era. Increasingly since the 1990s and the success of shows like *The Simpsons* (1989–) and *South Park* (1997–), the notion that animation is suitable for children's programming alone is seen as somewhat outdated. This is something to which Netflix itself can attest, having produced numerous adult-oriented animated shows including hits like *Bojack Horseman* (2014–20) and *Big Mouth* (2017–). In theory, then, Universal, DreamWorks and Netflix could have adapted the *Fast & Furious* films as a more adult-oriented show, hewing closer to the subject matter and tone of the source material. The fact that they instead targeted children is testament to the desire to expand the *Fast & Furious* brand.

Given television's history as a format built on advertising, branding has long been central to children's programming. Amy Ratelle (2018: 195) argues that since its inception, children's television animation in the United States 'was subsumed into a rapidly expanding consumer culture', something reflected in the lucrative toylines that were launched from the likes of *Real Ghostbusters*, *Rambo: Force For Freedom* and *Toxic Crusaders* (1991; based on the 1984 film *The Toxic Avenger*). As Ratelle (Ibid: 200) puts it, these shows and others were 'situated in a capitalist context from which it is nearly impossible to be extricated' and, in this sense, little has changed since the 1980s in terms of the relationship between children's entertainment and cross-promotion. The same impulse that drove these earlier examples is apparent in a modern show such as *Spy Racers*, but what is chiefly being advertised here is *Fast & Furious* itself, and by extension its merchandise and paratexts. This is consistent with Henry Jenkins's (2006) account of brand extension in the contemporary age of media convergence. He (Ibid: 69) notes that 'successful brands are built by exploiting multiple contacts between the brand and consumer', and that crucially 'the experience should … extend across as many media as possible' in order to develop and retain relationships with audiences.

Children's animated series are a vital tool for expanding the availability of these contact points to audiences that may be excluded by a franchise's core cinematic texts, securing them as future consumers of the broader range of texts and products on offer. To this point, Wells (2003: 29) attests that the animated adaptations of the 1980s and 1990s arose from a desire to 'extend the shelf-life of popular series by using what had become the visual language by which it was assumed children and young adolescents were addressed'. Similarly, with Cohn's admission that *Spy Racers'* producers wanted to 'extend the franchise for the younger end of the audience' in light of the films' presumed lack of appeal to children (Faughnder 2018), it becomes clear that part of the series' function within the *Fast & Furious* transmedia network is providing an entry point for young viewers into the array of products and texts associated with the franchise – ranging from the aforementioned games, tours and theme park attractions to numerous toys based on *Spy Racers* itself.

Having addressed the why, the next question is *how* have these shows historically adapted live-action feature films for younger audiences? One major method in the examples surveyed for this chapter is adding characters designed specifically to appeal to children, or significantly altering existing characters to achieve the same effect. This is a strategy employed by nineteen of the thirty-two series surveyed for this chapter, and it manifests in two main ways. One of these involves foregrounding child or teenaged characters to provide clear points of identification for young viewers. Most commonly this is done by adding new characters or expanding on existing ones, whether they be the offspring of the films' protagonists as in *The Mummy: The Animated Series* (2001–3), or as a 'next generation' of heroes taking the baton from their live-action predecessors, a strategy that is found in *Extreme Ghostbusters* (1997). A less common tactic is using de-aged versions of the film's leads, as with the cast of *Beetlejuice* (1989–91), who act out similar relationships and situations to their adult cinematic counterparts, albeit at a younger age. A show like *James Bond Jr*

(1991–2) contains elements of both approaches, featuring a lead character – the nephew of 007 – who, in the absence of his uncle, embodies most of the same characteristics and effectively becomes his ersatz juvenile substitute.

The second kind of character often foregrounded in these shows in order to appeal to a young audience is the non-human sidekick. While not specifically coded as children themselves, characters like the talking dogs of the K9 Corps in *Police Academy* (1988–9) and Gassie the alien in *Alienators: Evolution Continues* (2001–2, based on the 2001 film *Evolution*) provide their respective franchises with both a cute, merchandisable character as well as a source of comic relief to alleviate the tone of an action-heavy series. The ur-example of this trope, and the greatest testament to its effectiveness, is Slimer from *The Real Ghostbusters*. A minor antagonist from the original film, Slimer was elevated to a core protagonist of the show and became one of the most iconic elements of the franchise, to the point that the show was renamed *Slimer! And the Real Ghostbusters* with its fourth season.

The addition or promotion of comic side characters like Slimer is reflective of another adaptive strategy common to many of the series surveyed: an overall push towards comedy, especially evident in examples based upon more serious or action-heavy films. As Nichola Dobson (2018: 182) points out, comedy as a genre has tended to dominate animated television in the United States. This is something which applies equally to shows aimed at adults as it does to children, but which is inextricably linked to the decades long link between the format and children's entertainment. Indeed, another factor in the favouring of comedy over action in children's shows is the reoccurring discourse of concern over the latter's suitability for young audiences. This is an issue that has affected the production and reception of animated television in the United States for many decades, dating as far back as the 1968 cross-network decision to move away from 'realistic' action series and towards more comic material (Haynes 1978: 63). By the 1980s and 1990s, the period during which most of the animated film adaptations surveyed were produced, action-centric cartoons were once again becoming commonplace. Nevertheless, the legacy of these presumptions and concerns remained apparent in the content of the shows, with series like *Rambo* and *Godzilla: The Series* (1998–2000, based specifically on the 1998 American film) adding wisecracks and comic beats to their violent source material so as to render it more 'appropriate' for a younger audience.

*Spy Racers* contains evidence of both these strategies. Firstly, its protagonists are notably younger than those of the films. Whereas the movies' cast age from their thirties to their fifties over the course of the franchise, *Spy Racers*' leads range from thirteen to seventeen years old. This brings them much closer in age to the show's target audience, while also being (crucially) just old enough to drive. Moreover, in the lineage of earlier examples like *James Bond Jr*, the main character, Tony Toretto, is the cousin of Vin Diesel's Dom, placing him within the ubiquitous Toretto 'family' which lies at the heart of the films. Beyond this, the group as a whole is explicitly pitched as an equivalent of the films' core ensemble, with Tony regularly describing them as his 'family' much as Dom does with his team. Although the remaining members of *Spy Racers*' teenaged crew are not directly related to any of the live-action cast, characters like tough female racer Echo and comic relief-cum-tech expert Frostee have clear adult analogues in the films' Letty and Tej, respectively. Further, their expertise and interests have been adapted in step with their ages: Frostee is adept with drones and computer games rather than cars and weapons as those skills are more befitting of a child character in a children's show. In addition to focusing on younger characters, the show even dabbles in non-human sidekicks, such as Donut, a monkey who befriends the gang in the second season.

The animated series is also distinctly more comedic in tone than the films. A key part of this stems from the way in which *Spy Racers* avoids melodrama. While the *Fast Saga* incorporates elements of comedy, especially in the banter between members of the core ensemble, it retains a serious tone centred on the soap opera storylines pertaining to the tragedies and feuds that plague the Toretto family. The cast of the films regularly contend with the deaths, disappearances and betrayals of close friends and relations, and are subject to the attendant emotional stakes. In contrast, the gang in *Spy Racers* participate in generally light-hearted escapades mostly free of serious consequences or interpersonal drama. While the team suffer through arguments and spats, these are typically low-stakes conflicts without long-lasting consequences: Tony is accused of being a show-off, for example, and gets jealous of Echo for being the first to enrol in 'spy school'. On the rare occasion that they do face lasting personal consequences – as in the fourth season when they're framed for a crime and go on the run – this is neatly resolved by the end of the season, and its implications for their civilian lives are never examined. Tony is never subjected to the life-changing heartbreaks that Dom encounters on a film-by-film basis – not because the world in which he operates is less dangerous, or his enemies any less tenacious, but because of the desire to retain a light, comedic tone in a show aimed at a child audience.

What's more, the series also foregrounds a type of wacky comedy that is largely absent from the *Fast Saga* films which, as mentioned above, tend to limit their humour to the quips and insults traded between teammates. While this is also a factor in *Spy Racers*, a more prominent source of comedy is the group of government agents overseeing the crew's operations, who are allotted more outlandish, cartoonish personalities than any of the live-action cast members. Department head Ms Nowhere, contrasting with her cool-headed live-action counterpart Mr Nobody (Kurt Russell), is an excessively fastidious busybody known for wild fits of comic anger. The dogged enforcer Palindrome, played by Paul 'Big Show' Wight, is a clear parody of fellow wrestler Dwayne Johnson's character in the *Fast* films, known for ridiculous feats of strength and silly one-liners. Lastly, Ms Nobody's assistants, Gary and Julius, the show's most purely comedic characters, are tellingly allotted more screen time in each successive season. Their humour is essentially bathetic; imposingly built and clad in black suits and sunglasses, they appear outwardly threatening in the manner of archetypal mysterious government agents. However, they are frequently childish and immature, falling into flights of fantasy and fawning over cute animals, while also treating Ms Nobody and Palindrome as surrogate parents by season four. By bathetically contrasting their bureaucratic role and muscular, bald physicality, these agents' cuddly antics effectively poke fun at the nebulous government organizations and displays of arrogant masculinity that are so central to the later *Fast & Furious* films. All these elements combine to make a show that operates far more consistently in a comic milieu compared to the films that birthed it, and frequently verges on openly parodying its source material. By softening the portrayal of the government figures overseeing the young protagonists specifically, it also contributes to reducing the overall threat level and further demarcating *Spy Racers* as a children's show.

Along with the reduced ages of the characters, it's clear that *Spy Racers* is participating in many of the same strategies as its forebears in order to demarcate itself as suitable and entertaining for children. Of course, another key difference between the *Fast* films and the show is the ways in which they both handle action, with the movies' stunts and violence taking on a far more realistic dimension than those of the animated series. While aspects of this are clearly a result of the aforementioned concerns around the levels of violence appropriate for children's programming – sequences which would involve gunfire in the films instead utilize paint-guns – the differences in the treatment of action in the series are also crucially linked to the second key form of adaptation it undertakes: adapting for animation.

## Adapting for animation

In adapting live-action film franchises for animation, producers and creatives must decide how best to translate the visual properties of their source material to a new medium. Animation is a form which brings its own challenges and advantages in the field of visual storytelling. While allowing for the ongoing emergence of complex computer imaging software that can convincingly imitate live-action footage, it typically differs substantially from live-action in terms of its mise-en-scène and cinematographic properties. This is potentially problematic for a commercial endeavour which, like the shows in question, is predicated on a palpable sense of brand continuity to find its audience. Matthew Freeman (2014: 41) argues that the sustained commercial success of such brands is dependent on 'stylistic synchronicity' – the use of similar aesthetic traits to link transmedial iterations of the same franchise or brand. He (Ibid: 43) explains that 'a sense of textual or visual coherence across these products [is needed] to ensure that each indeed feels like it fits with the others'. Animation problematizes this due to its unique visual language and ontology necessarily clashing with that of the live-action source material in these cases, leading to several strategies being adopted by different series to reconcile this.

To that end, the majority of animated adaptations defer to the principle of stylistic synchronicity and hew as closely as the medium and the budget will allow to the visual brand of the live-action franchise. Writing on 1960s television animation, Sexton and Cook (2015) observe that many early action-based series utilized rotoscoping, a technique involving tracing over footage of live-action actors. This had the effect of pushing shows like *Journey to the Center of the Earth* and *Fantastic Voyage* 'toward the adaptation of qualities normally associated with another medium, live-action film' (Ibid: 108). While not necessarily rotoscoped, the relatively realistic and film-accurate designs of shows from *Rambo* and *RoboCop* to *Godzilla* and *The Mummy* clearly show that the overriding concern when designing these adaptations has been to ensure stylistic synchronicity with their live-action counterparts through graphic fidelity.

Regardless of intentions, the production time and budget afforded to these hand-drawn adaptations necessarily limit their ability to achieve this kind of fidelity. These constraints lead to noticeably stiff character models and a frequently static 'camera', with the animators unable to simulate the movements of real people, or the dynamic cinematography of an action film. This may explain why almost every example produced in the twentieth century – *Spy Racers*, *Camp Cretaceous* and the various *Star Wars* shows – is made using computer graphics. While 3D computer-animation has long been the industry standard for theatrical feature animation in North America, it is less common on television, where 2D processes still proliferate. It is noteworthy, then, that all three of these cinematic franchises have opted to use the digital tools now available to them to create three-dimensional worlds into which they can extend their fictional universes. These shows are still low-budget and low-tech in comparison to a contemporary Disney or DreamWorks feature film, but their added dimensionality means they are nonetheless capable of imitating the type of kinetic live-action camerawork that is associated with the original films. With computer imagery, artists are also able to approximate the appearance and physicality of actual actors and sets, enhancing their stylistic synchronicity. Furthermore, Chris Pallant (2011: 141) observes that digital animation is also able to *exceed* the limits of live-action cinematography as well as imitating it, achieving 'shots that could not have been done in a live-action film'. In doing so, animation's propensity for depicting the impossible is applied to a world that in many ways palpably resembles the photographic 'reality' of the source films.

This potential is evident in *Spy Racers*' approach to action, in a way which differentiates it from the live-action *Fast & Furious* franchise. While many of the earlier animated adaptations under discussion display visible signs of their limited budgets in their relative lack of detail and movement, unlike live-action film they are *not* limited in terms of *what* they can depict. Even the oldest and cheapest examples have been known to surpass their live-action sources in the fields of fantastical happenings and impossible action (Perlmutter 2014). Implemented in the modern day with a show like *Spy Racers* and augmented with the aforementioned capabilities of computer-animation, the propensity for these adaptations to outstrip their sources in terms of outlandish action is fully realized via a medium that can do so using the cinematographic language of the parent franchise.

As Lennart Soberon has noted elsewhere in this volume, the *Fast & Furious* films have continuously upped the ante with each instalment when it comes to the absurdity and spectacle of their action sequences. The cinematic Toretto gang has gone from the highway chases of *The Fast and the Furious* (2001), to a rocket-powered journey into orbit in *F9* (2021). While many of these stunts still utilize a degree of practical filming, they are increasingly reliant on computer-animated elements to make the action fully convincing. Their televisual counterparts, however, are fully untethered from reality. Digitally crafted from the ground up, they are able to participate in events unlikely to ever occur in a

*Fast & Furious* feature. Episodes have seen the gang battle giant robots, drive through flaming hurricanes, and fistfight a group of cyborgs inside an erupting volcano. While it may not be *impossible* to imagine these events taking place in the films, they certainly surpass anything they've attempted so far in their audacity and their embrace of science-fiction elements. This is aided by the fact that, being animated, the show's characters are even less subject to audience's conceptions of physical laws than Dom and company, thus demanding less suspension of disbelief.

The consistent sense of escalation Soberon identifies in the *Fast Saga* also applies to *Spy Racers*. Showrunner Tim Hedrick has said that 'when we approach a stunt scene, that's one thing that we always think of, it's like, if you saw this in the movies, how can we make this more?' (quoted in Kelley, 2020). This suggests that, as much as animation facilitates this escalation, it also to an extent *necessitates* it: 'It's completely different when they do those stunts in the movies', Hedrick continues, due to 'all these awesome practical car effects. When we do them in animation we want to heighten it' (Ibid). The implication here is that *Spy Racers* must strive towards ever more outrageous action sequences to retain interest.

*Spy Racers* seems aware of this imperative to escalate the action, something which is noticeable from one of its very first action sequences. In episode 1, not long after meeting the show's young crew, we see them engage in a high-speed car chase, trying to escape some enemy agents. During the chase, Echo swerves to avoid her pursuers and drifts underneath a passing truck. I highlight this particular stunt because it bears striking resemblance to a scene from the live-action *Fast & Furious Presents: Hobbs & Shaw* (2019), released earlier that same year, in which the title characters similarly swerve under a pair of trucks while pursued by a motorcyclist villain. The stunt in *Hobbs & Shaw* is augmented with slow-motion: it lasts almost twenty seconds, stretched far beyond its natural running-time in order to foreground its intricacy and difficulty. This is consistent with the way slow-motion is used in the franchise as a whole, and in action cinema more broadly. Meanwhile, the *Spy Racers* stunt takes place more or less in real time, lasting less than two seconds. What was in a live-action film the drawn-out centrepiece of a major sequence becomes, in an animated format, simply one in a line of action beats which comprise the episode. Though there are slightly more moving parts in the *Hobbs & Shaw* stunt, the magnitude by which it is extended versus its animated counterpart clearly reflects a sense that stunts in animation are worth less than those in 'live action', even when computer effects are clearly involved. The perceptual realism of *Hobbs & Shaw*'s world invites a suspension of disbelief that supports a focus on impossible stunts like this one, stunts which are par for the course in animated action scenes. Elsewhere in this single twenty-minute episode, for example, we see motorcycles jumping off cliffs, wingsuit flights, cars driving off exploding ships and more. Through its heightened and escalated action, it's clear that *Spy Racers* is designed to recreate the same spirit of excess and enormity that has become a trademark of the later *Fast & Furious* films. However, in these regards, it's also clear that the show surpasses its live-action source, something which is facilitated by, and symptomatic of, the process of adapting for the animated medium.

## Adapting for television

The final axis of adaptation affecting *Spy Racers* and its animated predecessors is the need to adapt for television. This is evident not only in the need to adapt stories, characters and worlds originally conceived for feature-length films to the particular formal demands of a television show, but also in the decisions each of these shows must make regarding their intertextual relationship with the original properties. Most importantly from a narrative standpoint, the creators must decide if and how the fictional world depicted in the television show will intersect with that depicted in the live-action film franchise. They must also establish the extent to which the events of one will affect the other. One factor that must be taken into account is that the television series as a storytelling medium has a unique set of properties which distinguish it from feature-length film. It offers creators the ability to tell a series of short, episodic stories, or conversely longer, fully serialized narratives. This in turn has historically affected the ways in which animated television adaptations have been positioned in relation to their cinematic parent franchises. In the streaming era, however, television's unique narrative properties have evolved along with its position in the broader media landscape, altering these relationships even further.

The narrative relationship between film franchises and their animated television adaptations has shifted significantly in the twenty-first century, coinciding with the streaming era and the move to a more cinematically imitative visual idiom in the form of computer-animation. Within the twenty-seven shows I've surveyed produced from 1967 to 2001, this relationship takes two distinct forms, both equally common and evenly historically distributed.

Thirteen of the series take place explicitly in a separate continuity from the films, with characters and events being consistently depicted in a way which is irreconcilable with the narratives seen in their live-action source material. For example, *Beetlejuice* depicts the movie's characters meeting at a much younger age, and *James Bond, Jr* features characters shown to have died in the original films. Conversely, fourteen of the shows surveyed ostensibly take place in the same storyworld as the films, depicting the continuing adventures of the characters or filling the narrative gap between cinematic sequels. Shows like the *Back to the Future* and *The Mummy* series pick up where the previous film in the franchise left off and, while there may be stray continuity errors in the ensuing episodes, the shows as a whole purport to follow the same versions of the characters to which viewers have become accustomed.

To an extent, each of these series represents an exercise in transmedia storytelling, defined by Henry Jenkins (2006: 95–6) as a story which 'unfolds across multiple media platforms, with each new text making a distinctive and valuable contribution to the whole'. Building on Jenkins's work, Colin Harvey (2014: 278) has argued for a broader definition, which would allow for shows like *Beetlejuice* and *James Bond, Jr* to be considered as transmedia storytelling despite not contributing to the storyworlds of the original. However, this criterion of continuity – of ostensible narrative consistency between texts – is nevertheless a useful tool for discerning between types of transmedia project and assessing how and why they differ from one another. To this end, Jens Eder (2015: p. 76) taxonomizes several transmedial strategies, introducing the term 'functional integration' to distinguish transmedia franchises in which 'the elements contribute to the understanding of the whole in their own media-specific ways and are, ideally, ordered according to some calculated temporal dramaturgy'.

While contemporary shows like the later *Star Wars* series, *Camp Cretaceous* and *Spy Racers* likewise fall into the category of 'functional integration', these more recent examples have one crucial difference: they do *not* include the feature film's leads as part of their main cast. Instead, they introduce new protagonists, whose adventures occur concurrently with those seen in the films. *Spy Racers*, for instance, focuses on Dom Toretto's cousin and his teenage friends, with Dom himself only appearing in the first season to establish the premise and setting as being consistent with the film franchise. While these newer shows apply functional integration just as many of their predecessors did, the ubiquity of this approach in the current era compels us to assess it as a unique strategy in and of itself. It also suggests that this strategy is to an extent informed by the media landscape in which these series were produced, just as aspects of *Spy Racers*' approach to adaptation are necessitated and facilitated by the need to adapt for both a child audience and the animated medium.

One aspect of contemporary children's animated television which distinguishes it from the earlier historical periods which have produced these adapted series is its openness to serialized storylines. Jason Mittell (2015: 18) writes that twenty-first-century series tend to present 'a cumulative narrative that builds over time, rather than resetting back to a steady-state equilibrium at the end of every episode'. While Mittell mainly refers to live-action shows aimed at adults, an analogous shift has taken place in North American children's animation. An increasing number of hit shows, from *Avatar: The Last Airbender* (2005–8) to *Steven Universe* (2013–19), have moved away from purely episodic narratives and into serialized stories and layered worldbuilding, characteristics all but absent from the Saturday morning cartoons that preceded them. Of the twenty-seven film adaptations in my survey which preceded *Clone Wars*, for example, only three contained elements of serialization. Conversely, all the *Star Wars* shows, *Spy Racers* and *Camp Cretaceous* are heavily serialized, telling continuous, season-long stories that include strong connective tissue between seasons. Streaming platforms like Netflix in particular facilitate this kind of continuity-heavy, serialized storytelling. Unlike televised cartoons, which are frequently syndicated and aired out of order, shows on streaming platforms can safely assume that even child viewers will be watching every episode in order, from the beginning, as this is what the platform's interface encourages them to do.

It is this serialization that allows shows like *Spy Racers* to establish more complex and carefully delineated relationships with their respective flagship film franchises that do not rely on the consistent presence of recognizable characters. Connections that the new characters and events depicted within the series may have with their cinematic counterparts can be revealed at a logical pace that benefits from and complements the films with whose release schedules they interweave. The clearest example of this in *Spy Racers* is in its first episode, which methodically introduces not only the new cast of characters but also their relationship with the established *Fast & Furious* storyworld. This is apt given Mittell's (2015: 56) assertion that 'the chief function of a television pilot is to teach us how to watch the series and, in doing so, to make us want to keep watching.' Both of these aims are accounted for by *Spy Racers*' deployment of the Dom Toretto character, voiced by a returning Vin Diesel, in its opening moments.

Before Dom arrives, for example, our introduction to his cousin Tony foregrounds their transmedial relationship using what Eder (2015: 77) would call 'strategies of indication'. We meet Tony stepping out of what looks to be a black Dodge Charger, Dom's signature vehicle in the films; and, in one of the first lines of dialogue, the teenager describes it as a 'ten second car', recalling a repeated phrase from the films. Sporting a shirt with a 'Toretto' patch on the pocket, which he wears for much of the series, he announces his ambition to 'break the record that Dom set on this very stretch of road', explaining, 'I was born to win … I'm a Toretto!'. Immediately, then, the audience is familiarized with his relationship to Dom, and by extension to the film franchise.

These links between the film and show are developed further with the arrival of Dom himself, just two minutes later. He is introduced through his voice alone, highlighting the most recognizable asset of Diesel as a performer in an animated context in which he's stripped of his physical presence. After giving Tony and his friends a characteristic pep-talk on what it means to be a Toretto, Dom is attacked and bundled into a car, prompting the gang to give chase. When they catch up, they find that the kidnapping was staged – it was a test prepared by Dom and Ms Nowhere, to see if the teens have what it takes to work as spies for the same mysterious organization represented by Mr Nobody in the *Fast* films. Thus, this scene introduces our second link to the franchise, while also justifying Dom's absence from the rest of the series: in a self-reflexive explanation that could equally apply to Diesel himself, Dom is too famous to get involved in spy work, stressing the need for a group of new, younger agents. In this way, despite the general absence of established characters from this point forward, the series is able to rely on its pilot episode to teach its viewers how to understand the series in terms of its intersections with the *Fast & Furious* films. It also gives those viewers familiar with that franchise a reason to watch: while you won't often see Dom Toretto, you will spend time with characters he cares about, and witness events that impact his world. We even get confirmation of this in the first season finale, in which Dom returns to rescue Tony when things get out of hand. Because *Spy Racers* is so heavily serialized, and because it is hosted on a platform which sends new viewers to the first episode directly, the producers *know* they can control how the vast majority of viewers are introduced to its world and its rules. This simply would not be the case with the syndicated animated series of the twentieth century, and it is this key difference that facilitates the more complex transmedial relationship between *Spy Racers* and the cinematic arm of the franchise.

This particular transmedial adaptive strategy – following a group of new characters whose adventures run parallel to the films – is also symptomatic of the increased prominence of convergent transmedia franchises in the contemporary media landscape as a whole. By moving the focus away from characters with convoluted onscreen backstories known to some – but not all – of the audience, shows like *Spy Racers* adhere to Jenkins' (2006: 96) maxim that for effective transmedia storytelling 'each franchise entry needs to be self-contained so you don't need to have seen the film to enjoy the game, and vice versa. Any given product is a point of entry into the franchise as a whole.' This is crucial for retaining appeal to new audiences, and especially child audiences whose exposure to older-skewing film franchises must be presumed to be limited. *Spy Racers*' showrunner Hedrick has acknowledged this impulse himself, claiming that despite an edict from Universal that it feature the Torettos in some capacity, he 'really wanted to come in and try to create a show that could stand on its own ... I wanted it to be if you've never seen *Fast & Furious*, that's fine' (quoted in Kelley 2020).

The shift in focus away from cinematic protagonists demonstrated by *Spy Racers* and its contemporaries reflects a world in which audiences are more transmedially literate than ever before, honed by and reflected in the enormous success of projects like the MCU and Disney's approach to the *Star Wars* franchise. Spin-off movies featuring entirely new casts like *Rogue One: A Star Wars Story* (2016) can rank among the highest-grossing entries in a franchise, and what's more, fans have come to *expect* connections between disparate media properties occupying the same fictional universe. Discussions over what constitutes 'canon' are central to the online fan bases of many contemporary transmedia franchises (Harvey 2015: 3–4). If a text is considered canon, it is invested with a sense of validity and significance, thus facilitating one of the primary goals of commercial transmedia storytelling, per Eder (2015: 72): 'to activate the public, to make it explore the represented worlds ... and to animate it to buy more products.' This sense of continuity is easier to maintain when the different branches of the franchise focus on discrete groups of characters who only occasionally overlap, as in the case of *Spy Racers* and its relationship to the films. Part of the *Fast Saga* 'family', the adventures of Tony and his crew are framed as implicitly no less valid than those of Dom and company. Through his brief appearances and infrequent mentions, it's made clear that the elder Toretto considers his nephew a vital part of his world, and by extension audiences are encouraged to do the same.

There are numerous ways in which *Spy Racers* has been shaped by its three axes of adaptation, including the youthful characters it foregrounds in order to adapt for children, and the heightened approach to action necessitated and facilitated by adapting for animation. However, it's the way *Spy Racers* adapts for television, using serialized storytelling to orient itself as a canonical transmedia offshoot running parallel to its parent film franchise, which separates the show from its animated predecessors and demarcates it as a unique product of its contemporary media moment. It remains to be seen whether *Spy Racers* will truly, as Jenkins (2006: 96) puts it, 'mak[e] a distinctive and valuable contribution to the whole' in the purest sense, by impacting noticeably on the film franchise itself. This has proven to be the case with the *Star Wars* franchise, with characters created for the various animated series making appearances in the live-action films and shows at the core of the brand. Regardless of whether we ever see Tony and company meet up with Dom on the big screen, though, *Spy Racers* makes its distinctive contribution on an industrial level if not a narrative one, expanding the horizons of what the *Fast & Furious* franchise can be, how it can operate and who it can reach.

## References

*Back to the Future* (1985), [Film] Dir. Robert Zemeckis, USA: Universal Pictures.
*Back to the Future* (1991–1992), [TV Programme] CBS.
*Beetlejuice* (1989–1991), [TV Programme] ABC.
*Big Mouth* (2017), [TV Programme] Netflix.
*Bojack Horseman* (2014–2020), [TV Programme] Netflix.
Dobson, N. (2018), 'TV Animation and Genre', in N. Dobson et al (eds), *The Animation Studies Reader*, 181–9, London: Bloomsbury.
*Dumb and Dumber* (1995–1996), [TV Programme] ABC.
Eder, J. (2015), 'Transmediality and the Politics of Adaptation: Concepts, Forms and Strategies', in D. Hassler-Forest and P. Niklas (eds), *The Politics of Adaptation*, 66–81, New York: Palgrave Macmillan.
*Extreme Ghostbusters* (1997), [TV Programme] Syndication.
*Fantastic Voyage* (1968–1969), [TV Programme] ABC.

Faughnder, R. (2018), 'Small Screen Gamble Pays off for DreamWorks Animation', *Los Angeles Times*, 30 October. Available online: https://www.latimes.com/business/hollywood/la-fi-ct-dreamworks-animation-television-20181030-story.html (accessed 23 September 2021).

Freeman, M. (2014), 'Transmediating Tim Burton's *Gotham City*', *Networking Knowledge*, 7 (1): 41–54.

*Godzilla* (1998), [Film] Dir. Roland Emmerich, USA: TriStar Pictures.

*Godzilla: The Series* (1998–2000), [TV Programme] Fox Kids.

Harvey, C. (2014), 'A Taxonomy of Transmedia Storytelling', in M. Ryan and J. Thom (eds), *Storyworlds across Media*, 278–94, Lincoln: University of Nebraska Press.

Harvey, C. (2015), *Fantastic Transmedia*, New York: Palgrave Macmillan.

Haynes, R. B. (1978), 'Children's Perceptions of "Comic" and "Authentic" Cartoon Violence', *Journal of Broadcasting and Electronic Media*, 22 (1): 63–70.

*James Bond Jr* (1991–1992), [TV Programme] syndicated (Claster Television).

Jenkins, H. (2006), *Convergence Culture*, New York: New York University Press.

*Journey to the Center of the Earth* (1967), [TV Programme] ABC.

*Jumanji* (1995), [Film] Dir. Joe Johnston, USA: TriStar Pictures.

*Jumanji* (1996–1999), [TV Programme] UPN.

*Jurassic World: Camp Cretaceous* (2020–22), [TV Programme] Netflix.

Kelley, S. (2020), '*Fast & Furious: Spy Racers* Producer Talks Vin Diesel, Family, and the Franchise Going to Space', *Den of Geek*, 9 October. Available online: https://www.denofgeek.com/tv/fast-and-furious-spy-racers-vin-diesel-family-going-to-space (accessed 23 September 2021).

*Madagascar* (2005), [Film] Dir. Eric Darnell and Tom McGrath, USA: DreamWorks Pictures.

Mittell, J. (2015), *Complex TV: The Poetics of Contemporary Television Storytelling*, New York: New York University Press.

*The Mummy: The Animated Series* (2001–2003), [TV Programme] The WB.

Pallant, C. (2011), *Demystifying Disney*, London: Bloomsbury.

Perlmutter, D. (2014), *America Toons in: A History of Television Animation*, Jefferson: McFarland.

*Police Academy* (1988–1989), [TV Programme] syndicated (Ruby Spears Enterprises).

*Rambo: First Blood Part II* (1985), [Film] Dir. George P. Costamos, USA: Tri-Star Pictures.

*Rambo: The Force of Freedom* (1986), [TV Programme] syndicated (Ruby Spears Enterprises).

Ratelle, A. (2018), 'Animation and/as Children's Entertainment', in N. Dobson et al (eds), *The Animation Studies Reader*, 191–202, London: Bloomsbury.

*The Real Ghostbusters* (1986–1991), [TV Programme] ABC.

*RoboCop* (1987), [Film] Dir. Paul Verhoeven, USA: Orion Pictures.

*RoboCop* (1988), [TV Programme] syndicated (New World Television).

*Rogue One: A Star Wars Story* (2016), [Film] Dir. Gareth Edwards, USA: Walt Disney Pictures.

Sexton, M. and M. Cook (2015), *Adapting Science Fiction to Television*, Lanham: Rowman & Littlefield.

*The Simpsons* (1989), [TV Programme] Fox.

*South Park* (1997), [TV Programme] Comedy Central.

*Star Trek: The Animated Series* (1973), [TV Programme] NBC.

*Star Wars: The Clone Wars* (2008–2020), [TV Programme] Cartoon Network.

*Steven Universe* (2013–2019), [TV Programme] Cartoon Network.

*The Toxic Avenger* (1984), [Film] Dir. Michael Henz and Lloyd Kaufman, USA: Troma Entertainment.

*Toxic Crusaders* (1991), [TV Programme] syndicated (Swenson Troma Entertainment).

*Turbo* (2013), [Film] Dir. David Soren, USA: 20th Century Fox.

Wells, P. (2003), 'Smarter Than the Average Art-Form: Animation in the Television Era', in C. Stabile and M. Harrison (eds), *Prime Time Animation*, 15–32, New York: Routledge.

12

# 'Zero tolerance for candy asses': World Wrestling Entertainment and *Fast & Furious* as transmedia storytelling

Robert Watts

On 26 April 2019, Vin Diesel posted a video on his Instagram account announcing the casting of World Wrestling Entertainment (WWE) star John Cena in the upcoming ninth instalment of the *Fast Saga*. Addressing the franchise's fans and musing on 'the responsibility of making something iconic and deserving of your loyalty' (Diesel 2019), he framed Cena's induction into the *Fast & Furious* 'family' by evoking the spirit of his deceased former co-star Paul Walker (referred to by Diesel as 'my brother Pablo'). Not prone to understatement, Diesel (Ibid) began, 'this sounds crazy but every blue moon I feel like Pablo up there sends me someone; another soldier for the fight for truth', adding that 'today someone came by the Toretto gym that speaks to what Pablo would have brought me.' A tilt of Diesel's camera revealed a smiling Cena in the background, silently waving his palm across his face in what WWE fans would recognize as Cena's signature 'You Can't See Me' wrestling taunt.

Cena is one of several WWE performers to have crossed over into the *Fast & Furious* 'universe' since Dwayne 'The Rock' Johnson's debut in *Fast Five* (2011), and his casting here can be seen as part of an array of textual and promotional convergences between the film franchise and WWE. These include the incorporation of WWE stars' signature gestures, catchphrases and wrestling moves within the films themselves, but also deeper intertextual references to and promotional tactics from professional wrestling culture. Not least among these is the converging of two 'feuds' – one between Johnson and Cena within the WWE space, and the other between Johnson and Diesel during their *Fast Saga* collaborations – that both involved a sustained blurring of boundaries between the fiction those spaces produce and the 'reality' of those who produce and perform it. Just as Diesel and his *Fast Saga* co-stars publicly conflate their on- and off-screen 'families' and personas (Diesel referring here to his workout space as the 'Toretto gym', after his character in the series), professional wrestling has long been a field in which such boundaries are strategically blurred. Real names and personal relationships are absorbed into wrestling's scripted storylines, while fictional conflicts are in turn incorporated into performances of the 'authentic' individuals behind these characters via social media and other public outlets (Ford 2016; Koh 2017; Litherland 2014; Ward 2019). Framed in this context, the casting of Dwayne Johnson's former on- and off-screen wrestling rival (Cena), endorsed in familial terms by his current on- and off-screen acting rival (Diesel), can be read as a strategically mediated moment of convergence: one that might channel fan affect and engagement from one narrative world directly into another.

This chapter will explore some of these commonalities and convergences in the textual production of both the *Fast & Furious* franchise and WWE, in order to consider what they might tell us about transmedia storytelling in the contemporary media ecology. That ecology is marked by trends towards increased conglomeration of major companies and studios, consolidation of media assets and intellectual properties (IP) and an economics of 'synergy' in which the most valuable IP is exploited across multiple media platforms. In such a competitive environment, it becomes particularly crucial for media producers to capture and retain what Henry Jenkins (2006: 63) refers to as 'loyals' – passionately engaged fans who are likely to follow their interests across multiple platforms or 'touch points'. After first outlining the uniquely transmedial nature of WWE's storytelling and its relationship to Hollywood, I will argue that in its engagement with WWE talent the *Fast & Furious* has proved particularly adept at absorbing wrestlers' existing star images, and attendant fan affect, into its own narrative world. The transmedia narratives of both WWE and *Fast & Furious* are publicly framed in terms of a brand 'universe', and a comparative analysis of the two brands reveals further commonalities in their marketing rhetorics. The second half of the chapter will explore how the concept of 'family' is used not only to structure dramatic tensions between characters and performers across these texts, but also to interpellate audiences into an overarching brand 'family'. In both cases, the term is frequently used to signal loyalty to the brand in question, for both the performers and their audiences. Family, I argue, emerges as a useful affective rhetoric of transmedia production, distribution and storytelling; with fans encouraged to re-enact in their consumption behaviours, the kinds of familial loyalty of the characters and performers they follow on screen.

## Wrestling with Hollywood: WWE, transmediality and kayfabe

There is a moment, early in Barry Blaustein's behind-the-scenes pro-wrestling documentary *Beyond the Mat* (1999), where WWE chairman Vince McMahon suggests to the filmmaker what his organization is 'really about'. 'We make movies', smirks McMahon with a performative swig of water and a raised eyebrow, in a clip widely mocked by fans as emblematic of McMahon's reluctance to be viewed as a lowly 'rasslin' promoter (he famously avoids the terms 'wrestler' and 'wrestling' in favour of euphemisms like 'superstar' and 'sports entertainment'). After inheriting the then-World Wrestling Federation (WWF) from his father in 1982, McMahon took the regional promotion national and then international: embracing technologies like cable, pay-per-view and VHS; spinning his performers' likenesses into an array of promotional paratexts including toys, magazines, music albums and cartoon series; and engaging in various promotional crossovers with celebrities from the more culturally legitimate realms of sport, music, film and television. As Holly Chard and Benjamin Litherland (2019: 27) suggest, during this expansion period McMahon sought to reposition WWE's brand of pro-wrestling as a 'subfield of popular culture rather than of sport'. In 2002, as the WWF became the WWE, McMahon launched the production company WWE Films (later renamed WWE Studios) as a way for his organization – now described in its corporate materials as an 'integrated media and entertainment company' – to 'expand its role within the film and television industries' (WWE Corporate 2002). In a press release, the incoming head of the new film division Joel Simon called WWE an 'untapped creative resource for Hollywood', noting that it had 'created a new breed of action-adventure hero, one with a ready-made audience' (Ibid). Across the various expansions of what is now branded as the 'WWE Universe', there is a clear sense that McMahon has long viewed proximity to Hollywood as a source of legitimacy for a business culturally derided as a 'fake' sport.

While there's a long history of scholarship on professional wrestling as a performative spectacle (Barthes 1972; Mazer 1998), this strategic alignment with other media forms has also seen it emerge as a topic of interest for scholars of media convergence and transmedia storytelling. Wrestling's hybridity of genres (taking in sport, soap opera, action, comedy), its blend of interactive live performance and scripted serial television production and a (deliberate) indeterminacy between the 'real' and the story-world all position it as a convergent medium that straddles a diverse array of pop cultural forms and modes simultaneously (Reinhard and Olson 2019). Sam Ford (2016: 170) sees wrestling as a particularly useful form through which to think about transmediality, given that it 'long thrived on existing across multiple locus points' including live events, weekly broadcast television, monthly pay-per-view and various forms of online and social media – all of which feed and progress a perpetual narrative of storylines, characters and feuds. For Ford, WWE is particularly instructive for scholars of transmedia because its storytelling 'benefits from having no single core primary text'.

In his foundational work on the concept, Henry Jenkins (2007) defines transmedia storytelling as the process where 'integral elements of a fiction get dispersed systematically across multiple delivery channels for the purpose of creating a unified and coordinated entertainment experience'. He also points out that most multimedia franchises are not designed as transmedial from the outset, but rather develop as a cluster of licensed paratexts, subordinate to some original 'master text' (spinoffs from a blockbuster film series, for example). By contrast, WWE's narrative canon is always inherently transmedial and intertextual, not least because wrestling's fictional characters and storylines co-exist with the 'real world' in real-time (Sciarretta 2019; Ward 2019). This intertextuality can thus extend to events in Hollywood cinema. When performers like Dwayne Johnson (The Rock), Terry Bollea (Hulk Hogan) or Dave Bautista (Batista) make professional excursions beyond the wrestling 'text', these experiences are also seen to have happened to the characters they play within it. In these instances, the wrestler-turned-actor will often return to the WWE space as a heel (villain) imbued with the arrogant swagger of one who has now 'transcended' the business. Such tactics serve as a useful form of transmedia cross-promotion, whereby the wrestler functions simultaneously as an ongoing character and a celebrity outsider lending Hollywood credibility to the wrestling text.

Within wrestling, this porousness between reality and story-world is often understood through reference to 'kayfabe'. A complex idea or code with roots in wrestling's carnival origins, kayfabe is generally associated with 'protecting the business' by concealing its predetermined nature (Ward 2019). Historically, to 'break kayfabe' was to let the mask slip, acknowledging the distinction between performer and performance. While that distinction, as well as wrestling's predetermined nature, has been widely acknowledged by McMahon and WWE since at least the late 1990s, Litherland (2014: 531) suggests that if we view kayfabe as 'the practice of sustaining the in-diegesis performance into everyday life' it persists today in more complex ways, and is particularly visible in the way wrestlers use social media to blur such boundaries. These flows between WWE's story-world and the 'real' spaces of social media are pertinent to a discussion of Johnson and Cena's respective crossovers into *Fast & Furious*. Like Vin Diesel – who is among the most-followed actors on Facebook – the two wrestlers command a huge online following and were key drivers of WWE's embrace of social media as one of its narrative 'touch points'. As the second half of this chapter will outline, Johnson and Cena have proven adept at using social media to blur boundaries of performer/performance, in the contexts of both their wrestling careers and their work with Diesel in transitioning into the *Fast Saga* universe.

While contemporary wrestlers like Johnson and Cena can deftly toggle between the performance of their 'real' and fictionalized wrestling personas, earlier eras presented obstacles for those seeking to extend their star image beyond the wrestling space. Chard and Litherland (2019) outline how Terry 'Hulk Hogan' Bollea's attempts to establish himself as a Hollywood leading man in the late 1980s and early 1990s were hampered by that era's adherence to more traditional forms of kayfabe. Acting under his ring name, the need to protect the specific star persona of 'Hulk Hogan' (as the WWF's top-drawing 'babyface' or hero) meant that critics and publicists had very little sense of Terry Bollea beyond the 'kayfabed' biography developed by McMahon. Hogan thus 'struggled to use his celebrity to migrate from the subfield of wrestling to the subfield of cinema, in part because his persona was not readily translatable to the frameworks of big screen stardom' (Chard and Litherland 2019: 43). Despite his failure to sustain a Hollywood career, Hogan nonetheless parlayed his brief dalliance with movie stardom into a successful second career act in wrestling (for the rival group WCW) as the arrogant heel character 'Hollywood' Hulk Hogan. While in reality fans had already begun to sour on his babyface routine, the exaggeration of his credibility as a cultural icon outside of wrestling (who does not *need* the wrestling fans anymore) helped provide Hogan's rationale for his character's 'heel turn'. While the limits of kayfabe inhibited his ability to migrate the 'Hulk Hogan' star image across pop cultural fields, wrestling's inherent intertextuality allowed it to productively absorb Bollea's failed excursion back into its rolling narrative of the Hogan character itself.

Even as WWE shifted away from the more protectionist form of kayfabe, numerous wrestlers have used all or part of their WWE persona for film roles, both within and beyond the WWE Films/Studios imprimatur. The most successful wrestler to transition between these fields (and the most useful analogue to Hogan's experience) is Dwayne Johnson. In his two breakthrough roles for Universal Pictures – *The Mummy Returns* (2001) and its spinoff *The Scorpion King* (2002) – Johnson is credited only by his WWE name 'The Rock', despite only the latter film having McMahon on board as a co-producer. WWE Films' initial press release in 2002 explicitly refers to the success of *The Scorpion King* as its founding impetus, and it seems fair to imagine Johnson as embodying the 'new breed' of action-adventure hero 'with a ready-made audience' that they had in mind (WWE Corporate 2002). That audience was certainly substantial, given that the sardonic, charismatic Rock character was a central protagonist of WWE's millennial 'Attitude Era' – one of the greatest boom periods in the history of the wrestling business.

By the time Johnson boarded *Fast & Furious* for 2011's *Fast Five* he had transitioned into using only his real name. However, this is not to say that he had distanced himself from his wrestling character (and by extension the sizeable wrestling audience). Unlike Bollea/Hogan, Johnson was able to reconcile his personal biography with his wrestling persona, which was pitched as a heightened extension of his real personality. Indeed, elements of his wrestling persona are integrated into all of Johnson's performances within the franchise, which around the time of his arrival shifts towards a greater emphasis on spectacular fight scenes and sardonic trash-talk between characters. In *Fast Five*, for example, Johnson's DSS agent Luke Hobbs clashes with Diesel's main protagonist Dom Toretto in a prolonged fight sequence notable for the way in which Hobbs counters Dom's punches with grappling and throws, deploying specific wrestling moves including a 'spear' and a 'sleeperhold'. The two combatants later reconcile – in wrestling parlance, the threatening antagonist Hobbs 'turning face' by saving Dom and aligning with the heroes – and in *Fast & Furious 6* (2013) the two perform together a version of a famous tag-team manoeuvre known as the 'Doomsday Device' in the film's final battle. Likewise, when Hobbs first faces off with his franchise frenemy Deckard Shaw (Jason Statham) in *Furious 7* (2015), Johnson performs his signature wrestling finisher (the 'Rock Bottom') to plant his adversary through a glass table.

The parallels between Hobbs and The Rock occur not just at the level of physical but also vocal performance. The *Fast & Furious 6* script incorporates wrestling-specific phrases such as 'guaran-damn-tee' (one of the many catchphrases of Johnson's WWE character), and from this second outing onwards Johnson notably shifts his performance of Hobbs' acerbic dialogue into a more 'Rock'-like cadence. Mimicking the call-and-response rhythms of his live wrestling 'promos', Johnson frequently draws out lines of dialogue into short, clipped fragments that allow Hobbs' threats and insults to land like punchlines. In an illustrative scene from *The Fate of the Furious* (2017; hereinafter *Fast Eight*), Hobbs and Shaw trade an escalating series of insults across their separate prison cells. 'Let me tell you something,' begins Hobbs, pausing to step forward. 'Me and you … one-on-one … no one else around …' – with another pause as Hobbs leans predatorily on the cell window, making his frame as large as possible – 'I will *beat* … your *ass* … like a Cherokee drum.' The scene plays out in the manner of two wrestlers building up a fight, and the measured pauses recall The Rock's crowd-pleasing verbal style (that he famously termed 'Sing-along with The Rock') whereby clipped, memorable insults are repeated as sound bites to encourage the live audience to chant along in participation.

The influence of Johnson's wrestling career becomes especially prevalent in franchise spinoff *Fast & Furious Presents: Hobbs & Shaw* (2019). An action buddy movie leaning into the knockabout chemistry of Johnson and Statham, *Hobbs & Shaw* strikes a more overtly comic tone than the (often comedically earnest) *Fast Saga*. It is also the only release in the series produced by Johnson's family-owned production company, Seven Bucks, and in many regards the film works to furnish the Hobbs character with aspects of Johnson's personal backstory as well as his wrestling persona.[1] Its plot sees the two former antagonists (who found a begrudging mutual respect in *Fast Eight*) bicker their way through a CIA mission to prevent cyberterrorist operative Brixton Lore (Idris Elba) from acquiring a deadly weaponized virus. The convoluted mission takes the odd-couple heroes on a journey from London to Ukraine and Russia, before they retreat for a final showdown in Samoa – the US-born Johnson's ancestral homeland, which is depicted here as Hobbs' family home. Within wrestling culture, Johnson is known as a member of the famous 'Samoan dynasty' centred on the Ano'ai family, of which he is considered a (non-blood) relative. The sense of Johnson's authorial command over the spinoff (relative to the *Fast Saga*) is further heightened by the casting of his 'cousin', WWE's top contemporary star Joe 'Roman Reigns' Ano'ai, as a member of Hobbs' Samoan family, who like Johnson physically re-enacts his signature wrestling moves and taunts within the film's diegesis.

Similarly, *Hobbs & Shaw*'s script is peppered with verbal and performative allusions to Johnson's wrestling past. Within the film's first ten minutes, Hobbs threatens to open 'an ice-cold can of whoop-ass' (catchphrase of The Rock's nemesis Stone Cold Steve Austin) and dismisses another character as an 'ass clown' (catchphrase of another former WWE rival Chris Jericho). Later, threatening Shaw, he describes his plan to 'take this chair, turn it sideways ...', which wrestling fans would recognize as the set-up to The Rock's signature call-and-response punchline from WWE ('and stick it straight-up your candy-ass'), a response omitted from this particular exchange. A subsequent scene between Hobbs and his young daughter sees her mocking his tendency to comically raise one eyebrow, a reference to another of The Rock's signature gestures within WWE ('the people's eyebrow'). Hobbs denies all knowledge of his habit, before flashing a quick people's eyebrow as the scene's payoff.

These reflexive nods and intertextual references to The Rock persona and the wrestling world might be taken as a way to establish *Hobbs & Shaw* as specifically a Johnson vehicle, as distinct from the ensemble appeals of *Fast & Furious*. They can also be seen as providing a particular form of spectacle appealing to wrestling's niche but sizeable audience. Indeed, both *Fast Eight* and *Hobbs & Shaw* were cross-promoted on WWE's television and online channels – the film's distributor, Universal, having long-standing ties with WWE through various television and streaming deals (NBCUniversal 2021). The promotion for the latter film included WWE-produced featurettes focused on Johnson and Reigns' relationship on set and the action sequences depicting their moves. These references not only work to channel wrestling fan interest and affect towards the movie franchise, making it feel as much a product of WWE's 'Universe' or extended 'family' to the *Fast Saga*, but they also allow Johnson himself to maintain a fairly seamless star image in line with what Christine Geraghty (2007) has termed 'the star-as-professional'. Here, the performer presents a relatively stable set of characteristics across roles and is thus seen to be playing a version of themselves, to some degree. In this instance, the stability extends across not just Johnson's film roles but to his continuing presence as an on-off wrestling character during the years when he was integrated into *Fast & Furious*.

In his navigation of transmedia stardom, Johnson succeeded where Hogan and other wrestlers have failed. Rather than migrating back and forth between the distinct fields of wrestling and Hollywood, Johnson was able to use each as an extension of the other, opening up avenues for transmedia synergy through formal cross-promotions as well as the more subtle channelling of fan affect from one narrative world into another. As the next section will explore, Johnson's use of social media to manipulate and blur boundaries between the movie star and the wrestler, and between his back- and front-stage performances, has been explored through the lens of a more modern 'kayfabe', reflective of wider shifts in celebrity culture (Litherland 2014; Ward 2019). I will explore how the concept of 'family' is used in both the WWE and the *Fast Saga* to similarly blur the line between the fictional (front stage) 'family' dynamics on screen and the real (back stage) 'family'; channelling and directing affects of loyalty and resentment amongst their audience 'families', in ways that will ultimately keep them invested in the overarching (transmedia) 'universe'.

## Family feuds: Worked shoots, loyalty and the 'family' as synergy

In April 2011, Johnson returned to WWE as the 'host' of the annual *Wrestlemania* event, chiefly to promote the upcoming release of *Fast Five*. Between then and the 2013 release of *Fast & Furious 6*, Johnson embarked on a two-year storyline with WWE's then-top star John Cena, culminating in his return to the ring for two 'dream' matches at subsequent *Wrestlemania* events (the first of which remains WWE's highest-grossing pay-per-view event of all time). The feud was designed to position Cena, as the company's current marquee attraction, as needing to defeat his predecessor The Rock to legitimize his position and legacy. The Rock had been an on/off character for much of the preceding decade while Johnson's movie career took off, and during this time Cena had publicly criticized Johnson for being an opportunistic part-timer while Cena carried the company day-to-day. This off-screen grievance (real or otherwise) was folded into the fictional storyline as the impetus for the feud, which in Johnson's absence was sustained through dozens of personal jibes between the two over Twitter around Johnson's supposed lack of engagement with WWE (Litherland 2014). As *Wrestlemania* approached in 2012, the two came face-to-face on the 27 February episode of WWE's weekly TV broadcast *Raw*, where Cena brought the online discourse into the physical space, pointing to the audience and declaring: 'These people love The Rock, I was one of these people, until I got to meet Dwayne Johnson. Dwayne Johnson is a self-centred, egotistical see-through son of a bitch that wouldn't give a rat's ass if this company closed its doors tomorrow' (WWE Raw 2012). With Johnson visibly bristling at the comments, Cena channelled this playful subversion of kayfabe towards its end product, adding: 'April 1st, when the "millions" see John Cena vs The Rock, John Cena's gonna be eyeing up Dwayne Johnson – and I don't like Dwayne Johnson' (Ibid).

The dropping of real names, and allusions to non-kayfabe events or incongruities within the wrestling text, are common features of a promotional tactic in wrestling known as the 'worked shoot', designed to destabilize the viewer's sense of what is real versus staged. As Wilson Koh (2017) outlines, the worked shoot is an amalgamation of the wrestling argot 'work' (something predetermined, part of the kayfabed performance) and 'shoot' (an unplanned occurrence or legitimate opinion breaking the kayfabe). Drawing on Barthes' (1975) concept of *jouissance*, Koh (2017: 461–2) sees the worked shoot as a 'rapturous moment of viewing' which works against the grain of the 'front-stage' performance such that the consumer 'does not know what is authorised and what is not'. In the Cena-Rock confrontation, the tactic was effective in playing off Cena's wrestling persona as a loyal company man, whose clean-cut, patriotic and moralistic image (with a sideline in irreverent toilet humour) appealed primarily to WWE's younger audiences. As a result of this image, he was often booed by wrestling's older hard-core audience for a perceived lack of edge and authenticity, an unsolicited response he typically brushed off in his 'front-stage' performance with a smile and a wink. In implying a disjuncture between 'The Rock' and 'Dwayne', and channelling his company-man image into what could be interpreted as an expression of authentic 'back-stage' grievance, Cena attempted to signal to the audience that this was *both* a fictional and an authentic grudge at the same time.

In framing Johnson (the performer) as somehow disloyal or inauthentic in moving away from his wrestling character and roots, Cena also tapped into a common rhetoric within WWE of the 'family'. As a kind of travelling roadshow, WWE performers often refer to their colleagues as a working family, and in the social media age wrestlers whose contracts are terminated are often eulogized in familial terms on Twitter by those who remain, in what can read like a form of professional grieving. The term is also frequently incorporated into WWE's corporate materials. In a press release announcing Nick Khan's appointment as company president in 2020, Khan said he was 'looking forward to expanding my relationship with Vince McMahon and the entire team at WWE, and becoming a full-time member of the WWE family' (WWE Corporate 2020). This interpellation into the 'family' is also extended to the audience: on 22 July 2019 'Reunion' episode of *Raw*, a returning Stone Cold Steve Austin toasted a procession of past and current wrestlers by saying 'it's all family', before raising his beer to the audience and adding 'and you guys are family' (WWE Raw 2019). Within WWE, the term 'family' is used both expansively (to encapsulate any involvement with WWE's brand across its production, performance and consumption) and restrictively (to imply a boundary that can be crossed when someone 'leaves', betrays or is banished from that family). Just as Austin's speech implied that any past character is always welcome back into the 'family' fold, the Cena-Rock feud was built around the idea that Dwayne Johnson's competing loyalties had led to a familial neglect that fans were encouraged to resent (as members of that family), but in a way that ultimately channelled their interest towards the real product being sold (*Wrestlemania*).

By allowing himself to be accused of familial disloyalty by Cena, Johnson was able to create a productive tension between his cinematic and wrestling work, one that he has actively built into his WWE persona, his film star image and his social media activity. Ward (2019: 485) notes Johnson's skill in adapting to audience responses across these media fields to shape his star image, arguing that both 'the wrestling character of The Rock and the star persona of Dwayne Johnson have evolved in a fluid synergy through a range of performative platforms'. According to Ward, Johnson 'sees the cultivation of his own star persona as an active, collaborative process'. Thus, rather than simply defending his status as a member of the 'WWE family' within that one space, Johnson used social media to heighten engagement in the issue, and increasingly incorporated wrestling references into his performances in *Fast & Furious* during this period. This synergistic approach to managing his star image sees Johnson attempt to 'spread' the issue across different media realms. In doing so he was not only able to signal to wrestling fans in his film work that he's *still a wrestler*. He was also able to play up the notion that his stardom is *bigger than wrestling* in advance of his return to the WWE space.

It is notable that during Cena's own transition out of full-time wrestling and into Hollywood (and specifically *Fast & Furious*), he tried to signal loyalty to both 'families', tweeting about enjoying the 2021 edition of *Wrestlemania* as an 'observer' but nonetheless 'with the WWE family', meaning its fans (Cena 2021). In the advance promotion for *F9* (2021) Cena spoke frequently of the 'family atmosphere' on set. Here, he compared *Fast & Furious* to WWE in having to 'earn your respect' before being 'welcomed into the family' (Lawrence 2019), noting that: '[whenever] new performers come in [to WWE], we always size them up and question their passion. The *Fast* legacy and the family is the same way ... you need to know the responsibility to fans across the world' (Boone 2020). Ahead of *F9*'s opening weekend, Cena also signalled his intention to return to the WWE ring, just as Johnson had done a decade earlier (Romano 2021). Across these various exchanges, the term 'family' is used to signal a performer's loyalty to both a franchise brand and its fandom. In promoting the idea that the WWE and *Fast & Furious* 'families' share a similar ethos, Cena therefore contributed to a growing sense of synergy between the two brands.

Through the lens of modern kayfabe, we might then view certain 'back-stage' events within the production of the *Fast & Furious* 'universe' in terms of how they are used to build engagement, synergy across texts and channel fan affect into the 'front-stage' performance. Specifically, I refer to the 'Candy Ass' feud' between Johnson and co-star Vin Diesel (Bryant 2017), and how its aftermath deployed ideas of familial loyalty/disloyalty in much the same way as Cena and Johnson's 'worked shoot'. In August 2016, towards the end of the production of *Fast Eight,* Johnson made a now-deleted Instagram post suggesting that some of his male co-stars 'conduct themselves as stand up men and true professionals, while others don't. The ones that don't are too chicken shit to do anything about it anyway. Candy Asses' (Cobb 2016). In much the same way Cena implied their WWE rivalry was *both* real and staged, Johnson added that when fans watch the movie 'and it seems like I'm not acting in some of these scenes and my blood is legit boiling – you're right. Bottom line is it'll play great for the movie and fits this Hobbs character that's embedded in my DNA extremely well' (Ibid). In an example of his synergistic approach to managing his star image, Johnson simultaneously positions Hobbs as an extension of his true self whilst also summoning one of The Rock's old catchphrases, hashtagging the post 'Zero Tolerance For Candy Asses' (Bryant 2017). The anonymous Candy Ass was widely speculated as being Diesel, later confirmed in an interview where Johnson revealed the two had ended up having to shoot their joint scenes separately (Eells 2018). Speaking a year later, Johnson told *Rolling Stone* that after hashing things out with Diesel there was 'no ill will there, just because of all the clarity we have', before circling back to cheekily embellish the sound bite: 'Actually, you can erase that part about "no ill will". We'll just keep it with the clarity' (Ibid). For Johnson, there is value in maintaining both his reputation as a consummate professional *and* the idea of unresolved tension between himself and Diesel. Indeed, he reframes this tension in other interviews as 'unfinished business between Hobbs and Dom', thereby seeming to tease a possible return to the main franchise in the future (ET Canada 2019). As with the Cena feud, Johnson's promotional work handles the controversy in a way that simultaneously builds into his own personal brand, as well as the ongoing storytelling imperatives of the franchise.

Johnson's departure from *Fast & Furious* to shoot the *Hobbs & Shaw* spinoff was itself absorbed into the feud to position him as being disloyal to the 'family', again in a similar dynamic to the Cena feud within WWE. Here, *Fast & Furious* cast member Tyrese Gibson, who has portrayed the wisecracking Roman Pearce since the series' first sequel *2 Fast 2 Furious* (2003), launched a barrage of Instagram posts attacking Johnson: for delaying the launch of *F9* by agreeing to the spinoff, threatening to quit *F9* if Johnson were to be cast in it, and accusing Johnson and his own family's production company of having 'broke up the #FastFamily' (Stefansky 2017). Posting a picture of the original cast with the hashtag #OriginalFastFamily, Gibson said that 'what makes us great is when you see us all TOGETHER we don't fly solo' (Stefansky 2017). Johnson responded variously that his goal was always to 'elevate the franchise and build it out', and that he wouldn't be in *F9* because 'the plan has always been for the *Fast & Furious* universe to grow and expand' (ET Canada 2019). As the 'universe' of the franchise expands into spinoffs and an increasing array of intertexts, and the 'original' family publicly redraws its boundaries in the face of perceived challenges to Vin Diesel's authority (real or manufactured), there is a sense that authorship over the *Fast & Furious* 'universe' itself begins to feel contested. It is at this point Diesel casts Johnson's nemesis John Cena as his own character's long-lost brother, sent by his late 'brother Pablo', and Cena builds his promotional campaign around asserting the importance of familial loyalty to the film series – just as he did with the WWE where Johnson was cast as the prodigal son who 'sold out' his family.

For fans of the film franchise, there is perhaps no way of knowing how genuine these public displays of tension, petty jibes and accusations, and hints at future directions actually are. It is unclear the degree to which, as with modern kayfabe in WWE, the in-diegesis performance of the *Fast Saga* is being extended into media spaces traditionally coded under a different register of authenticity. The squabbles over who does or does not authentically belong in the '*Fast* Family' mirror the emphasis on loyalty to a (largely non-biological) 'family' in the text of the film series itself. As with wrestling's worked shoot, there is a *jouissance* in not being quite sure what is or is not 'authorized' here, of destabilizing the distinction between back – and front-stage performances. In an interview with *Men's Health* magazine coinciding with *F9*'s launch, Diesel framed the Johnson feud as emerging from his own 'method' instincts, delivering 'tough love' on set as a producer (D'Agostino 2021). Indeed, he claimed: '[W]e're going to take Dwayne Johnson, who's associated with wrestling, and we're going to force this cinematic world, audience members, to regard his character as someone that they don't know'. The result, according to Diesel, is that 'Hobbs hits you like a ton of bricks. That's something that I'm proud of, that aesthetic. That took a lot of work' (D'Agostino 2021). The idea that producer Diesel would make this kind of artistic choice four films into Johnson's run in the franchise might cast further scepticism on how the discourse is being conditioned here. But as with WWE's profitable use of such ambiguities, there is always another end product coming within the franchise, be it further sequels, spinoffs or other transmedia expansions towards which this interest can be directed.

## Conclusion: Kayfabe and 'family' as passionate engagement

One thing Johnson, if not all involved, seem to realize is that these dramas of 'unfinished business' and family feuds can be mobilized in service of what Adam Arvidsson and Tiziano Bonini (2014: 159) have called 'passionate engagement'. Arvidsson and Bonini use the term in their discussion of a new paradigm of audience value, where the goal for producers begins to shift away from getting 'eyeballs' on any particular media product (a feature film, a pro-wrestling pay-per-view) towards the creation of reliable, passionately engaged 'publics' that build certain consumption habits into their self-identity, and who will follow a story or brand across various different products and forms (a transmedia 'universe'). Helen Morgan Parmett (2016: 4) elsewhere describes passionate engagement as a 'marketing and branding discourse typically associated with the emotional and affective investments of audiences harnessed through forms of new media interactivity'. In this chapter, through a focus on the work of Dwayne 'The Rock' Johnson, I have suggested that both the 'WWE Universe' and the '*Fast & Furious* Universe' have become adept in harnessing such investments across different media touch points (including social media) to sustain passionate engagement with their ever-expanding, ongoing transmedia franchises.

As indicated in the introduction, these promotional tactics can be viewed in the context of a highly conglomerated media ecology, increasingly focused on maximizing the value of franchise brands and other studio-owned IP. The synergistic relationship between WWE and *Fast & Furious* is certainly made easier through both brands' ties to NBCUniversal (NBCU) and its parent company, Comcast. As I have explored elsewhere, WWE has in recent years been shifting away from its old pay-per-view model (dependent on marquee matches that might draw more casual viewers) towards monetizing its core 'loyal' audience through its SVOD (Subscription Video On-Demand) service the WWE Network (Watts 2019). In 2021, WWE sold their US streaming rights to NBCU, and the Network was absorbed into their own 'Peacock' SVOD (NBCUniversal 2021). In a 2020 interview with *Total Film*, Diesel framed shifts in the *Fast & Furious* universe as moving in a similar direction. The spinoffs Diesel viewed as 'inevitable' and as something 'Universal deserves ... because of how much they've invested in this little saga, and it'd be good to give back to Universal' (Shephard and Farley 2020). While maintaining some distance between Diesel's artistic product and the wider franchise, he still emphasized the transmedia story-world in terms of a familial lineage: 'for the fans, should *Fast 10* parts one and two be the conclusion, it would be nice for this world to continue for generations to come' (Ibid). And like WWE's interpellation of their audience into a loyal brand 'family', the official *Fast Saga* website invites fans to 'Join the Family' by signing up for exclusive offers and access to content and events surrounding the series.[2]

In their discussion of Hulk Hogan's transmedia excursions in the 1980s and 1990s, Chard and Litherland (2019: 22) also argue for a rethinking of professional wrestling's role in the broader popular media landscape not as a niche genre 'but as a central and vitally important space in which industry logics are tested, developed, and explored'. While Vince McMahon and WWE have clearly longed since that earlier era to be thought of as more like the 'movies', it is useful to consider the degree to which in this media ecology the movies have also become more like WWE. McMahon's company expanded and thrived by repositioning itself not as a singular product (professional wrestling) but a fluid, transmedial and convergent narrative world ('sports entertainment'). Similarly, in an era where the industrial value of the singular, core cinematic text diminishes amidst the rise of serial, franchise and transmedia narratives, the *Fast Saga* evolved from a mid-budget film series about street racing into its own complex (and often absurd) blockbuster 'universe' encompassing spinoffs, animated series, games, live stage shows and more. The *Fast Saga*, like WWE, thrived by adapting to the conditions of a shifting media ecology to maximize loyal fan engagement. Dwayne Johnson's celebrity – in straddling both story-worlds – serves as a useful case study, generating productive continuities across the media brands, as well as internal tensions that destabilize these texts in interesting (and potentially productive) ways. This chapter has used Johnson's transmedia stardom to mount a comparative analysis of seemingly distinct branded media universes. Through the conceptual lenses of 'family' and 'kayfabe', it points to the value of such a comparative approach in unpicking and contextualizing these broader trends and flows of the convergent media age.

## Notes

1  Seven Bucks Productions was founded in 2012 by Johnson and his ex-wife Dany Garcia, and since 2017 her brother Hiram Garcia has served as its president of production.
2  See https://www.thefastsaga.com/join-the-family/ (accessed 25 June 2021).

## References

Arvidsson, A. and T. Bonini (2014), 'Valuing Audience Passions: From Smythe to Tarde', *European Journal of Cultural Studies*, 18 (2): 158–73.

Barthes, R. (1972), 'The World of Wrestling', in R. Barthes (ed), *Mythologies*, 15–25, New York: Hill and Wang.

Barthes, R. (1975), *The Pleasure of the Text*, New York: Hill and Wang.

*Beyond the Mat* (1999), [Film] Dir. Barry Blaustein, USA: Universal Pictures.

Boone, J. (2020), 'John Cena Says It's "Not True" That He's Playing the Villain in *Fast 9* (Exclusive)', *ET*, 31 January. Available online: https://www.etonline.com/john-cena-says-its-not-true-that-hes-playing-the-villain-in-fast-9-exclusive-140700 (accessed 25 June 2021).

Bryant, K. (2017), 'The Rock and Vin Diesel's "Candy Ass" Feud: A Comprehensive Timeline', *Vanity Fair*, 10 April. Available online: https://www.vanityfair.com/style/2017/04/dwayne-the-rock-johnson-vin-diesel-fast-and-furious-feud-timeline (accessed 25 June 2021).

Cena, J. (2021), [Twitter] 'Transitioning to an Unfamiliar Perspective Is Always Difficult to Self and Surroundings. Perspective May Change (From Focus to Observer) but Purpose [...]', 10 April. Available online: https://twitter.com/johncena/status/1380948511114489861?lang=en (accessed 25 June 2021).

Chard, H. and B. Litherland (2019), '"Hollywood" Hulk Hogan: Stardom, Synergy, and Field Migration', *Journal of Cinema and Media Studies*, 58 (4): 21–44.

Cobb, K. (2016), 'According to a Pissed-off Dwayne Johnson, Someone on the Set of *Fast Eight* Is a "Candy Ass"', *Decider*, 9 August. Available online: https://decider.com/2016/08/09/dwayne-the-rock-johnson-goes-on-a-fast-8-facebook-rant (accessed 25 June 2021).

D'Agostino, R. (2021), 'Vin Diesel Is 53 and Still Shifting Up', *Men's Health*, 22 June. Available at: https://www.menshealth.com/entertainment/a36663682/vin-diesel-f9-interview/ (accessed 25 June 2021).

Diesel, V. (2019), [Instagram] 'Thank you Pablo', 26 April. Available online: https://www.instagram.com/p/BwsrZnDnB8s/ (accessed 25 June 2021).

Eells, J. (2018), 'Dwayne Johnson: The Pain and the Passion That Fuel The Rock', *Rolling Stone*, 4 April. Available online: https://www.rollingstone.com/movies/movie-features/dwayne-johnson-the-pain-and-the-passion-that-fuel-the-rock-630076/ (accessed 2 May 2022).

ET Canada. (2019), [YouTube] 'Dwayne Johnson Says He's Not in *Fast and Furious 9*', 30 January. Available online: https://youtu.be/6rQoeoxPIbc (accessed 25 June 2021).

Ford, S. (2016), 'WWE's Storyworld and the Immersive Potentials of Transmedia Storytelling', in B. W. L. Dehry Kurtz and M. Bourdaa (eds), *The Rise of Transtexts: Challenges and Opportunities*, 169–83, London: Taylor and Francis Group.

Geraghty, C. (2007), 'Re-examining Stardom', in S. Redmond and S. Holmes (eds), *Stardom and Celebrity: A Reader*, 98–110, London: Sage.

Jenkins, H. (2006), *Convergence Culture: Where Old and New Media Collide*, New York: NYU Press.

Jenkins, H. (2007), 'Transmedia Storytelling 101', *Confessions of an Aca-Fan*, 21 March. Available online: http://henryjenkins.org/blog/2007/03/transmedia_storytelling_101.html (accessed 20 August 2021).

Koh, W. (2017), '"It's What's Best for Business" – "Worked Shoots": And the Commodified Authentic in Postmillennial Professional Wrestling', *Quarterly Review of Film and Video*, 34 (5): 459–79.

Lawrence, D. (2019), 'New Family Member John Cena Says *Fast & Furious 9* Experience Has Been "Really Special"', *Entertainment Weekly*, 3 October. Available online: https://ew.com/movies/2019/10/03/john-cena-furious-9-experience/ (accessed 6 August 2022).

Litherland, B. (2014), 'Breaking Kayfabe Is Easy, Cheap and Never Entertaining: Twitter Rivalries in Professional Wrestling', *Celebrity Studies*, 5 (4): 531–3.

Mazer, S. (1998), *Professional Wrestling: Sport and Spectacle*, Jackson: University Press of Mississippi.

*The Mummy Returns* (2001), [Film] Dir. Stephen Sommers, USA: Universal Pictures.

NBCUniversal. (2021), 'Press Release: Peacock to Become the Exclusive Home of WWE Network in the U.S', *NBCUniversal.com*, 25 January. Available online: https://www.nbcuniversal.com/press-release/peacock-become-exclusive-home-wwe-network-us (accessed 25 June 2021).

Parmett, H. M. (2016), 'It's HBO: Passionate Engagement, TV Branding, and Tourism in the Postbroadcast Era', *Communication and Critical/Cultural Studies*, 13 (1): 3–22.

Reinhard, C. D. and C. J. Olson (eds) (2019), *Convergent Wrestling: Participatory Culture, Transmedia Storytelling, and Intertextuality in the Squared Circle*, London: Routledge.

Romano, N. (2021), 'John Cena Confirms Rumours of a WWE Return: "I Haven't had My Last Match"', *Entertainment Weekly*, 24 June. Available online: https://ew.com/tv/john-cena-wwe-return/ (accessed 25 June 2021).

Sciarretta, E. (2019), 'The Use of Social Media as Part of a Transmedia Storytelling Strategy in WWE's Professional Wrestling', in G. Meiselwitz (ed), *Social Computing and Social Media: Design, Human Behavior and Analytics, HCII 2019 LNCS 11578*, 556–70, Cham: Springer.

*The Scorpion King* (2002), [Film] Dir. Chuck Russell, USA: Universal Pictures.

Shephard, J. and J. Farley (2020), 'Vin Diesel Suggests *Fast and Furious 10* Could Be Split into 2 Parts', *GamesRadar*, 5 February. Available online: https://www.gamesradar.com/fast-and-furious-10-vin-diesel-interview-part-1/ (accessed 25 June 2021).

Stefanksky, E. (2017), 'Tyrese Gibson Calls The Rock a "Clown" for Breaking up the *Fast & Furious* Family', *Vanity Fair*, 7 October. Available online: https://www.vanityfair.com/hollywood/2017/10/tyrese-gibson-dwayne-the-rock-johnson-fast-and-furious-feud (accessed 25 June 2021).

Ward, D. (2019). '"Know Your Role": Dwayne Johnson & the Performance of Contemporary Stardom', *Celebrity Studies*, 10 (4): 479–88.

Watts, R. (2019), '"What's Best for Business": The WWE *Cruiserweight Classic* and Managing Renegade Audiences through Affective Economics', in C.D. Reinhard and C.J. Olson (eds), *Convergent Wrestling: Participatory Culture, Transmedia Storytelling, and Intertextuality in the Squared Circle*, 149–63, London: Routledge.

WWE Corporate (2002), 'WWE Creates New Los Angeles-Based Film Division', 31 July. Available online: https://corporate.wwe.com/news/company-news/2002/07-31-2002 (accessed 25 June 2021).

WWE Corporate (2020), 'WWE Names Nick Khan President and Chief Revenue Officer', 5 August. Available online: https://corporate.wwe.com/news/company-news/2020/08-05-2020 (accessed 25 June 2021).

*WWE Raw* (2012), [TV Programme] USA Network, 27 February.

*WWE Raw* (2019), [TV Programme] USA Network, 22 July.

# Filmography

## Main saga: The *Fast Saga*

*The Fast and the Furious*, 2001, 106 min, USA
*Director*: Rob Cohen
*Production Company*: Universal Pictures, Original Film, Mediastream Film BMBH & Co. Productions KG, Ardusty Entertainment
*Producer*: Neal H. Moritz (Producer); Jimmy Star (Assistant Producer); Wayne Johnson (Assistant Producer); Creighton Bellinger (Associate Producer); Doug Claybourne (Executive Producer); John Pogue (Executive Producer)
*Script*: Ken Li (magazine article 'Racer X'); Gary Scott Thompson (Story and Screenplay); Erik Bergquist (Screenplay); David Ayer (Screenplay)
*Cinematography*: Ericson Core
*Film Editor*: Peter Honess
*Music*: BT
*Cast*: Paul Walker (Brian O'Conner); Vin Diesel (Dominic Toretto); Jordana Brewster (Mia Toretto); Michelle Rodriguez (Letty Ortiz); Chad Tyler Lindberg (Jesse); Johnny Strong (Leon); Matt Schulze (Vince); Rick Yune (Johnny Tran); Ted Levine (Sgt. Tanner); Noel Gugliemi (Hector); Ja Rule (Edwin)

*2 Fast 2 Furious*, 2003, 108 min, USA
*Director*: John Singleton
*Production Company*: Universal Pictures, Original Film, Mikon Productions GmbH & Co KG, Ardustry Entertainment
*Producer*: Neal H. Moritz (Producer); Heather Lieberman (Co-Producer); Michael Fottrell (Executive Producer); Lee R. Mayes (Executive Producer)
*Script*: Garry Scott Thompson (Story); Michael Brandt (Story and Screenplay); Derek Haas (Story and Screenplay)
*Cinematography*: Matthew F. Leonetti
*Film Editor*: Bruce Cannon, Dallas Puett
*Music*: David Arnold
*Cast*: Paul Walker (Brian O'Conner); Tyrese Gibson (Roman Pearce); Eva Mendes (Agent Monica Fuentes); Chris 'Ludacris' Bridges (Tej Parker); MC Jin (Jimmy); Cole Hauser (Carter Verone); James Remar (Agent Markham); Thom Barry (Agent Bilkins); Devon Aoki (Suki); Amaury Nolasco (Orange Julius); Michael Ealy (Slap Jack); Mark Boone Junior (Detective Whitworth)

***The Fast and the Furious: Tokyo Drift***, 2006, 104 min, USA
*Director*: Justin Lin
*Production Company*: Universal Pictures, Relativity Media, Original Film, MP Munich Pape Filmproductions
*Producer*: Neal H. Moritz (Producer); Amanda Lewis (Co-Producer); Ryan Kavanaugh (Executive Producer); Lynwood Spinks (Executive Producer); Clayton Townsend (Executive Producer); Grace Morita (Associate Producer, Tokyo); Chiaki Yamase (Associate Producer, Tokyo); Kazutoski Wadakura (Line Producer, Tokyo)
*Script*: Chris Morgan
*Cinematography*: Stephen F. Windon
*Film Editor*: Kelly Matsumoto, Dallas Puett, Fred Raskin
*Music*: Brian Tyler
*Cast*: Lucas Black (Sean Boswell); Shad 'Bow Wow' Moss (Twinkie); Nathalie Kelley (Neela); Sung Kang (Han Lue); Brian Tee (Takashi); Zachery Ty Bryan (Clay); Brian Goodman (Major Boswell); Leonard Nam (Morimoto); Keiko Kitagawa (Reiko); Vin Diesel (Dominic Toretto)

***Fast & Furious***, 2009, 107 min, USA
*Director*: Justin Lin
*Production Company*: Universal Pictures, Original Film, Relativity Media, One Race Productions, Dentsu
*Producer:* Neal H. Moritz (Producer); Vin Diesel (Producer); Michael Fottrell (Producer); Michael K. Ross (Producer); Ricardo Del Rio (Co-Producer, Mexico); Amanda Lewis (Executive Producer); Samantha Vincent (Executive producer)
*Script*: Chris Morgan
*Cinematography*: Amir Mokri
*Film Editor*: Christian Wagner, Fred Raskin
*Music*: Brian Tyler
*Cast:* Paul Walker (Brian O'Conner); Vin Diesel (Dominic Toretto); Jordana Brewster (Mia Toretto); Michelle Rodriguez (Letty Ortiz); Gal Gadot (Gisele Yashar); Sung Kang (Han Seoul-Oh, aka Han Lue); Tego Calderon (Leo); Don Omar (Rico Santos); Shea Whigham (Agent Stasiak); John Ortiz (Arturo Braga/Ramon Campos); Laz Alonso (Fenix Calderon)

***Fast Five***, 2011, 130 min, USA
*Director:* Justin Lin
*Production Company*: Universal Pictures, Original Film, One Race Productions, Dentsu
*Producer*: Neal H. Moritz (Producer); Vin Diesel (Producer); Michael Fottrell (Producer); Michael K. Ross (Producer); Amanda Lewis (Executive Producer); Justin Lin (Executive Producer); Samantha Vincent (Executive Producer); Fernando Serzedelo (Line Producer, Brazil)

*Script*: Chris Morgan
*Cinematography*: Stephen F. Windon
*Film Editor*: Kelly Matsumoto, Fred Raskin, Christian Wagner
*Music*: Brian Tyler
*Cast*: Paul Walker (Brian O'Conner); Vin Diesel (Dominic Toretto); Jordana Brewster (Mia Toretto); Tyrese Gibson (Roman Pearce); Chris 'Ludacris' Bridges (Tej Parker); Gal Gadot (Gisele Yashar); Sung Kang (Han Seoul-Oh, aka Han Lue); Matt Schulze (Vince); Tego Calderon (Leo); Don Omar (Santos); Dwayne Johnson (Agent Luke Hobbs); Elsa Pataky (Agent Elena Neves); Eva Mendes (Agent Monica Fuentes); Joaquim de Almeida (Hernan Reyes)

*Fast & Furious 6*, 2013, 130 min, USA
*Director*: Justin Lin
*Production Company*: Universal Pictures, Relativity Media, Original Film, One Race Productions, Dentsu, Fuji Television Network, Universal Studios, F & F VI Productions AIE, BBC Films
*Producer:* Neal H. Moritz (Producer); Vin Diesel (Producer); Clayton Townsend (Producer); Amanda Lewis (Executive Producer); Justin Lin (Executive Producer); Chris Morgan (Executive Producer); Samantha Vincent (Executive Producer); Alexandar Dorstal (Line Producer, Russia)
*Script*: Chris Morgan
*Cinematography*: Stephen F. Windon
*Film Editor*: Kelly Matsumoto, Dylan Highsmith, Christian Wagner, Greg D'Auria, Leigh Folsom Boyd
*Music*: Lucas Vidal
*Cast:* Paul Walker (Brian O'Conner); Vin Diesel (Dominic Toretto); Jordana Brewster (Mia Toretto); Michelle Rodriguez (Letty Ortiz); Tyrese Gibson (Roman Pearce); Chris 'Ludacris' Bridges (Tej Parker); Gal Gadot (Gisele Yashar); Sung Kang (Han Seoul-Oh, aka Han Lue); Tego Calderon (Leo); Don Omar (Santos); Dwayne Johnson (Agent Luke Hobbs); Elsa Pataky (Elena Neves); Shea Whigham (Agent Stasiak); Gina Carano (Agent Riley Hicks); John Ortiz (Arturo Braga); Luke Evans (Owen Shaw); Jason Statham (Deckard Shaw)

*Furious 7 (aka Fast & Furious 7)*, 2015, 137 min, USA
*Director*: James Wan
*Production Company*: Universal Pictures, Original Film, One Race Productions, Media Rights Capital, China Film Group Corporation, Dentsu, Fuji Television Network, Quebec Production Services Tax Credit, Colorado Office of Film, Television & Media, Abu Dhabi Film Commission
*Producer*: Neal H. Moritz (Producer); Vin Diesel (Producer); Michael Fottrell (Producer); Brandon Birtell (Co-Producer); Adam McCarthy (Co-Producer);

F. Valentino Morales (Associate Producer); Amanda Lewis (Executive Producer); Chris Morgan (Executive Producer); Samantha Vincent (Executive Producer); Hiram Garcia (Consulting Producer)
*Script*: Chris Morgan
*Cinematography*: Stephen F. Windon, Marc Spicer
*Film Editor*: Christian Wagner, Dylan Highsmith, Kirk Morri, Leigh Folsom Boyd
*Music*: Brian Tyler
*Cast*: Paul Walker (Brian O'Conner); Vin Diesel (Dominic Toretto); Jordana Brewster (Mia Toretto); Michelle Rodriguez (Letty Ortiz); Tyrese Gibson (Roman Pearce); Chris 'Ludacris' Bridges (Tej Parker); Lucas Black (Sean Boswell); Sung Kang (Han Seoul-Oh, aka Han Lue); Jason Statham (Deckard Shaw); Dijmon Hounsou (Mose Jakande); Tony Jaa (Kiet); Ronda Rousey (Kara); Nathalie Emmanuel (Ramsey); Dwayne Johnson (Agent Luke Hobbs); Elsa Pataky (Agent Elena Neves); Kurt Russell (Mr Nobody); John Brotherton (Sheppard); Ali Fazal (Safar); Luke Evans (Owen Shaw); Noel Gugliemi (Hector)

***The Fate of the Furious (aka F8 and Fast & Furious 8)***, 2017, 136 min, USA
*Director:* F. Gary Gray
*Production Company*: Universal Pictures, Original Film, One Race Productions, China Film Group Corporation, Dentsu, Fuji Eight Company Ltd,
*Producer*: Neal H. Moritz (Producer); Vin Diesel (Producer); Michael Fottrell (Producer); Chris Morgan (Producer); Cliff Lannin (Co-Producer); Amanda Lewis (Executive Producer); Samantha Vincent (Executive Producer); Sharon Lopez (Associate Producer, Cuba Unit); Finni Johannsson (Line Producer, Second Unit, Iceland)
*Script*: Chris Morgan
*Cinematography:* Stephen F. Windon
*Film Editor*: Christian Wagner, Paul Rubell
*Music*: Brian Tyler
*Cast*: Vin Diesel (Dominic Toretto); Jordana Brewster (Mia Toretto); Michelle Rodriguez (Letty Ortiz); Tyrese Gibson (Roman Pearce); Chris 'Ludacris' Bridges (Tej Parker); Nathalie Emmanuel (Ramsey); Tego Calderon (Leo); Don Omar (Rico Santos); Dwayne Johnson (Agent Luke Hobbs); Elsa Pataky (Agent Elena Neves); Charlize Theron (Cipher); Jason Statham (Deckard Shaw); Kurt Russell (Mr Nobody); Scott Eastwood (Little Nobody); Luke Evans (Owen Shaw); Krisofer Hivju (Rhodes); Helen Mirren (Magdalene Shaw)

***F9 (aka F9: The Fast Saga and Fast & Furious 9)***, 2021, 143 min, USA
*Director*: Justin Lin
*Production Company*: Universal Pictures, Original Film, One Race Production, Perfect Storm Entertainment, China Film Group Corporation, Roth/Kirschenbaum Films

*Producer*: Vin Diesel (Producer); Neal H. Moritz (Producer); Justin Lin (Producer); Samantha Vincent (Producer); Joe Roth (Producer); Clayton Townsend (Producer); Jeff Kirschenbaum (Producer); Piya Pestonji (Producer, Second Unit, Thailand); Josh Henson (Co-Producer); Scott Shapiro (Associate Producer); Alexander Vegh (Associate Producer); Kevin Elam (Associate Producer); Sophio Bendiashvili (Line Producer, Second Unit, Georgia); Bacho Meburishvili (Line Producer, Second Unit, Georgia); Thunn Pestonji (Line Producer, Second Unit, Thailand)
*Script*: Justin Lin (Screenplay and Story); Daniel Casey (Story and Screenplay); Alfredo Botello (Story)
*Cinematography*: Stephen F. Windon
*Film Editor*: Dylan Highsmith, Kelly Matsumoto, Greg D'Auria
*Music:* Brian Tyler
*Cast*: Vin Diesel (Dominic Toretto); Jordana Brewster (Mia Toretto); Michelle Rodriguez (Letty Ortiz); Tyrese Gibson (Roman Pearce); Chris 'Ludacris' Bridges (Tej Parker); Sung Kang (Han Seoul-Oh, aka Han Lue); Lucas Black (Sean Boswell); Nathalie Emmanuel (Ramsey); Tego Calderon (Leo); Don Omar (Rico Santos); John Cena (Jakob Toretto); Charlize Theron (Cipher); Kurt Russell (Mr Nobody); Scott Eastwood (Little Nobody); Luke Evans (Owen Shaw); Shea Whigman (Agent Sasiak); Helen Mirren (Magdalene Shaw/Queenie); Shad Moss (Twinkie); JD Pardo (Jack Toretto)

# Spinoffs

***Fast & Furious Presents: Hobbs & Shaw***, 2019, 137 min, USA
*Director*: David Leitch
*Production Company*: Universal Pictures, Dentsu, Seven Bucks Productions, Chris Morgan Productions
*Producer*: Dwayne Johnson (Producer); Jason Statham (Producer); Chris Morgan (Producer); Hiram Garcia (Producer); Kathy Chasen-Hay (Associate Producer); Nicole Furia (Associate Producer); Steven Chasman (Executive Producer); Ainsley Davies (Executive Producer); Dany Garcia (Executive Producer); Kelly McCormick (Executive Producer); Ethan Smith (Executive Producer)
*Script*: Chris Morgan (Screenplay and Story); Drew Pearce (Screenplay)
*Cinematography*: Jonathan Sela
*Film Editor*: Christopher Rouse
*Music:* Tyler Bates
*Cast*: Dwayne Johnson (Luke Hobbs); Jason Statham (Deckard Shaw); Vanessa Kirby (Hattie); Idris Elba (Brixton Lore); Cliff Curtis (Jonah Hobbs); Helen Mirren (Magdalena Shaw/Queenie); Joe 'Roman Reigns' Anoa'I (Mateo Hobbs); Josh Mauga

(Timo Hobbs); John Tui (Kal Hobbs); Eddie Marsan (Professor Andreiko); Eliana Su'a (Sam Hobbs); Lori Pelenise Tuisano (Sefina Hobbs); Eiza Gonzalez (Margarita/Madame M); Ryan Reynolds (Agent Victor Locke); Kevin Hart (Air Marshal Dinkley)

## Short films

**The Turbo Charged Prelude to 2 Fast 2 Furious**, 2003, 6 min, USA
*Director*: Phillip G. Atwell
*Production Company:* Universal Pictures, Original Film
*Producer:* Chris Palladino
*Script:* Keith Dinielli
*Film Editor:* Scott Meyer
*Cast:* Paul Walker (Brian O'Conner)
*Distributor:* Universal Pictures Home Entertainment

**Los Bandoleros**, 2009, 20 min, USA
*Director:* Vin Diesel
*Production Company:* One Race Productions, Terrero Films, Universal Pictures
*Producer:* Vin Diesel (Producer); Jessy Terrero (Producer); Samantha Vincent (Producer); Josh Goldstein (Executive Producer); John Nguyen (Executive Producer); Jalina Steward (Executive Producer); Thyrale Thai (Executive Producer); TJ Mancini (Co-Executive Producer); Juan Basanta (Local Producer, Dominican Republic); Linel Hernandez (Line Producer, Dominican Republic); Maria Jose Ripoll (Coordinating Producer)
*Script:* Vin Diesel; TJ Mancini (Co-Writer and Screenplay)
*Cinematography:* Shawn Kim
*Film Editor:* Justin Bourret, Sonia Gonzalez-Martinez
*Cast:* Vin Diesel (Dominic Toretto); Michelle Rodriguez (Letty Ortiz); Sung Kang (Han Lue); Tego Calderon (Leo); Don Omar (Rico Santos); Juan Fernandez (Elvis)

## Animated series

*Fast & Furious: Spy Racers*, 2019–21, 23–24 min episodes, USA: Netflix.
*Creator:* Tim Hedrick, Bret Haaland
*Executive in charge of Production:* Gregg Goldin
*Production Company:* DreamWorks Animation Television, One Race Productions, Original Film, Universal Animation Studios, Universal Television

*Producer:* Neal H. Moritz (Executive Producer); Vin Diesel (Executive Producer); Chris Morgan (Executive Producer); Tim Hedrick (Executive Producer and Show Runner); Bret Haaland (Executive Producer and Show Runner); Joseph R. Alessandra (CG Supervising Producer); Chris Belcher (Line Producer); Katie Ely (S1-S3 Line Producer); Ben Cawood (SVP Development for S1 & S2)
*Art Direction:* Christine Bian, Joel Fajnor
*Series Music:* Ryan Lofty, Jay Vincent
*Music (Theme Song):* 'Chasing Legacy' performed by Shaylin Becton and Tha Vil and produced by Timbaland, Federico Vindver and Angel Lopez for BEATCLUB
*Main Cast:* Tyler Posey (Tony Toretto); Charlet Chung (Margaret 'Echo' Pearl); Jorge Dias (Cisco Renaldo); Camille Ramsey (Layla Gray); Luke Youngblood (Frostee Benson); Renee Elise Goldsberry (Ms. Nowhere); Tru Valentino (Gary)

# Index

*2 Fast 2 Furious* 6–7, 10, 12, 43–5, 47, 51, 88, 97–8, 124–5, 137, 245

action
    driving 9, 13, 21, 30, 51, 96, 125, 131, 224
    escalating action 9, 12–18, 48–53, 222–4
    fight sequences 16, 19, 39, 41, 46–7, 51–2, 124–7, 136, 145, 162, 164, 167, 170, 181, 238–9
    incorporating new styles 12–18, 38, 44–8, 50–3
    set pieces 11, 48–53, 207, 222–4
adaptation 3–4, 20, 23, 29, 106, 201
    animation 213–18, 220–6
affect 57–60, 64–5, 67, 71, 241, 246
    fan affect 63, 189, 234, 240–1, 244
audiences. *See also* fandom
    child and youth 95, 214–19, 226, 228, 242
    domestic (USA) 1, 5, 19, 97, 196
    international 8, 19, 115, 122, 197, 203
    Mainland China 194–5, 197–8, 200–8
    wrestling 234–5, 238–43
authenticity 25–6, 57, 62–3, 65, 175, 177–80, 182–4, 186–9

Beltrán, Mary 8, 23, 27, 44, 74–5, 85–6, 89, 92, 95–7, 99–100, 114–15, 124
*Better Luck Tomorrow* 8–9
bodies 64, 68, 85, 126, 136, 143, 158
    ageing 67, 160, 162, 168–9
    gendered 98, 123, 129, 145, 151–2
    hardbody 104, 108–11, 113, 115–16, 143–4, 159–60, 162, 164–5, 168, 170
Brewster, Jordana. *See under* Mia Toretto
Bridges, Chris 'Ludacris'. *See under* Tej Parker
bromance 28–9, 127–30, 137, 176–7
    between Brian and Dom 125–6, 131–5, 175–6, 180–90

Candy Ass feud 240, 244–6
celebrity 29, 64, 104, 107, 175, 177–80, 187, 190, 236–7, 241, 247
Cena, John 17, 87, 193–4, 201, 206–7, 233–4, 237, 241–5. *See also* Jakob Toretto
'cinema of attractions' (Tom Gunning) 58–62, 67, 70–1
Cipher 15, 94, 147–8, 153

Diesel, Vin. *See also* Dominic Toretto
    *Bloodshot* 104, 106, 184, 188
    as director 105–9, 113, 115
    *Multi-Facial* 105–7, 108, 113, 115–16
    multiracial protagonist 23, 74, 85–7, 99, 105–6, 115
    as producer 1, 14, 21, 23, 25, 103–4, 106–8, 189, 246. *See also* One Race
    *Riddick* franchise 10, 104, 106
    *Saving Private Ryan* 106, 115
    social media 21, 25, 27, 29, 166, 176, 185–9, 234, 237, 246
    *xXx* franchise 104, 106, 202, 210
diversity
    data 75–81, 86, 100
    racial 28, 73–5, 82–7, 90, 93–5, 98–100, 113–15, 122, 124–5
Dyer, Richard 104, 136, 163, 177–80, 189

Emmanuel, Nathalie. *See under* Ramsey
ensemble 43, 90, 92, 94, 97, 110, 158, 162, 167, 170, 175, 187–8, 219, 240

*F9* (aka *F9: The Fast Saga* and *Fast & Furious 9*) 1–2, 7–8, 16, 22–5, 54, 61, 67, 87, 137, 155, 168, 193, 206, 222, 243–5
fandom 6, 10, 19, 25, 104, 158, 166, 194, 201, 228, 237, 240, 243
    fan-driven franchise 11, 17, 21–6, 48, 233

global fandom 23, 96, 115, 195, 203–4, 244
  reaction to Walker's death 63, 134, 186, 205
*The Fast and The Furious* 3–7, 11, 37–8, 43, 45, 47, 50, 58–9, 74, 85, 88, 106, 115, 121–2, 126, 130, 134, 143, 146, 149–50, 157, 165, 176, 180–1, 196, 222
*The Fast and the Furious: Tokyo Drift* 6–7, 8–12, 14, 24, 43, 61, 66, 89, 107–8, 124, 161
  action 11, 29–30, 44–5, 47, 49, 67
  race/ethnic representation 8, 9, 23, 89
  visual style 9, 11
*Fast & Furious* (*Fast Four*) 7, 10–14, 16, 18, 20–1, 24–5, 28, 30, 43, 45–7, 66, 68, 87, 90, 95, 103–4, 106–8, 112–13, 116, 121, 131–2, 151, 186, 198, 246
*Fast & Furious 6* 7, 11, 13–14, 16–17, 19, 43, 45–7, 66, 91–2, 94, 124–5, 143, 146–7, 151–3, 157, 181, 194, 197, 199, 204, 238, 241
*Fast & Furious Presents: Hobbs & Shaw* 3, 7, 8, 19, 43, 45–7, 66, 92, 94, 124, 129, 161, 163–5, 202, 204, 223–4, 239–40, 245
*Fast & Furious: Spy Racers* 3, 107, 213–29
*Fast* family 21–2, 24, 90, 202, 205, 245
*Fast Five* 1, 5, 7, 12–19, 43, 45–8, 50, 52, 66, 84, 91–4, 97, 110, 121, 132–3, 142–3, 147, 149, 151–3, 157, 161, 185, 193–4, 207, 233, 238, 241
*The Fate of the Furious* (aka *F8* and *Fast & Furious 8*) 7, 14, 43, 45–7, 73, 78, 93, 124, 141, 162, 168–9, 184, 193, 209, 239
fatherhood 142–5
feminist 159, 163
  postfeminist 127, 142, 144, 152, 154–5
Fleury, Hartzheim, & Mamber 2, 8, 20, 195–7, 203–4
franchise era 4, 8, 19–20, 26, 95, 195, 197, 203–4
friendship
  between Brian and Dom 123–4, 129–36
  between Diesel and Walker 183–90
  between Gibson and Walker 185–6
  between Pearce and O'Conner 124–5
Fritz, Ben 2, 19–20, 95
*Furious 7* (aka *Fast & Furious 7*) 1, 7, 14–15, 19, 23, 43–4, 46–8, 50–1, 57, 61–3, 65–70, 73, 92, 94, 97–8, 125, 134–5, 141, 143, 154, 161, 176, 181, 183, 188, 193, 195–7, 199, 202–8, 238

genre 4, 12–13, 15–16, 19, 37–8, 40, 43–8, 50, 53, 78, 84, 109–10, 126–9, 136, 143, 158–63, 167, 168, 176, 194, 218, 235, 247. *See also* rebranding the franchise
  buddy comedy 11, 47, 87, 89, 97, 12629, 161, 176, 239
  heist 13, 38, 46, 115, 176, 179
  spy thriller 5, 13–16, 38, 46, 48, 50
  superhero film 16, 30, 47, 142, 167, 204
Gibson, Tyrese 87, 97–8, 185–6, 245. *See also* Roman Pearce
global marketplace 6, 11, 14, 18, 193–7, 201, 208
  Mainland China 8, 14, 23, 29, 193–212

Hobbs, Agent Luke 17–20, 86, 92, 94, 97, 124, 129, 132–3, 157, 161–2, 164, 238–40, 244, 246. *See also* Dwayne Johnson
homoeroticism 68, 123, 125–7, 129, 136

intersectionality 28, 103, 107, 116

Jenkins, Henry 10, 197, 217, 225, 228–9, 234, 236
Johnson, Dwayne 16–21, 25, 28–9, 86, 92, 94, 126, 144, 157–8, 161–3, 165, 168–70, 202–6, 209, 220, 233–4, 236–7. *See also* Agent Luke Hobbs
  multiracial 86, 92
  *The Other Guys* 18, 127
  *Scorpion King* 18, 238
  *Skyscraper* 144, 204
  social media 21, 234, 237, 240, 242–6. *See also* Candy Ass feud
  wrestling career 18, 29, 233–40, 243

Kang, Sung 67, 90. *See also* Han Seoul-Oh

Latinx (portrayal of) 23, 81, 85–6, 90, 95–7, 99, 111, 114
Li, Kenneth 3–4. *See also* 'Racer X'
Lin, Justin 5, 8–12, 21, 23–5, 29–30, 46, 124–5
*Los Bandoleros* 28, 68, 103–4, 107–16

marketing 23–4, 26, 57, 164, 175, 187–8, 197, 199, 201, 203, 213, 234, 246
  brand family 12, 21–2, 24, 94, 234, 247
  brand identity 2, 17, 20, 26–7, 53, 62, 98, 163, 203, 207–8, 213–17, 221, 228–9, 235, 243–6
  social media 22, 24, 178, 185–6, 234, 236–7
Marvel Cinematic Universe (MCU) 1, 2, 4–5, 10, 14, 16, 20, 26, 95, 104, 167, 175, 200, 203, 213, 228
masculinity 28, 98, 103–4, 107–17, 127–30, 136–7, 144, 149–50, 152, 157–63, 165, 168–70, 220
  hierarchies 98, 136, 147, 151, 160–3, 167
  as performance 127–8, 142, 146, 159, 163, 176
  stardom 17, 104, 164, 169
Morgan, Chris 5, 8–12, 21, 202
motherhood 28, 144, 153–5
Mr Nobody 24, 46, 94, 220, 227

Neves, Elena 28, 129, 137, 143, 147–8, 151–5

O'Conner, Brian 4–6, 11, 17, 28–9, 57, 61–2, 67–70, 87, 89, 110, 121–37, 143, 150–4, 175–6, 180–1, 184, 186–8, 206, 209. *See also* Paul Walker
  action sequences 13, 52, 58–9, 63, 71
One Race 20, 106, 115, 117, 202
Ortiz, Letty 11, 13, 20, 25, 28, 68–9, 95–6, 111–13, 131, 141, 143, 154–5, 157, 219. *See also* Michelle Rodriguez
  action sequences 124–5, 150–2
  death and resurrection 14, 25, 43, 68, 71, 108, 132, 151, 205

parenthood 142–4, 152, 155, 184, 220
Parker, Tej 6, 90, 97, 219
Pataky, Elsa 129, 143. *See also* Elena Neves
Pearce, Roman 6, 17, 87, 89–90, 97–8, 124–5, 245
*Point Break* 4, 121, 126–7, 157, 176
Purse, Lisa 16, 38, 40, 74, 87, 97, 99

quantitative analysis
  dialogue networks 75, 82–3, 85, 87–94, 96, 98
  inequality 76, 80

race
  multicultural 73–4, 81, 85, 98–9, 109, 115, 124
  multiracial 74, 76, 85–7, 89, 92, 98–9, 105, 115–16
'Racer X' (*Vibe* article) 3, 4, 23, 24
Ramsey 94–5, 141
rebranding the franchise 5, 12–18, 44–8, 50–3
representation 8, 11, 12, 23, 28, 73–100, 123, 129, 135, 142–59, 178, 181, 189–90, 200, 209
  diversity data 74–87, 94–5, 98
  as visibility 75, 93, 95, 97–100, 169, 187
rivalry. *See also* Candy Ass feud
  cast members 158, 164–5, 245–6
  fight sequences 51, 113, 124–6, 164–70, 238–9
The Rock. *See under* Dwayne Johnson
Rodriguez, Michelle 20, 124–6, 186, 209. *See also* Letty Ortiz

Seoul-Oh, Han 12, 24–5, 67, 90, 108, 124–5, 129, 209. *See also* Sung Kang
  #Justice4Han 24–5
  death and resurrection 9–11, 19, 60–1, 66
Shaw, Deckard 14, 19–20, 24–5, 48, 52, 94, 124, 157, 161–2, 164, 169, 199, 238–40. *See also* Jason Statham
Shaw, Hattie 94, 129, 199
Shaw, Owen 13–14, 17, 48, 94, 181, 199
spinoffs 3–4, 6, 8, 10, 12, 19, 26, 45, 92, 94, 121, 124, 161, 199, 204, 213, 236,

238–9, 245–7. *See also* adaption, *Hobbs & Shaw* and *Spy Racers*
games 3, 106, 217, 247
live show 3, 213, 217, 247
theme parks 3, 20, 29, 213, 217
*Star Wars* franchise 2, 4–5, 25, 34, 62, 104, 197, 198, 213, 215, 221, 225–6, 228
stardom 104, 195, 237, 247
  in action genre 17–19, 207
  emphasis on stars 17–20, 64, 94–5, 107, 203–6, 240, 243
  international markets 5, 195, 203, 205–6
Statham, Jason 16, 19–20, 25, 28, 48, 157–8, 161–3, 165, 168–70, 199, 204–5, 239. *See also* Deckard Shaw
*The Expendables* 19, 168
street racing 2–4, 6, 12–15, 27, 37–8, 46–8, 50, 58–9, 63, 66, 87, 95–6, 103, 121, 130, 141, 146, 150–1, 194, 247

Tasker, Yvonne 126, 142, 145, 157–9, 163, 167, 168
Toretto, Dominic. *See also* Vin Diesel
  Christianity 68, 103, 109, 112–14, 116
  ethnic ambiguity 85–6, 97, 103, 115–16, 137
  as father 113, 148, 152–5, 161
  as Latinx 86–7, 95, 137

as patriarch 109–10, 113, 116, 141–3, 146, 153
wrench 146
Toretto, Jakob 67, 87. *See also* John Cena
Toretto, Mia 67, 86–7, 121, 125, 129–35, 143, 146, 150, 152–5, 181
transmedia 2–4, 14, 27, 29, 107, 179, 197, 213, 215, 217, 221, 225, 227–9, 246–7
WWE 234–6, 240–1
*The Turbo Charged Prelude to 2 Fast 2 Furious* 6

visual effects 28, 57–9, 175, 222
  action sequences 11–12, 15, 57, 66–7, 70–1, 221, 223–4
  Weta Digital (also posthumous Paul Walker) 57, 61–5, 134

Walker, Paul 4, 28–9, 74, 97, 137, 175. *See also* Brian O'Conner
  death 57–8, 61–5, 69–70, 94, 104, 134,154, 176–7, 181, 183–90, 205–6, 233
  eyes 63, 121, 132
  as white protagonist 74, 87, 89–90, 92, 94, 97–9, 157
Warner, Kristen 74, 80–1, 99
World Wrestling Entertainment (WWE) 18, 29, 233–7

www.ingramcontent.com/pod-product-compliance
Lightning Source LLC
Chambersburg PA
CBHW062124300426
44115CB00012BA/1800